# Fundamentals of Tree-Ring Research

# FUNDAMENTALS
## OF TREE-RING RESEARCH

James H. Speer

The University of Arizona Press    Tucson

## THE UNIVERSITY OF ARIZONA PRESS

© 2010 The Arizona Board of Regents
First published as a paperback edition 2011

www.uapress.arizona.edu

Library of Congress Cataloging-in-Publication Data
Speer, James H., 1971–
Fundamentals of tree-ring research / James H. Speer.
p.   cm.
Includes bibliographical references and index.
ISBN 978-0-8165-2684-0 (cloth : alk. paper)
ISBN 978-0-8165-2685-7 (pbk. : alk. paper)
1. Tree-rings.   2. Dendrochronology.   3. Trees—Growth.   4. Wood.   I. Title.
QK477.2.A6S64   2010
582.16—dc22      2009044485


Manufactured in the United States of America on acid-free,
archival-quality paper and processed chlorine free.

16   15   14   13   12   11      8   7   6   5   4

*I dedicate this book to my wife Karla, who helped with many aspects of this book throughout the entire process.*

# Contents

# Figures

# Tables

# Preface

I have envisioned writing this book since I was an undergraduate student at the University of Arizona in the Laboratory of Tree Ring Research. In my introductory dendrochronology class, taught by Tom Swetnam, we used a photocopy of a book written by Hal Fritts that was no longer in print. That book was the famous *Tree Rings and Climate*, but during the 1990s the only way to acquire the text was from a photocopy directly from the author. Thankfully, Blackburn Press reprinted the book in its entirety in 2001, and it is once again available to new students of dendrochronology. Another book that was often suggested for the novice dendrochronologist was *An Introduction to Tree-Ring Dating* by Marvin Stokes and Terah Smiley. Fritts' book was written at a high level with the explicit focus of dendroclimatology, whereas Stokes' and Smiley's book was a basic introduction that specifically used a dendroarchaeological project to explain the techniques of dendrochronology. I have written this book as a basic introduction to the breadth of dendrochronology, including some of the principles and physiological background that one needs to conduct dendrochronological research. The second half of the book has chapters dedicated to each of the subdisciplines of dendrochronology, providing a basic bibliography for one to start dendrochronological research in any of the applications within the field.

I further saw a need for this book while teaching and organizing the North American Dendroecological Fieldweek since 1997, along with teaching my own dendrochronology class at the university level since 1999. The students consistently asked the same questions about the field, and I hope that this book answers those questions. In teaching at the North American Dendroecological Fieldweek, I realized that every laboratory has its own perspective on the field, although the Tucson Lab has wide-reaching influence because so many people spend some time at that laboratory for aspects of their training in the field. My own training in dendrochronology came from four years at the Laboratory of Tree-Ring Research in Tucson at the University of Arizona, and therefore my perspective is from that institution. I have contacted researchers in other countries to try to ensure the inclusion of the best literature from around the world, but admittedly my perspective is based on my own research in North America.

I hope that readers find this book useful as a reference and as a primary starting point for work in dendrochronology. It is the result of five years of dedicated reading and writing along with the input from 22 other dendrochronologists through reviews of different stages of the book.

# Acknowledgments

I thank the many dendrochronologists that have given input on this text, for without their help this work would be much diminished: Rex Adams, Parveen Chhetri, Ed Cook, Lori Daniels, Jeff Dean, Dieter Eckstein, Esther Fichtler, Hal Fritts, Holger Gärtner, Henri Grissino-Mayer, Richard Guyette, Tom Harlan, Steve Leavitt, Kathy Lewis, Dave Meko, Steve Nash, Bill Patterson, Fritts Schweingruber, Greg Wiles, Connie Woodhouse, Tom Yanosky, and Qi-bin Zhang. I would especially like to thank my wife, Karla Hansen-Speer, who edited this text multiple times, provided line drawings for some of the graphics, helped with all of the issues involved in bringing a book to print, and posed as my model for some of the photographs.

# Abbreviations

| | |
|---|---|
| DBH | diameter at breast height |
| EPS | expressed population signal |
| ITRDB | International Tree-Ring Data Bank |
| NAO | North Atlantic Oscillation |
| PCA | principal component analysis |
| PDO | Pacific Decadal Oscillation |
| PDSI | Palmer drought severity index |
| SOI | Southern Oscillation index |
| SSS | subsample signal strength |

# 1
# Introduction

Dendrochronology is one of the most important environmental recording techniques for a variety of natural environmental processes and a monitor for human-caused changes to the environment such as pollution and contamination. The word *dendrochronology* has its roots in Greek; *dendro* means tree and *chronology* means the study of time. Dendrochronology examines events through time that are recorded in the tree-ring structure or can be dated by tree rings. Because the tree becomes the instrument for environmental monitoring, it serves as a long-term bioindicator that extends for the lifetime of the tree. Dendrochronology can be applied to very old trees to provide long-term records of past temperature, rainfall, fire, insect outbreaks, landslides, hurricanes, and ice storms, to name only a few applications. Wood from dead trees can also be used to extend the chronology of tree rings further back in time. Trees record any environmental factor that directly or indirectly limits a process that affects the growth of ring structures from one season to the next, making them a useful monitor for a variety of events.

## Some Interesting Applications of Dendrochronology

The discipline of dendrochronology is used to mark time or record environmental variability in the structure of the wood from trees growing in seasonal climates, such as in the mid and high latitudes, and some tropical trees growing in environments with a pronounced wet or dry season. Because many environmental variables can affect tree growth, different records can be gained from a variety of tree species on a site and on a variety of sites in a region. Dendrochronologists have been able to develop interesting records that contribute to many areas of modern culture, from boundary disputes to forensic science. Sellards et al. (1923) used tree rings to settle a boundary dispute between the states of Oklahoma and Texas along the Red River. The old boundary line between the states was defined as the river, but the river changed its course since that boundary was drawn. The state of Texas asked Sellards to examine the establishment dates of the trees in the floodplain to demonstrate that the boundary line had moved, supporting their attempt to reclaim the land back to the original channel of the river. Tree rings were used as forensic evidence in a murder case by dating the age of a root that grew over a buried corpse (Thomas Harlan, personal communication). Finally, a carving on an aspen (*Populus tremuloides*) tree stem supposedly made by Ted Bundy (the infamous serial killer) was dated to 1976, a time he was reported to be in the region, thus causing investigators to intensify their search for Bundy's victims in this area (Thomas Swetnam, personal communication). This was an unusual use of dendrochronology because the carving was only in the bark of the tree and not in the wood. Aspens produce rings in the bark (although not as continuously as in the wood), which were counted to establish the date.

Tree rings have been used to help elucidate strange atmospheric events such as the Tunguska Event that occurred on June 30, 1908 (Vaganov et al. 2004). One of the main hypotheses of what caused this event that flattened 80 million trees over 2150 km² in Siberia is the arrival of a large meteoroid that disintegrated in the atmosphere from 5 to 10 km above the surface of the Earth. This is the largest impact event in the written history of the Earth. Vaganov et al. (2004) examined tree rings at the time of the impact and found that the cells growing during the end of 1908 were deformed. They concluded that this was likely caused by a forceful impact on the trees and suggested an upward adjustment of previous estimates to the amount of force that was exerted on the trees from this event.

One of the more remarkable stories in dendrochronology comes from attempts to date the Stradivari violin called the Messiah, which has a label date of 1716 (fig. 1.1). The Messiah violin is considered one of Antonio Stradivari's crowning achievements. It is a well-preserved instrument that has a distinct red hue to its finish. This instrument would be valued between 10 and 20 million dollars if it could be authenticated as the true Messiah violin, but if it was made by a copyist in the 1800s, it would be worth far less. This instrument is housed in the Ashmolean Museum in Oxford, England. Initial tree-ring dating on the Messiah suggested that the instrument was the original Stradivari (Topham and McCormick 1997, 1998, 2001), but others (including one dendrochronologist) claimed the violin was made after Stradivari died in 1737 (Pollens 1999, 2001). To settle the controversy, Dr. Henri Grissino-Mayer of the University of Tennessee was asked to assemble a team of experts and examine the rings a second time in an attempt to date the violin.

Dendrochronologists cannot conclusively demonstrate that the instrument was made by Stradivari. Dendrochronology, however, can be used to disprove the possibility of it being a Stradivari instrument by finding growth rings in the wood of the instrument that postdate Stradivari's death in 1737. The Messiah violin was made from a spruce tree and had 120 rings showing on the top of the instrument. Grissino-Mayer et al. (2002, 2003, 2004) worked at dating this violin against European reference tree-ring chronologies and against chronologies developed from other known Stradivari instruments. They demonstrated that the last rings in the instrument dated to 1687, which was consistent with two other instruments made by Stradivari: the Archinto (dating to 1686) and the Kux/Castelbarco violas (dating to 1684).

## Some Basic Principles and Definitions in Dendrochronology

Many proxy records (alternate sources of information from natural phenomena) of climate and the environment exist, such as pollen, ice cores, lake varves (annually layered sediment), coral layers, and speleothems (calcium carbonate dripstone from caves)(Bradley 1999), but dendrochronology provides the most reliable dating with the highest accuracy and precision of any of these paleorecords. The practice of **crossdating**, matching the pattern of wide and narrow rings to demonstrate dating between trees, which was developed by A. E. Douglass in the early 1900s (Douglass 1909, 1917, 1920, 1921, 1929, 1941), is now being used for some of the other proxy records that form regular (sometimes annual) increments, such as ice cores, corals, rings in clam shells, and otoliths (the bony structure in the ears of fish) as a check on the dating of those records (Black et al. 2005).

**Figure 1.1** The Messiah violin. Any object that is made of wood and has enough rings in a sensitive series can potentially be dated using tree rings. In an unusual example, the Stradivari Messiah violin was dated using dendrochronology. (Photo by Peter Biddulph)

The science of dendrochronology has a few basic principles and concepts that have been demonstrated repeatedly by scientific evidence from multiple disciplines and supported experimentally by dendrochronological research. These principles are the subject of chapter 2, but I summarize some of them here because it is difficult to discuss dendrochronology without the use of some of these terms.

The main principle of crossdating suggests that variation in ring width is driven by limited environmental factors needed for growth; matching these narrow rings provides the quality control required by dendrochronologists, allowing the assertion of annual resolution and the ability to provide exact calendar years for every tree ring in a sample. This principle is strengthened by the concept of **replication**, which states that reliable dates must be supported by enough samples to assure the probability of being erroneous is sufficiently minute. For example, for most sites in the southwestern United States, 20 overlapping tree records (**sample depth**) are usually sufficient for a reliable **chronology** (a site-level representation of tree growth). Good chronologies have been developed with as few as 10 trees sampled on sites with a consistent site-level chronology, and many chronologies have been developed with more than 100 tree samples. By sampling two cores from each tree, statistics can be used to calculate the amount of year-to-year agreement within trees as well as between trees. Two cores per tree also enable the researcher to start the crossdating process within a tree to better represent overall tree growth. If a cross section can be taken from a tree, there is an opportunity to examine numerous radii around the section. This sampling protocol of 20 trees with two cores per tree results in 40 cores represented in a site-level chronology; a **site** is defined as a spatially proximal group of trees with similar environmental conditions such as slope, aspect, and climate.

Tree-ring width responds to a similar set of environmental factors that limit tree growth. This is the well-known biological principle of **limiting factors**. Because ring width is influenced by anything that limits tree growth, the dendrochronologist must consider what problem is to be addressed, then find the particular sites and trees that provide the necessary information. This procedure is one of the most important principles and is called **site selection**. Dendrochronologists label tree-ring chronologies as **sensitive** when their ring-width patterns vary markedly from year-to-year, while chronologies that have similar amounts of growth every year are called **complacent** series. For climate studies, sensitive trees are targeted because their ring variation is likely to better reflect climate than complacent trees. Climate is essentially the primary limiting factor that imparts the year-to-year variability that makes crossdating possible. The history of dendrochronology in chapter 3 introduces the pioneers in the field that were the first to recognize and apply many of these basic principles.

## Subfields of Dendrochronology

Because tree-ring width can vary with anything that affects tree growth, annual records of many natural phenomena can be developed. The term *dendrochronology* refers to the science of dating tree rings and studying their structure to interpret information about environmental and historical events and processes (sensu Kaennel and Schweingruber 1995). Many subfields within dendrochronology have been developed and subsequently named by keeping the base of the word *dendro* and adding a secondary prefix to describe the specific field being studied. For example, dendroclimatology uses the variation in tree-ring structure and width to infer information about past climate, while dendroarchaeology uses the date of the outside tree ring from a beam to study the timing and process of archaeological construction (see table 1.1 for a brief synopsis of the many subfields of dendrochronology, which are discussed in greater detail in chapters 7–11).

## Limitations of Dendrochronology

As with all research, dendrochronology has certain limitations that must be acknowledged (table 1.2). Annual tree rings (fig. 1.2) can form in any forest that has one yearly growth

**Table 1.1**  Subfield of dendrochronology. Many of the subfields also have subheadings (written in bold) that more specifically describe the discipline. Dendrochronologists often identify themselves as practitioners of one or more of these subfields.

| Subfield | Description |
| --- | --- |
| **Dendroarchaeology**<br>See chapter 7 | Tree-ring samples from beams and posts in archaeological dwellings are dated to provide construction dates for the dwellings. The position of these beams in the dwelling can be used to study the timing of construction and expansion of dwellings and to better understand human behavior in these cultures. Correlation with regional master chronologies can also help to identify the dendro-provenance of archaeological and historical wood objects. |
| **Dendroclimatology**<br>See chapter 8 | Samples from trees can provide short- or long-term records of past climatic variability for the lifetime of the trees. Most often temperature, precipitation, and drought indices are reconstructed, although anything that affects the processes of tree growth such as number of cloudy days, relative humidity, or wind strength can be reconstructed as well if they limit tree growth. Information from dendroclimatology has provided important information about past climate change and help us understand what the future climate might be like. This subfield also includes **dendrohydrology**, which is the reconstruction of water level or streamflow, although this is often separated out as its own subdiscipline. |
| **Dendroecology**<br>See chapter 9 | Because trees are an important functional feature of many ecosystems, they can be used as a natural record of ecological processes, such as tree-line movement, successional processes through the establishment and death of trees, fire occurrence (**dendropyrochronology**), insect outbreaks (**dendroentomology**), synchronous fruiting (masting) in trees (**dendromastecology**), or movement of invasive tree species. |
| **Dendrogeomorphology**<br>See Chapter 10 | The vertical structure of a tree enables it to gather the most light while standing up straight so that land movement can be reconstructed by the tilting of a tree and the resultant reaction of wood (thicker growth rings produced to straighten the stem of a tree). Also tree death or establishment can be used to date geologic phenomena such as landslides, mudflows, seismic activity along faults (**dendroseismology**), glacial activity (**dendroglaciology**), or volcanic events (**dendrovolcanology**). |
| **Dendrochemistry**<br>See chapter 11 | Trees absorb chemicals along with water from soil and gases from the atmosphere. These chemicals are deposited in the wood in the stem, roots, and branches and can be used as a record of contamination, nutrient availability, and pollution. Stable isotopes can also be measured in wood structure to reconstruct past temperature, humidity, and the source of water or growing conditions of the trees. |

**Table 1.2** The general limitations of dendrochronology along with solutions to those limitations.

| Limitation | Solution |
| --- | --- |
| Young trees | Finding old trees in unique sites, buried wood, or archaeological samples to extend a chronology |
| Calibration data sets | Conducting studies close to available climate or ecological data sets or establishing monitoring stations for future calibration data sets in remote areas; regionalized climate data are also being used to examine broad-scale climate response in areas without local climate stations |
| Lack of ring formation in the tropics | Looking for a chemical or stable isotopic signal in tropical woods; examining wood anatomy of many tropical species to find some with annual ring formation |
| Lack of a physiological understanding of how tree rings form | Conducting more wood anatomy, tree physiology, and biochemical studies to better understand the growth of tree rings |

**Figure 1.2** A cross section of an ash (*Fraxinus* sp.) tree. Note the dark-colored heartwood near the center of the tree and the suppressed rings in the 1930s and the 1950s (at arrow). The split is a natural break in the wood due to the cross section drying out after it was sampled. (Photo by the author)

period followed by a dormant period, but some locations, such as many tropical areas, do not have the seasonality to allow the formation of annual rings. Crossdating must be used to verify the dates of every ring in a sample. This technique is time consuming, takes special skills, and requires much patience to learn and apply properly.

The development of wood through cambial activity that forms xylem and phloem in the trees is a very complex process that has been the topic of an entire book (Larson 1994). Tree physiologists have not been able to explain the exact biochemical processes that occur from photosynthesis to the formation of tree rings. Some physiologists have argued that because we do not completely understand the mechanisms that occur from the assimilation of abiotic elements from the environment to the formation of the tree ring, we should not be conducting dendrochronological studies. However, countless analyses of the correlation between tree growth and environment variables have demonstrated consistent predictable results indicating that, despite our lack of understanding of the exact mechanisms, we know that tree growth does reflect environmental variables. Over 100 years of productive research in dendrochronology supports its validity and importance in environmental reconstruction.

The development of well-dated tree-ring chronologies for the reconstruction of environmental variables is restricted by the location of sensitive tree-ring series (Fritts 1976). Trees are not ubiquitous on the landscape, and even when they are present, dendrochronologists must choose specific sites that are likely to record the environmental variable that they wish to study. Furthermore, many reconstructions depend upon calibration and verification data sets, such as modern temperature and precipitation records, to create a statistical model to reconstruct past climatic variations (Stahle et al. 1998a). These constraints geographically limit dendrochronology to areas where the trees produce datable annual rings and where local paired climate or ecological data exist for calibration of the trees' response. These calibration data enable a scientifically meaningful reconstruction, and independent verification data allow the researcher to determine the validity of the reconstructions. Still, tree-ring data can be useful even when calibration data are not available. For example, the variability of rings in petrified wood demonstrates variability in climate millions of years ago, and long-term growth suppressions and releases in tree rings can demonstrate stand dynamic processes.

We can use trees to interpret past environmental phenomena, but trees are biological entities that are driven by their own physiology and biochemistry that create filters on the climatic or ecological processes that they record in their annual rings. Trees, therefore, are not strict monitors of the environment, and these biological factors must be considered when interpreting tree-ring data.

In comparison with many other proxy data, dendrochronological data provide a relatively short record, with only three tree-ring chronologies in the world that extend back 10,000 years or longer. These were developed from bristlecone pine (*Pinus longaeva*) in California (Ferguson et al. 1985), oak (*Quercus* spp.) in Ireland (Pilcher et al. 1984), and oak in Germany (Becker 1993, Friedrich et al. 2004). Dendrochronological records for any particular area are further constrained by the need for well-preserved wood samples that represent a range of time scales. For example, most wood in the eastern United States will decay on the forest floor within 20 to 50 years, while wood found on a lava flow in the western United States may last for 1000 years without much decay of the heartwood (Grissino-Mayer 1995). Very little wood can survive decay for longer than hundreds or thousands of years, thus limiting the length of our tree-ring records. Some researchers have begun to use subfossil (buried but not permineralized) wood that may extend their chronologies back 15,000 years or more (Roig et al. 2001, Guyette and Stambaugh 2003). Petrified wood also provides a possible source of information on climatic variability from millions of years in the past as long as the rings are well preserved (Chaloner and Creber 1973, Falcon-Lang 1999), although it is important to not overinterpret the climate information that can be gleaned from fossilized wood (Falcon-Lang 2005).

## Objective

This book introduces the fundamental principles, concepts, and methods of dendrochronology and provides the basic instruction, theoretical framework, and biological and ecological background for the practitioner of tree-ring research. While portions of this information were presented elsewhere (Stokes and Smiley 1968 [reprinted as Stokes and Smiley 1996], Fritts 1976 [reprinted as Fritts 2001], Phipps 1985, Schweingruber 1996), here I have compiled this knowledge into a single basic user manual and easy reference book that covers the breadth of the field. Whether you are a graduate student incorporating tree-ring chronologies into your thesis or dissertation, a professional land manager who is looking for environmental information, or a layperson who has heard about dendrochronology and wants to learn more, this book is a practical resource that will provide you a strong start in the field of dendrochronology.

No previous volume has presented a comprehensive history of dendrochronology that incorporates old world and new world pioneers in dendrochronology. Chapter 3 contains a more complete history of dendrochronology that draws from European, American, Russian, and Asian dendrochronologists up to the 1950s. An understanding of wood anatomy is becoming more important in this field as we push the geographical bounds of past research and start to study tree species growing in moist environments, such as the tropics and the deciduous forests of the eastern United States. I provide a quick primer on the aspects of wood growth and structure that underlie the study of tree rings in chapter 4. The core of this book is the field and laboratory methods that are incorporated in chapters 5 and 6. I present a basic founding in field practices and provide some greater depth in working with the programs and statistics that are important to dendrochronology. Broad overviews and useful starting points for all of the major subfields in dendrochronology are given in chapters 7–11. Each chapter describes some specialized methods in each subfield, and the bibliography includes entries for the subfields as a starting point for research. Finally, chapter 12 describes what I see as some frontiers in dendrochronology where researchers are gaining the most ground. Dendrochronology is still a young science, and there are many exciting frontiers yet to be explored.

## Summary

I have heard many discussions about the status of dendrochronology. People ask if it is a discipline, a tool, or an application. The answer depends upon who is doing the research and how they approach their work. I, among others, see dendrochronology as a thriving discipline with its own governing body of principles, theoretical advancements, and areas of important contributions to society. Some may simply use it as a tool to obtain dates or longer-term records of past phenomena. Other researchers may work mainly on advancing theory in different fields but call on the techniques of dendrochronology to advance their understanding within their discipline. Through my experience teaching dendrochronology classes in the university setting and coordinating and teaching the North American Dendroecological Fieldweek, I have found that that a basic set of knowledge exists that is new to and important for the starting practitioner of dendrochronology.

The text is meant to present the principles and methods needed to work independently through basic research projects in dendrochronology. This book is not intended as the final word in dendrochronology, and any practitioner of these methods should delve deeply into the primary literature and other resource books available in the field. I attempted to cite most of the pertinent literature throughout the text and to lead the reader to useful internet resources that are available in dendrochronology. I hope that you will find this book useful, whatever your intended application.

# 2
# Some Basic Principles and Concepts in Dendrochronology

Dendrochronologists follow some basic principles and concepts that describe sampling protocols, model how environmental factors are incorporated in tree growth, and form basic procedures of how to date tree rings and build chronologies. We also make some basic assumptions about the natural world in the way that we conduct research. In this chapter, I will discuss some of the assumptions, guiding principles, and core concepts in the field of dendrochronology.

Some basic terminology associated with dendrochronology will be introduced first. The **signal-to-noise ratio** is an important measure of the amount of desired information recorded in the chronology versus the amount of unwanted information and random variation also included in the tree-ring record. The noise can come from environmental factors not of interest to the researcher. For example, growth releases due to mortality of neighboring trees (processes involved in gap dynamics) are considered noise to a dendroclimatologist, whereas they are the signal of interest for the dendroecologists interested in reconstructing forest succession.

**Calibration** is the process of comparing a known record of some environmental variable to the tree-ring chronology for the purpose of determining tree growth response to that variable. We use meteorological data (such as monthly temperature, precipitation, or the Palmer drought severity index) as a calibration data set for climate reconstruction. Similarly, dendrochronologists use a record of past fruiting of trees as a calibration data set for mast (synchronous fruiting in trees) reconstruction or the historical records of insect populations to identify the growth pattern associated with insect outbreaks. Part of this independent data can be withheld from the original model and used to verify the reconstruction. This step is important to determine how accurate reconstructions may be.

## Principle of Uniformitarianism

The principle of uniformitarianism is a basic assumption of geology and most other natural sciences. It can be succinctly stated as, "The present is the key to the past." This means that the processes occurring today are the same processes that occurred in the past. The classic example states that by collecting the sediment washing down a stream over a certain time period one could extrapolate how long it would take the entire mountain to erode away, because the principle of uniformitarianism assumes that the processes that determine the rate of erosion remain the same through time. This basic assumption enables estimates of the rate of change in natural systems. Dendrochronologists use the principle of uniformitarianism when we reconstruct past climate. Researchers realize that the climate is changing through time and that this change (such as the availability of carbon dioxide) may alter how a tree responds to climate, but this is the best estimate that can be provided until further information is added to the model.

Dendrochronologists use calibration data sets such as meteorological data, historical records of insect outbreaks, or masting to build mathematical models of how trees respond to these environmental factors. Once such a model is developed (usually with regression analysis), it provides an understanding of how the trees respond to the variable of interest. The model can then be inverted to reconstruct that variable into the past for the lifetime of the trees. For this reconstruction to be possible, dendrochronologists have to assume that the processes affecting the tree's response to these environmental factors have not changed from the calibration time period to the period of reconstruction. This is a common assumption made in the natural sciences, but it has some drawbacks of which the researcher should be aware.

The trees' responses to the environment do vary with age. Seedlings are more sensitive to environmental factors and are more likely to perish because of limited moisture availability or temperature extremes. Young trees often go through a period of juvenile growth during which they produce larger-than-average growth rings. Dendrochronologists should be aware of and control for these tree responses as they build chronologies and reconstruct environmental factors over the lifetime of the trees.

Humans have changed the environment, which may change how a tree responds to climate variations. We live in a world of elevated carbon dioxide in the atmosphere; prior to the industrial revolution the normal level of carbon dioxide was 280 ppm, while the current level is close to 380 ppm. This amount of carbon dioxide in the atmosphere is outside the natural range of variability recorded over the past 100,000 years by ice cores. Most of the calibration climate data has been recorded during a time of elevated carbon dioxide, and tree response to variability in temperature and precipitation may be moderated by the amount of carbon dioxide in the atmosphere, as carbon dioxide is a key component in the process of photosynthesis. This may affect climate calibrations and the resulting climate reconstructions.

There are some ways to reduce the risk of violating the assumptions of the principle of uniformitarianism. For example, tree-ring series can be truncated to remove juvenile growth. This shortens the resultant chronology and reduces sample depth further back in time, but it results in more reliable reconstructions. Series can also be detrended by fitting curves such as a negative exponential or a cubic smoothing spline (described at the end of this chapter and in chapter 6) to the ring-width measurements to remove trends through time. But none of these treatments deal with the calibration problem of living in a time of an altered climate. We know that our assumption that present processes have not changed through time is not always correct, but uniformitarianism is a productive starting point in the analysis of past climates and environmental variability. Researchers must be aware of these assumptions and work to overcome such limitations to understand the natural world.

## Principle of Crossdating

The principle of crossdating is the basic tenet of dendrochronology. It is the main tool by which the exact year of growth of every annual ring is determined. Without crossdating, a simple ring count is likely to produce error due to locally absent or false rings. Crossdating is imperative when ring-width measurements are compared to annual phenomena such

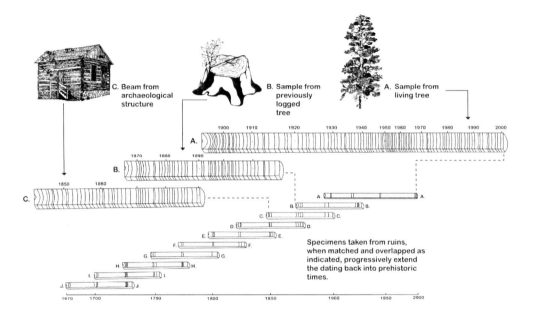

**Figure 2.1** Crossdating is the basic principle of dendrochronology and provides the annual resolution of the dated rings. (Modified from Stallings 1949)

as meteorological data or when reporting past events with annual accuracy. Without exact annual dating of the tree rings, accurate calibration is impossible because the chronology will be misdated by one or more years. For example, the temperature data from 1973 may be erroneously compared to the annual ring grown in 1972 or 1974, and the result is a degraded or nonexistent climate signal. Because of the importance of crossdating, all samples should be visually crossdated first before they are statistically checked with a program like COFE-CHA (discussed in chapter 6). Annual resolution is the trademark of dendrochronology, so every effort should be made to ensure annual resolution and to provide quality control of the dating.

The history of the principle of crossdating is relatively long. The French naturalists Duhamel and Bufon first used crossdating to identify the 1709 frost ring in a series of samples collected in 1737. Alexander Catlin Twining rediscovered the process in 1827, and Charles Babbage wrote about it in great length in 1838. But it was not until 1904, when A. E. Douglass laid out the basic methodology of skeleton plotting and the refined technique of the memorization method, that crossdating was really tested and documented.

Crossdating matches the pattern of wide and narrow rings in a tree to determine the location of real ring boundaries based on anatomical wood structure, providing a check of the actual date of a specimen (fig. 2.1). In this sense, a tree core is like a bar code with varying widths of lines representing each year. The patterns from one tree can be matched with those of other trees to determine if all of the rings are represented in a sample. This technique shows where rings are missing from a sample or where a tree might have formed two or more rings in one year. Crossdating results in accurate dates for every single ring in the tree-ring record.

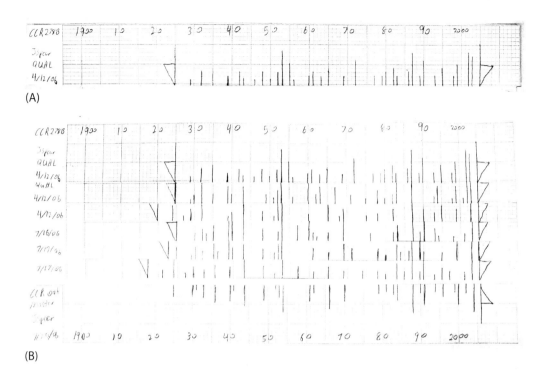

(A)

(B)

**Figure 2.2** (A) Single skeleton plot showing the beginning and end arrows that represent the innermost date and bark date, respectively. Notice on the left side, the sample ID, dendrochronologist's name, species, and date are recorded. (B) Once multiple skeleton plots are completed on a site, they can be taped together and a master chronology can be drawn from them (as seen in the inverted plot at the bottom of the graphic).

There are many ways to date tree rings, but the most repeatable and tested techniques are those originally developed by Douglass. The method of **skeleton plotting** assigns each year of growth to a vertical line on a piece of graph paper (usually graph paper with five lines per centimeter is used). The length of the line represents the importance of the ring to the signal of the chronology. Narrow rings are more important for recording limiting environmental factors, so more attention is usually given to the rings that are below average in width. Therefore, the more narrow a ring, the longer the line marked on the skeleton plot (fig. 2.2).

Because of the age-related growth trend, which will be discussed below, and the individual variability of growth in the tree through time, the dendrochronologist uses a process of mental standardization in which the relative width of the ring is determined by comparing the ring of interest to three rings on either side. Only seven rings are compared at a time, and the narrowest rings are noted on the skeleton plot. This mental standardization keeps long-term trends or short-term suppressions from dominating the signal in the chronology.

The skeleton plot allows for a range of line lengths from 0, indicating an average or larger than average ring width, to 10, which is usually reserved for a ring found to be absent through crossdating. The sample about to be dated should be visually scanned to determine the size of the smallest and largest rings across the entire cross section to set the overall scale of the skeleton plot. The smallest rings in the sample will have a line length of nine boxes, and the entire range from 1 to 9 should be used for all samples. The resultant plots illustrate the inter-annual ring-width variability within the wood sample whether the wood is complacent, with very similar ring widths, or sensitive, containing much variability in ring width.

Many beginning dendrochronologists have a difficult time with this apparently arbitrary determination of the length of the line on the skeleton plot, but after some practice, most researchers and students produce very similar skeleton plots. The process can be duplicated by a computer program, showing that it is not a purely subjective process (Cropper 1979). However, dating should always be performed visually and can be checked with various computer methods.

Skeleton plotting allows two different trees growing at vastly different rates to be compared to determine if all of the rings are represented (see chapter 5 for specific details in marking the wood and making a skeleton plot). A **master chronology**, a record of ring widths representing the stand level signal, can also be developed from the individual tree skeleton plots. For a ring to be represented on the master chronology it has to appear on 50% of the plots, and the length of the lines are averaged together (usually only counting the trees that represent that ring). The master chronology is drawn upside down from the orientation of a regular plot so that it is easy to check the date of subsequent plots against it. In the stack of skeleton plots, the rings that are represented on most of the samples become marker rings on the master chronology. This is usually done by lining up the skeleton plots so that they share the same time axis along the bottom, and any ring that is consistently marked on half of the samples in a given year is averaged onto the master skeleton plot. Dead wood can then be dated against this master chronology. One clear advantage of skeleton plotting over the list method is that samples with unknown outside dates can be dated using skeleton plots.

The **list method** is a technique used to develop the chronology of marker rings without the added steps of plotting them on graph paper (Yamaguchi 1991). The skeleton plot provides more data and a clear graphic representation of the samples, making the dating of difficult samples more probable. Also, the list method can only date complete samples from living trees, as the outer ring provides the starting point for the list. The list method, therefore, is not of any use in dating archaeological samples or fire scars from dead wood. The list method is a faster procedure and can be more efficiently used in wood with a clear pattern of rings. When developing the list, the researcher starts at an anchor in time, which is the outside of the sample with the known coring date. Care should be taken to develop the master list only from good-quality cores in which the samples are complete and the tree was living. The date of each small ring is noted on a piece of paper while counting back from the bark of the tree so that a list of marker rings is generated (fig. 2.3). Those rings that are consistently noted between samples are the reliable marker rings that can be used to date other cores.

The **memorization method** is generally used once the master chronology is known for a set of samples (Douglass 1941). The master chronology may have been produced from skeleton plots, the list method, or a published chronology. The marker rings in the chronology are memorized (sometimes with a written aid) and the tree rings are counted back from the bark to the inside of the core. Each time a narrow ring is encountered it is mentally checked with the list of previously derived marker rings. If the narrow ring is a marker ring and should be

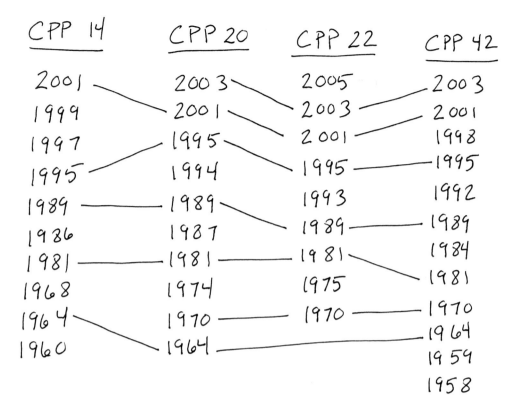

**Figure 2.3** Marker rings recorded using the list method. Five rings (2001, 1995, 1989, 1981, and 1964) all appear as important marker rings that occur between all of the samples that are recording growth at the time. Note that the marker rings from sample CCP22 stop at 1970 because this core does not extend earlier than this time. One can list the inside ring date in a box at the beginning of the list to indicate when the sample started recording.

narrow, then continue dating the sample. If the ring is not a marker ring, it is usually best to count to other marker rings to check the dates across a couple marker rings. The chronology of marker rings would be consistently off from the master in the case of a missing or false ring. If the whole chronology appears to be shifted forward in time by one year, then the wood representing the period in time where that pattern started to diverge from the master should be examined to identify the missing ring.

## Principle of Limiting Factors

The principle of limiting factors states that the most limiting environmental factor controls the growth of the organism. This is based on Liebig's law of the minimum, which is a simplification of the actual physiological response of a tree to environmental forcing, but it can be used as a first approximation of the environmental factor that is most likely to be recorded in a given tree-ring chronology (fig. 2.4). For example, trees growing in the semi-arid

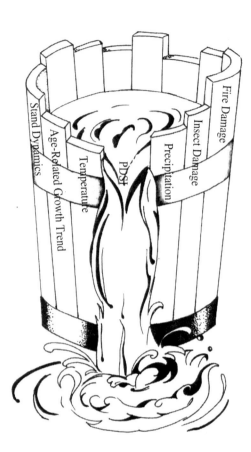

**Figure 2.4** Liebig's Law of the Minimum states that whatever factor is most limiting to growth will control the rate of growth for that organism. In this illustration of the concept, the slat labeled PDSI (Palmer drought severity index) is the most limiting factor for plant growth; therefore, availability of moisture to the plant will control the ring width. It should be noted that the limiting factor may change over time.

environment of southern Arizona are normally limited by the amount of rainfall each year and actually stop growth in the middle of the summer, when the soil moisture is depleted and very little rain falls to sustain the trees. But those same trees start to grow again when the monsoon rains come in late summer and replenish the water. Trees growing at high elevation tend to be limited by temperature, whereas defoliated trees are limited by the reduction in their photosynthetic potential. Tree growth can also be limited because of a lack of access to nutrients in the soil. Gardeners often experience the benefits of fertilizing plants with nitrogen to increase growth.

A limiting factor dominates the growth for each year and is the main variable recorded in ring width, creating a series of rings that vary in width from one year to the next (fig. 2.5). It is possible, however, that this limiting factor changes through a plant's life, making reconstructions of environmental factors more tenuous. When one variable was limiting but then

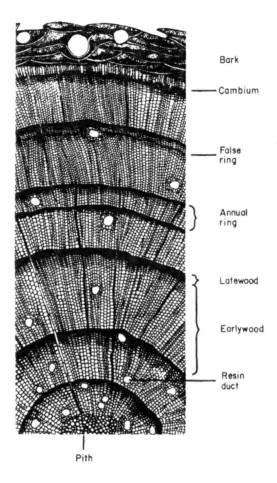

Bark

Cambium

False
ring

Annual
ring

Latewood

Earlywood

Resin
duct

Pith

**Figure 2.5** Pine cross section. Conifer trees in temperate areas produce one ring per year. These rings can be broken into the earlywood portion (open cells with thin cell walls) and the latewood portion (cells with thick cell walls and a smaller lumen). Other features that are present are the pith, resin ducts, cambium, and the bark. The variation in ring width is generally driven by climate and results in the pattern of wide and narrow rings that we use to crossdate the wood samples. Sometimes a false ring may be present, as in this sample, where the tree growth slows because of a reduction in the limiting factor for growth of the tree, such as precipitation. When that environmental factor limiting growth returns (e.g., when it rains), the tree resumes growth and the cells grade back to earlywood structure with thinner cell walls. (From Fritts 1976)

occurs in abundance, another limiting factor is likely to control growth. Also, trees may be limited by multiple factors at one time, complicating the physiological response of the tree.

## Principle of the Aggregate Tree Growth Model

The principle of aggregate tree growth suggests that trees record everything that affects their growth and provides a conceptual model for how to envision these effects, ultimately providing a tool to tease apart the disparate effects of the environment on tree growth. Although trees can be severely limited by one factor, they are most likely recording multiple factors that limit their growth. The aggregate tree growth model (equation I; Cook 1985, 1992) is used to conceptualize this response and to try to understand the different variables that can affect tree growth:

$$R_t = f(G_t, C_t, D1_t, D2_t, E_t) \qquad\qquad [\text{I}]$$

where $R_t$ is ring width at year $t$, $G_t$ is the age- (or size-) related growth trend, $C_t$ is climate, $D1_t$ is the endogenous disturbance within the stand, $D2_t$ is the exogenous disturbance from outside the stand, and $E_t$ is the error term incorporating all of the signal that is not controlled for by the above variables.

This conceptual model demonstrates that ring width for each year is dependent upon a complex array of variables that contribute to growth. Trees have an intrinsic age-related growth trend, respond to current climate conditions and reflect the previous year's climate, and are affected by disturbances from within and outside of the stand. The age-related (also known as size-related) growth trend results from a tree putting the same volume of wood on an ever-increasing cylinder. When a radius of the tree is examined, ring-width often decreases in size with age of the tree. In an open-grown pine tree, this trend can be modeled with a negative exponential curve, while the ring-width pattern from trees grown in a dense forest may be dominated by competitive effects from neighboring trees more than this age-related growth trend. Finally, some variability always remains that cannot be explained, and this is incorporated in the model by the error term. Recent research has begun to explore the information that is contained in the error term by looking at variables such as biological constraints to growth (for an example with mast reconstruction, see Speer 2001). Calling this the error term is not the most accurate wording, as it incorporates all variables not explicitly identified in the model not just errors in measurement.

The aggregate tree growth model demonstrates the complexity incorporated in each year's growth, but it can also be used as a tool to explore the different layers of response. The age-related growth trend can be removed from the chronology through basic standardization techniques that will be discussed later in this chapter. The climate variables can be removed by running a regression analysis between ring widths and the climate variables to which the tree responds. The residuals from that analysis (that is, the variability not accounted for by the regression model) can be analyzed to determine what environmental factors are present beneath the age-related growth trend and climate variables that have been removed, assuming the appropriate calibration data set is available to build such a model.

## Concept of Autocorrelation

Autocorrelation is the correlation of a variable with itself over successive time intervals. All biological organisms are subject to autocorrelation because of the continuity and unidirectional flow of the progression of time and the development of growth (fig. 2.6). The needles of conifers produced in one year because of a favorable climate are maintained on a tree the following years, adding to the photosynthetic potential of that tree (fig. 2.7; LaMarche 1974, LaMarche and Stockton 1974). Therefore, the previous year's climate affects the current year's growth. This is the most obvious example of autocorrelation, but any biological organ-

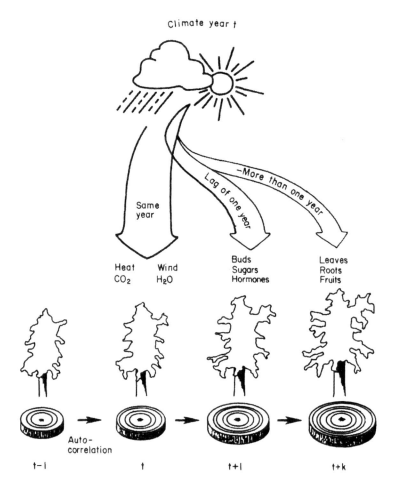

Climate year $t$

Same year

Lag of one year

—More than one year

Heat  Wind  Buds  Leaves
$CO_2$  $H_2O$  Sugars  Roots
Hormones  Fruits

Auto-correlation

$t-1$    $t$    $t+1$    $t+k$

**Figure 2.6** Tree growth often includes autocorrelation, which is the statistical characteristic that the current year's growth is affected by the previous year's growth. Autocorrelation can be driven by the biological activities of the tree in that the current year's climate will affect the heat, rainfall, and carbon dioxide ($CO_2$) levels for this year's growth, but it also affects the following year's growth through development of new buds, sugars, and hormones. Finally, the climate from that same year will affect growth even further into the future by the development of leaves, roots, and fruits.

ism produces cells, proteins, and sugars that can be used in subsequent years, creating autocorrelation in the response of that organism to environmental variables. Autocorrelation can become a problem because most statistical analysis (such as regression analysis) assumes that the data are not autocorrelated because it can artificially increase correlation statistics. Fortunately, this component can be described and removed by determining the variance of the current year's growth that is explained by the previous year's growth. This one-year lag is described by a first-order autoregressive model. The correlation to growth two years prior is described by a second-order autoregressive model, and this continues back in time until no significant autoregressive signal can be detected.

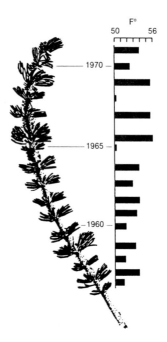

**Figure 2.7** Needle retention in bristlecone pine at upper treeline related to summer temperature (from LaMarche and Stockton 1974). Bristlecone pine trees retain their needles for many years, in this case 16 years, resulting in good growing conditions in the past affecting the current year's photosynthetic potential.

## Concept of the Ecological Amplitude

Ecological amplitude is the pattern of vegetation on the landscape that is controlled by the range of climate variables to which a species responds (Lomolino et al. 2006). The microclimate of a site is also modified by topography, slope, and aspect, which affect the local distribution of species. Based on this idea, a tree species should be less stressed at the center of its range and more stressed near the margins of the range, where the climate is assumed to be harsher for that species. Therefore, for climate-related research it is often better to sample a species near the edge of its range to find trees that are more likely to record the climate variable of interest. These ecotones, or edge regions, are also the areas where change in tree growth is more likely to occur in the face of a changing climate, making ecotones important sample sites. For example, black gum (*Nyssa sylvatica*) is at the northern limit of its range distribution in New Hampshire (fig. 2.8), so samples taken from this species at this location are likely to be more sensitive to temperature if that is the limiting climatic factor at the northern edge of its ecological amplitude. Samples taken from just north of the Everglades in Florida, at the southern end of black gum's ecological amplitude, are not likely to be limited by lower temperatures but may be limited by competition with other species or by an excess of precipitation and soil moisture.

*Nyssa sylvatica*

500    0    500   1000  1500  Kilometers

**Figure 2.8**  The light-gray area represents the range of black gum. (From Little 1971; http://esp
.cr.usgs.gov/data/atlas/little/nysssylv.pdf)

## Principle of Site Selection

Given that trees record all of the variables that affect their growth, dendrochronologists
use the concept of site selection to maximize the signal recorded in the trees they sample.
Sites should be located where the trees are most likely to be stressed by the variable that the

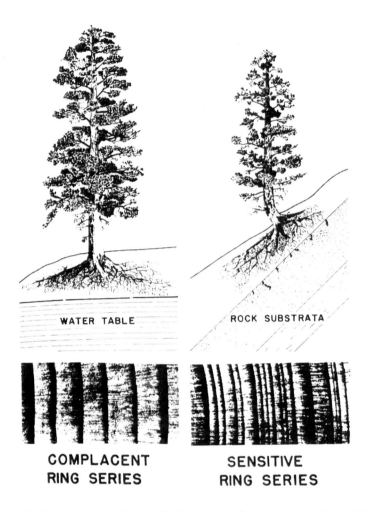

WATER TABLE

ROCK SUBSTRATA

**COMPLACENT
RING SERIES**

**SENSITIVE
RING SERIES**

**Figure 2.9** Specific sites are selected from which trees are likely to record the variable of interest. A tree with the same size rings is considered to have a complacent ring-width series (left) and a tree with a lot of variability in growth is considered to have a sensitive tree-ring series (right). (From Stokes and Smiley 1968)

researcher is interested in reconstructing (fig. 2.9). For example, if a precipitation reconstruction is needed, then trees located in an arid environment should be sampled. Trees that are growing on the edge of their ecological amplitude, such as the extreme lower elevation of species in a semi-arid environment, are more likely to record drought events. A temperature signal is likely to be recorded at high elevation or high latitude, where low temperatures during the growing season can limit growth. Similarly, historical documentation of insect outbreaks or fire history is used to guide initial sampling of trees to demonstrate the tree-ring response to these phenomena.

Trees that are growing at the center of their ecological amplitude with favorable climate year round are likely to produce complacent growth, in which each ring is a similar width. If a tree is complacent, it does not record much environmental variability that could be used for crossdating. The tree is likely to be a poor environmental recorder. However, it may be limited by its biological ability to grow, which could be genetic or driven by other physiological factors that might be of interest to a dendrochronologist, such as masting. The opposite of complacent growth is sensitive growth, in which the tree demonstrates considerable variability in year-to-year growth and is thus recording some environmental variable (fig. 2.9). All of these factors must be considered when choosing a site to sample for a given research project.

## Principle of Replication

Replication is the use of multiple samples to develop an accurate stand-level chronology or the use of many samples back in time to provide good sample depth throughout the chronology. This principle was recognized by many of the early researchers in the field, such as Twining (1833) and Babbage (1838). By taking multiple samples on a site and matching the ring-width pattern between these trees, valid crossdating for the stand can be demonstrated. Averaging the growth between two cores from one tree and between 20 trees on a site can remove individual tree variability and yield a stand-level signal. Averaging across many samples enables dendrochronologists to change the spatial scale over which a study is conducted, essentially stepping up from the individual tree to the stand and even regional level (fig. 2.10). Replication provides the basis for crossdating and contributes to the robustness of environmental reconstructions. The appropriate sample depth can be determined by using the expressed population signal (EPS) statistic described in chapter 6.

## Concept of Standardization

By fitting curves to trends in ring series, standardization removes age-related growth trends and other long-term variability that can be considered noise (fig. 2.11). Note that the long-term trend could be the signal that climatologists are interested in when they examine long-term changes in climate, but it is noise to an ecologist who is studying shorter-term variability in forest dynamics. This process also removes differences in growth rates between samples and produces a series mean equal to 1.0.

The most conservative technique of standardization is the negative exponential curve that is common in the growth of many trees and is geometrically mandated by adding the same volume of wood on the surface of an ever-increasing cylinder. The negative exponential curve is deterministic, meaning that it follows a model of tree growth. Other standardization techniques are empirical, meaning they are chosen through experimentation to find the best fit to a series of data. A cubic smoothing spline is an example of an empirical model that uses a flexible curve that is allowed to adjust at a regular interval (Cook 1985; fig. 2.12). When using these forms of standardization, the researcher should be cognizant of the signal that is being removed from the record. A 40-year cubic smoothing spline, for example, removes 50% of the variance at 40 years, leaves 99% of the variance at 12.67 years, and leaves 1% of the variance at 126.17 years so that very little century-length signal is left in the resultant chronology (see table 2.1 for data on other splines). Splines provide a more organic fit to the data

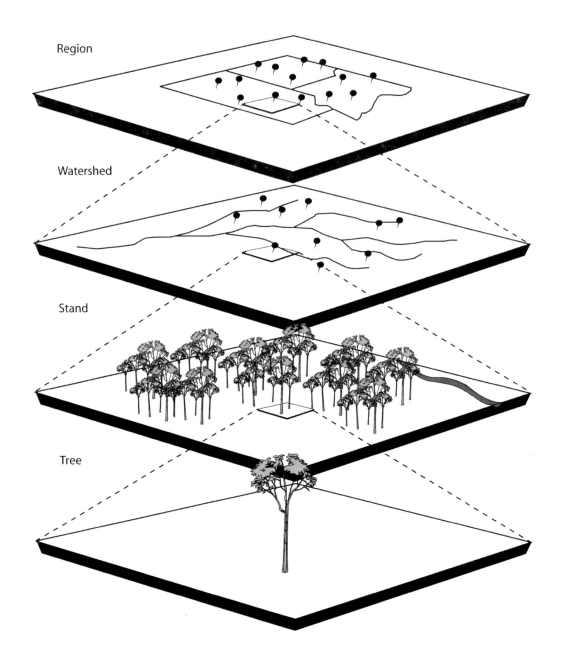

**Figure 2.10** Sampling scale. By taking replicate samples, we can average out individual tree variability and change the analysis level to higher spatial scales (such as the stand, watershed, or regional levels). (Modified by Bharath Ganesh-Babu from Swetnam and Baisan 1996)

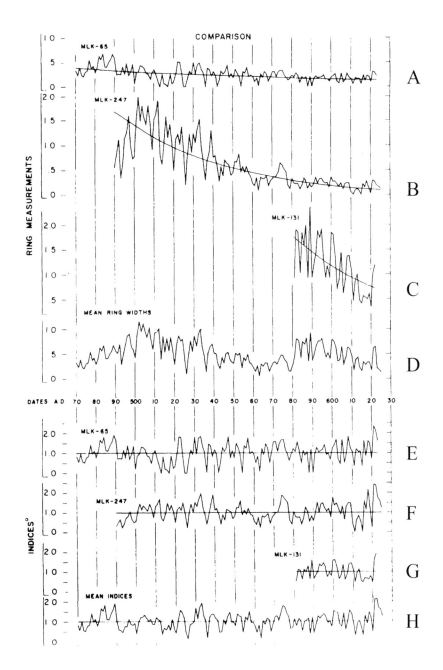

**Figure 2.11** Standardization. The juvenile growth effect results in a higher level of growth when a tree is young. If cores from three trees (A–C) are averaged together without regard for this age-related growth trend, the resultant chronology (D) will mainly record when these younger trees are incorporated into the chronology. If, however, the series are standardized with a negative exponential curve and index chronologies are generated by dividing the measured ring width by the model curve fit value, then these index chronologies (E–G) can be averaged together to generate a master chronology that maintains its interannual variability and enhances the stand level signal (H). (Modified from Fritts 1976)

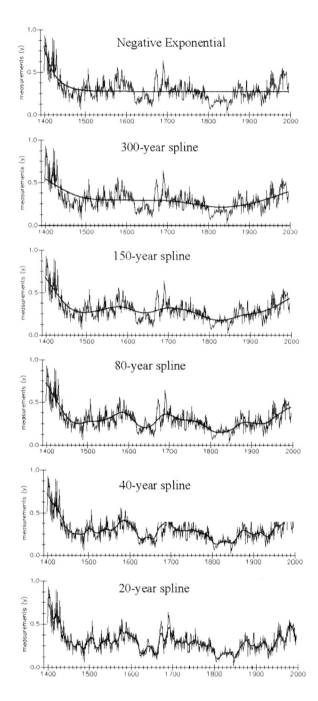

**Figure 2.12** Standardization with a negative exponential curve and cubic smoothing splines. Each curve represents the same set of ring-width measurements back to 1400. A negative exponential curve is fit to the ring widths, followed by a series of shorter cubic smoothing splines (300, 150, 80, 40, and 20 years) and the resultant curve fit is shown as the smooth black line. Note that increasingly shorter wavelengths are removed from the master chronology.

**Table 2.1**    The frequency of the variance that remains using different cubic smoothing splines

| Spline Length | Leaves 99% of variance at | Leaves 50% of variances at | Leaves 1% of the variance at |
|---|---|---|---|
| 20 | 6.34 years | 20 years | 63.09 years |
| 40 | 12.67 years | 40 years | 126.17 years |
| 60 | 19.01 years | 60 years | 189.26 years |
| 80 | 25.35 years | 80 years | 252.35 years |
| 100 | 31.69 years | 100 years | 315.43 years |
| 150 | 47.53 years | 150 years | 473.15 years |
| 200 | 63.37 years | 200 years | 630.87 years |
| 300 | 95.06 years | 300 years | 946.20 years |
| 400 | 126.75 years | 400 years | 1261.73 years |
| 500 | 158.44 years | 500 years | 1577.17 years |

than straight line or exponential curves, but they do remove different amounts of variance at different temporal scales.

Standardization is a powerful technique that can be used to minimize noise in a chronology and increase the signal of interest, but it is also a complex issue and probably one of the more controversial steps in dendrochronological analysis. New techniques are being developed for the standardization of tree-ring series and are further discussed in chapter 6.

## Summary

The principles and concepts described in this chapter help dendrochronologists to work through the process of developing valid dendrochronological reconstructions. Some studies are starting to show that our perception of concepts such as ecological amplitude and what we expect a site should be recording are not necessarily as we suppose (Tardif et al. 2006; Speer, unpublished data). The patterns that we observe on the landscape are more complex than some of the basic models presented in this chapter, but these principles help to guide our sampling and chronology development and are a good first approximation of the factors that drive dendrochronological sampling methods. The next chapter explores the history of dendrochronology and discusses the people who developed many of these principles.

# 3
# History of Dendrochronology

Dendrochronology is a young discipline in the realm of the sciences, with many new frontiers left to be investigated. The first Laboratory of Tree Ring Research was founded at the University of Arizona in 1937 by A. E. Douglass. The subfield of dendroecology became a major area of research only in the 1970s, and today new research is being conducted using stable isotopes from tree rings to examine trees' physiological responses to climate change. Despite these fairly recent beginnings, the idea that trees produce annual rings had been suggested since the time of Theophrastus in 322 BC (Studhalter 1956). In this chapter, I describe the development of the field and many of the basic concepts that we still use today.

## The Early Years

In the 1400s and 1500s, some famous naturalists recognized the annual character of tree rings and started to look to the environment for causes of variation in ring growth (table 3.1). In the late 1400s, **Leonardo da Vinci** (fig. 3.1) described annual ring formation and suggested that the growth of tree rings is related to weather (Stallings 1937, Sarton 1954, Corona 1986). "The rings in the branches of trees that have been cut off show the number of its years and which years were damper or drier according to the greater or lesser thickness of these rings" (Kemp and Walker 2001; translation of Leonardo da Vinci's Treatise on Painting).

From 1580 to 1581, **Michel de Montaigne** traveled through Germany, Switzerland, and Italy and kept a diary of his journey. While in Italy, he reported on a conversation that he had with an unnamed carpenter who noted the annual nature of tree rings.

> The artist, a clever man, famous for his ability to make mathematical instruments, taught me that every tree has inside as many circles and turns (*cerchi e giri*) as it has years. He caused me to see it in many kinds of wood which he had in his shop, for he is a carpenter. The part of the wood turned to the North is the straightest, and the circles there are closer together than in the other parts. Therefore when a piece of timber is brought to him he is able, he claims, to tell the age of the tree and its situation (the orientation of the section). (Translation of the original Italian text by Sarton 1954)

## The 1700s and the 1709 Frost Ring

Many other early scientists had recognized tree-ring growth and used tests to demonstrate that trees produce rings annually. French naturalists **Henri Louis Duhamel du Monceau** and **George Louis Leclerc de Buffon** discovered in 1737 that a conspicuous frost-damaged ring occurred 29 years in from the bark of several newly felled trees in France, recording

**Figure 3.1** Leonardo da Vinci (1452–1519) mentioned that trees put on annual rings and respond to local climatic conditions in the *Trattato della Pittura* (*Treatise on Painting*), which he worked on from 1482 to 1498 in Milan at the court of Ludovico Sforza. (Image from the Library of Congress, no. unk84025089)

the 1709 marker ring. This year was significant in dendrochronology because of its frequent use as a marker ring by early dendrochronologists across Europe. **Carl Linnaeus** noted the 1709 frost ring when he examined wood samples in Sweden (Linnaeus 1745, 1751). Burgsdorf and de Candolle also noted this frost ring in other countries, demonstrating how important this type of marker ring is in dating tree rings. Duhamel went on to conduct early experiments in pinning trees (the process of creating a small wound in the tree that can later be sampled to examine growth since the wounding) and used aluminum foil as an early type of dendrometer band around the tree to examine the annual growth of trees in 1751 and 1758 (Studhalter 1956).

In 1785 **Friedrich August Ludwig von Burgsdorf** examined tree growth over a blaze marking a trail that was cut into a tree in 1767. He found 18 rings had formed since the blaze was cut, thus demonstrating annual growth in this oak (*Quercus* sp.) tree in Germany. Burgsdorf also noted the 1709 frost ring in beech (*Fagus* spp.) and other trees in Germany (Studhalter 1956). **Alphonse de Candolle**, a Swiss botanist, discovered the 1709 frost ring when examining

**Table 3.1** The early dendrochronologists sorted by the dates that they used tree rings

| Scientist | Location | Year | Contribution | Reference |
|---|---|---|---|---|
| Theophrastus | Greece | 322 BC | Noted that trees put on new growth every year | Schweingruber (1996) |
| Leonardo da Vinci | Italy | 1452–1519 1482–1498 | Noted the relationship between climate and tree growth. Wrote the *Trattato della Pittura* mentioning tree rings | Sarton (1954) |
| Michel de Montaigne | Italy | 1581 | The idea of counting tree rings to attain tree age was related to Montaigne by an unnamed carpenter | Sarton (1954) |
| Carl Linnaeus | Sweden | 1707–1778 | Counted rings to determine the age of trees | Webb (1986), online article |
| Duhamel and George Louis Leclerc de Buffon | France | 1737 | Counted rings to determine the date of a conspicuous frost ring | Dean (1978), Webb (1986) |
| A. C. Twinning | Connecticut, United States | 1827 | Used crossdating and noted the common signal across a site | Dean (1978) |
| Theodor Hartig | Germany | 1837 | Set up the ecological basis for dendrochronology in Germany | Schweingruber (1996) |
| Charles Babbage | England | 1838 | Noted the concepts of competition, complacency, replication, reaction wood in trees, parent trees, climate reconstruction, and specific tree-ring patterns from storms and floods | Babbage (1838), Heizer (1954), Zeuner (1958) |
| Jacob Kuechler | Texas, United States | 1859 | Used modern principles of site selection by choosing trees on low ridges with good drainage and used tables to note ring characteristics, demonstrating an early example of crossdating | Dean (1978) |
| Robert Hartig | Germany | 1867 | Used tree rings to date events of hail, frost, insect damage, and examined trees that were killed by pollution | Schweingruber (1996) |

| Name | Location | Year | Description | Reference |
|---|---|---|---|---|
| A. L. Child | Nebraska, United States | 1871 | Compared tree growth in red maple to meteorological data for spring and summer | Webb (1986) |
| A. Stoeckhardt | Western Europe | 1871 | Examined forest damage from air pollution | Eckstein and Pilcher (1990) |
| Jacobus C. Kapteyn | Denmark | 1880–1881 | Examined the relationship between tree growth in oaks and rainfall | Webb (1986) |
| F. Shvedov | Ukraine | 1892 | Examined black locust trees for a dendroclimatic analysis that he used for prediction | Kairiukstis and Shiyatov (1990) |
| B. E. Fernow | New England, United States | 1897 | Wrote a paper on determining the age of blazing on trees by counting the tree rings | Webb (1986) |
| A. E. Douglass | Arizona, United States | 1904 | Developed crossdating as a tool and was persistent in developing chronologies and training future dendrochronologists | Webb (1983), Nash (1999) |
| Bruno Huber | Germany | 1940 | Spent considerable time dating wood samples and worked on new statistical techniques to quantify the strength of dating of different specimens | Schweingruber (1996) |

**Figure 3.2** Alexander Catlin Twining (1801–1884) noted the application of using tree rings to examine climate in 1827. (Image from http://www.rootsweb.com/~ctnhvbio/Twining_Alexander.html)

juniper (*Juniperus* spp.) tree rings in France in 1839–1840. Candolle went further by suggesting a number of early methods that could be used to crossdate rings, although much of his work dealt with average ring widths over a period of time rather than maintaining the annual resolution of the rings (Studhalter 1956).

## The 1800s: Tree Rings Become Common Knowledge

**De Witt Clinton** in 1811, while he was mayor of New York City, counted rings from trees growing on the earthen mounds near Canandaigua, New York. He estimated that the trees had about 1000 rings, and concluded that the mounds were created by prehistoric Native Americans and not by early Europeans. This was the first recorded archaeological use of tree rings, although Clinton did not exactly date the wood to obtain more reliable bounding dates on the structures. His ring count of 1000 rings seems greatly exaggerated considering the tree species in this area, although he was able to test whether the structure was made prior to or after European colonization (Zeuner 1958).

**Alexander Catlin Twining** (fig. 3.2) used replicated samples from many trees harvested for the building of a wharf in New Haven, Connecticut. This early account is unique because Twining conducted dating across multiple samples and related the growth to climate.

> In the year 1827, a large lot of hemlock timber was cut from the north eastern slope of East Rock, near New Haven, for the purpose of forming a foundation for the wharf which bounds the basin of the Farmington Canal on the East. While inspecting and measuring that timber, at the time of its delivery, I took particular notice of the successive layers, each of which constitutes a year's growth of the tree; and which, in that kind of wood, are

**Figure 3.3** Charles Babbage (1791–1871) wrote an article in the Ninth Bridgewater Treatise in 1838 about the potential for dendrochronology applied to buried wood, although his tree-ring comments were restricted to "Note M: On the Age of Strata, as Inferred from the Rings of Trees Embedded in Them." (Image from http://encyclopedia.laborlawtalk.com/Charles_Babbage)

very distinct. These layers were of various breadth, indicating a growth five or six times as full in some years as in others, preceding or following. Thus every tree had preserved a record of the seasons, for the whole period of its growth, whether thirty years or two hundred,—and what is worthy of observation, *every tree told the same story*. Thus, if you began at the outer layer of the two trees, one young and the other old, and counted back twenty years, if the young tree indicated, by a full layer, a growing season for that kind of timber, the other tree indicated the same. (Twining 1833: 391–392; italics in original)

Twining went on to foreshadow the use of tree rings to reconstruct climate beyond modern records. He also suggested that different genera would have a different climate response:

It would be interesting . . . to compare the sections of one kind of tree with that of another kind from the same locality, or to compare sections of the same kind of tree from different parts of the county. Such a comparison would elicit a mass of facts, both with respect to the progress of the seasons, and their relation to the growth of timber, and might prove, here-after, the means of carrying back our knowledge of the seasons, through a period coeval with the age of the oldest forest trees, and in regions of the country where scientific obser-vation has never yet penetrated, nor a civilized population dwelt. (Twining 1833: 393)

The Englishman **Charles Babbage** (fig. 3.3) wrote at length about the application of tree rings in determining the age of geological strata in his 1838 paper "On the Age of Strata, as Inferred from Rings of Trees Embedded in Them" (Heizer 1954). He discussed, with exam-ples, the concept of crossdating (the process of matching ring widths to obtain exact dates of annual growth) and went further to mention that distinctly small rings are due to climatic variability. Babbage (1838) also discussed competition, complacency, replication, reaction wood in trees, the concept of parent trees, climate reconstruction, and specific tree-ring patterns from storms and floods. He also formulated a research agenda using stem analysis to understand the growth throughout an entire tree and suggested that tree-ring patterns found in the roots should be the same as those found in the canopy.

In the following passage, Babbage wrote about the climate response of trees and their ability to record climate through time: "These preeminent effects are obvious to our senses; but every shower that falls, every change of temperature that occurs, and every wind that blows, leaves on the vegetable world the traces of its passage; slight, indeed, and imperceptible, perhaps, to us, but not the less permanently recorded in the depths of those woody fabrics" (Babbage 1838: 258).

Babbage described the principle of crossdating with an example of the trees' response to climate: "If we were to select a number of trees of about the same size, we should probably find many of them to have been contemporaries. This fact would be rendered probable if we observed, as we doubtless should do, on examining the annual rings, that some of them conspicuous for their size occurred at the same distances of years in several trees. . . . The nature of the season, whether hot or cold, wet or dry, might be conjectured with some degree of probability, from the class of tree under consideration" (Babbage 1838: 258–259).

The concept of the effect of local ecology on tree-ring response was also noted by Babbage: "Some [trees] might have been protected by adjacent large trees, sufficiently near to shelter them from the ruder gales, but not close enough to obstruct the light and air by which they were nourished. Such a tree might have a series of large and rather uniform rings; during the period of its protections by its neighbour; and these might be followed by the destruction of its protector" (Babbage 1838: 260).

One of the more important principles in dendrochronology is the concept of replication, which Babbage also realized could be used to examine broad-scale climate patterns: "But the effect of all these local and peculiar circumstances would disappear, if a sufficient number of sections could be procured from fossil trees, spread over considerable extent of country" (Babbage 1838: 260–261).

From 1837 to 1877, **Theodor Hartig** taught botany at the University of Braunschweig in Germany, where he laid the ecological groundwork for later dendrochronological research in Germany done by Robert Hartig (his son) and Bruno Huber (Schweingruber 1988, 1996). Theodor Hartig started a tradition of ecological examination in Germany that included the use of tree rings. Much of the present-day dendroecological research in Europe has grown from this foundation.

**Jacob Kuechler**, a German immigrant to the United States with an interest in weather, used crossdating to examine three post oak (*Quercus stellata*) trees from Texas in 1859. Kuechler's (1859) own publication is in German, but an editorial by Cleveland Abbe (1893) related an investigation made by Kuechler and reported on work by Colonel William W. Haupt. Kuechler used modern principles such as site selection by choosing trees on low ridges with good drainage as well as tables to note ring characteristics, demonstrating an early example of crossdating (Stallings 1937, Glock 1941).

Many of these early researchers recognized the climatic application of tree rings, and other researchers in the late 1800s noted additional applications that could be studied using tree rings. In 1866 the German botanist **Julius Ratzeburg** was probably the first to document an insect outbreak due to the effect of defoliation by caterpillars on tree rings (Ratzeburg 1866). He was able to assign absolute dates to the outbreak event by examining tree rings (Studhalter 1956). In 1882 **Franklin Hough** also discussed the possibility of dating insect outbreaks from damage the insects caused to trees (Studhalter 1956). Some of the first work in examining forest damage from air pollution was conducted by **Adolph Stoeckhardt** in Western Europe (Stoeckhardt 1871). This early investigation provided the lead for current researchers to examine and quantify the effects of air pollution (Eckstein and Pilcher 1990). **Elias Lewis** (1873) frequently counted the number of rings on fallen trees or stumps to determine the local growth rate of a species and then used that number to estimate the age of living trees based on their diameter and this age-diameter relationship. This was an early use of tree rings to estimate age structure in a forest stand, although today we realize that diameter is not always a good predictor of age (Studhalter 1956).

**John Muir**, the famous American naturalist, noted the annual nature of tree rings and that they could be used for geomorphic reconstructions, specifically determining the age of glacier-carved structures in the Sierra Nevada of California. He also expressed interest in having the time to study such phenomena with tree rings in *My First Summer in the Sierra*, passages from his journals written during his first visit to the Sierra Nevada in 1869:

> Have been sketching a silver fir that stands on a granite ridge a few hundred yards to the eastward of camp . . . a fine tree with a particular snow-storm story to tell. It is about one hundred feet high, growing on bare rock, thrusting its roots into a weathered joint less than an inch wide, and bulging out to form a base to bear its weight. The storm came from the north while it was young and broke it down nearly to the ground, as is shown by the old, dead, weather-beaten top leaning out from the living trunk built up from a new shoot below the break. The annual rings of the trunk that have overgrown the dead sapling tell the year of the storm. Wonderful that a side branch forming a portion of one of the level collars that encircle the trunk of this species (*Abies magnifica*) should bend upward, grow erect, and take the place of the lost axis to form a new tree. (Muir 1911 compiled in Cronon 1997: 235–236)

In another passage, Muir wrote, "Young pines, mostly the two-leaved and white-barked, are already springing up in these cleared gaps [avalanche tracks in the Sierra Nevada]. It would be interesting to ascertain the age of these saplings, for thus we should gain a fair approximation to the year that the great avalanches occurred. Perhaps most or all of them occurred the same winter. How glad I should be if free to pursue such studies!" (Muir 1911 compiled in Cronon 1997: 280).

The recognition of the formation of annual rings in trees, their record of the climate and insect outbreaks, and their dependence upon microsite differences was common knowledge to foresters in the 1880s, as evidenced by repeated discussion of annual rings in a textbook called *The Elements of Forestry*:

> In cross sections made years afterwards, the record of the seasons for a long period may be determined, at least in effect, by the width of the rings of annual growth. We sometimes find, at recurring intervals, a narrow ring, perhaps in every third year, that may have been

caused by the loss of leaves from worms that appear at that interval, and that have thus left their record when every other proof of their presence has perished. We have seen sections of trees in the museums of Schools of Forestry, in which these proofs were recorded through a century or more of time, and the years could be definitely fixed by counting inward from the year when the tree was felled. (Hough 1882: 70)

Franklin Hough (1882) went on to discuss the calculation of basal area increment for the purpose of quantifying the amount of growth in each year. He also discussed the microsite variations that affect tree-ring growth. "The rate of growth in wood differs greatly, according to the soil, elevation, aspect, climate, humidity, temperature, prevailing winds, and other causes" (Hough 1882: 75). The growth rings of multiple species are also shown in many figures throughout the text. From this textbook, it must be concluded that knowledge of the annual growth rings of trees and their response to the environment was common knowledge at this time. Hough (1882), however, described counting rings for this record—a practice still common in forestry today—rather than the process of crossdating.

In 1881 **Arthur Freiherr von Seckendorff-Gudent** collected tree samples from 6410 Austrian black pines (*Pinus nigra*) throughout Austria, Hungary, and Slovenia and used many of the basic principles in modern dendrochronology, including crossdating and replication (Wimmer 2001). He took the analysis further by noting the response of the trees to local climate (Seckendorff 1881).

When counting the tree rings on the disks, particular sequences of tree rings were repeatedly found in most of the trees. As an example, on most disks we found the 1871 ring showing a wide latewood, and the narrow 1802 ring. The tree rings of 1862 and 1863 were very close and significant due to their obvious difference in the strength of the latewood.

These significant tree-ring formations, which I named *characteristic tree-rings*, were an excellent tool to determine the age even on trees grown on very poor sites. From the many discovered characteristic *tree-rings* we always found at least a few on each disk.

. . . This method of age determination also helped to avoid counting false rings.

A comparison of tree-ring characteristics with temperature and precipitation for the dated years shows the relationship between tree growth and climate. Although, local site conditions are the major factor for tree-ring formations, the effect of particularly warm and cold years with low and high rainfall cannot be neglected. This influence (climate) may be smaller or bigger in a growing region, whether the climate is more of local or more of regional character.

Very hot and wet summers, such as the hot summer in 1811 (a good vine year) and the hot and also wet year of 1846 are characterized with extreme tree-ring formations. While the 1811 ring is distinct because of its weak (small) latewood, the year 1846 is significant because of its wide latewood.

. . . For now it is sufficient to state that climate has an effect on the formation of tree-rings and this effect can be softened by local site conditions but not revoked completely. (Seckendorff 1881 as translated in Wimmer 2001)

**Robert Hartig** used tree rings to date events of hail, frost, and insect damage and publishing 34 papers from 1869 to 1901 on the anatomy and ecology of tree rings while he was a professor at the University of Munich (Studhalter 1956, Schweingruber 1988). Hartig conducted a great deal of work in wood anatomy and was one of the first to look at the physiological basis for ring formation. Hartig (1888) categorized the rings of conifers into three sections: the spring zone, summer zone, and autumn zone. These divisions were later made into earlywood and latewood that we still use today (Studhalter 1956).

Hartig also examined trees that were killed by pollution and noted the long-term growth decline before their death, which made ring identification on the outside of the sections impossible. He was able to find the rings represented on the stem near the canopy of the tree and used these samples to crossdate the samples at the base and determine which rings were missing. Further work on hail, frost, and insect outbreaks was conducted by K. Rubner (1910) and I. W. Bailey (1925a, 1925b).

**F. Shvedov** worked on an early precipitation analysis using two black locust (*Robinia pseudoacacia*) trees. He found a 3- to 9-year cyclicity in the data and was able to correctly predict upcoming droughts in 1882 and 1891 (Shvedov 1892). His early work in dendroclimatology in Odessa in the Ukraine sets Shvedov apart as one of the early founders of dendroclimatology (Kairiukstis and Shiyatov 1990).

**Jacobus C. Kapteyn**, a Dutch astronomer, used crossdating on more than 50 oaks collected from Holland and Germany to examine climatic patterns that might be recorded in those trees. Although his work was completed in 1880, it was not published until 1914 (Kapteyn 1914). He concluded that spring and summer rains were the most important climatic variables that affect tree growth in this area of Europe. Kapteyn was ahead of his time, employing modern practices such as crossdating, replication, and standardization. He used a 15-year running average to smooth his data and noted that he was removing any cycles greater than 15 years that might have been included in the wood. Kapteyn tested for missing rings using crossdating and identified precipitation cycles of about 12.5 years in his final chronologies (Schulman 1937).

## The Early 1900s, Douglass, and Huber

**A. E. Douglass** (fig. 3.4) was the first researcher to use crossdating "... persistently and extensively ..." (Studhalter 1956) and has been named the "undisputed ... father of dendrochronology" (Schweingruber 1988). He developed the repeatable process of crossdating that is the cornerstone of dendrochronology today. Douglass was an astronomer by training and assisted Percival Lowell in finding sites with clear skies for observatories in the southwestern United States (Webb 1983). Douglass later had a disagreement with Lowell because he would not publicly support Lowell's hypothesis that patterns on the surface of Mars were man-made canals.

On a horse-drawn carriage trip in 1901 near Flagstaff, Arizona, Douglass noticed that a cross section from a ponderosa pine (*Pinus ponderosa*) tree showed a variation in width of the rings. In 1904 he had the opportunity to examine a number of pine cross sections and found a distinct pattern of small rings on the first, third, sixth, ninth, eleventh, and fourteenth rings in from the bark. He documented what is now called the Flagstaff Signature, consisting of small rings in 1899, 1902, and 1904. During later research he noticed that rings from a tree in Prescott, Arizona (50 miles southwest of Flagstaff), had a similar pattern of small rings. This

**Figure 3.4**  A. E. Douglass (1867–1962) in the storage room of the Laboratory of Tree-Ring Research underneath the football stadium at the University of Arizona in 1940. (From Webb 1983)

pattern was repeated on numerous logs in the area, and after years of work, Douglass found that the pattern was repeated throughout the southwestern United States (Webb 1983).

Douglass moved to Tucson, Arizona, in 1906 and took up a position as an assistant professor of physics and geography at the University of Arizona. While at the university, he continued his work with tree rings, taught physics, and continued his astronomical pursuits, including acquiring funding for Steward Observatory. Douglass was interested in reconstructing a long-term record of sunspots. Knowing that sunspots were related to energy fluctuations in the sun and that the sun provides energy for the Earth's climate system, Douglass hypothesized that one could measure variations in solar intensity recorded in tree rings. He was later able to demonstrate that the trees could be recording cycles driven by climatic parameters (Douglass 1909) and that they were recording rainfall (Douglass 1914).

Douglass collected many species of trees from locations in California, Oregon, South Dakota, New Mexico, and Arizona from his base at the University of Arizona. He later collected more samples from England, Germany, Austria, Norway, and Sweden in the fall of 1912 during his sabbatical. In 1915 Douglass collected his first giant sequoia (*Sequoiadendron giganteum*) from a grove near Hume, California, in the same location that was sampled by **Ellsworth Huntington** in 1911. The sequoia collections yielded a 3000-year chronology that extended back to 1305 BC. By 1919, Douglass had collected 230 tree samples from the United States and Europe and he had measured 75,000 rings (Webb 1983).

Douglass had the right combination of skills and talent for dendrochronology. He was painstakingly meticulous, and he had a memory for dates. He memorized the entire chronology for the Southwest during his efforts to date the archaeological structures in this region.

**Figure 3.5** A. E. Douglass and his students in 1946. From left to right: Fred Scantling, Sid Stallings, A. E. Douglass, Edmund Schulman, and James Louis Giddings. (Image from Nash 1999)

Douglass also developed techniques that are still used today to facilitate dating, such as skeleton plotting (see chapter 5).

Douglass formed the world's first tree-ring laboratory in 1937, at the University of Arizona, when space underneath the football stadium bleachers was allocated as a temporary housing for the lab. The Laboratory of Tree-Ring Research is still located there today. Douglass trained a number of students (fig. 3.5), most notably Edmund Schulman, Ted Smiley, Florence Hawley, James Giddings, and Emil Haury, who sustained the field of dendrochronology. It is due to all of their efforts along with those of their European counterparts, Bruno Huber, Walter Liese, Bernd Becker, Dieter Eckstein, and Fritz Schweingruber, that dendrochronology is a highly regarded field of research today. I will discuss these later contributions to the field of dendrochronology in chapters 7–11, which describe the methods and analyses applicable to each subdiscipline.

**Bruno Huber** was one of the main researchers in Europe to spend considerable time and energy in dating tree samples, publishing more than 39 dendrochronology papers from 1938 to 1970. Huber was a professor of forest botany at the Technical University of Dresden and the University of Munich from 1899 to 1969 (Schweingruber 1996). He was aware of Douglass' work and concluded that the more complacent growth in trees from central Europe was due to the more temperate and humid climate of the region. Despite these difficulties, Huber was able to produce accurate chronologies and worked on new statistical techniques to quantify the strength of dating of different specimens (Liese 1978). Samples taken from old structures that contained wooden beams and posts were used by early European researchers, including Huber, to extend their chronologies back in time. Huber used oak beams from medieval buildings in Franconia to extend his chronology back to 1000 (Zeuner 1958). Huber

(1935) also examined wood anatomy and determined that fluid from the roots in ring-porous trees (wood types with large pores at the beginning of each ring, such as oak trees) travels up the stem 10 times faster than in diffuse-porous trees (wood types with disbursed pores, such as maple trees) even though ring-porous trees only use their earlywood pores in the present year to transport fluid, while diffuse-porous trees use several years of scattered pores to transport fluid. Around the same time, K. Brehme, another German researcher, developed a chronology from larch (*Larix* spp.) trees in the Bavarian Alps extending back to 1300, and Wellenhofer and Jazewitsch used oak (*Quercus* spp.) trees from the Spessart Mountains in western Germany to build a chronology back to 1391 (Zeuner 1958).

**Edmund Schulman** was one of Douglass' early students who made his own contributions to dendrochronology. He conducted early work in dendroclimatology and expended much of his energy in finding old trees to produce long chronologies for climate reconstructions. These explorations led him to find the bristlecone pines (*Pinus longaeva* and *Pinus aristata*) that are now considered to be the oldest living organisms that are not clonal (Schulman 1954). Schulman (1956) also published the first chronologies from South America, with the Chilean incense cedar (*Austrocedrus chilensis*) and the Chile pine (*Araucaria araucana*).

**Florence M. Hawley** was another of Douglass' students in the 1930s, and she completed her PhD at the University of Chicago in 1934. She extended Douglass' work to the southeastern United States, trying to date mound-builder artifacts from Tennessee and Mississippi. Hawley developed some of the first chronologies from the southeastern United States under much scrutiny because of the belief at the time that trees in the eastern deciduous forest would not produce datable tree rings. She continued this research as a professor of anthropology at the University of New Mexico.

## The Modern Era and International Organization

Since the 1950s and 1960s with the careers of Douglass, Schulman, and Huber, many prominent dendrochronologists have made great strides in the science, including Dieter Eckstein, Fritz Schweingruber, Bernd Becker, Mike Baillie, Gordon Jacoby, Hal Fritts, and Ed Cook, who each published more than 100 papers in dendrochronology through 2006 (as determined from Grissino-Mayer's online Bibliography of Dendrochronology; see the internet references in appendix E). The number of publications has risen dramatically to more than 11,000. I discuss the contributions to the field by many of the modern practitioners in the second half of this book.

International organizations that encourage dendrochronological research, teach dendrochronology, and provide venues for tree-ring research presentations have developed in the last century, with a great influx of members and meetings over the past 20 years. The Tree-Ring Society is the oldest association of dendrochronologists and was founded by A. E. Douglass in 1935. The society's journal *Tree-Ring Bulletin* was first published in 1934 and has since changed its name to *Tree-Ring Research*. The Tree-Ring Society now has more than 200 members from more than 30 countries. The Association for Tree-Ring Research started in 2003 and provides a network for European dendrochronologists. A second tree-ring journal called *Dendrochronologia* was first published in 1983 and is another major outlet for dendrochronological literature. A new organization called the Asian Dendrochronology Association started in 2006.

A. E. Douglass started conducting annual meetings on dendrochronology in 1934, which continued to run in 1935, 1936, 1937, 1939, and 1941. These first meetings included researchers from Arizona and New Mexico who had an interest in archaeology and climatology. The Tree-Ring Society continued to meet at various venues through the intervening years, including a notable meeting in Tucson in 1974 when the idea of regular international meetings arose and another major meeting occurred in Norwich, England, in 1980. Regular international meetings on dendrochronology started at the international conference in Ystad, Sweden, in 1990. These International Conferences on Dendrochronology included the 1994 meeting in Tucson, which had 207 participants from more than 35 countries, and meetings in Mendoza, Argentina (2000); Quebec City, Canada (2002); Beijing, China (2006); and Rovaniemi, Finland (2010). Smaller conferences have been developed around the world to encourage local research, with EuroDendro being the longest running of these conferences. Their first meeting was in Lourmarin, France in 1989, followed by meetings in Liège, Belgium (1990); Travemünde, Germany (1994); Moudon, Switzerland (1996); Savonlinna, Finland (1997); Kaunas, Lithuania (1998); Malbork, Poland (1999); Gozd Martuljek, Slovenia (2001); Obergurgl, Austria (2003); Rendsburg, Germany (2004); Viterbo, Italy (2005); and Hallstatt, Austria (2008) (Dieter Eckstein, personal communication). Other regional conferences have been developed, such as the Southeast Asian Dendrochronology Conference (1998), the Asian Dendrochronology Conference (2007), and the Ameridendro Conference (2008).

Fritz Schweingruber started an International Dendroecological Fieldweek in 1986, and Paul Krusic began the North American Dendroecological Fieldweek in 1990 (Speer 2006). These fieldweeks continue to be some of the main educational opportunities for researchers who do not have access to local dendrochronology courses. The success of the fieldweek model has led to the development of the South American Dendrochronological Fieldweek (begun in 2005), a Southeast Asian Fieldweek, and a summer course in Turkey.

A more lasting contribution of this international collaboration in dendrochronological research is the development of the International Tree-Ring Data Bank (ITRDB; Grissino-Mayer and Fritts 1997). This data archive and computer forum arose from the international meeting in 1974, during which participants expressed the need for a repository of tree-ring chronologies so that the work of individual researchers can be passed along and preserved. Hal Fritts founded the ITRDB and was its main proponent in its early years. In 1990 the National Oceanographic and Atmospheric Administration took over the operation of the ITRDB and founded the World Data Center Paleoclimatology A program in Boulder, Colorado. The databank currently holds more than 2000 chronologies from six continents. In 1988 the managers of the ITRDB started a computer forum to enhance communication between tree-ring researchers around the world. Today this forum has more than 600 members from 32 countries who subscribe to the listserve. All of these international organizations, meetings, fieldweeks, and the ITRDB continue to foster an international tree-ring community.

## Summary

The field of dendrochronology grew out of the work by the researchers mentioned in this chapter. From this work, we have accumulated knowledge over time and continue to improve dendrochronology as a science. New applications, longer records, and larger spatial analyses are continually added. In chapters 7–11 I describe each subfield in greater depth and discuss the recent history of dendrochronological research. Because the number of researchers and the amount of research has increased so tremendously since A. E. Douglass' time, it is difficult to synthesize all of that work into one volume. I hope that the references in the remainder of this book will serve as a first step toward the varied publications in dendrochronology.

# 4
# Growth and Structure of Wood

Tree rings are composed of individual cells that constitute the building blocks of the tree. One must understand the cellular level of tree growth in order to accurately identify the individual tree rings. A basic understanding of tree physiology is also important for comprehending the biological processes that link the environment to ring formation. Tree rings are the end result of a complex sequence of assimilation of natural resources by the tree. A cascade of chemical reactions and cell division ultimately produces the annual ring that contains the information dendrochronologists analyze. Salisbury and Ross (1992) and Kozlowski and Pallardy (1997) are suggested resources for further information.

## Tree Physiology

Gymnosperms (plants that produce naked seeds) are more primitive than angiosperms (flowering plants) and have less-developed and fewer cell types. Gymnosperms, also known as softwood trees or conifers, transport water from the roots to the leaves through tracheids, long narrow cells that comprise growth rings, in the outer living part of the xylem in the area of the sapwood, the region with living parenchyma cells. Angiosperms, also known as hardwood or deciduous trees, more efficiently transport most of the water and nutrients from the soil to the leaves in specialized, capillary-like cells called vessels. These vessels are larger in diameter than tracheids and transport water more efficiently, but they are more prone to embolism, air bubble formation during conduction that blocks water movement.

Angiosperms are further divided into monocotyledons (or monocots) and dicotyledons (dicots). A cotyledon is a seed leaf or a leaf that breaks out of the seed; monocots produce one such leaf, whereas dicots produce two. The monocots (such as palms and yucca plants) produce vascular bundles of xylem and phloem tissue, but they do not produce a vascular cambium that results in growth around the stem of the plant that would otherwise produce annual rings. Therefore, monocots are not useful for dendrochronology, although researchers may be able to quantify the age of some monocots through incremental height growth patterns as the tree grows taller. Dicots, on the other hand, often produce annual rings around the circumference of the tree from cell division in the vascular cambium.

Most gymnosperms and dicots in seasonal climates produce one ring per year. The ring can be divided into **earlywood** and **latewood**. Earlywood is defined as cells that have large lumen (the opening in the center of a dead cell) relative to the cell walls. Latewood cells are always flattened and have a more compact lumen relative to the cell walls and consequently appear darker (fig. 2.5). Earlywood is usually produced in spring and early summer, whereas latewood is formed in the late summer. However, this timing varies with species and environmental conditions.

**Apical meristem** (or primary meristem) are located at the tips of branches and roots and are the origin for elongation of branches, roots, and height growth in a tree. **Secondary meristem** is produced in most gymnosperms and dicots and enables a tree to grow in circumference through time and produce tree rings. Cell division occurs in the **vascular cambium** (often simply called the cambium), which is a narrow layer of meristematic cells between bark and wood. During cell division, **xylem** is produced toward the inside of the tree, becoming the wood structure that supports the tree, and **phloem** is produced toward the outside of the tree and becomes the inner bark. A **cork cambium** forms the outer bark of most trees. The walls of all woody cells continue to thicken up to a cell-type-specific extent within a few days or weeks before the cells die, lose their protoplasm, and start to function for the tree as conducting or strengthening tissue.

Water transport is driven by **transpiration** (the evaporation of water) through the stomata in the leaves of the tree and the cohesion of water molecules throughout a connected column from the leaves all the way down to the roots. Transpiration is the pump that drives water (and subsequently nutrient) uptake in the roots. The phloem cells remain alive much longer than the xylem cells and transport the products of photosynthesis (sugars and hormones) down the tree.

Less frequently, a series of thin-walled ray cells are also produced during cell division in the cambium, resulting in a radial cell component that connects the outside of the tree to the inside. Heartwood forms in the middle of the stem as a result of an active production of substances, mainly phenols, that are deposited to fill the cells and guarantee that the wood is resistance to decay (fig. 4.1). The lighter colored outer wood is called the **sapwood** and in conifers is the area that transports water up the tree from the roots to the canopy.

Visualize a tree as a series of stacked cones representing a complete sheath of wood that is put on the tree each year. The tree grows upward by cell division at the apical meristem (or shoot tip) and outward from cell division in the secondary meristem, causing the cones to stack upward and grow outward. When a dendrochronologist cores a tree, a sample is removed from bark to pith, collecting the full number of rings produced at the height of the core. The **pith** is the bundle of cells produced by the upward growth of the apical meristem, allowing trees to reach to greater heights and creating the cambium initials that start secondary thickening of trees (fig. 4.2).

## Basic Wood Structure

All wood samples can be examined from three distinct views, or planes, which provide a different perspective on the cells that compose the wood (fig. 4.3). The **cross-sectional view** (also called the **transverse view**) is what we see on the surface of a stump when a tree is cut down. In this view, you can clearly see the cross section of the **tracheids** in coniferous trees, which are elongated tubelike cells that make up the majority of the wood and function to transport fluids and nutrients vertically in the xylem of the tree. This is the view that dendrochronologists examine most frequently. If you look at a side view along a cut from the bark to the pith of the tree, you are examining the **radial view** of the section (think of the radius of a circle). In this case, you can see the full length of the tracheids, but the ring boundaries are often obscured. The last view is a cut down the outside of the tree, basically parallel to the pith column. This is the **tangential view** (tangent, or perpendicular, to the radius), which can often be seen in furniture as the veneer cut from a tree. Each view provides a different perspective that a wood anatomist can use to identify the type of wood being examined.

## Cell Features and Types

Gymnosperms, such as pine (*Pinus* spp.), spruce (*Picea* spp.), and juniper (*Juniperus* spp.)(fig. 4.4), produce simpler wood structure (figs. 4.5 and 4.6) than hardwoods and are mainly composed of elongated tracheids that are connected by bordered pits between the tracheids. Resin ducts may occasionally occur. Tracheids make up most of the cells in conifer wood and function as structural and conducting elements, transporting nutrients along with water from the roots. Bordered pits are evident on the tracheids' cell walls that allow water transport from one tracheid to another. Parenchyma is another cell type that can be found in gymnosperms. These cells are alive and have a complete protoplast in the lumen of the cell. In a cross-sectional view, they can be identified as a normal cross section of a tracheid cell, except that the **vacuole** (central cavity of the cell) is dark with cell material. Finally, resin ducts that transport resin throughout the tree to seal off wounds can be found on the cross-sectional view of many conifers (fig. 4.7). Because of the function of this resin, conifers are relatively resistant to decay. Thickening of the cell walls and flattening of the cells are the main indicator of annual ring structure in coniferous wood. Bordered pits in the tracheid walls and resin ducts can be present, but pits do not occur in all conifers.

Angiosperms have more complex wood structure than gymnosperms (fig. 4.8). Fibers provide the key structure and support for the tree, but angiosperms also produce vessels that are used for the main water transport in the tree. Angiosperms may have large and small vessels along with fibers, tracheids, and parenchyma cells (fig. 4.8), all of which are evident in cross section. Pits are very evident in hardwood species in the radial section and allow for water transport between individual vessels. Parenchyma cells are more common in hardwoods, and they actually form the ring boundary in some genera of diffuse-porous species. A three-dimensional wood block of a hardwood sample shows that vessels dominate the view, but fiber cell size is still important for differentiating ring boundaries in some genera (fig. 4.9). Rays form perpendicular to the ring boundaries and are very prominent in hardwoods, providing efficient transport and storage of nutrients, photosynthetic products, and some metabolic wastes to the heartwood (fig. 4.10).

## Forms of Wood Structure

Two main wood structures can be identified: the nonporous woods of the gymnosperms and the porous wood types of the dicotyledon group of the angiosperms (fig. 4.11). The dicots are further broken into ring-porous, semi-ring-porous, and diffuse-porous wood types (fig. 4.12). In **nonporous** wood structure the ring boundaries can be identified by examining the size and cell wall thickness of the tracheids.

The presence of vessels differentiates gymnosperm wood from angiosperm wood. Vessels are an advanced evolutionary trait of angiosperms that enable the trees to more efficiently transport water upward. They can be large or small (fig. 4.13), and their distribution in the ring can help a dendrochronologist identify the ring boundaries. Large vessels occur at the beginning of the growth ring in ring-porous genera. Small vessels may form as solitary individuals, as vessel multiples, vessel chains, nested vessels, or as wavy bands and can occur anywhere in the ring (fig. 4.14).

**Ring-porous** wood structure is defined by a row of vessels that are produced at the beginning of the growing season before leaf-out. Because these vessels are formed early in the growing season when photosynthates have yet to be produced, the tree uses stored reserves from the previous growing season. Ring-porous genera, such as oak (*Quercus* spp.) and ash (*Fraxinus* spp.), are the most distinct of the angiosperms with an obvious row of vessels occurring at the beginning of the growth ring (known as the earlywood zone; fig. 4.15).

**Semi-ring-porous** genera, such as hickory (*Carya* spp.) and elm (*Ulmus* spp.), have some vessels that form at the beginning of the ring but also have smaller vessels distributed throughout the ring (fig. 4.16). The earlywood zone is not as consistent and distinct as with ring-porous genera.

**Diffuse-porous** genera, such as maple (*Acer* spp.), birch (*Betula* spp.), and aspen (*Populus* spp.), have small vessels distributed throughout the ring that have no relationship with the ring boundaries (fig. 4.17). This varied distribution of vessels often obscures the ring boundaries, making ring identification in diffuse-porous genera particularly difficult. These trees also produce a large number of vessels, but the vessels have nothing to do with the annual ring structure, are generally smaller, and can be randomly distributed throughout the rings. In some cases, 80% of the microscopic field of view is taken up with these vessels. Because the vessels are not associated with the ring boundaries, the cell wall thickness of the fibers should be examined to determine the ring boundaries, similar to analysis of nonporous species.

## Reaction Wood

Trees growing on a slope or those that are tilted produce **reaction wood** to maintain or re-obtain their vertical orientation. Gymnosperms produce **compression wood** on the down hill side of the tree that is composed of thick-walled and rounded tracheids. Angiosperms produce **tension wood** on the uphill side of the tree with reinforced cell walls acting to pull the tree up straight (fig. 4.18). The differing responses cause the pith to be displaced upslope from center in a conifer and downslope from center in a hardwood tree. In cross section, the cell walls may be obviously thickened in compression wood (fig. 4.19), while in the radial view, spiral thickening along the outer surface of the tracheids may be evident in tension wood only under high magnification. I demonstrate in chapter 10 how reaction wood can be used to determine the date of mass movements, such as landslides.

## Growth Initiation and Absent Rings

Growth hormones (such as auxin and cytokinin) trigger cell division, cell elongation, and fruit development. During years of good environmental conditions, growth hormones are produced in abundance at the apical meristem and are transported down the stem in the phloem of the tree, initiating growth all along the cambium (fig. 4.20). In stressful years, however, insufficient growth hormone production may fail to initiate growth for some parts of the stem, especially near the base of the tree (fig. 4.21). The results of this phenomenon are locally absent rings that are only present in certain regions of the stem. Growth hormones tend to move from the tip of the branches to the tips of the roots, so that a tree is more likely to be missing rings near its base.

Ring-porous genera often produce vessels at the beginning of the growing season before leaf-out, suggesting that these vessels develop from cambial derivatives that overwintered in an undifferentiated state. This phenomenon likely results in the observation that ring-porous trees usually do not produce locally absent rings. However, ring-porous trees can produce rings so closely packed together that it can be difficult (if not impossible) to differentiate the ring boundaries.

## Growth Throughout the Year

Trees continue to grow throughout the year, with different parts of the tree developing at different times of the year (fig. 4.22). Krueger and Trappe (1967) examined growth in three parts of Douglas fir trees. They found that most stem-diameter increase occurs from March through November, although some of that activity could be due to water draw-up. Shoot elongation frequently occurs over a shorter period of time (May through August in this example), but root growth can occur in just about any month of the year. This activity throughout the year gives trees the potential to record climate from many different times of the year.

## Ring Anomalies

Rings are produced in many different forms that may confuse a dendrochronologist, but close examination of a full cross section usually enables the appropriate identification of these problem rings (Speer et al. 2004). A tree may produce **micro rings** that are only two cells wide, with one cell of earlywood and one cell of latewood in gymnosperms (fig. 4.23a). Micro rings are difficult to find on a cross section, but a well sanded surface and the aid of crossdating can help the dendrochronologist to locate them.

**False rings** occur when limiting factors reduce growth rates and cause the tree to shut down during some part of the year, but as that limiting resource returns the tree continues to grow. False rings can be used to record various environmental events such as severity of monsoon events in precipitation-limited climates. In northern Michigan, false rings have been documented as being more frequent in trees that are growing quickly and located in codominant or intermediate canopy positions (Copenheaver et al. 2004). In most cases, these false rings can be identified because the cell walls gradually thicken into a pseudo-latewood, but then they gradually thin back out (fig. 4.23b). By following an individual **radial file** (a row of cells radiating out from the center of the tree that originated from an individual cambium cell), this cell wall thickening into the false ring can be observed, and then gradually the cell walls thin back to earlywood cell widths. This contrasts with the abrupt transition in cell wall thickness associated with a true annual ring. In conifers, if you can find one radial file that does not shut down completely, this is likely to be a false ring boundary.

Some trees (especially in tropical climates) form **diffuse ring boundaries** when growing conditions are optimal and the tree is never forced to cease growing for part of the year. Therefore, annual boundaries are diffuse without any real change in cell wall thickness between years (fig. 4.23c). Often the ring in the second year is composed largely of latewood cells because the tree never enters dormancy and it continues to produce thick cell walls in anticipation of the end of the growing season.

Dendrochronologists prefer to have **circuit uniformity** in the cross sections of trees that they examine. A well-formed tree has the same amount of growth around the circumference of the cross section that is cut from a stump of a tree, so that taking a core sample from any place around the stem yields the same number and width of rings (see chapter 5 for more details on sampling methods). When viewing the cross section, it should appear as a bull's eye target with a regular pattern of rings around the center (as seen in fig. 1.2). Many tree species do not have circuit uniformity, so care must be taken to collect measurements of what would be the average amount of growth for each year. Teak (*Tectona grandis*) trees and some juniper (*Juniperus*) species produce a lobed growth pattern around the circumference so that it is difficult but not impossible for the researcher to determine normal growth on the stem of the tree (fig. 4.1). Some trees that do not exhibit circuit uniformity have **pinching rings** around the circumference of the cross section. In this case, one or more rings pinch out so that two different cores from the same tree at the same height yields vastly different ring counts (fig. 4.23d and 4.23e). If too many rings pinch out too frequently, it is very difficult (if not impossible) for the dendrochronologist to locate these missing rings, even with crossdating.

These ring anomalies can occur in any of the wood types (nonporous, ring-porous, semi-ring-porous, and diffuse-porous), although I know of only one site that has produced a locally absent ring in a ring-porous species. Trees with ring-porous wood structure conduct most of their water in the vessels in that single year of growth, although some water is transported in small latewood vessels and tracheids in a relatively (compared to gymnosperms) reduced area of sapwood. Rings can be very small with little more than earlywood vessels produced over a series of years, making ring identification difficult (fig. 4.24).

Cell division is continuous along a radial file but can occur at different rates around the circumference of the tree. The different rates of growth are not a problem when the ring is continuous around the circumference of a cross section, but when rays interrupt the rings it is possible for them to become misaligned. A dendrochronologist examining a series of rings in an oak tree, for example, should match the width of the rings on either side of the ray before visually crossing the ray to follow the rings on the other side (fig. 4.25).

Other ring anomalies may be found in the wood as well. Some of these are caused by environmental conditions, and others are caused by interactions with other organisms. In the mid and high latitudes, **frost rings** occur when the air temperature drops well below freezing during the growing season. There are two competing hypotheses about how frost rings form. Some suggest that frost rings can form when water freezes in the lumen of a cell and explodes the cell. Later, as the cambium differentiates, these crumpled tracheids get crushed, producing a distinctive frost ring (fig. 4.26; Bailey 1925, Glock 1951). Another explanation is that the water in the stem near the ground or in the ground itself freezes, but transpiration from the canopy continues to draw water, collapsing the outermost conducting cells that are not yet lignified—similar to the collapse of a straw when drawing on a thick milkshake. These distinct frost rings can be observed in the wood of high-elevation trees and, as noted in the history of dendrochronology (chapter 3), can become important marker rings.

Some aphids suck sap from sieve cells, damaging the cambium and producing **pith flecks**. These can be observed in cross section as a cluster of bubbly-textured wood (fig. 4.27). This aphid damage cannot be used as a marker ring unless it results from an unusual outbreak of the insect, so that the damage makes a distinct ring that is synchronous between trees.

**Fire scars** are another distinctive anatomical feature that is caused by localized cambial mortality due to the high temperature of a fire. Charcoal is not necessarily a part of the fire scar, as the scar is formed where the cambium was killed off because of the high temperature. The bark often sloughs off after the cambium has been killed, leaving exposed wood. The living cambium on either side of the scar then grows quickly, completing the scar structure in the tree. Fire scars can be identified based on distinct cellular characteristics (see Smith and Sutherland 2001). Living cambium cells on the edge of the dead cambium differentiate at an accelerated rate to cover the injured area and seal off the damaged wood (fig. 4.28). This results in a distinctive growth curl after the fire scar occurred. Based on a close examination of the area where the scar occurs in the tree ring, dendrochronologists can determine the season of the fire, based on how much of the ring was developed before the injury (see chapter 8 for more details). Multiple fire scares in conifers usually occur on one aspect of the tree because the wound caused by the first fire event makes the tree more susceptible to scarring by subsequent fires.

## Summary

With this basic knowledge of wood anatomy, cell structure, and tree growth, you can start to analyze tree rings and to differentiate ring boundaries. Sample collection and preparation is explored in the next chapter. The most important process for identifying ring boundaries is to have a good polished cross-sectional surface with which to work. The ring boundaries can only be identified if the structure of each individual cell can be seen under a microscope. Therefore, before a sample can be analyzed, the surface must be prepared properly.

**Figure 4.1** A juniper from Jordan with lobate growth demonstrating poor circuit uniformity, where the rings pinch out around the circumference of the section. Notice the darker inner wood, called heartwood, and the lighter outer wood, called sapwood. See figure 1.2 for an example of good circuit uniformity. (Photo by the author)

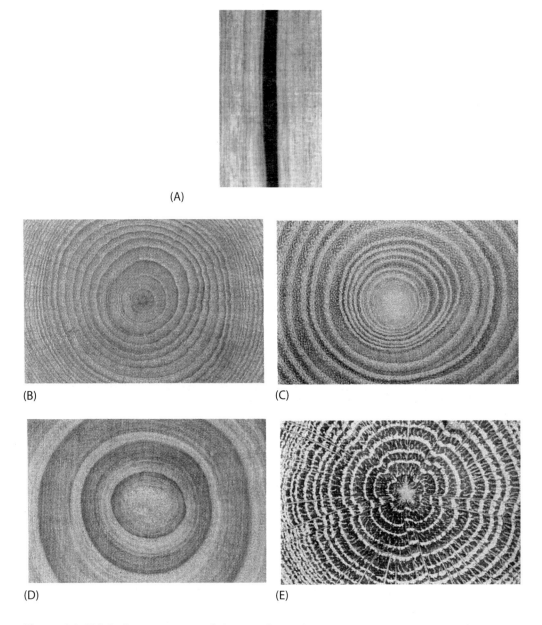

(A)

(B)                              (C)

(D)                              (E)

**Figure 4.2** Pith is the very center of the tree that is formed by the terminal leader as the tree extends in height each year. If the pith is hit when coring the tree, dating the year that ring formed will provide the exact age of that tree at that height. (A) Longitudinal section of butternut with a chambered pith, and cross sections of (B) beech, (C) catalpa, (D) sumac, and (E) oak. (From Hoadley 1990)

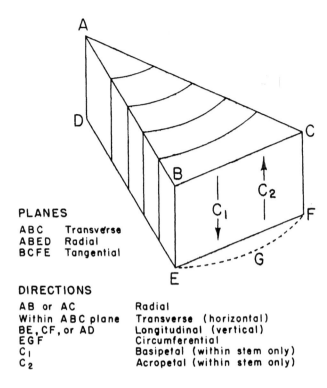

**PLANES**

| | |
|---|---|
| ABC | Transverse |
| ABED | Radial |
| BCFE | Tangential |

**DIRECTIONS**

| | |
|---|---|
| AB or AC | Radial |
| Within ABC plane | Transverse (horizontal) |
| BE, CF, or AD | Longitudinal (vertical) |
| EGF | Circumferential |
| $C_1$ | Basipetal (within stem only) |
| $C_2$ | Acropetal (within stem only) |

**Figure 4.3** Planes of wood structure. Wood samples can be sectioned to expose three primary surfaces used in wood identification: the cross-sectional (or transverse) view, radial view, and tangential view. (From Fritts 1976)

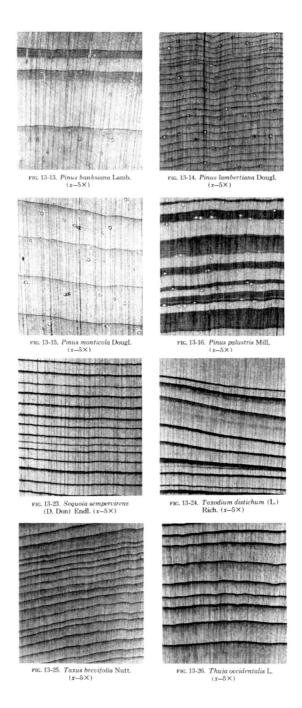

FIG. 13-13. *Pinus banksiana* Lamb.
(x–5×)

FIG. 13-14. *Pinus lambertiana* Dougl.
(x–5×)

FIG. 13-15. *Pinus monticola* Dougl.
(x–5×)

FIG. 13-16. *Pinus palustris* Mill.
(x–5×)

FIG. 13-23. *Sequoia sempervirens*
(D. Don) Endl. (x–5×)

FIG. 13-24. *Taxodium distichum* (L.)
Rich. (x–5×)

FIG. 13-25. *Taxus brevifolia* Nutt.
(x–5×)

FIG. 13-26. *Thuja occidentalis* L.
(x–5×)

**Figure 4.4** Examples of gymnosperm species with coniferous growth: pine (*Pinus* spp.), Douglas-fir (*Pseudotsuga menziesii*), coast redwood (*Sequoia sempervirens*), bald cypress (*Taxodium distichum*), hemlock (*Tsuga* spp.), yew (*Taxus brevifolia*), cedar (*Thuja* spp.), and California nutmeg (*Torreya californica*). (From Panshin et al. 1964)

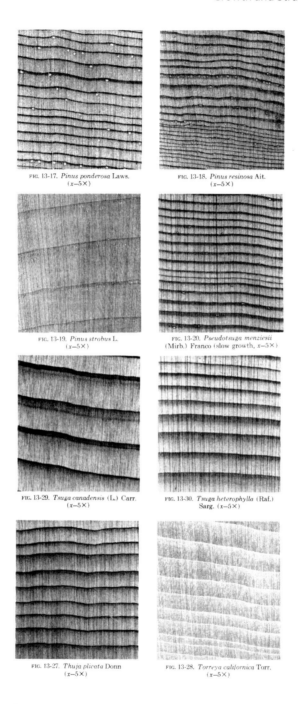

FIG. 13-17. *Pinus ponderosa* Laws. (x–5×)

FIG. 13-18. *Pinus resinosa* Ait. (x–5×)

FIG. 13-19. *Pinus strobus* L. (x–5×)

FIG. 13-20. *Pseudotsuga menziesii* (Mirb.) Franco (slow growth, x–5×)

FIG. 13-29. *Tsuga canadensis* (L.) Carr. (x–5×)

FIG. 13-30. *Tsuga heterophylla* (Raf.) Sarg. (x–5×)

FIG. 13-27. *Thuja plicata* Donn (x–5×)

FIG. 13-28. *Torreya californica* Torr. (x–5×)

**Figure 4.4** *(Continued)*

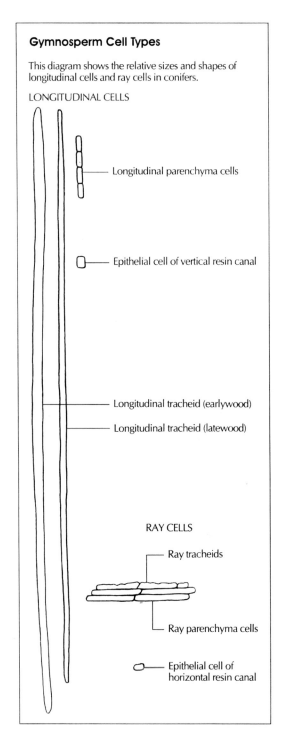

**Figure 4.5** Gymnosperms only have a few cell types: tracheids, parenchyma cells, ray cells, epithelial cells, and resin canals. (From Hoadley 1990)

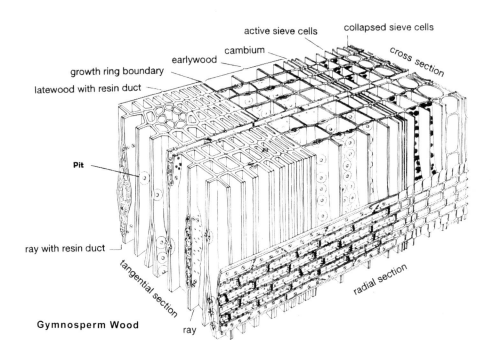

active sieve cells

collapsed sieve cells

cambium

cross section

earlywood

growth ring boundary

latewood with resin duct

Pit

ray with resin duct

tangential section

radial section

Gymnosperm Wood

ray

**Figure 4.6** Gymnosperm wood structure. In coniferous wood, the diameter of the cell, cell wall thickness, and size of the lumen determine the ring structure. (From Schweingruber 1996)

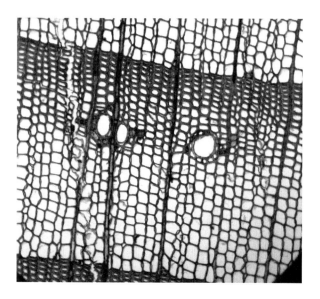

**Figure 4.7** Resin ducts in a gymnosperm. Resin ducts are produced in most conifers. The resin duct is a large hollow vessel that is surrounded by guard cells. When the guard cells relax, they allow resin to flow through the duct. The tree uses this resin to seal off wounds. (Photo by the author)

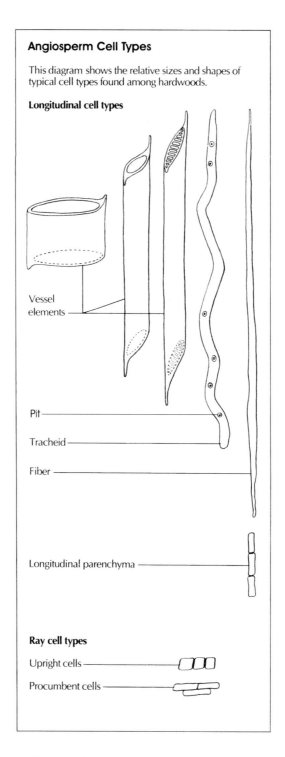

**Figure 4.8** Angiosperm cells types. Angiosperms have more complex cell types: vessel elements, tracheids, fibers, parenchyma, ray cells, and pits. (Modified from Hoadley 1990)

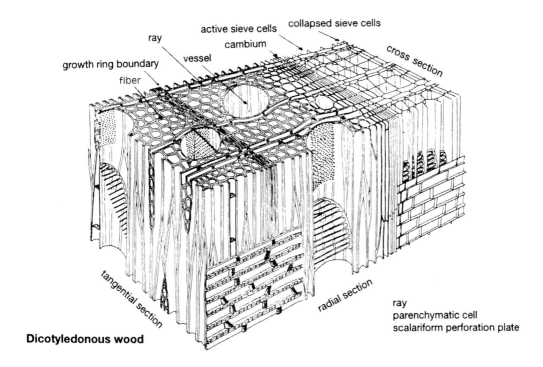

**Figure 4.9**  Dicotyledonous angiosperm wood structure. Angiosperms, such as this diffuse-porous wood, have different cellular structure than gymnosperms and are composed of multiple vessels and more prominent rays. Ring boundaries, however, may still be defined by the size of the fibers, size of the lumen, and thickness of the cell walls. (From Schweingruber 1996)

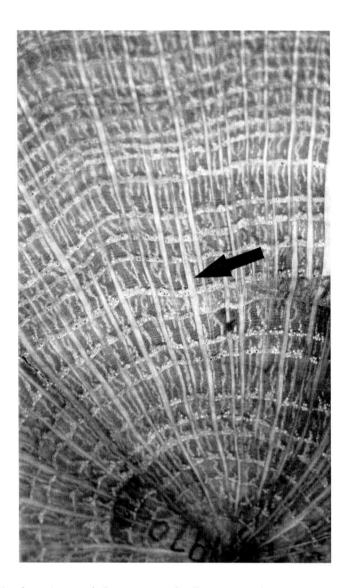

**Figure 4.10** Wood rays in an oak. Rays are wood cell structures that transport materials horizontally (radially) through the tree and are most evident in ring-porous and diffuse-porous tree species. (Photo by the author)

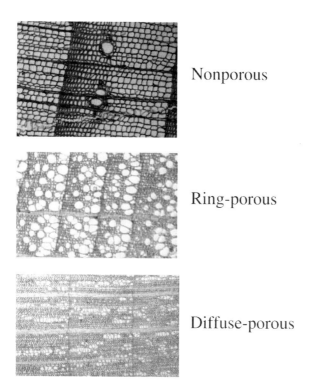

Nonporous

Ring-porous

Diffuse-porous

**Figure 4.11** Gymnosperm versus angiosperm wood types. Gymnosperm woods are nonporous, and angiosperm woods are either ring-porous, with a row of vessels at the beginning of each ring, or diffuse-porous, with vessels distributed throughout the ring. All of these tree samples were growing from right to left in these images. (Photos by the author)

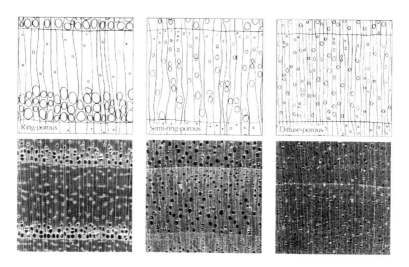

**Figure 4.12** Classification of ring porosity. Gradation from ring-porous wood to diffuse-porous wood, with semi-ring-porous as an intermediate stage. (From Hoadley 1990)

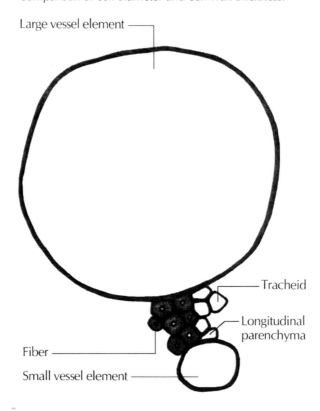

This diagrammatic transverse view of hardwood longitudinal cell types gives an approximate comparison of cell diameter and cell-wall thickness.

Large vessel element

Tracheid

Longitudinal parenchyma

Fiber

Small vessel element

**Figure 4.13** Relative size of hardwood cells and wall thickness in ring-porous species. In diffuse-porous species, there may be less disparity in size of the cells. (From Hoadley 1990)

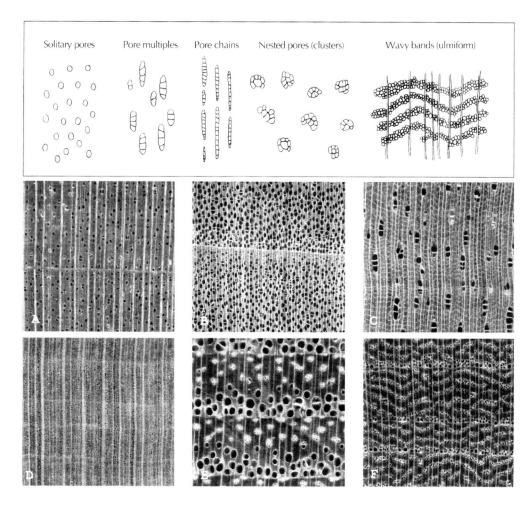

**Figure 4.14** Pore arrangement in angiosperms. Pores can be arranged in many different patterns in angiosperm wood. This arrangement helps with wood identification. (A) *Acer*, with solitary pores; (B) *Populus*, with pore multiples; (C) *Dyera*, with pore multiples; (D) *Ilex*, with pore chains; (E) *Gymnocladus*, with nested pore clusters; and (F) *Ulmus*, with wavy bands. All images are at 15× magnification. (From Hoadley 1990)

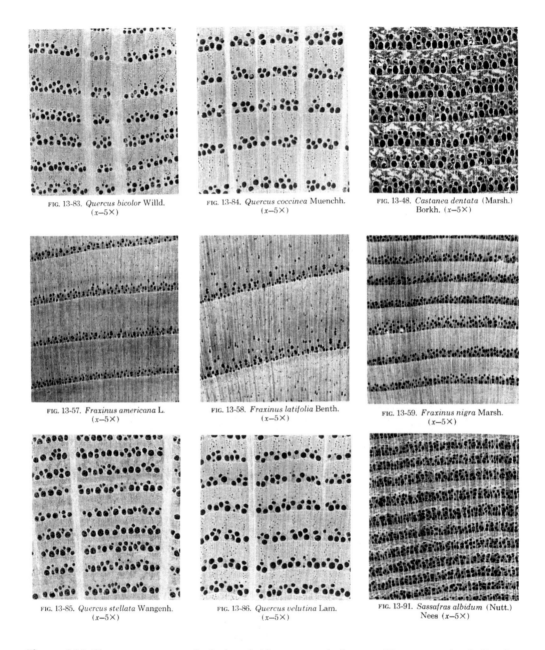

FIG. 13-83. *Quercus bicolor* Willd. (x–5×)

FIG. 13-84. *Quercus coccinea* Muenchh. (x–5×)

FIG. 13-48. *Castanea dentata* (Marsh.) Borkh. (x–5×)

FIG. 13-57. *Fraxinus americana* L. (x–5×)

FIG. 13-58. *Fraxinus latifolia* Benth. (x–5×)

FIG. 13-59. *Fraxinus nigra* Marsh. (x–5×)

FIG. 13-85. *Quercus stellata* Wangenh. (x–5×)

FIG. 13-86. *Quercus velutina* Lam. (x–5×)

FIG. 13-91. *Sassafras albidum* (Nutt.) Nees (x–5×)

**Figure 4.15** Ring-porous genera include oak, (*Quercus* spp.), chestnut (*Castanea* sp.), ash (*Fraxinus* spp.), and sassafras (*Sassafras* sp.). (From Panshin et al. 1964)

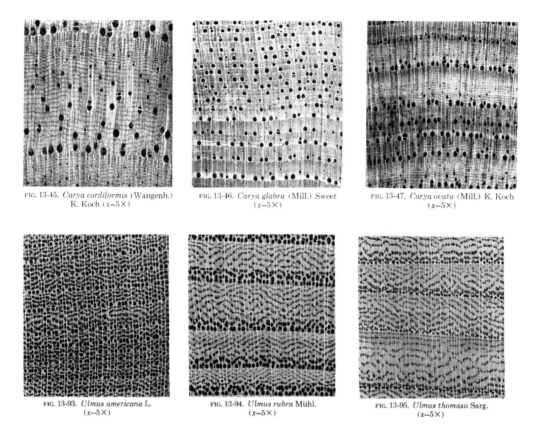

FIG. 13-45. *Carya cordiformis* (Wangenh.) K. Koch (x–5×)

FIG. 13-46. *Carya glabra* (Mill.) Sweet (x–5×)

FIG. 13-47. *Carya ovata* (Mill.) K. Koch (x–5×)

FIG. 13-93. *Ulmus americana* L. (x–5×)

FIG. 13-94. *Ulmus rubra* Mühl. (x–5×)

FIG. 13-95. *Ulmus thomasii* Sarg. (x–5×)

**Figure 4.16** Semi-ring-porous genera include hickory (*Carya* spp.) and elm (*Ulmus* spp.). (From Panshin et al. 1964)

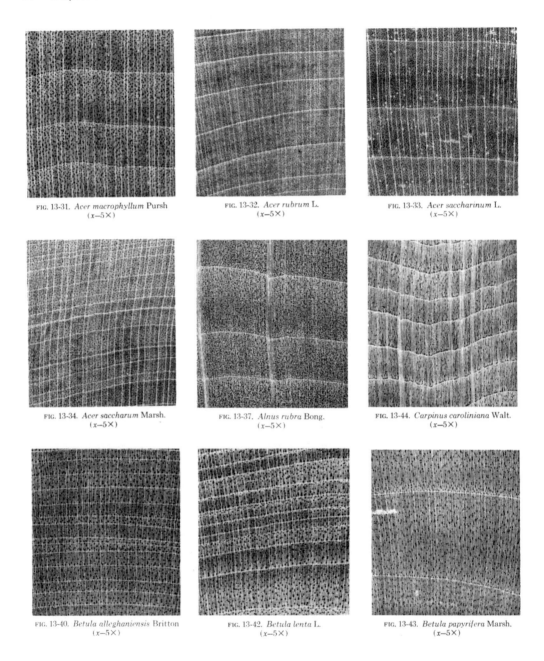

FIG. 13-31. *Acer macrophyllum* Pursh
(x–5×)

FIG. 13-32. *Acer rubrum* L.
(x–5×)

FIG. 13-33. *Acer saccharinum* L.
(x–5×)

FIG. 13-34. *Acer saccharum* Marsh.
(x–5×)

FIG. 13-37. *Alnus rubra* Bong.
(x–5×)

FIG. 13-44. *Carpinus caroliniana* Walt.
(x–5×)

FIG. 13-40. *Betula alleghaniensis* Britton
(x–5×)

FIG. 13-42. *Betula lenta* L.
(x–5×)

FIG. 13-43. *Betula papyrifera* Marsh.
(x–5×)

**Figure 4.17** Diffuse-porous wood showing no association between the pores and the ring boundaries. Genera include maple (*Acer* spp.), alder (*Alnus* sp.), musclewood (*Carpinus* sp.), and birch (*Betula* spp.). (From Panshin et al. 1964)

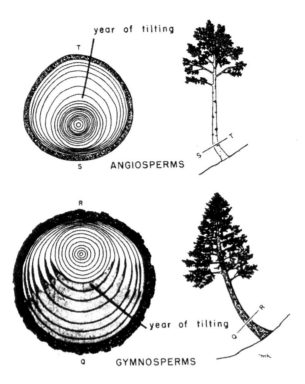

**Figure 4.18** Reaction wood. Angiosperms and gymnosperms react differently to the pull of gravity on a steep slope. Angiosperms put tension wood on the uphill side of the tree to pull the tree back up straight, whereas gymnosperms produce compression wood on the downhill side of the tree to push the tree back up straight. Both of these types of reaction wood produce larger rings, and smaller rings are produced on the opposite side of the tree. This reaction can be used to determine the date when a slope shifted, causing the tree to react. (From Fritts 1976)

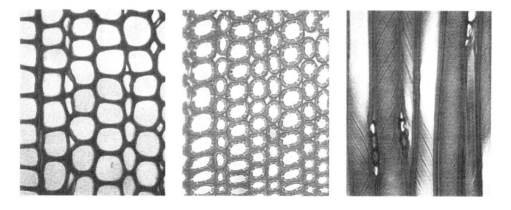

**Figure 4.19** Microscopic cross-sectional view of compression wood in a conifer (center). Note the cell-wall thickening of this pine compared to the normal cells in the image on the left. The image on the right shows the spiral thickening of tension wood from the tangential view. (From Hoadley 1990)

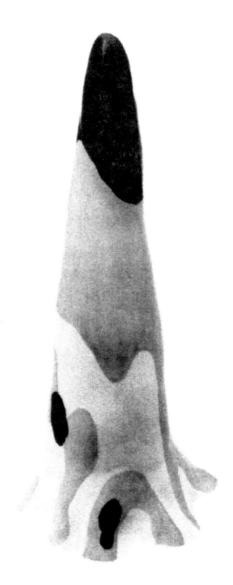

**Figure 4.20** The auxin model of tree growth: the darker area at the top of the modeled stem is new auxin production, whereas the lighter shades of gray represent past years of auxin production. Auxin is a growth hormone produced in the canopy of the tree. Auxin triggers cell division in the canopy, driving the production of tree rings through secondary growth. In stressful years, not enough auxin is produced, resulting in a lack of secondary growth initiation and causing areas around the stem to not form a ring during some years. This also explains pinched rings around the circumference of a cross section. (From Nogler 1981 as cited in Schweingruber 1996)

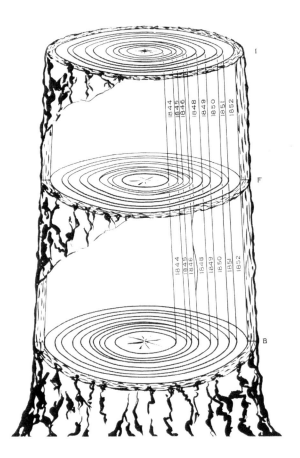

**Figure 4.21** It is important to think of tree-ring production in three dimensions. Each ring is formed on the trees like a sheath wrapping around the stem. Based on the environmental conditions and the growth hormones produced in each year, a ring may be absent around a cross section or vertically from one section to another. The absence of rings is why crossdating is important for determining the complete chronology for each tree and stand. (From Stokes and Smiley 1968)

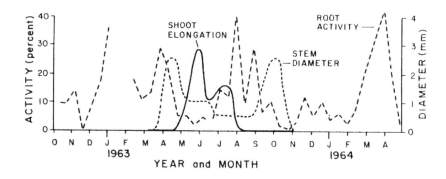

**Figure 4.22** Tree growth throughout the year. Trees have the capacity to grow some part of the organism in just about any month of the year. These measurements were made on growth of the stem, shoots, and roots on Douglas-fir trees. (Data from Krueger and Trappe 1967, graphic from Fritts 2001)

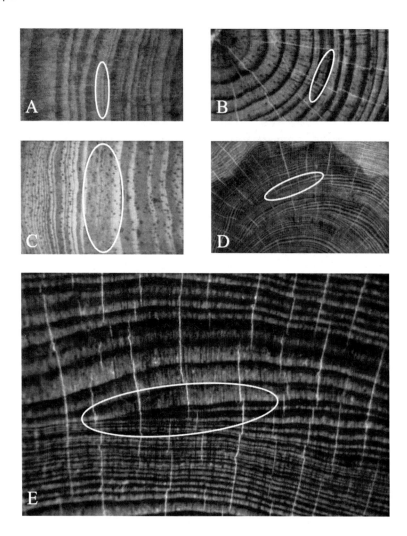

**Figure 4.23** Ring anomalies in *Pinus occidentalis*. Trees can produce a whole series of anomalous ring forms that need to be properly identified for successful crossdating. (A) Micro rings may be only a few cells wide. (B) False rings form when tree growth begins to shut down because of limited environmental resources, but starts again because of the return of input from the limiting factor. (C) Diffuse ring boundaries arise when the normal process causing trees to go dormant for part of the season do not occur. The pictured sample is from the Dominican Republic at 19.5°N latitude, where trees are dormant during the January–March dry season, in other words, they stop growing because of lack of moisture. If a year has unusually high precipitation during the dry season, the tree is not forced to become dormant and continues to grow, producing a diffuse ring boundary and no clear distinction from one year to the next. (D) Pinching rings are produced when the tree is damaged or nutrients are limiting so that growth is not initiated all the way around the stem. (E) Five normal-sized rings pinch to very small size and some disappear completely. (Photos by James H. Speer)

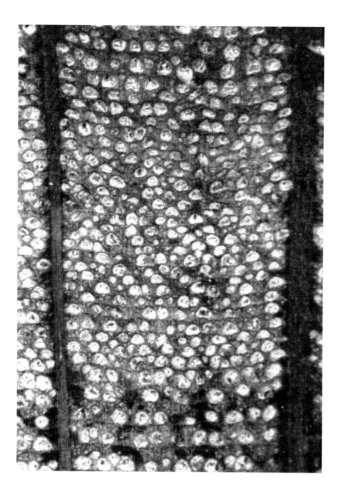

**Figure 4.24** Suppressed ring-porous wood growth. Ring-porous trees (in this case an oak) always produce pores at the beginning of the growing season, but those pores may be packed so tightly that the determination of ring boundaries is difficult. This section shows about 36 rings. (From Baillie 1982)

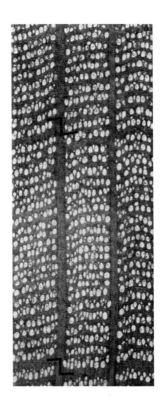

**Figure 4.25** Offset of wood growth across rays. Radial files produce cells at their own rate. When crossing a ray, it is possible for the ring not to be strictly aligned. Therefore, it is important to follow the same ring when crossing a ray. This is done by a quick mental crossdating check to make sure that the ring widths are the same size on either side of the ray for several of the surrounding rings. (From Baillie 1982)

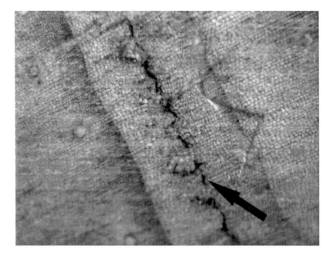

**Figure 4.26** Frost rings occur when freezing temperatures are reached during the growing season. The cold temperatures make the water in the cell lumen expand and destroy the integrity of the cell walls so that the cells become crushed. (Photo by the author)

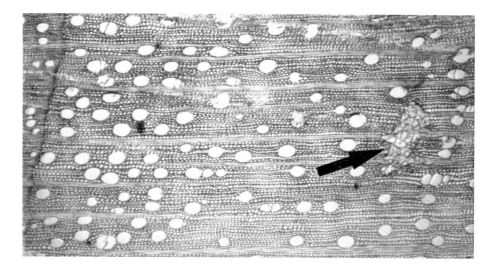

**Figure 4.27** Aphid damage to cells of a red maple (*Acer rubrum*) tree. The aphids are active in the cambium layer and move vertically up and down the tree, feeding on the newly developing wood and damaging the meristematic tissue. (Photo by the author)

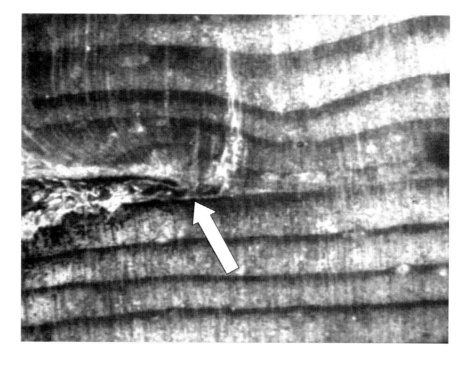

**Figure 4.28** Fire scar in ponderosa pine. From the left, the area where dead cambium meets the living cambium is visible. The accelerated growth of the living cambium cells creates the growth curl, healing over the injured area to the left. (Photo by the author)

# 5
# Field and Laboratory Methods

Good research starts with well-planned and well-executed field practices. Two important components of fieldwork addressed in this chapter are basic field methods for sampling dendrochronological projects and designing a sampling scheme so that the patterns observed in the environment can be accurately described. Fieldwork always brings up surprising circumstances and unexpected situations that you will have to adapt to in the field. While this chapter describes some basic field practices, modification of sampling plans may be needed due to the field area and its specific challenges.

## Gear

The basic tools for dendrochronological fieldwork include at least two increment borers, straws in which cores are stored, map tube for holding cores and straws, diameter tape, Sharpie permanent markers, golf tees or chopsticks for clearing wood stuck in a borer, field notebook, rope, compact drill kit, rifle cleaning kit, digital camera, global positioning system, and hand saw. Along with this basic gear, it is good to have a field vest to keep all of the gear organized. With these tools, you can sample most basic dendrochronological projects and travel relatively lightly. Field equipment changes depending upon the project. For example, a stand-age structure study requires two 100-m measuring tapes to lay out plots, whereas a fire history study may require a chainsaw to take cross sections. Table 5.1 gives a list of recommended field gear.

A golf tee is the perfect tool for removing small pieces of wood that may remain in the borer tip or for widening paper straws that might have been crushed. A bamboo skewer, chopstick, or dowel can serve the same purpose. A rope may be necessary to remove a stuck increment borer (see the Spanish windlass technique below). A digital camera is an important piece of equipment to record the site characteristics, tree characteristics, and field methods. WD-40 should be used to clean the increment borer, unless sampling for a chemical or isotope analysis. A sharpening kit (with a small wedge stone and a cone sharpening stone) should be on hand for sharpening dull or chipped increment borers. A cruiser pack (an empty backpack frame often used while hunting) with bungee cords is an excellent piece of equipment to carry out a large number of cross sections. Beeswax can be used to lubricate the increment borer when coring hardwood trees. When the borer is just removed from a tree, it is warm from friction. The beeswax can easily be melted onto the warm borer tip at this time. WD-40 can also be used as a lubricant and to break down excess sap when coring pitchy pine trees, but it should only be used when necessary. Fingerless gloves are recommended to obtain a better grip on the borer while leaving your fingers free for the delicate work of packaging a core into a straw. Finally, always carry lots of water, a first aid kit, and a two-way radio for unforeseen issues that might arise in the field.

**Table 5.1** Basic checklist of gear needed for dendrochronological sampling. Portions of this equipment will be needed for different field projects, but this list should provide a good foundation

| Equipment | Project | Notes |
|---|---|---|
| Increment borer | all | bring duplicates in case of breakage or jamming |
| Map tube | all | for storage of samples |
| Straws | all | paper or plastic |
| Permanent markers | all | fine point and ultrafine point Sharpie® work very well |
| Diameter tape | all | diameter at breast height (DBH) is a standard forestry measure that is often taken as part of tree description |
| Masking tape | all | for joining straws or making minor repairs |
| Hand lens | all | for examining rings in the field |
| WD-40® | all | for cleaning increment borers and for lubrication |
| Beeswax | all | for lubrication and water barrier on borers |
| Hand saw | all | for taking small wood sections |
| Golf tee, chopstick, or dowel | all | for removing pieces of wood from the tip of the increment borer |
| Long 9/16-inch drill bit with handle | all | for drilling out jammed wood; do not use this from the cutting end, and be careful of the cutting tip |
| Rifle cleaning kit for a .22 with cloth pads | all | for cleaning increment borers; paper towels and a spoon can also be used to clean the borer shaft |
| Weight lifting or bicycling gloves | all | fingerless gloves for hand protection while preserving the dexterity of your fingers |
| Rope | all | for starting a borer or for removing a stuck borer from a tree with the Spanish windlass technique |
| Backpack | all | for holding all gear |
| Field vest | all | provides easy access to the frequently used gear |
| Compass | all | for orienteering and field measurement |
| Knife | all | always helpful, but do not use on the increment borer tip |
| Nylon climbing rope | all | useful for the Spanish windlass technique or to help with laying out plots |
| Sharpening kit | all | for resharpening increment borer bits; mainly used in camp on long field trips or in the lab between trips |
| First aid kit | all | always have one on hand for minor injuries and possible broken limbs |
| Camera | all | very important for documenting field sites and field techniques |
| Topographic maps | all | important for mapping sample locations and for orienteering |
| GPS unit | all | important for mapping locations of field samples |
| Chainsaw | fire history | for taking larger cross sections |

*(Continued)*

**Table 5.1**    (*Continued*)

| Equipment | Project | Notes |
|---|---|---|
| Chaps | fire history | safety protection for the legs |
| Helmet with ear protection and face shield | fire history | safety protection for the head |
| Gloves | fire history | safety protection for the hands |
| Plastic wedges | fire history | for keeping chainsaw cuts open when cutting whole sections |
| Scrench chainsaw tool | fire history | for work on the chainsaw |
| Round sharpening file | fire history | for sharpening dull chainsaw blades |
| 2-in-1 fuel and oil can | fire history | for carrying extra fuel and oil |
| Small pry bar | fire history | for prying out cut cross sections |
| Plastic wrap or fiber tape | fire history | to securely wrap fire history samples so that no pieces are lost and to protect delicate samples |
| Cruiser pack with bungee cords | fire history | empty frame pack for carrying out many cross section samples |
| 50- to 100-m measuring tapes | stand-age structure | for setting up plots |
| Boomerang increment borer handle | optional | for coring on trees with deep fissures in the bark; this is a homemade item of a bent increment borer handle |
| Increment borer starter | optional | for helping to push the borer into the tree with your body mass |

Paper or plastic straws may be used to protect the core. Paper straws are difficult to find and do not work very well under extremely wet conditions, but they allow the core to dry without molding. Plastic straws are convenient because they can be found at any fast-food restaurant, but care should be taken to slit the straw so that air can circulate. Masking tape may be used to hold plastic straws together or longer clear plastic straws can be used for longer cores. The clear plastic straws also allow cursory examination of the cores to see broad ring patterns or if the core is broken in many pieces. Plastic straws can also be sealed with a stapler or melted shut with a lighter. Paper straws can be joined by pinching the paper straw against the core and then sliding, with a twisting motion, a second straw over the first.

Whenever a core is packaged in a straw, the straw should be labeled with a site designation (usually three letters), a tree number (usually two, sometimes three numbers), and an A or B for the first and second core taken from a tree. For example, a second core taken from the third tree sampled from Shakamac Park might be labeled SHA 03 B. The date, your initials, the tree species, and any other relevant field notes can also be recorded on the straw. Following the U.S. convention, the tree genus and species is noted with the first two letters of the genus and the first two letters of the species, for example *Pinus ponderosa* is PIPO.

It is always important to take sufficient field notes to provide a complete site description for later publications that may come out of your work (see Appendix D for sample field note cards). It often takes much time and effort to get into the field and to locate a field site, so as much information as possible should be collected while you are in the field. The vegetation should be noted for the canopy as well as the shrub and even the herb layer, as this understory vegetation can often reveal information about the long-term moisture conditions on the site. Slope, aspect, and the location of trees relative to each other and prominent landmarks are also important pieces of information that should be recorded. A global positioning system is a good tool to locate and later map the locations of specific trees that have been sampled. Occasionally the importance of individual samples requires that they be tagged with a permanent marking, such as an aluminum tag with a specific sample identification number. In this case, it is good to carry a lightweight hammer and nails. A digital camera can also be used to collect data in the field and is a great way to record the appearance of the sampled trees.

A good case study of proper field techniques can be observed with the current effort to extend the bristlecone pine (*Pinus longaeva*) chronology further back in time (Tom Harlan, personal communication). Individual trees in the White Mountains of California can live to be more than 4000 years old. Many previous sampling trips provided a very long chronology from these amazing trees, with such noted historical figures as Edmund Schulman, Val LaMarche, and Wes Ferguson having taken samples from this area. Tom Harlan and colleagues are trying to extend that chronology and are completing an exhaustive sampling protocol throughout the high-elevation zones of the White Mountains. To locate the oldest samples, the researchers have documented the locations of past and current samples and mapped the locations of old versus young samples. Currently, they are trying to increase the sample depth between 6000 and 10,000 BC. By relocating previously sampled trees of great age and locating remnant wood in the correct time period, Harlan has been able to continue to collect very old wood and extend the chronology. While working on this project, however, the researchers have found it difficult to relocate old samples due to poor field notes and proper archiving of those notes and the samples. Because of these difficulties, the current workers are very aware of the need for good notes. Every sample that is collected today is permanently marked with a metal tree identification tag nailed into the wood. A photograph of the tree or log is taken with a white board stating the tree ID, its location in latitude and longitude (from a global positioning system measurement), the date of the photograph, and the initials of the field team collecting the samples. This quality of documentation ensures that the samples can be relocated in the future and that this chronology can continue to be developed.

## Field Methods

### Site Selection

The first important consideration in choosing where to sample is site selection (see the Principle of Site Selection in chapter 2). Often the study area is outlined by local land managers or by the goals of the research. Once the study area is determined, specific sites need to be chosen that will adequately represent the area and topic that is being examined. Individual sites can be chosen through a random selection technique to represent the broader landscape, or targeted sampling can be used to explore specific signals.

## Random versus Targeted Sampling

When in the field, observe how the environment is likely to affect the site on which you are working. Much science consists of observing patterns and, from that, determining the process that drives that pattern. It is important, therefore, to observe the patterns on the landscape and to document those patterns in your field sampling. The sampling protocol may control what can be observed on the landscape, so researchers should be explicit about their sampling protocol.

Often, random sampling is used to facilitate the extrapolation of conclusions to the broader landscape. Square or circular plots are randomly located to sample a representative area of the forest type. Random sampling locations in a field area can be determined either before going into the field by using geographic information system or the random number generator function in Excel or while in the field using a compass bearing and a random number generator, which is available on most advanced calculators. Randomly choosing plots before going into the field is useful because it removes the bias of the observer who gravitates, however unconsciously, toward good trees. Another advantage of choosing plots before going into the field is the ability to develop a stratified random sampling regime so that samples are spread over different vegetation types. This method requires time spent in the field to locate the preselected plots with a global positioning system. It is also possible to generate random samples in the field by finding a stand that you want to quantify, then randomly selecting a compass bearing and distance by using a random number generator for a value between 1° and 360° and then from 1 to 100 m distant. Once the randomly generated spot is located, the transect or plot can be started at that point.

In many of the applications of dendrochronology, targeted sampling is necessary. If the purpose is a climate reconstruction, the oldest trees located in the most climatically stressful areas should be targeted, because not all trees and all landscape positions record the same climate signal. We need to select trees that are sensitive to climate, record a coherent stand-level signal, and have the longest record available. A few young trees can also be sampled to ensure that the outer rings are well represented, because older trees may be suppressed on the outside. For reconstruction of surface-fire-regime fire history, the specific trees recording the longest and most complete fire histories need to be targeted. In this example, a general reconnaissance should be conducted so that the researcher knows the samples that are available in the field site. The trees that yield the longest and most complete fire history based on a count of externally visible fire scars and wood preservation should be sampled. Fire history in a stand-replacing fire regime can be sampled following the methods of a stand-age structure in which the establishment date approximates the age since the last fire (Heinselman 1973). Finally, if studying gap dynamics in a dense forest, the fallen gap-making trees need to be targeted to acquire death dates, and trees immediately within and responding to that gap should be sampled to record the date of gap occurrence.

## Plots, Transects, or Targeted Sampling

Some basic decisions have to be made about how to sample the trees on the landscape. This decision varies based on the research goal. Circular and square plots work well for sampling a given area for stand-age structure. Circular plots are easy to set up from a given center point and a known radius and require fewer decisions about whether a tree is considered inside the plot or outside of it. Square plots are a little more difficult to lay out with tape measures and a compass, but the process results in plots that have a well-defined sampling area. Transects functionally become long rectangular plots and allow sampling across gradients (such as an elevation, aspect, or moisture gradient). A nested band transect is useful for sampling stand-age structure. For this type of transect, a tape measure can be run out 50 m. Everything within 1 m of either side of the tape should be cored at ground level. To increase the sample depth in the older age classes, all trees greater than 20-cm diameter at breast height (DBH) within 2 m of either side of the tape and all trees greater than 30-cm DBH within 3 m of either side of the tape should be sampled as well. These size categories change depending upon the forest type being sampled and the purpose of the study.

## Coring a Tree

The first question that most lay people and forest managers ask is whether coring the tree causes damage to the tree. The simple answer is yes, coring the tree opens up the tree to pathogens that can cause rot and discoloration in the tree, but the tree has natural defenses to combat injuries where the bark is broken. Many conifer trees exude pitch into the core hole, sometimes even within a few hours, effectively sealing off the hole. Angiosperm trees compartmentalize the wound by creating a barrier that stops the spread of fungus once it comes into the tree. The main issue associated with coring is that the researcher leaves behind a hole in the tree that is likely to cause some local discoloration of the wood around the bore hole. If the trees are of great economic importance, such as orchard trees, a fungicide can be sprayed in the bore hole until bark grows over the opening, but this is costly and takes a lot of time. It is possible to go back and find some of the original trees that A. E. Douglass cored in the 1920s, and they are doing fine today.

The height at which a tree cored is dependent upon the question being asked. If a researcher is interested in the exact age of the trees for examination of successional processes in a stand-age structure, the trees should be cored at the base so that the sample is taken as close to the point of germination as possible. This yields the most accurate age of the tree. A number of problems exist, however, with sampling this close to the root collar of the tree. Many trees have lobate growth at the base that is associated with root activity just under the soil. This irregular growth could confound a climate reconstruction. Also, it is more difficult to core a tree at the base because you are restricted to using your upper body strength to take a core. The increment borer handle can also hit the ground while trying to core at the base. To avoid this, an area can be excavated at the base of a tree so that the handle can turn freely. Shorter borer handles can also be used to get closer to the base, or a borer handle can be bent to create Brown's "bent boomerang borer handle" (also known as the Quad B) that bends back toward the operator and allows the person coring to get closer to the ground or to core deeper in between large fissures in the bark (Brown 2007). Another option is a power borer, which uses a large chainsaw engine connected to a drilling attachment that converts the motion of the chain into torque like a drill. These machines can be dangerous, as they create a lot of torque, and they are not sold in most stores. The power borer is driven by a large chainsaw head (such as a Stihl 460 or larger) that is attached to an Atom Drilling Attachment (available from Seago International Inc., Hickory, North Carolina). The increment borer shaft connects through a special chuck that can be purchased from forestry catalogs.

Heart rot due to root disease, basal injury, or browsing by animals is more likely to be encountered at the base of the tree than at breast height. Unless tree establishment dates are needed, dendrochronologists usually take cores at approximately breast height (1.4 m), even though the initial years of tree growth will not be represented because the tree would not have grown to breast height in its first years. Coring at breast height is advantageous because the whole body can be used to build momentum for coring, and the most common forestry measure in North America is DBH, so that samples taken at this height can tie into the extensive data and literature compiled by forest researchers.

Two cores should be taken from all trees sampled so that crossdating can begin at the tree level, in other words, the two cores from the same tree can be dated and compared with one another. More cores can be taken to obtain a solid core or to try to get older rings in a tree. When these two cores are averaged together, a better estimate of overall tree growth is obtained.

If the tree is growing on a slope, the cores should be taken parallel to the contour to avoid reaction wood in the tree. Conifer trees produce larger rings (compression wood) on the downhill side of the tree to keep the tree growing upright. In hardwood trees, the larger rings (tension wood) develop on the uphill side of the tree. Therefore, a core taken parallel to the contour avoids the larger rings of reaction wood and represents the average ring growth at that height in the stem. When two people take cores from the same tree at the same time, the cores should be taken at different heights so that the increment borers do not meet inside the tree and damage each other.

To start an increment borer, push the bit into a fissure in the bark of the tree as you turn the handle in a clockwise direction (fig. 5.1). The fissure in the bark gives a starting place and allows you to avoid coring through a thicker area of bark. On trees located near roads, however, grit may accumulate in the fissures, which could dull the increment borer. Starting a borer is an easy process in softwoods, but it can be exceedingly difficult in trees with smooth bark such as young sugar maple and beech or in hardwood trees such as oak or hickory. To aid in starting a borer in hardwood trees, you can also use an increment borer starter, which consists of a metal plate that can be positioned against your chest and a shaft that fits into the opening on the increment borer bit at the handle. This allows you to push with your chest as you turn the borer by hand. The starter also helps to ensure that you are coring straight into the tree, perpendicular to the stem. If the borer wobbles as you core into the tree, an irregular core will be cut until the shaft of the borer is solidly seated inside of the tree.

Once the borer is started, the borer handle simply needs to be turned in a clockwise direction until the tip of the borer has passed the center of the tree. You can measure how far you have cored into the tree by holding up the spoon (that is, the core extractor of the borer) so that the knob on the spoon is at the borer handle and the blade of the spoon is along the side of the tree, parallel to the increment borer shaft. With larger trees, this may take a second person standing back to observe if the spoon makes it to the halfway point into the tree.

Two hands should always be kept on the borer handle to ensure that even pressure is applied along the shaft. Do not bend the increment borer shaft. As you core into the tree,

**Figure 5.1** When starting an increment borer, push the borer into the tree with equal pressure on the shaft of the borer as you turn it into the tree. Starting an increment borer is especially difficult on smooth-barked hardwood trees. A starter may be used when coring a hard tree. It is made of a metal plate that can be placed against the chest and a shaft that is inserted into the increment borer bit at the handle. This allows you to push with your chest as you turn the handle of the borer. (From Jozsa 1988)

feel the resistance to turning the increment borer. If the borer starts to turn easily, you may have cored into a pocket of rot in the tree and are at risk of getting the borer stuck. Stop and remove the core and then the borer from the tree. If, as you core into the tree, it becomes very difficult to turn the borer—more than you would expect from the friction of having more of the borer shaft in the tree—the core may be twisting up inside the shaft and you are at risk of a jammed increment borer. Stop and remove the core. A jammed borer usually is the result of a poorly sharpened bit, but it can be exacerbated by rot in the tree. It takes a lot of time to clear a jammed increment borer, so it is better not to get to that point.

*Testing for a Compressed Core.* It is possible to stop coring to check the depth of the core in the shaft of the increment borer to see if it is jamming up. This procedure is only recommended when coring softwoods such as pine. If coring is stopped for any period of time in hardwoods, the wood fibers relax back on the borer and there is a risk of breaking the borer when you start to core again. On a conifer, you can stop and push the spoon into the shaft of the borer until you feel resistance on the spoon, which means that you have hit the bark of the core in the shaft. Hold your thumb and forefinger on the spoon at the opening of the shaft, marking the depth of the spoon (fig. 5.2a). Then carefully extract the spoon, making sure that you are not taking part of the bark with you. Put the spoon up to the tree bark along the increment borer shaft (fig. 5.2b). The distance from the bark to the handle of the borer should be the same distance that you measured inside of the shaft for the depth to the core. If your marking thumb is one or more inches from the handle of the borer (fig. 5.2c), then you have a jammed core and should remove the core and the borer immediately.

*Taking and Packaging a Core.* The increment borer bit cuts and pushes away the wood surrounding a pencil-sized core of wood inside the tree, so that once the borer is completely turned into the trunk, the only area of the core still connected to the tree is the inner disc of material just at the cutting tip (fig. 5.3). The inside shaft of the increment borer is tapered to a smaller diameter at the tip, so that the spoon, inserted into the shaft, is forced to pinch into the end of the core (fig. 5.4). When the increment borer is then turned a half or a full turn in the counter-clockwise direction, the core is broken off inside the tree and can be extracted by pulling the spoon out of the borer shaft.

At this point, the core is placed into a straw to protect it and maintain the proper order of any wood fragments that come out of the increment borer. The shaft of the increment borer should be used as a third hand holding the core while you package it into a straw (fig. 5.5). Remove the spoon only far enough out of the shaft to slide the exposed core into the straw. Pinch down the end of the straw to seal the core in the paper straw or use masking tape to close plastic straws. Do not simply fold over the end of the paper straw, because it may open in the map tube. Do not leave the tape as a flagged end because it will become stuck on other cores in the map tube and take up more space than is needed. The straw is then labeled with the site designation, the tree number, and the side of the tree that the core was taken from (usually coded as an A or B core).

Once the cores are neatly packaged in straws, they should be placed in the map tube to protect them from breakage or getting lost. Remember that plastic straws should be slit to ventilate the cores and to keep mold from forming. These cores can be removed from the map tube at the end of the day and bundled together in newspaper or with string so that they can air dry. Once the cores have been bundled in newspaper, they can be placed on the dashboard of the field vehicle to help them dry out.

*Removing an Increment Borer from the Tree.* When removing the increment borer from the tree, turn the borer in a counterclockwise direction. The borer should gradually come out of the tree as you turn it. A borer may become stuck in a tree if left too long because the wood that was pushed out of the way relaxes back on the shaft of the borer. If this occurs, apply a sharp backward jerking force on the borer as you turn the borer counterclockwise so that the spiral threads of the borer bite back into the wood of the tree (fig. 5.6). As a last resort, a rope can be used to create a Spanish windlass to remove a stuck borer (see the next section). Note that the clip that keeps the handle of the increment borer connected to the shaft can vibrate

**Figure 5.2** Measuring for compressed wood in an increment borer. In pine trees, you can use the spoon to measure if the wood of the core is binding up inside of the increment borer shaft. In panel (C), the thumb marking the depth of the core in the shaft is about 2 inches from the handle, when measured against the tree. This means that the core has twisted and jammed up inside the borer and should be removed immediately. (Photos from Henri Grissino-Mayer; Grissino-Mayer 2003)

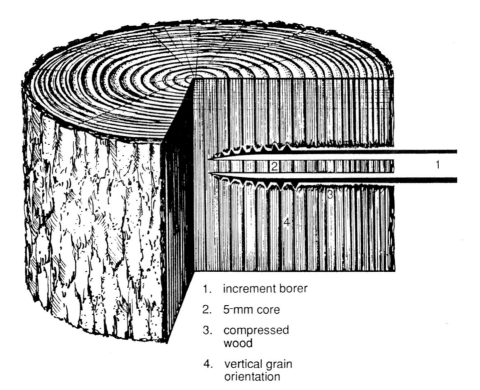

1. increment borer
2. 5-mm core
3. compressed wood
4. vertical grain orientation

**Figure 5.3** When coring a tree, as the borer is turned into the tree, it cuts away the wood around the increment borer and compresses the wood away from the borer. The core stays in its original position as the wood is cut away from the outside of the core, so that when the core is extracted, there is a full sample of rings from the bark to the pith. Note the space between the core and the wall of the shaft that allows the spoon to pass up to the tapered tip of the borer. (From Jozsa 1988)

loose or come undone. Be very careful when pulling back on the increment borer handle to ensure that this clasp is engaged or the handle can come off in your hands, which could be dangerous when coring on steep slopes. Some tape or a rubber O-ring can be used to ensure that this clasp does not come loose.

*Spanish Windlass Technique for Retrieving a Stuck Borer.* A borer may become stuck in a tree if it encounters a pocket of rot or if left in the tree for too long. If you cannot get the borer unstuck by pulling and turning the handle, you can use a Spanish windlass to remove the stuck borer. This technique can be very dangerous as much tension is put on the rope and the increment borer handle during this procedure, so the utmost caution should be exercised.

For this procedure, you need to have a tree directly behind you and a rope. Take the rope and wrap it around the handle and clip of the borer, making sure that the clip will not release prematurely. Then take the rope and wrap it around the tree directly behind the borer. Bring the end of the rope back and tie the rope to itself (fig. 5.7). You have now made one continuous loop of rope linking the tree and the borer. As you turn the borer, the rope twists and

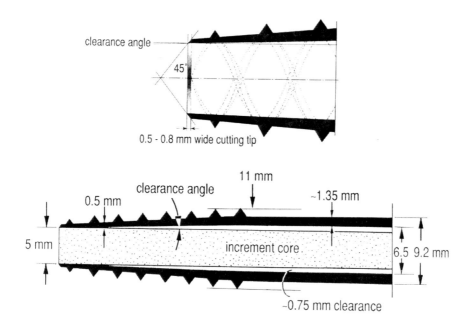

**Figure 5.4** The tip of the increment borer shaft is tapered so that the diameter of the core is smaller than the diameter of the inside of the increment borer. This allows the spoon to pass by the core and to pinch into the core near the pith of the tree. (From Jozsa 1988)

shortens, eventually providing the tension needed to remove the borer from the tree. This produces a lot of tension pulling the borer out of the tree, so when the borer bit gets into the bark, the borer is forcefully pulled from the tree. Hold onto the borer handle and be careful not to get hit by the handle or the bit of the borer. Make sure that you do not let go of the handle of the borer because the borer can fly through the air in an uncontrolled fashion and possibly hurt someone or damage the increment borer bit. Some researchers release the tension on the windlass before the borer leaves the wood, but be certain that the borer bit is in solid wood at this point so that you do not have to go through the process of retying the windlass.

## Cleaning an Increment Borer

Increment borers are made of steel and are susceptible to rusting. If the borer shaft becomes rusty, the metal will be weakened and the cutting edge can be pock-marked from the breakdown of the metal by the rust. To avoid these problems, increment borers should be cleaned with a dewatering agent (such as WD-40) and paper towels or steel wool. A .22 rifle cleaning kit can be used to clean inside the shaft of the borer, but one should take care not to push the brush to far past the cutting edge or it may be damaged. I prefer using the spoon of the increment borer with a postage-stamp-sized piece of paper towel wrapped around the teeth of the spoon. The cleaning agent should be sprayed along the outside and inside of the shaft, with special attention paid to the tip of the borer. Then the piece of paper towel can be run up and down the inside of the shaft. The paper towel usually comes off of the spoon teeth

**Figure 5.5** To extract the core from the tree, turn the borer a half turn in the counterclockwise direction, which breaks the wood off inside the tree, allowing you to pull the core out with the spoon. Once the spoon is extracted with the core on it, slide paper or plastic straws over the core from the bark end. It is easier if the core is left in the borer so that only a few inches of the core can be seen while the straw is slid over the core. The shaft of the borer acts as a third hand and reduces the possibility of losing pieces of the sample. (Photo by the author)

and then can be pushed out the cutting end of the borer (as long as the piece is not too large). Repeat this process until the paper towel comes out clean. This cleaning process should be done at the end of each field trip at a minimum and could be done at the end of each field day, especially if coring trees that tend to be moist, such as in the eastern deciduous forest in the spring.

## Sharpening an Increment Borer

The tip of an increment borer becomes dulled through regular use and could become chipped if it encountered a rock or some metal. This cutting edge is the most important component in getting a good straight core without many breaks or twisting. The tip should be inspected regularly through a microscope or with a hand lens to check its condition. The tip of an increment borer is tapered so that the core that is cut is a smaller diameter than the inside of the borer shaft. This allows the spoon to pass by the core and attach at the tip of the core so that it can be removed. If the tip of the borer is sharpened back too far, this taper is removed and the borer is ruined. Increment borers can be sent for professional sharpening, but they remove so much metal that this can only be done two or three times before the borer can no longer be used.

**Figure 5.6** Normally an increment borer can be extracted by turning the handle in a counterclockwise direction with equal pressure along the shaft of the borer. When the borer becomes stuck in a pocket of rot, you have to pull and turn at the same time while being careful that the handle clip on the borer shaft does not release, resulting in a backward fall. (From Jozsa 1988)

A sharpening kit can be purchased from forestry catalogs or at some better hardware stores. The kit should include three whet stones (rectangular, wedge, and conical stones) that are about 3 inches long and some honing oil. Increment borers can be sharpened under a microscope so that you can closely watch how you are affecting the cutting edge of the borer, or in the field you can work on the borer in your lap and check the cutting edge periodically under a hand lens. Sharpening the tip of an increment borer is a delicate process. It is best if you can get some instruction from someone who is skilled at it, but I describe the general procedure below.

**Figure 5.7** The Spanish windlass technique uses the force generated from a twisting rope to provide backward pull on the increment borer, enabling removal of a stuck borer from a tree. Connect the rope around the handle of the increment borer and a tree directly in line with the increment borer, then twist the handle of the borer counterclockwise. The increment borer will come out of the tree quickly when most of it has been rotated out of the tree, so be careful with this technique. Keep a tight grip on the borer to control it as it comes out so that you or the borer does not get hurt. (Photo by Karla Hansen-Speer)

The rectangular stone is only used in dire circumstances when the tip of the increment borer is chipped, and the tip of the borer must be worked back below that chip. Put some honing oil on the whet stone, and hold the stone perpendicular to the shaft. Rub the stone back and forth to grind down the tip past the bottom of the chip in the cutting edge. If the chip is more than 1/8 inch deep, then the borer cannot be fixed.

For a dull increment borer that does not have chips out of the tip, start with the wedge stone to sharpen the tip and the threads of the borer. The stone should be held at a 37–45° angle to the axis of the shaft. A 37° angle makes a sharper borer, but it will not hold its edge as long. A 45° angle holds its edge longer, but it may be more difficult to start in some wood types. The wedge stone should be used to sharpen the outer bevel of the cutting tip while the borer shaft is continually rotated. Do not hold the borer steady and work back and forth on one part of the cutting tip, because the cutting tip is a circle and you will wear down one side. Instead, through constant rotation of the borer shaft and swiping the wedge stone in the opposite direction of that rotation, you can sharpen that rounded edge. Some pressure can be applied as long as you are careful to be consistent in the amount of metal removed around the circumference of the cutting tip.

The conical stone is only used to remove the tiny metal burs that are bent into the shaft during this sharpening process. Insert the conical stone into the end of the cutting tip and gently rotate it to remove these burs. The stone is not really sharpening the inside of the cutting tip; only the outer edge does the cutting, and the conical stone should not touch all of the inside edge of the cutting tip at any time. If you put too much pressure on the cutting tip and force the conical stone into the tip, it will flare out the tip of the borer and ruin it. Only a little work with the conical stone is needed, and then the cutting edge can be checked for sharpness.

When looking at the cutting tip through a microscope, you should see the shiny metal surface where you sharpened around the tip. To check the sharpness of the tip, turn the tip of the borer on a small folded stack of paper towels. It should cut out a series of small disks. If it does not, then the borer is not sharp enough. This test should be done carefully, because if the borer is sharp and you don't use enough paper towels, you will cut little disks out of your finger, which is not a pleasant experience.

The threads of the borers can also be sharpened in a similar manner to the tip of the increment borer. Use the wedge stone and constantly rotate the borer while running the stone in the opposite direction along the edge of the threads. This needs to be done on both sides of the threads, and increment borers have either two or three threads that need to be sharpened.

Take care in handling a sharpened increment borer. It is easy to cut your fingertips on the sharpened threads. It is also easy to damage a newly sharpened tip, so be careful as you return the increment borer shaft to the handle for storage. Also, when coring in the field make sure that grit and stones do not come in contact with the tip of the increment borer.

## Laboratory Methods

Once the cores are brought in from the field in their paper or plastic straws, the laboratory work begins. This consists of preparing the wood by drying, mounting, and sanding the cores; analyzing the cores through such methods as skeleton plotting; and measuring. In chapter 6 I discuss the analysis of wood using computer and statistical methods.

## Preparing Core Samples

While the cores are still in their straws, they can be placed in a drying oven at 60°C for 24 hours, in a fume hood with continuous airflow for a week, or on high in a microwave oven for 20–25 seconds. If you are lucky enough to live in a dry climate, cores can also be air dried as long as the plastic straws are well ventilated. If the core is glued to a mount when it is still wet, it will develop cracks as it dries and shrinks, making it difficult to be certain that no wood was lost in the field. Drying the cores on too high of a temperature may cause some wood types to twist. Also if the research project is examining wood chemistry or isotopic analysis, a high drying temperature may volatilize some chemicals in the wood.

Once the core is dried, it is mounted on a prefabricated wooden core mount (for a review of laboratory techniques, see Stokes and Smiley 1968, Phipps 1985). The best mounts are narrow enough to view two mounted cores side by side in a stereozoom microscope at 20× magnifica-tion. Professionally manufactured core mounts can be purchased that are made from poplar wood and measure 1.25 cm × 0.75 cm × 1.2 m. The mounts have a half circular groove routed into them to take the 4.3- and 5.15-mm cores that are the standard dimensions of increment cores. The cores should be mounted using water-soluble white glue so that they can be removed from the mount and remounted, if necessary, by soaking them overnight in a water bath.

*Mounting Cores.* Before the core is mounted, all of the information from the straw should be copied onto the core mount. This should include the sample ID, tree species, date the sample was taken, and initials of the person taking the core. Once the mount is prepared, a line of glue can be extruded into the core mount groove and the core can be carefully mounted in the groove. The core has two cross-sectional views and two radial views. Imagine the circular core squared on four sides: two opposite sides are cross-sectional views and two are radial views (fig. 5.8; see chapter 3 for a description of these wood sections). Care must be taken to mount a cross-sectional view facing up; otherwise the ring boundaries may not be evident after sand-ing. The radial view of the core is often coarse because of the torn tracheids or shiny because of the side view of the long tracheids (fig. 5.9). Also, the tangential view can be examined to align the tracheids so that their long axis is mounted vertically. String, binder clips, masking tape, or heavy weights can be used to hold the cores in place as the glue dries (fig. 5.10d, e). If you do not restrain the core, it will soak up moisture from the glue and curl out of the core mount. The glue usually dries in about two hours. I personally prefer using string as it allows you to pull the core tightly into the core mount and is flexible enough to provide pressure wherever the core is broken. The string can also be reused many times. One drawback of using string is that it leaves fibers behind that can be observed under the microscope when the core is being examined. For drying the glue quickly, some researchers at the University of Arizona micro-wave their cores on high for 20–25 seconds, which drives off the moisture in the glue.

*Untwisting Cores.* Cores may become twisted if the increment borer had a dull or nicked tip. If a twisted core is mounted without treatment, then the core will vary between the cross-sectional

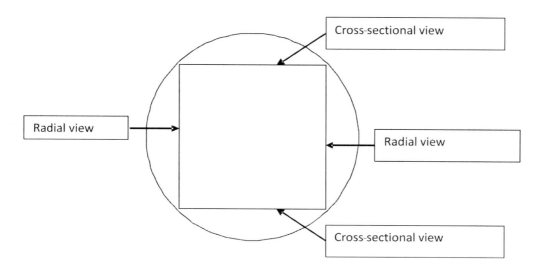

**Figure 5.8** Schematic of the different sides of a core. The circle represents looking at the end of a core, where the core has two cross-sectional views and two radial views. The researcher must take care to mount a cross-sectional view facing up in the core mount, or the rings will not be clear. (Drawing by Karla Hansen-Speer)

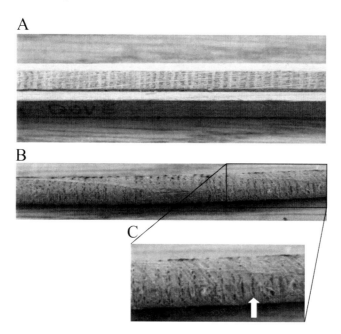

**Figure 5.9** The core should be mounted with the cross-sectional view facing up. (A) A core correctly mounted with rings facing up. (B) An unmounted core. (C) The arrow points to an example of torn tracheid. The tracheids are torn on the radial view so that the surface looks rough or shiny. The vertical fibers on the end of the core can also be used to determine proper orientation of the core. (Photos by Tony Campbell)

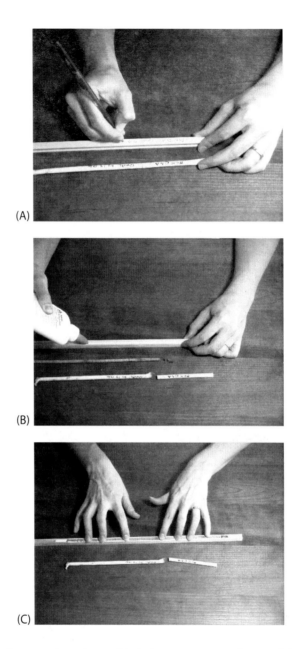

(A)

(B)

(C)

**Figure 5.10** Once the cores have been dried, they are mounted on prefabricated wooden core mounts with water-soluble white glue. (A) The information from the straw is written on the side of the core mount. (B) The core should be delicately removed from the straw and can be used as a guide for how much glue should be extruded into the groove. (C) The core should be firmly pressed into the groove. (D) The core is then secured to the core mount to keep it from curling as it absorbs the moisture from the glue. String, tape, binder clips, or weights can be used to hold the cores in place while the glue dries. (E) The string can be tied off and the mount should sit for at least two hours before it can be sanded. (F) Once the string is removed all of the cores are ready for sanding. (Photos by the author)

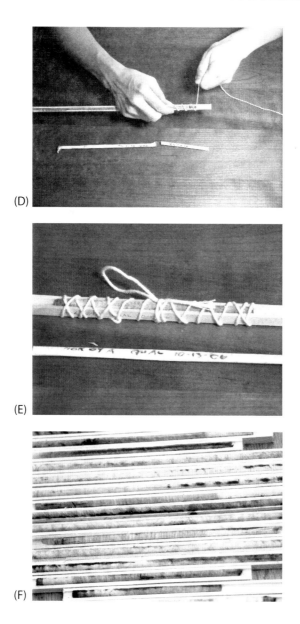

(D)

(E)

(F)

**Figure 5.10** (*Continued*)

view and the radial view as you move along the core mount. You can use a low-pressure steam jet generator (or a tea kettle with a molded aluminum foil spout to direct the steam; fig. 5.11) to moisten and heat the core so that it can be untwisted. Gentle continuous pressure should be applied to the core counter to the direction of twist while the core is moved back and forth through the jet of steam. This process usually takes about 30 seconds for each twist. Be careful not to burn your fingertips. The technique is especially difficult with short lengths

**Figure 5.11** If a core is twisted (usually due to a nicked or dull increment borer), then the core can be straightened over a jet of steam. (Photo by the author)

of core. Cores can also be microwaved with a wet paper towel for a short period of time to get the same effect of moistening and heating the core so that it can be untwisted.

*Sanding Cores.* Once the glue is dry, the core needs to be sanded using a belt sander with progressively finer sandpaper from ANSI 50 grit (125–149 μm; mainly used for hardwoods), 120 grit (105–125 μm), 220 grit (53–74 μm), 320 grit (32.5–36.0 μm), and 400 grit (20.6–23.6 μm) (fig. 5.12; Orvis and Grissino-Mayer 2002). The first sanding grit is used to flatten the core surface for subsequent polishing and takes the longest. The progressive sequence of finer sandpaper allows efficient removal of the striations created from the previous sanding belt as the core is polished to a better finish. The final surface should be polished so that each individual cell of the cross-sectional view can be clearly seen under a microscope with 7–40× magnification. A 4 inch × 24 inch belt sander with a flat top for sanding cores is often used, although some researchers use an orbital sander and others even use a drill press with a sanding disc attached to it. The drill press technique has merits because you can look down on the core surface as you sand it to determine when it has been sanded enough.

It is also possible to use a razor blade to create a clean surface on the cores. A sharp, stainless steel scalpel with a steady hand and polishing with superfine steel wool can create a clean

**Figure 5.12** Cores and cross sections should be surfaced using progressively finer grades of sandpaper from 50 to 400 grit. Use a dusk mask, ear plugs, and eye protection while using an electric sander. (Photo by Michael Glenn)

surface. This stainless steel scalpel technique is particularly useful for dendrochemistry and isotopic analysis because contamination from sawdust should be avoided.

I use a belt sander and invert it so that the belt faces up and clamp the sander handle to the table. This creates a flat, stable surface on which to sand the cores. It is a good practice to change the angle of the core between sanding grits (sanding along the length of the sander, then switching to a 45° angle from the axis of the sander) so that you can see the striations from the previous belt (fig. 5.13). Once those striations are removed, you can move on to the next finer sandpaper.

Hand sanding film at 30, 15, or 9 μm can be used to provide a finer polish to the finished surface. The ANSI grit rating of sandpaper is a general value of the roughness of the surface even though many different sized particles may be used in the sandpaper. Sanding film with a micron rating is made of particles with a specific size as determined by a geologic sieve; therefore, the sanding film provides a better surface than the equivalent sandpaper grit.

Be careful not to sand the surface of a core down too far. About half of the core should be left when all sanding is done, so that the largest area of wood can be looked at under the microscope. The final polish on the cross-sectional view is most important for allowing the proper identification of ring boundaries. Some researchers use ethanol or isopropyl alcohol on pine trees to remove excess resin. The surface can also be buffed with suede leather, but if it is too polished, then it may be difficult to make pencil marks on the surface. Many researchers have experimented with wood dyes to bring out the ring boundaries, but in my

**Figure 5.13** Cores can be sanded on a belt sander (a 4-inch × 24-inch belt sander recommended for the surface area that it provides) with progressively finer grits (50, 120, 220, 320, and 400 grits) to polish the cross-sectional view until the individual cells are apparent under a microscope at 40× magnification. In this picture the operator is sanding the core at a 45° angle from the axis of the sander so that he can see the striations made from the previous grit. Once those striations are sanded off of the core, it is time to move on to the next finer grit. Repeated visual examination of the core helps determine when the core has been sanded enough. Of course, the final test is to examine the core under the microscope. (Photo by the author)

experience, a well-polished surface (even on maple wood) is superior to any dye for the identification of ring boundaries.

## Preparing Cross Sections

Cross sections can be sanded with the same belt sander that is used on cores. First, the sample needs to be securely mounted to the table. Four layers of Masonite peg board can be used as a working surface. Cut dowels into pieces about one inch long to fit into the peg holes. Put multiple cross sections on the peg board and use the short dowels to securely fasten each sample to the board. These dowels, placed around the circumference of the section, enable you to sand the sample while it stays in place. A friction pad (rubberized pad) can also be used to hold the sample in place.

**Figure 5.14** Sander belts lose efficiency before the grit is worn down as they become covered in a layer of resin and dust from the wood. Sander belts can be cleaned using a rubber gum eraser that can be purchased at most woodworking stores. The eraser pulls the sawdust from within the grit of the sandpaper and clumps it together, shooting it from the sander. If cleaned, sander belts can be reused some 20 or more times before the grit wears down. (Photo by the author)

The same series of sandpaper used on cores is also used on cross sections, but if the surface of the cross section is particularly uneven from the original chainsaw cut, you may start with a coarse 50-grit (125- to 149-μm) sandpaper or cut a clean surface with a band saw to remove the saw cuts. Once a flat surface is obtained, continue to work through the finer grits of sandpaper. While sanding, always keep the sander flat on the sample and keep it in continual motion. Do not start or stop the sander on the section because this will gouge the wood. The sander should be running when it is placed on the sample and running when it is removed from the sample.

A thick gum eraser can be used to clean sandpaper belts, greatly extending their usable life (fig. 5.14). These large erasers can be purchased at woodworking supply stores. Hold the eraser against the belt surface while it is running. The gum from the eraser clumps up the sawdust and resin, removing them from the spaces between the sanding medium on the belts. This cleaning should be done after the use of any grit belt and before the belt is removed from the sander.

## Analysis of Cores and Cross Sections

At this stage, the cores and cross sections have been prepared and are ready for visual analysis and crossdating. The goal of crossdating is to assign calendar dates to each annual ring, and one way to start is to mark a visual ring count of the decades on the wood. Use a number 2 pencil to initially denote the decades because these will probably need to be erased and changed as the analysis continues. Start the inspection from the outside of the tree (bark side) if you know the date of death or cutting or from the inside (pith) if the sample has an unknown death date.

Starting from the pith, cores can be marked from zero as the innermost ring of the tree with every 10th ring marked with a single pencil dot to designate the decade year. Every 50th ring receives two dots, a 100th ring receives three dots, and a millennial ring gets four dots (fig. 5.15). When the core is briefly scanned it is easy to count up the total number of rings, and the dendrochronologist can refer to this relative time scale if there is any question about the dating of the core. This is a conservative technique that does not assume an accurate date of the wood until those pencil marks are erased and real calendar years are marked on the samples.

Another technique is to start from the outermost, bark-side ring and use it as an anchor in time for when the tree was cored, counting back from that outermost ring and assuming calendar years as you work backward in time. This is a faster technique because it does not require remarking the wood, but it can be misleading because these are not truly dated rings until the process of crossdating is complete. In this process, one dot is still used for decade rings, two dots for 50-year rings, three dots for century rings, and four dots for millennial rings, but in this case the millennial mark coincides with 2000 and the first century mark coincides with 1900. If you are working with dead wood with an unknown outer date, you still have to use the relative marks from the inside of the core until the core is crossdated against a master chronology.

### Skeleton Plotting

Skeleton plotting is the basic technique invented by A. E. Douglass in the early 1900s and used by many dendrochronologists around the world for the first attempt at dating a sample (Stokes and Smiley 1968). Most dendrochronologists today use the same plotting paper of five squares to a centimeter as Douglass originally used. When two samples of wood are compared, they may be growing at different rates, which would prevent a productive comparison of these two cores. Time can be put on a standard scale by using graph paper in which each vertical line represents one calendar year so the cores can be compared against each other. This can also be thought of as a two-dimensional plot with time on the x-axis going from old on the left to the present on the right and an inverse scale of the narrowness of the ring on the y-axis, ranging from 0 (for average or larger width) to 10 (for an absent ring). This also reduces the bulky sample to a concise record of the narrow marker rings that can be compared between samples, stored for future reference, and compiled into a master chronology.

A **marker ring** is a ring that is consistently narrow or has identifiable characteristics and is consistent between different trees. Graph paper is used as the standard scale for comparisons

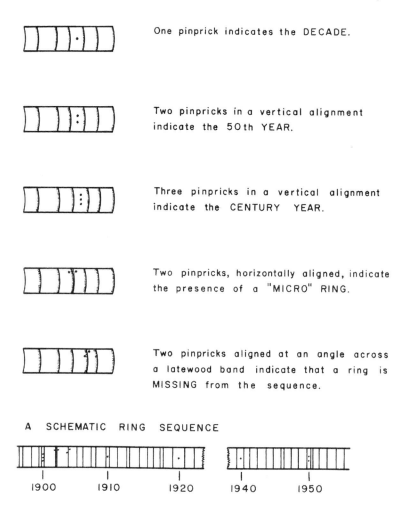

One pinprick indicates the DECADE.

Two pinpricks in a vertical alignment indicate the 50th YEAR.

Three pinpricks in a vertical alignment indicate the CENTURY YEAR.

Two pinpricks, horizontally aligned, indicate the presence of a "MICRO" RING.

Two pinpricks aligned at an angle across a latewood band indicate that a ring is MISSING from the sequence.

A   SCHEMATIC   RING   SEQUENCE

1900     1910     1920     1940     1950

**Figure 5.15** A systematic method of marking the wood provides a temporal frame of reference so that you do not lose count of the rings. One dot is used on every decade year, two dots every 50 years, three dots every 100 years, and four dots every millennium. This allows for quick scanning of the wood to determine the date anywhere along the sample. Micro and missing rings are indicated with dots across ring boundaries. (From Stokes and Smiley 1968)

between trees where each line represents one year. A line is drawn for the years representing narrow rings that are responding to a limiting environmental factor. Extraordinarily big rings can be marked with a "b" on the skeleton plot and may be as reliable for crossdating as narrow rings.

Dating by use of skeleton plots and the other methods described later are much more efficient and quicker than measuring the rings and relying on statistics to find the match. Visual dating allows the dendrochronologist to use all aspects of the wood, such as color, latewood thickness, and marker rings, to determine the dating of the sample of wood. The computer program COFECHA (discussed more in chapter 6) was created by the late Richard

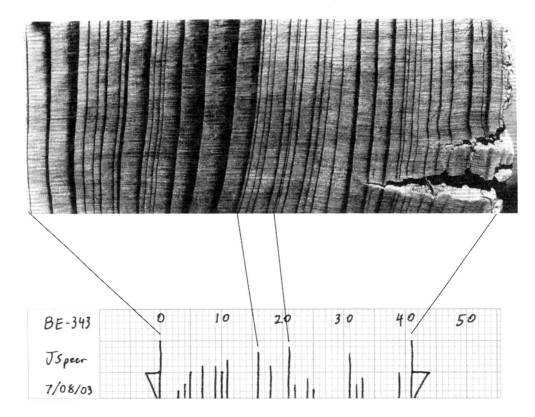

**Figure 5.16** Making a skeleton plot from a sample of wood. The plot illustrates time on a standard scale of each line representing one year. The more significant smaller marker rings are represented by longer lines on the plot. Beginning and end flags are drawn to show the inside and outside dates on the sample. Calendar years or a relative dating scale is marked along the top of the paper with every 10th ring marked with a date. Begin plotting from left to right, pith to bark. The sample ID, your name, and the date that the plot was created should be written in the blank space on the left of the plot. (Photo from Stokes and Smiley 1968)

Holmes as a second check of the chronology developed by a dendrochronologist. Until the 1980s, most dates were independently checked by a second dendrochronologist before they were assumed to be accurate and published. Today, the second check that is normally used is the COFECHA program, as long as the visual dating was done independently of this statistical tool.

When preparing a skeleton plot, cut a sheet of 8½ × 11-inch graph paper on the long axis into thin strips that are 15 squares high (fig. 5.16). Dendrochronologists try to use the same graph paper that Douglass did in the early 1900s so that all of our plots can be compared to each other. This graph paper has five lines per centimeter. Along the length, 110 years can be marked on this sheet, and additional sheets can be glued on to accommodate longer cores. The empty white margin of the paper on the left should be used to write the sample ID, your name, and current date. The top third (five lines) of the paper should be marked with a regular count, either starting at year zero on the left and marking every tenth year or starting with the outside date on the right and marking every decade going back in time. Either way, time progresses from left to right. A triangular flag is used to designate the inside date and outside date of the core. These flags are important because they provide the establishment date (or inside-most date) and death date (or sampling date), respectively.

Because of the age-related growth trend discussed in chapter 2, some standardization process must take place while making a skeleton plot. Otherwise, all plots would start off with no narrow marker rings at the beginning and the length of the lines (designating narrower marker rings) gradually gets longer toward the outside of the plot paper. While this is an accurate representation of the growth curve of the tree, it does not provide useful interannual variability for dating. To remove this trend and any possible suppression and release events from forest dynamics, use a mental standardization process. Compare the ring being dated to three rings on either side of it. If the focal ring is relatively narrow compared to surrounding rings, it receives a vertical mark on the skeleton plot paper. Another technique compares the ring in question only to the rings before it, that is, those closer to the pith, because this prior growth may affect the current year's growth, making them a more accurate comparative pool. This also controls for autocorrelation, as mentioned in chapter 2.

The bottom 10 lines of the skeleton plot paper are used for drawing the marker rings, with a line that is 10 boxes tall representing the narrowest possible ring in the core and a line that is one box tall representing one that is only marginally narrower than average. Any ring that is of average width or wider gets no mark on the plot. Rings that are significantly wide, however, can be marked with a "b" on the plot designating them as a big ring. These wider rings can also be used as marker rings in dating samples. Dendrochronologists usually concentrate on narrower rings because narrow rings are controlled by the limiting factor (as mentioned in chapter 2). The narrower the ring, the more significant that ring is as a marker, resulting in a longer line on the skeleton plot. Many students making their first skeleton plots are concerned about an absolute scale for the length of the line on the plots. The length of the line is really an arbitrary designation that has to be determined by the person making the plots. But after some experience with the range of possible ring widths, most plots converge to a similar pattern.

Cropper (1979) made a computer program that could use the information from skeleton plots to date cores, demonstrating that this is a repeatable process that can be quantified. More recently, Tom Harlan commissioned a new crossdating program called Crossdate that makes electronic skeleton plots just as we do on graph paper, compares plots to a master chronology, and provides statistics on the best matches. This program was written for and is particularly useful when working on bristlecone pine samples that are dated against a 10,000-year master chronology, which is more than 15 m long when marked out on graph paper.

Much of the interannual pattern used for dating is in the marker rings, but the spaces between those rings also represent much of the pattern. Because of the mental standardization and for the precision of the dating pattern, it is important that no areas have four or more rings in a row marked as small. If more than four rings in an area are small, that area is considered suppressed and only the smallest ring(s) in that area should be used as marker rings. If there were four marker rings in a row, shifting the plot back and forth would match up marker rings in four separate positions, obscuring the annual resolution needed for crossdating. On the other hand, double and sometimes triple small years can be important dating markers.

When I work on a new site, I usually draw skeleton plots for at least 10 cores from that site. I compare these plots to each other and determine if all of the rings are represented on each core by matching up the marker rings. I start off by matching the two plots from within the same tree. Dating within trees (from the two cores from the same tree) is expected to be stronger than dating between trees. If one or more of the plots do not match the others, I go back to the wood to find where the problem in dating lies in that particular core. At every place where two plots disagree (for example, only one plot shows a narrow ring), I go back to the wood to check both plots. This variation in plots may not be a dating error, but could be due to the individual ecological response of the tree or even differences (such as compression wood) on the side of the tree being examined. If many decades of marker rings are consistently off in one direction, however, it is likely to be a dating error.

The quality of the match is difficult to determine and is something of an arbitrary determination, but repeated attempts to date a sample by trained dendrochronologists produce the same results. The date of an unknown sample should be checked through the length of the entire master chronology (the master plot for the site containing the average widths for the narrow rings). A researcher recognizes some locations where the marker rings match up better than others. Mark these dates on the plot as possible dates, then go back to them at the end and determine which represents the strongest match.

The result of these checks is a correctly dated set of cores from which a master chronology can be built. As a first step in developing a master chronology, overlap the individual plots each one above the previous so that they are very precisely aligned with all of the yearly line marks corresponding to one another. The master chronology plot is made in a mirror image of the other plots (fig. 2.2b). The blank space on the left side of the master plot paper contains information about the site and master plot status. The dates, however, are real calendar dates that are listed along the bottom of the plot paper. The lines representing the narrow marker rings run from the top of the plot paper down to a maximum of 10 boxes on the graph paper. The mirror-image characteristic of the master chronology enables regular skeleton plots to be easily compared with it in order to identify matching dates. A line is drawn on the master plot each time the ring in question is represented on at least 50% of the individual tree plots. For example, if 1974 appears as a narrow ring in 5 of 10 plots, that ring should be marked on the master chronology. The length of the line on the master is calculated by taking the average length of the lines represented on the individual tree plots. Do not count the cores not showing a narrow ring for those years in the average, but make a slightly longer line if that ring is represented on nearly every skeleton plot.

The master chronology, then, is a continuous time series containing all marker rings that agree between trees for the length of the chronology. This is the best tool that can be used to date remaining samples.

## List Method

The list method is another way to determine marker rings, if the outside date of the sample is known. The researcher can count back the rings from the bark to the pith, marking calendar years on the core according to the previously mentioned dot notation. Each time a narrow ring is noted, the date is written in a vertical list under the sample ID (fig. 2.4). Once the researcher has done this for 5 to 10 cores, he or she can go back to the lists and determine which rings are consistently narrow among the samples. At this early stage, as with skeleton plots, one should be careful that none of the samples are consistently off from the others, which would represent an initial dating error. Once a list of marker rings is developed, the researcher can use these marker rings to quickly date the rest of the samples.

## Memorization Method

The memorization method starts with known marker rings that may have been developed from a skeleton plot or the list method (Douglass 1941). The narrow marker rings can be memorized or written down as a list. Newly surfaced cores are counted back from the known outside date, and the calendar years are marked on the core using the dot notation. Every time a narrow ring is seen, it is checked against the marker rings. If the ring should be narrow, then the dating is still accurate. This process is continued to the inside of the sample. If the dating of the wood is off by a year or more from the marker rings, then the researcher checks other marker rings in the sample. If these rings are consistently off in one direction from the master chronology, a dating error has been located. The time period when the marker rings started to become different from the master should be examined for possible micro, false, or locally absent rings.

## Combining Dating Methods

I usually build my master chronology from 10 cores using the skeleton plot method and then date the remaining cores using the memorization method. When building the master, I start with the oldest cores in the collection so that I develop the longest possible master chronology representing the entire length of the chronology. Skeleton plotting takes some time, but it is the best technique for building a strong working master chronology, permanently recording that master, and providing a basis for dating. The memorization method allows for quick dating of the subsequent cores but relies on a valid master chronology. After measuring the tree-ring widths, I check all of my dates using COFECHA (see chapter 6). The final verification of a master chronology is to check its dating against other master chronologies from the surrounding area. The remote possibility exists that every tree in the chronology is missing the same ring or that the outside date is off by a year. Comparison to another master chronology might also help demonstrate crossdating in sections of the chronology with low sample depth. This second check of the whole chronology against another master can confirm the dating. At that point, I am confident that the dates have no error and are accurate and precise with annual resolution.

## Measuring Methods

Most dendrochronology projects require ring-width measurement for a quantitative analysis for comparison with climate data or some other calibration data set. Other projects, such as archaeological dating or fire history, simply require crossdating and do not need the samples to be measured. One of the benefits of measuring all samples is that the program COFECHA

**Figure 5.17** The Velmex Measuring System is the standard instrument for measuring ring width. It is a movable stage, rigged with an optical encoder, that works in conjunction with a stereo-zoom microscope that has a crosshair reticle in one eye piece. The print button is depressed each time the crosshair lines up with a ring boundary, sending the measurement from the QuickCheck device to the computer file. These measurements are retained in the virtual memory of the computer until the file is saved to the hard disk. (Photo by the author)

can provide the validation on the visual crossdating. These measured ring widths can also be contributed to the International Tree-Ring Data Bank (see appendix E for Web addresses), which is a repository of worldwide tree-ring chronologies. This databank also provides other master chronologies to which dating can be compared.

*Measuring Systems.* Many systems exist that can be used to obtain accurate measurements of tree rings. Most of these systems have a moving stage whose location is determined by rotation of a lead screw or by an optical linear encoder. These systems include the Bannister measuring stage, Measurechron, Henson measuring stage, Zahn measuring stage, LinTab measuring system, and Velmex measuring system. All of these systems are used in conjunction with a stereozoom microscope supported by a boom stand (fig. 5.17). The Bannister, Measurechron, Henson, and Zahn measuring stages all count the number of rotations of the lead screw to determine the width of each ring. One drawback from this type of system is that the screw can wear over time; if the technician measuring a core measures past the end of a

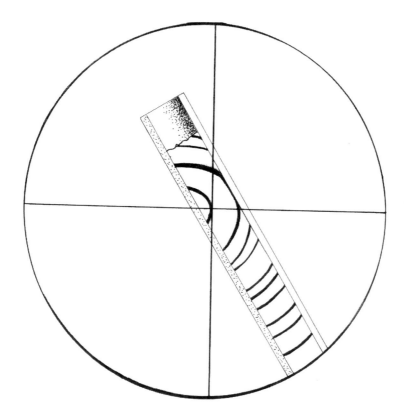

**Figure 5.18** Rings should be measured perpendicular to the current ring boundary at an area of average ring width for that year. The core needs to be repositioned at the end of each measurement while rings near the pith that exhibit a distinct curvature are measured. (Drawing by Karla Hansen-Speer)

ring, error can be incorporated in the measurement by turning the screw back. This can be avoided by backing off from the ring boundary and measuring back up to it. The Bannister, Henson, and Zahn systems are no longer made and it is difficult to find replacement parts for them. The Velmex and LinTab measuring systems have a movable stage that is advanced by a lead screw connected to a handle, but an optical linear encoder actually determines the exact location of the stage and measures its position to an accuracy of 0.01, 0.002, or 0.001 mm depending upon the precision of the instrument.

The microscope should have a crosshair reticle in one of the eye pieces, and this crosshair is lined up with a ring boundary so that the vertical hair is tangent to the curve of the ring boundary. Measurements are made along a core or cross section perpendicular to the ring boundary or along a radial file (a row of cells that are produced from the same cambial initials). The average width of the ring is measured based on the observable ring area. For example, if a ring pinches across the field of view, the average width of that ring is measured. Because it is necessary to measure perpendicular to the ring boundary, the core must be repositioned to take the curvature of the ring near the pith of a core into consideration (fig. 5.18).

Other measuring systems use digital images that are produced by scanning the sample on a flat-bed scanner. WindDendro and LignoVision are two such programs. They both provide automated measuring options that can speed the time it takes to measure samples. The drawback of these systems is that the accuracy of the program depends upon the resolution of the scanned image. Close supervision by the operator is needed to ensure that all of the rings are accurately measured. Micro rings can easily be missed by these automated processes. Wood samples that do not have very distinct ring boundaries, such as those of diffuse-porous woods, are not very well recognized by these systems and the cost of the programs can be prohibitive.

*Measuring Rings.* The best technique for measuring rings is to measure perpendicular to each ring boundary. As a core approaches the pith, it often shows much curvature at the center, and the core has to be adjusted in between each measurement to stay perpendicular to the previous ring boundary (fig. 5.18). The microscope that is connected to the measuring machine must have a crosshair reticle in one of its eye pieces. This crosshair is the target that is used to mark the ring boundary. The vertical crosshair should be tangent to the previous ring boundary, and the horizontal crosshair should reach the next ring boundary without going off of the wood sample.

Many researchers prefer to use a video capture system on a trinocular microscope to send the image from the microscope to a monitor. Crosshairs can be attached to the video monitor by using fishing line that has been colored black with a permanent marker. The image moves across the monitor in real time so that measurements can be made on the video screen. This arrangement reduces the eye strain of continually looking through a microscope for hours at a time. Some resolution is lost between the microscope and the video monitor, so this system is not the best for very narrow rings. Also there can be some parallax between the crosshairs and the image on the monitor so the researcher has to remain still while measuring each ring.

*Pith Indicators.* A pith indicator can be used when a core has missed the pith, but the pith age is required for analysis (Applequist 1956). An example of this is when conducting a stand-age structure analysis, and establishment dates are of interest. A pith indicator (Appendix C) is a series of concentric rings. The proper set is chosen based on the average size of the inner most rings on the core. The curvature of the rings is matched up to the curvature of the concentric circles, and the number of rings that are missing to the pith are counted. This is a rough estimate for the actual pith date, but is a better guess than simply using the inner ring date.

## Work Time Distribution

Each step of a project, from collection to analysis, takes a certain amount of time, and it can be useful when planning a project to have an idea about the time one can reasonably expect to spend on each part. The data collection process takes much less time than the laboratory procedures (not counting travel time to the site). Crossdating takes the most time, including the check of the dating that can be done with the COFECHA program. Measuring the cores

**Table 5.2**    Average work time in person-hours to collect, process, and build a chronology that is from 200 to 400 years in length from 20 trees

| Task | Mean Minimum | Mean | Mean Maximum | Mean Percentage |
|---|---|---|---|---|
| Collection | 11 | 15 | 23 | 9 |
| Specimen preparation | 7 | 12 | 17 | 7 |
| Dating | 51 | 72 | 120 | 42 |
| Measuring | 30 | 39 | 53 | 23 |
| Dating check with COFECHA | 10 | 17 | 28 | 10 |
| Basic climate response analysis | 3 | 5 | 8 | 3 |
| Project supervision | 8 | 11 | 15 | 6 |
| Total | 120 | 171 | 264 | 100 |

*Source:* Modified from Fritts (1976)

also takes considerable time, but the analysis can progress relatively quickly once these steps are completed. Table 5.2 lists the number of person-hours that it takes for each stage of a standard project that is completed by a skilled dendrochronologist with relatively straightforward wood.

## Summary

Solid field and laboratory methods will provide the basis for a good study. The time spent in the field is relatively small, and field sites are often difficult and expensive to get to, so it is important that we collect an adequate number of samples while on the site. Sample preparation cannot be emphasized enough. Ring identification depends upon being able to observe the individual cells to determine the ring boundaries. Good sample preparation with a very clear surface is paramount to good dating. Finally, accurate crossdating is the most important aspect of dendrochronology, so every effort should be made to achieve accuracy. Some researchers have been tending toward the sole use of COFECHA (described in the next chapter) or other statistical computer programs to achieve crossdating of their samples. This approach is not the best practice because the measurements can be adjusted (by inserting missing rings) to improve the dating, but there is no indication of what is the correct dating for the sample. The dating is in the wood, so visual crossdating with a second statistical check of that dating is the best practice to ensure accurate dating of samples.

# 6
# Computer Programs and Statistical Methods

Dendrochronologists use a suite of custom computer programs that incorporates both standard and complex statistical routines and tools that facilitate crossdating, climate analysis and reconstruction, biological response modeling, and tree-ring data editing. Many of these programs were written beginning in the 1960s and 1970s and are, therefore, DOS-based programs that run in a DOS shell in the Microsoft Windows operating environment. Richard Holmes rewrote these programs or wrote many new programs for the Macintosh operating system and created the Mac-compatible Dendro Program Library, a set of routines that helps dendrochronologists explore tree-ring data. Some programs also have migrated in the other direction. ARSTAN, a program that conducts autoregressive time series standardization of tree-ring data, was initially written for the Macintosh by Edward R. Cook of Columbia University and then ported to the personal computer in the late 1980s and early 1990s. Currently, the most up-to-date versions of ARSTAN are first made available to run on Macintosh computers.

Many other programs have been developed for Macintosh computers, Unix systems, or the SAS statistical package, but I will not describe those programs in this chapter. More information about these programs and applications can be obtained through the ITRDB computer forum archives. Most of the programs mentioned below are free and can be downloaded from Henri Grissino-Mayer's Ultimate Tree Ring Web Pages (see appendix E for Web addresses).

In the following sections, I describe some useful statistics followed by descriptions of the main dendrochronology programs in the approximate order of their use. I explain the purpose of the program and, in some cases, provide a keystroke tutorial that walks through the execution of the main programs. I also provide some basic interpretations that explain the output for the main programs. Some of this information is published elsewhere in a different format and by different authors. I cite these references at the beginning of each section so that the reader can also examine those publications.

My intent in this chapter is to provide the basic tools needed to conduct analysis, not to provide an exhaustive description of the programs and their output. See the cited references for more detailed description of the programs. Many of these programs can run as a black box using the program's default settings, where the user does not need to understand the internal (often statistically complex) operations executed by the program. Please try to educate yourself as much as possible about how each program functions and the proper parameters for the specific project in mind. Also, refer to some of the classic literature published on dendrochronological methods, such as Fritts (1976) and Cook and Kairiukstis (1990), for further reading.

## Statistics in Dendrochronology

### Series Intercorrelation

A tree-ring series from one core might be correlated against the master chronology, or two cores can be compared to each other. The **series intercorrelation** can be the average of every series back to the master chronology, and in this case it represents the common stand-level signal recorded for a site (equation II). The intercorrelation is calculated between two series, such as a core ($x$) and the master chronology ($y$), using

$$r_{xy} = \frac{\sum_{t=1}^{t=n}(x_t - m_x)(y_t - m_y)}{(n-1)S_x S_y} \quad [\text{II}]$$

where $x_t$ is the index value for a core at year $t$, $y_t$ is the index value for the master chronology at year $t$, $m_x$ is the mean index value for the core, $m_y$ is the mean index value for the master, $s_x$ is the standard deviation for the core, $s_y$ is the standard deviation for the master, and $n$ is the number of years being compared. This equation adjusts for the variance between the core and the master chronology as well as simply comparing the size of the rings in each year.

### Mean Sensitivity

**Mean sensitivity** is a measurement of the year-to-year variability in tree-ring width ranging from 0 to 1 (equation III). If every ring were the same width, the series would have a mean sensitivity of 0. If every other ring were absent, then the mean sensitivity would approach 1. For dating tree rings, it is possible to have series that are too complacent and other series that are too sensitive to date accurately. From personal experience, a series with a mean sensitivity around 0.1 is so complacent that it is difficult to date, and a mean sensitivity of greater than 0.4 is so sensitive that it becomes extremely tricky to date due to frequent micro or absent rings next to very wide rings. Mean sensitivity around 0.2 is generally accepted as series that are sensitive enough for climate reconstruction. The equation to calculate average mean sensitivity for a series is

$$ms_x = \frac{1}{n-1}\sum_{t=1}^{t=n-1}\left|\frac{2(X_{t+1}-X_t)}{X_{t+1}+X_t}\right| \quad [\text{III}]$$

where $X_t$ is ring width in year $t$, $X_{t+1}$ is ring width in the following year, and $n$ is the number of years being compared.

### Gleichläufigkeit (Sign Test)

The **Gleichläufigkeit** score ($G$) is a measure of similarity between two chronologies based on the first difference between successive tree rings (Eckstein and Bauch 1969, Schweingruber 1988). In other words, it tests whether two chronologies are increasing in growth at the same time or decreasing in growth at the same time. This examination of annual trends enables the researcher to compare the trend of cores for dating and to compare the ring widths (equations IV and V). G-scores have been incorporated into the programs CDendro, CATRAS, and TSAP, or they may be calculated by hand using the following equations:

$$\Delta_i = (x_{i+1} - x_i) \qquad [IV]$$

when $\Delta_i > 0 : G_{ix} = +\frac{1}{2}$
$\Delta_i = 0 : G_{ix} = 0$
$\Delta_i < 0 : G_{ix} = -\frac{1}{2}$

then
$$G_{(x,y)} = \frac{1}{n-1} \sum_{i=1}^{n-1} \left| G_{ix} + G_{iy} \right| \qquad [V]$$

where $\delta_i$ is the change in ring width; $x_i$ is the ring width in year $i$; $x_{i+1}$ is the ring width in the following year; $G_{ix}$ is the value added to the G-score reflecting whether ring width is increasing, staying the same, or decreasing in each interval for series $x$; $G_{iy}$ is the value added to the G-score for series $y$; and $n$ is the number of years being compared. This is a flexible measure that allows comparison between two cores, a core and a master chronology, or two separate master chronologies depending upon how series $x$ and series $y$ are defined.

Figure 6.1 shows an example that compares two cores to calculate the G-scores. Each core's increase or decrease is calculated for every year-to-year change, and then these

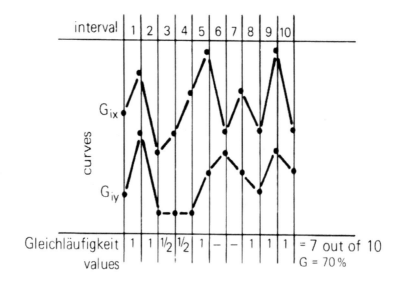

**Figure 6.1** An example of calculating the Gleichläufigkeit value. If an interval increases for one core it receives a $+\frac{1}{2}$ value, and if the same interval increases on the second core it also receives a $+\frac{1}{2}$ value, giving a total G-value for that interval of 1. The calculation is conducted for each interval, with a constant value being scored as 0 and a decreasing interval scored as $-\frac{1}{2}$. All of these intervals are summed over time throughout the chronology, resulting in the overall G-value. (From Schweingruber 1988)

G-scores are added together for each year-to-year change. This sum on an annual basis is then added up for the entire length of the core, and the result is the G-score between those two cores. For example, if one tree is increasing in growth in the first year and the second core is also increasing in growth for that year, the chronologies score a 1 for that year. If one tree is decreasing in annual trend while the other core is increasing, then those chronologies score a 0 for that year. Finally, all of these annual scores are summed. In figure 6.1, 7 of 10 intervals are trending in the same direction so the chronologies score $G = 70\%$.

## Running $\bar{r}$

The **running $\bar{r}$** (pronounced running r-bar) is a statistic that can be used to examine the signal strength throughout the chronology. It is calculated by taking the average correlation between all series in a 100-year window with 50 years of overlap throughout the entire chronology. Because it is a running correlation between series, it is a good measure of the common signal strength through time and is dependent upon the sample depth (Cook et al. 2000).

## Expressed Population Signal

The **expressed population signal** (EPS) is a measure of the common variability in a chronology that is dependent upon sample depth (equation VI; Wigley et al. 1984, Briffa and Jones 1990). It is calculated using the following equation:

$$EPS_t = \frac{t * r_{bt}}{t * r_{bt} + (1 - r_{bt})} \qquad [VI]$$

where $t$ is the average number of tree series using one core per tree and $r_{bt}$ is the mean between-tree correlation. When the EPS value drops below a predetermined level (usually 0.85), the chronology is starting to be dominated by the individual tree-level signal rather than a coherent stand-level signal (fig. 6.2). The chronology can still be well dated and useful for dating studies, such as in archaeological research, but it may produce large confidence limits in a climate reconstruction. This chronology measure is often used by European dendrochronologists and has recently come into use by American dendrochronologists as well.

## Subsample Signal Strength

The **subsample signal strength** (SSS) is a measure of the amount of signal captured by a subsample of cores from some master chronology (equation VII; Wigley et al. 1984, Briffa and Jones 1990). This calculation enables the researcher to quantify the variance in common between a subset of samples and the master chronology, which is particularly important as sample depth decreases in a climate reconstruction further back in time. SSS is calculated using the following equation:

$$SSS = \frac{t'\left[1 + (t - 1)\bar{r}\right]}{t\left[1 + (t' - 1)\bar{r}\right]} \qquad [VII]$$

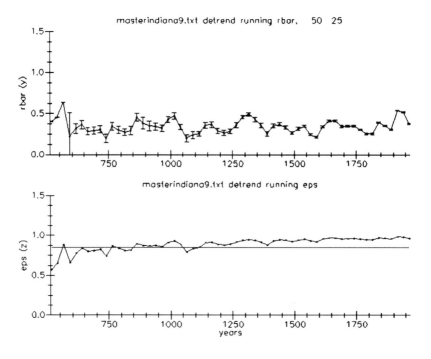

**Figure 6.2** (A) Running $\bar{r}$ and (B) running expressed population signal (EPS) analysis for the Newberry Crater Lava Flow ponderosa pine chronology. (P. Clark and J. Speer, unpublished data)

where $t'$ is the number of cores (if one core per tree) or trees (if two cores per tree) in a subset of the whole population, $t$ is the number of cores or trees in the full set, and $\bar{r}$ is the mean interseries correlation for the chronology.

## Measuring Programs

Many programs have been developed to measure tree rings, such as TRIMS, MEDIR, PJK, and MeasureJ2X. These programs take ring-width data that are fed to the computer through a data recording box, such as Accurite or QuikCheck. Each program has some good features and many have some bothersome quirks, as is the case with all computer programs. TRIMS, MEDIR, and PJK have been used for decades and do an excellent job as an interface to record tree-ring widths. They also have some minor data editing features that enable the user to correct measuring mistakes while still working at the measuring system. Currently, MeasureJ2X is the measuring program that is recommended when buying a new Velmex measuring system, so I explain its use in greater detail below.

### MeasureJ2X

MeasureJ2X is written in JAVA language and, therefore, can be used on a Macintosh or personal computer. It is one of the few programs that were written professionally, so it must be purchased. It has a graphical user interface that presents a program that functions like

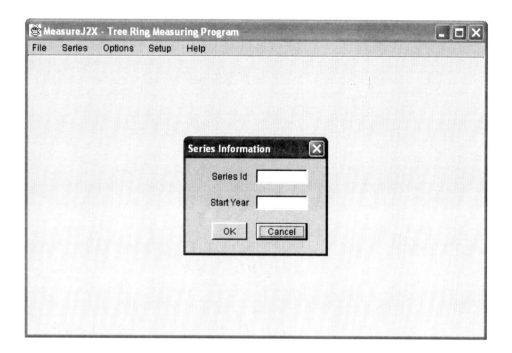

**Figure 6.3** Initializing a new series in MeasureJ2X.

most of the Microsoft package of programs. One can open files, save them, start new files, see statistics on cores already measured, and do some editing of measurement files. MeasureJ2X still has some limitations, such as the inability to rename folders, so it is best to create any necessary folders before you start to measure (see the MeasureJ2X User Guide, which is available online through the Voortech website).

*Keystroke Tutorial for MeasureJ2X.* Set the core up on the measuring stage as described in the Measuring Rings section of chapter 5. MeasureJ2X has menu options of File, Series, Options, Setup, and Help (fig. 6.3). To start a new series, go to the Series menu and choose New. The screen illustrated in figure 6.3 then appears and requests the series ID and start year for that core. When entering series IDs, always enter the same number of site and tree characters so that later programs can differentiate between cores from the same tree. For example, it is standard to have a three-character site designation and a two-digit tree number followed by an A or B for two cores taken from the same tree. The program ARSTAN can then average these core-level measurements together, resulting in a tree-level chronology, but for that to happen a standard site and tree code must be adhered to. Once these data are entered, click OK and go to the initialization of measurements.

The next screen that appears is the measuring window (fig. 6.4). The sample ID appears at the top of that internal window (in this case TES01) and the first year to be measured is displayed on the screen as well (in this case 1895). The program needs to be initialized at this time, which entails sending a beginning measurement from which all other measurements

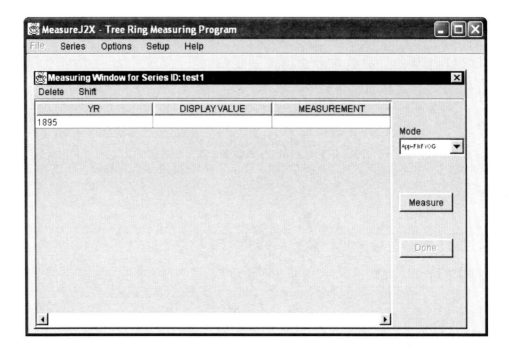

**Figure 6.4** Measuring window in MeasureJ2X.

will be calculated. Click on the Measure button on the right of the screen. The new window asks for an initial measurement. It is good to reset the measurement to zero at this stage and click OK. A new box shows what the initial measurement was. Click OK on that as well. Now the program is initialized and waiting for measurements. Turn the dial on the measuring machine, which moves the stage and the sample, until the crosshair is at the next ring boundary. Push the Print button on the remote, which sends the measurement to the computer. The display on the screen of the Display Value shows the cumulative measurement for that core and the measurement that is the width of the individual ring (usually in millimeters but it can be changed to inches). This procedure is repeated for each ring on the core. All of the measurements are displayed on the screen along with the year of each ring. The Quick-chek box beeps each time a measurement is entered and a second beep should be heard (if your computer has internal speakers) for each decade year that is measured. It is important to pay attention to this second beep and to use the decade years as landmarks so that a mistake in measuring can be identified within the decade being measured.

Once all measurements are completed, it is important to note that the data are in the computer memory and have not been saved permanently to the hard drive. Click the Done button on the screen and then close out the measuring window by clicking the small × in the top-right corner of the window. Be very careful that the measuring window is being closed and not the entire program window. If the program is closed the measurements are lost. Once the measuring window is closed, save the file by going to the File drop-down menu and clicking Save. At this point another series can be initialized by clicking Series and New

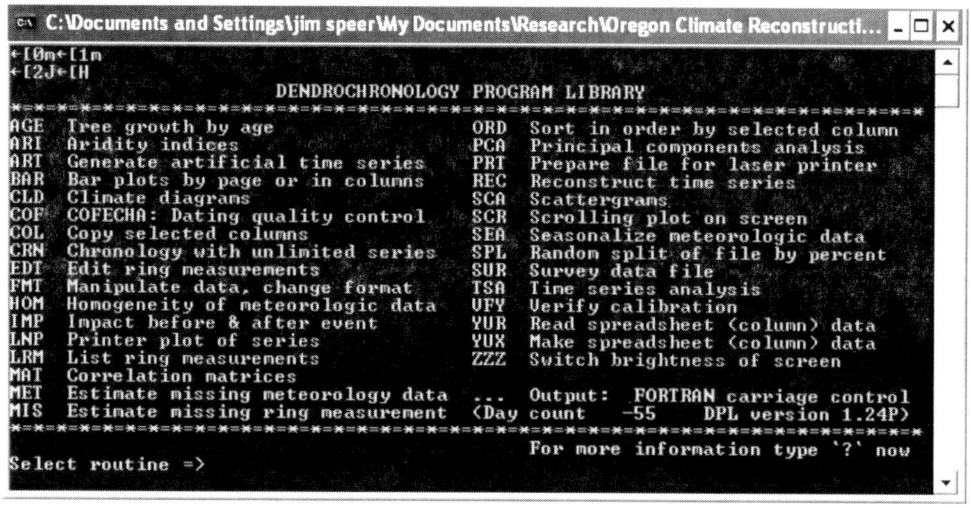

```
C:\Documents and Settings\jim speer\My Documents\Research\Oregon Climate Reconstructi...

←[0m←[1m
←[2J←[H
                    DENDROCHRONOLOGY PROGRAM LIBRARY
*=*=*=*=*=*=*=*=*=*=*=*=*=*=*=*=*=*=*=*=*=*=*=*=*=*=*=*=*=*=*=*=*
AGE   Tree growth by age              ORD   Sort in order by selected column
ARI   Aridity indices                 PCA   Principal components analysis
ART   Generate artificial time series PRT   Prepare file for laser printer
BAR   Bar plots by page or in columns REC   Reconstruct time series
CLD   Climate diagrams                SCA   Scattergrams
COF   COFECHA: Dating quality control SCR   Scrolling plot on screen
COL   Copy selected columns           SEA   Seasonalize meteorologic data
CRN   Chronology with unlimited series SPL  Random split of file by percent
EDT   Edit ring measurements          SUR   Survey data file
FMT   Manipulate data, change format  TSA   Time series analysis
HOM   Homogeneity of meteorologic data VFY  Verify calibration
IMP   Impact before & after event     YUR   Read spreadsheet (column) data
LNP   Printer plot of series          YUX   Make spreadsheet (column) data
LRM   List ring measurements          ZZZ   Switch brightness of screen
MAT   Correlation matrices
MET   Estimate missing meteorology data ...  Output:  FORTRAN carriage control
MIS   Estimate missing ring measurement (Day count   -55     DPL version 1.24P)
*=*=*=*=*=*=*=*=*=*=*=*=*=*=*=*=*=*=*=*=*=*=*=*=*=*=*=*=*=*=*=*=*
                                        For more information type '?' now
Select routine =>
```

**Figure 6.5** The Dendrochronology Program Library version 1.24p contains 31 Fortran programs that can be accessed by their three letter designation in this command-line-driven DOS window. Many of the more commonly used programs, such as EDRM, COFECHA, YUX, and FMT, have been extracted as stand-alone programs.

(as above); when this file is saved, the program will append these new measurements to the bottom of the last file measured.

It is possible to delete or shift the series in the measuring window if a mistake occurs. To delete one or more rings, highlight the ring-width measurements in the Measurement column. Click Delete and choose to leave the first year or the last year fixed in time. Any other edits should be conducted in the EDRM or EDT programs (discussed below).

## Dendrochronology Program Library

The Dendrochronology Program Library (DPL) is a compilation of DOS programs that have been developed by multiple users and provides useful tools for dendrochronology. This program library has also been ported to the Macintosh operating system. Historically it was a package of 31 programs, some of which have been so useful that they have been taken out and now stand alone, including COFECHA, EDT (now called EDRM), FMT, and YUX (fig. 6.5). Many old versions of Dendrochronology Program Library are being used in research labs today. The modern version contains 20 programs (fig. 6.6), many of which are useful for filling gaps in data, converting and displaying meteorological data, or generating a climate reconstruction.

## FMT

The FMT program enables the researcher to change the file format as well as do some basic file reorganization such as putting the series in alphanumeric order. The first set of menus

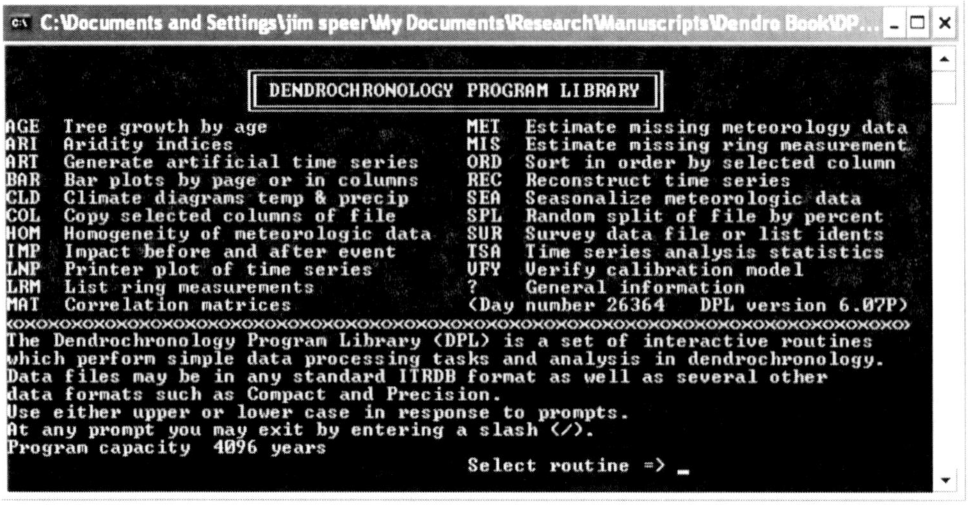

**Figure 6.6** The Dendrochronology Program Library version 6.07p contains 20 Fortran programs that can be accessed by their three letter designation in this command-line-driven DOS window.

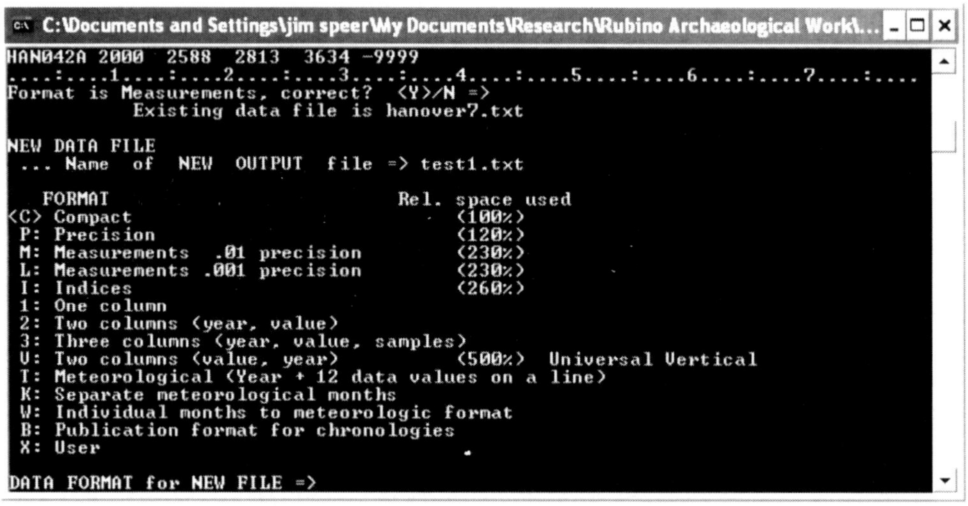

**Figure 6.7** Formatting options in FMT.

gives options to change the format of the file between any standard dendrochronological format such as compact, measurement (in 0.01- or 0.001-mm precision), index, one column, or two column (fig. 6.7). The compact format was developed when the computers that were used to measure tree rings had very limited hard drive space. This format removes all of the spaces between ring-width measurements. The computer can read the file based on space delimitation but the operator cannot read the measurements in the file because they all run

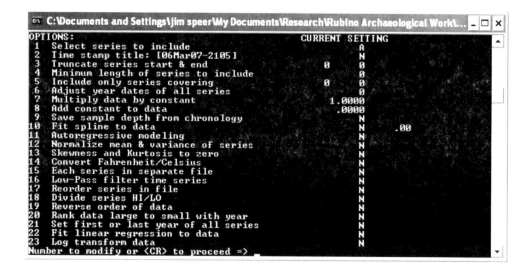

**Figure 6.8** Twenty-three functions that can be performed on data in the FMT program. Option 17 allows the series to be reordered based on alphanumeric sequence of the core identifications.

together. The measurement format has also been called decadal or Tucson format. The file is presented with each line representing a decade, and the first column holds the ring width for that decade year. The second column is the first year in the decade, and this continues through the ninth year of the decade in the last column. This format is easy for the user to read and determine the ring widths, however, the decimal places have been removed to conserve space and the end-of-file marker designates where the decimal should occur. A $-9999$ marker means the file has 0.001-mm precision and the decimal place should be three characters from the right reported value. An end of file marker of $-999$ means that the file has 0.01-mm precision and the decimal place should be two characters from the right. The index format includes the ring-width index and the sample depth that went into that calculation. It is also more compact than the measurement or decadal format and is difficult to read. The second set of menus provides 23 options for procedures that can be conducted on the series (fig. 6.8). I find option 17 for reordering the series to be the most useful tool in this package.

## COFECHA

Historically, dendrochronologists at the University of Arizona dated a sample of wood with skeleton plots, removed their marks on the wood, and had a second dendrochronologist skeleton plot the wood to check the dates. If their two dates differed, they would confer and find the problem. This quality control and second check on all dates produced from the University of Arizona helped to establish the reliability of dendrochronology as a dating technique. In today's research climate with expectations of high productivity, researchers do not have the time to completely check each other's dates. Therefore, Richard Holmes developed the quality-control computer program called COFECHA (Holmes 1983).

COFECHA was never intended to be the only attempt to date a sample of wood or to replace crossdating. COFECHA provides a statistical match between segments of each core and the master chronology that is made of the measurements that are entered into the program. However, if half of the cores going into the program are not properly dated prior to statistical analysis, the master chronology will be uncertain; therefore, it is essential that the researcher crossdates the wood samples before using COFECHA. By using COFECHA as the sole method of dating, an operator will not know what good dating for that tree species and site type looks like and will not discern that there is a problem. The operator can adjust the measurements and produce a chronology with acceptable statistics, but the resulting chronology is not necessarily well dated. The result will be inaccurate dates and poor correlations with calibration data, such as temperature and precipitation records.

I attended a professional presentation in which a researcher claimed that trees in a hardwood forest did not have any relationship with climate. When asked about his dating, he replied that he had not yet checked the quality of dating with COFECHA and gave no indication that the samples were dated by any other means. Because of this lack of time spent dating the samples, the researcher made an inaccurate conclusion and extrapolated it to the hardwood forest.

Dating of wood samples is the foundation of dendrochronology, and as such, dendro-chronologists should do everything in their power to properly date samples and check their dating quality. Two attempts at dating are necessary to provide the quality control that has been the hallmark of good dendrochronological research. The first attempt should include a visual dating method during which the researcher learns the wood; visual dating can include skeleton plots, the list method, or the memorization method from a known chronology. The second check on the dating can be done by another researcher using visual dating or by a statistical check such as with COFECHA. See chapter 5 for detailed descriptions of skeleton plots, the list method, and the memorization method for primary dating of samples.

COFECHA is a program in DOS, with all of its simplicity and quirks (Holmes 1983, Grissino-Mayer 2001). It has also been ported to the Macintosh operating system. For those who have not used DOS programs frequently, input file names can be no longer than eight characters and cannot have spaces or nonalphanumeric characters in a file title, and the program is command-line driven (meaning you have to type your responses). It is best if the program COFECHA is placed in the same directory as the files to be analyzed, so that you do not have to type in the directory chain each time the program is run and a long directory name such as My Documents would confound COFECHA. COFECHA leads the operator through default options with most of the command steps. On the command line, COFECHA often provides answer options such as <Yes>/No. The option that is in brackets is the default option and pressing Enter chooses that answer. Proper use of these default responses can facilitate efficient use of this program.

COFECHA works by statistically creating a master chronology with the cores that the operator enters into the program. This means that if undated series are entered into the program, then the master chronology will be compromised. COFECHA takes the ring-width measurements that were obtained from a measuring stage and, by default, fits a 32-year cubic smoothing spline to the cores for standardization. Next, it averages all of the index series for all of the cores together to create the master chronology. It then removes the core that is about to be analyzed, cuts it into 50-year segments with 25 years of overlap (by default), and statistically correlates each segment against the master chronology. If the correlation is below

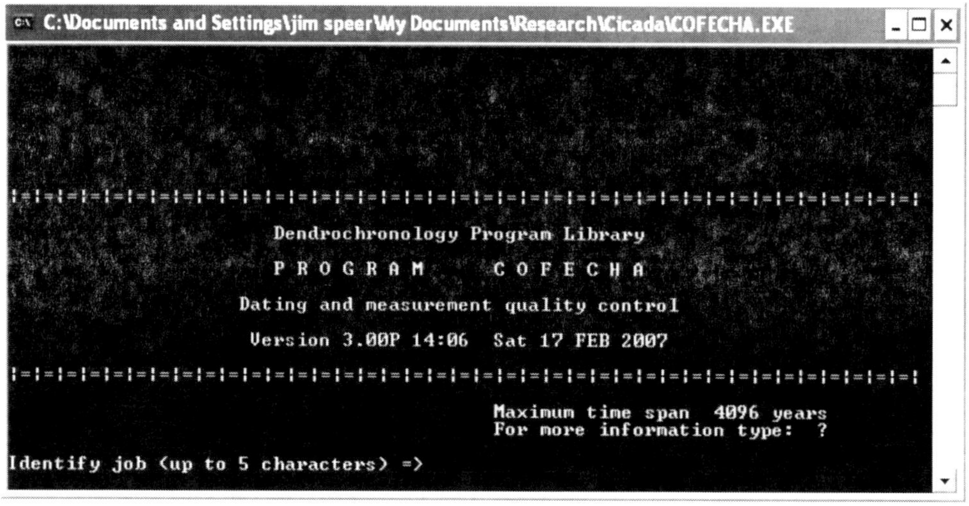

**Figure 6.9** Introductory screen of COFECHA in a DOS command line box.

the specified confidence level, which is set at 99% by default, then COFECHA checks from −10 to +10 lag years for a better match. If the program finds a better match, it reports a B flag in the output; if it does not find a better match, it reports an A flag for that segment, simply meaning that it has a low correlation. This is the basic concept of how COFECHA works, and I describe the specific keystrokes in running the program in the following section.

## Keystroke Tutorial of COFECHA

To start the program, double-click on COFECHA.EXE in the directory (for more information on COFECHA see Holmes 1983, Grissino-Mayer 2001). A DOS command box for the program opens (fig. 6.9). The first entry that the program asks for is a five-digit identifier for the program run. This identifier will be added as a prefix to any subsequent file created by this program and should enable you to later (say, 10 years down the road) understand what the file contains. I usually use a three-letter site designation with possibly one letter for species if I have sampled multiple species on a site, and a number at the end that can progress each time a new run is started (such as MORQ1 for Mogan Ridge *Quercus* first run). COFECHA usually has to be run many times per site before a chronology is finished. Next the program asks for the existing input file name. Remember that the file name must be eight digits or less and not include any spaces or odd characters. COFECHA can read files in many different formats: compact, measurement, indices, Accurite measurements, meteorological, spreadsheet, single column of values, two columns of values, or a user-defined protocol. COFECHA automatically recognizes most of these formats and asks if it has identified the correct format. If it has identified the file type, simply hit Enter. If it has not, then the file format is not compatible with COFECHA and needs to be corrected.

Next the program asks for the file name containing samples to run as undated tree-ring series. COFECHA can attempt to date undated series by breaking the series into 50-year

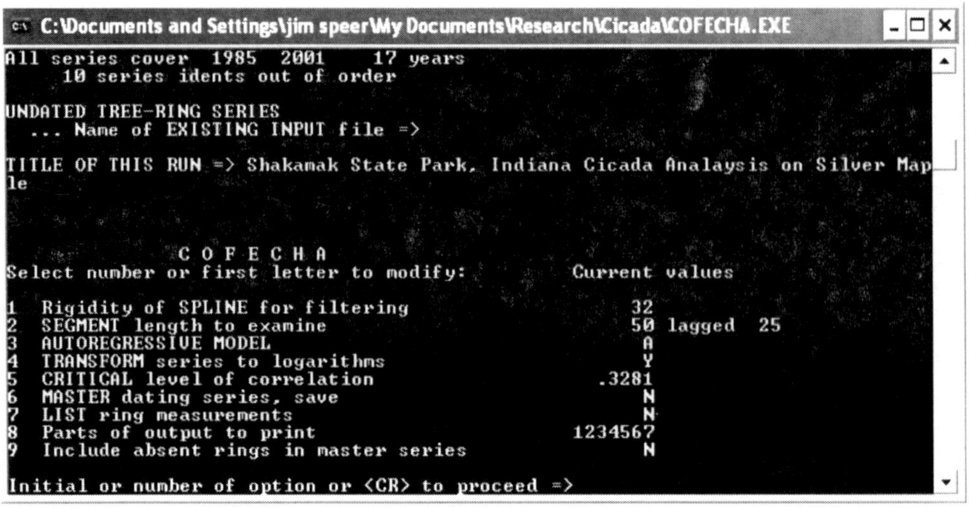

**Figure 6.10** Command-line-driven DOS box for COFECHA showing the series summary at the top of the screen, the line for undated tree-ring series input file, the title of this run line with data entered, and the table that offers options to control the analysis.

segments and statistically testing each segment against the master chronology while not including it in the master chronology. The output from this option appears as Part 8 in the COFECHA output near the bottom of the .out file. Assuming that you do not want to enter undated series into COFECHA, simply press Enter. The next option is a title for this run, which can be 36 characters including spaces and odd characters. The title should be an informative description for each run. It is useful to type out the site name, species, and any other notes for this run in the title. Remember that you might be looking back at these files in 10 years and not have any idea what the very short file names mean. This is your chance to mark the file with needed information. When finished entering the title for this run, press Enter to get to the next stage of the program.

The heart of COFECHA is the table that allows you to change the spline length for creation of the master chronology, change the segment length and overlap, run an autoregressive model, change the critical level of correlation (which is based on the segment length or $N$), decide whether to save the master dating series, list the ring-width measurements in the output, list the parts of the output to include, and decide whether to calculate absent rings in the master series (fig. 6.10). The default options in this program are listed on the right side of the screen and are usually applicable to most projects. Richard Holmes tested a series of spline lengths in creating the master chronology and found that the 32-year cubic smoothing spline is the most appropriate spline length for enhancing the interannual variability that leads to strong dating. The segment length is optimal for providing a high $N$ for statistical tests and providing the flexibility to pinpoint where missing or false rings may occur in the chronology. These segments are lagged, by default, at 25 years, again making it possible to pinpoint dating problems.

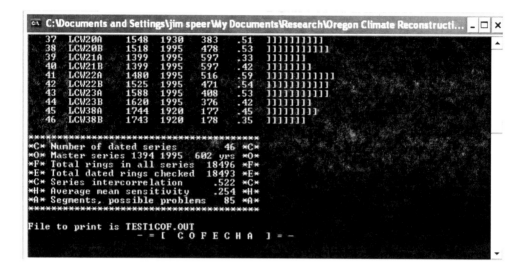

**Figure 6.11** The end of the information that flashes on the screen while COFECHA runs. In the top half of the screen is the summary of how each core correlated with the master chronology and a graphical representation is in the right column. The box in stars contains the summary statistics for the chronology that will also be reported on the first page of the COFECHA output.

To make changes in the main table in COFECHA, use the program submenus that are keyed by the number associated with the function. To adjust any of the values in this table, simply type the number on the left side of the screen that correlates to that object. For example, to make a change from a 50-year segment with a 25-year overlap to a 30-year segment with a 10-year overlap, type 2 and press Enter. A submenu then opens and asks for the length of the segment. Type 30 and press Enter. A prompt comes up asking for the lag between segments. Type 10 and press Enter. Because the segment length has been reduced from 50 to 30 years of comparison, the critical level automatically adjusts from 0.3281 to 0.4226. As I mentioned, however, the default options in this table work well for most analyses.

To run the program, press Enter once you have made any necessary changes in the table. The program then executes and very quickly displays on the screen the progress of the program and finally the correlation of each core with the master, as shown by a series of brackets, where each bracket represents a 0.05 overall correlation (fig. 6.11). This flashes by on the screen and the program exits automatically. An output file with the result of the run is placed in the directory from which the program was run. The file name begins with the prefix that you entered at the beginning of this run, the three letters COF to designate this as a COFECHA file, and the suffix .out.

## Reading the Output of COFECHA

The output file contains all of the summary statistics about the master chronology, the correlation of each core with that master, and some descriptive statistics for each core. The first

```
[]  DENDROCHRONOLOGY PROGRAM LIBRARY                           Run LCWEX  Program COF  22:29  Thu 22 FEB 2007  Page   1
[]
[]  P R O G R A M    C O F E C H A                                                      Version 3.00P    26352
------------------------------------------------------------------------------------------------------------------

QUALITY CONTROL AND DATING CHECK OF TREE-RING MEASUREMENTS

Title of run:           Sample Cofecha Run for the Lava Cast For

File of DATED series:   lcwexample.rwl

CONTENTS:

     Part 1:  Title page, options selected, summary, absent rings by series
     Part 2:  Histogram of time spans
     Part 3:  Master series with sample depth and absent rings by year
     Part 4:  Bar plot of Master Dating Series
     Part 5:  Correlation by segment of each series with Master
     Part 6:  Potential problems: low correlation, divergent year-to-year changes, absent rings, outliers
     Part 7:  Descriptive statistics

RUN CONTROL OPTIONS SELECTED                          VALUE

        1  Cubic smoothing spline 50% wavelength cutoff for filtering
                                                     32 years
        2  Segments examined are                     50 years lagged successively by  25 years
        3  Autoregressive model applied               A   Residuals are used in master dating series and testing
        4  Series transformed to logarithms           Y   Each series log-transformed for master dating series and testing
        5  Critical correlation, 99% confidence level  .3281
        6  Master dating series saved                 N
        7  Ring measurements listed                   N
        8  Parts printed                             1234567
        9  Absent rings included in master series     N

Time span of Master dating series is  1394 to  1995    602 years
Continuous time span is                1394 to  1995    602 years
Portion with two or more series is     1397 to  1995    599 years

     >> WARNING:  Year  1850 absent in    1 of    45 series; Master Series value  -.011
     >> WARNING:  Year  1980 absent in    1 of    39 series; Master Series value   .490

                    ********************************************
                    *C*  Number of dated series          46  *C*
                    *O*  Master series 1394 1995   602 yrs  *O*
                    *F*  Total rings in all series    18495  *F*
                    *E*  Total dated rings checked     18492  *E*
                    *C*  Series intercorrelation        .520  *C*
                    *H*  Average mean sensitivity       .254  *H*
                    *A*  Segments, possible problems      88  *A*
                    ********************************************

ABSENT RINGS listed by SERIES:          (See Master Dating Series for absent rings listed by year)

     LCW04A    1 absent rings:   1804
     LCW06A    2 absent rings:   1935  1940
     LCW06B    1 absent rings:   1935
     LCW08B    2 absent rings:   1930  1936
     LCW11A    1 absent rings:   1899
     LCW13A    1 absent rings:   1935
```

**Figure 6.12** COFECHA output page 1.

page of the output provides the program name and version, the date of the run, the title that was entered, as well as the file name used in the analysis, the parts included in the output, and the control options that were selected during the run (fig. 6.12). The bottom half of the page contains the summary statistics for the chronology, starting with the time span of the master chronology, the entire continuous time span for the chronology, and the portion of the chronology with a sample depth of two or more series. Next, COFECHA provides a warning of any rings that are inserted as absent.

The table bracketed by asterisks in Part 1 is the most important summary of the COFE-CHA run, much of which should be reported in a research paper. The table presents the number of dated series, master chronology length, total number of rings in all series, and total number of dated rings (as in those that overlap with at least one other chronology), series intercorrelation, mean sensitivity, and segments with possible problems. The series intercorrelation is a measure of the stand-level signal, and mean sensitivity is a measure of the year-to-year variability in the master chronology. These two statistics should be reported in any publication, as they are the most comparable measure of site-level signal and sensitivity between sites. Finally, a complete list of any absent rings is listed by core.

Part 2 of the COFECHA output is a graphic representation of the length of the chronology (fig. 6.13). It also summarizes the sequence number (which can provide an easy way to navigate the COFECHA output), beginning and end years of each series, and total number of years in each series.

Part 3 contains the master chronology in a three-column format, including the year, index value, and sample depth (fig. 6.14). Remember that COFECHA standardizes the series with a cubic smoothing spline of your choice or the default 32-year spline. Each core is standard-ized, and then the master chronology is created by averaging together the index series for each core. Because the master chronology in Part 3 records the index value for each year, it can be used to identify extremely small rings that may be missing in other cores.

I find the sample depth to be the most useful column in this part of the output because it is the only place where sample depth is recorded for the master chronology. This informa-tion can be used to determine where the master chronology has enough samples included in the chronology to provide an accurate stand-level signal. A general rule is to have a mini-mum sample depth of 10 cores for a well-replicated stand-level signal, although 20 is more robust and chronologies have been used with fewer cores. A site's sensitivity to climate will determine how many cores are necessary to average out the individual tree-level noise and to reinforce the stand-level signal. Earlier in this chapter I described the EPS, which is a sta-tistical measure of adequate replication. In order to maintain sufficient sample depth, many years often have to be cut from the final analysis because there are not enough overlapping series to demonstrate a stand-level signal. It is important to note, however, that as long as there is agreement of dates between series (at least two cores for a time period), then it may be possible to record events at the tree level for those cores and have some confidence that the dating is accurate.

Part 4 is a graphical representation of the master chronology that provides a good way for quickly observing the dates of narrow rings and determining how small the rings are compared to the rest of the chronology (fig. 6.15). An @ symbol indicates an average ring, uppercase letters indicate wider-than-average rings, and lowercase letters indicate smaller-than-average rings. The closer to the end of the alphabet, the larger (uppercase) or smaller (lowercase) the ring is. In the example given in figure 6.15, a lowercase s for 1652 means that this ring is extremely small and is actually one of the smallest rings in the chronol-ogy. An uppercase C for 1670 means that the ring is larger than but not much different than the mean. An @ symbol at 1678 indicates that this ring is of average width for this chronology.

Part 5 summarizes the correlation of each segment against the master chronology (fig. 6.16). Remember that to date the core, COFECHA took all of the measured series and, by default, broke them into 50-year segments with 25 years of overlap. Then it statistically cor-related each segment to the master chronology, minus the core being analyzed, at the date those rings were assigned. This part of the output reports the correlation of each 50-year segment to the master for each core with 25 years of overlap in the segments. COFECHA also marks poor correlations with either an A or a B flag. An A flag next to a segment correlation means that segment correlated below the critical level designated in this COFECHA run. A B flag means that COFECHA found a better correlation for that segment in a 20-year window of −10 to +10 years from the place where it is currently dated. This section is use-ful because it displays the correlation of each segment to the master and is the only place in COFECHA where all of the correlations for all of the segments are reported. Part 6 reports poorly correlated segments, but not the results of the highly correlated segments. One has to refer back to Part 5 for that information.

Part 6 presents each core separately, with a closer look at how well it correlates to the master, and reports any measurements that are outliers (fig. 6.17). The core name is given in

Time scale: 1000  1100  1200  1300  1400  1500  1600  1700  1800  1900  2000

| Ident | Seq | Beg year | End year | Yrs |
|---|---|---|---|---|
| LCW01A | 1 | 1689 | 1995 | 307 |
| LCW01B | 2 | 1676 | 1995 | 320 |
| LCW02A | 3 | 1399 | 1995 | 597 |
| LCW02B | 4 | 1399 | 1995 | 597 |
| LCW03A | 5 | 1414 | 1937 | 524 |
| LCW03B | 6 | 1431 | 1930 | 500 |
| LCW04A | 7 | 1527 | 1995 | 469 |
| LCW04B | 8 | 1563 | 1995 | 433 |
| LCW05A | 9 | 1558 | 1995 | 438 |
| LCW06A | 10 | 1744 | 1995 | 252 |
| LCW06B | 11 | 1767 | 1995 | 229 |
| LCW08A | 12 | 1417 | 1995 | 579 |
| LCW08B | 13 | 1397 | 1995 | 599 |
| LCW09A | 14 | 1751 | 1995 | 245 |
| LCW09B | 15 | 1721 | 1995 | 275 |
| LCW10B | 16 | 1788 | 1995 | 208 |
| LCW10C | 17 | 1526 | 1647 | 122 |
| LCW11A | 18 | 1539 | 1995 | 457 |
| LCW11B | 19 | 1546 | 1995 | 450 |
| LCW12A | 20 | 1727 | 1995 | 269 |
| LCW12B | 21 | 1681 | 1995 | 315 |
| LCW13A | 22 | 1669 | 1995 | 327 |
| LCW13B | 23 | 1610 | 1995 | 386 |
| LCW14A | 24 | 1614 | 1995 | 382 |
| LCW14B | 25 | 1658 | 1995 | 338 |
| LCW15A | 26 | 1417 | 1995 | 579 |
| LCW15B | 27 | 1428 | 1970 | 543 |
| LCW16A | 28 | 1394 | 1995 | 602 |
| LCW16B | 29 | 1472 | 1995 | 524 |
| LCW17A | 30 | 1451 | 1995 | 545 |
| LCW17B | 31 | 1399 | 1995 | 597 |
| LCW18A | 32 | 1680 | 1995 | 316 |
| LCW18B | 33 | 1712 | 1995 | 284 |
| LCW19A | 34 | 1754 | 1995 | 242 |
| LCW19B | 35 | 1764 | 1995 | 232 |
| LCW19C | 36 | 1764 | 1995 | 232 |

```
.    .    .    .    .    .    .    .    .    .    .    <=====================================>  .    . LCW20A   37 1548 1930  383
.    .    .    .    .    .    .    .    .    .    .<==============================================>. LCW20B   38 1518 1995  478
.    .    .    .    .    .    .    .    <==========================================================>. LCW21A   39 1399 1995  597
.    .    .    .    .    .    .    .    <==========================================================>. LCW21B   40 1399 1995  597
.    .    .    .    .    .    .    .    .    .  <==================================================>. LCW22A   41 1480 1995  516
.    .    .    .    .    .    .    .    .    .    . <==============================================>. LCW22B   42 1525 1995  471
.    .    .    .    .    .    .    .    .    .    .    .  <========================================>. LCW23A   43 1588 1995  408
.    .    .    .    .    .    .    .    .    .    .    .    . <====================================>. LCW23B   44 1620 1995  376
.    .    .    .    .    .    .    .    .    .    .    .    .    .    .   <=================>  .    . LCW38A   45 1744 1920  177
.    .    .    .    .    .    .    .    .    .    .    .    .    .    .   <=================>  .    . LCW38B   46 1743 1920  178

:    :    :    :    :    :    :    :    :    :    :    :    :    :    :    :    :    :    :    :    :
1000      1100      1200      1300      1400      1500      1600      1700      1800      1900      2000
```

**Figure 6.13** Part 2 of COFECHA lists and graphically depicts the length of each core.

PART 3:  Master Dating Series:  Sample Cofecha Run for the Lava Cast For

| Year | Value | No | Ab |
|---|---|---|---|
| 1400 | -1.519 | 7 | |
| 1401 | .100 | 7 | |
| 1402 | 1.662 | 7 | 2 |
| 1403 | .514 | 7 | |
| 1404 | 1.597 | 7 | |
| 1405 | 2.050 | 7 | |
| 1406 | .816 | 7 | |
| 1407 | -.745 | 7 | |
| 1408 | -.384 | 7 | |
| 1409 | .233 | 7 | |
| 1410 | -2.045 | 7 | |
| 1411 | -.891 | 7 | |
| 1412 | .201 | 7 | |
| 1413 | -1.246 | 7 | |
| 1414 | -.957 | 8 | |
| 1415 | -.345 | 8 | |
| 1416 | -.668 | 8 | |
| 1417 | -.168 | 10 | |
| 1418 | .312 | 10 | |
| 1419 | .945 | 10 | |
| 1420 | 1.020 | 10 | |
| 1421 | 1.633 | 10 | |
| 1422 | .806 | 10 | |
| 1423 | 1.951 | 10 | |
| 1424 | .505 | 10 | |
| 1425 | -.958 | 10 | |
| 1426 | -.197 | 10 | |
| 1427 | -.217 | 10 | |
| 1428 | -3.401 | 11 | |
| 1429 | .802 | 11 | |

| Year | Value | No | Ab |
|---|---|---|---|
| 1450 | -.824 | 12 | |
| 1451 | -.385 | 13 | |
| 1452 | -.589 | 13 | |
| 1453 | .729 | 13 | |
| 1454 | .894 | 13 | |
| 1455 | .231 | 13 | |
| 1456 | .726 | 13 | |
| 1457 | -.338 | 13 | |
| 1458 | -.284 | 13 | |
| 1459 | -.043 | 13 | |
| 1460 | -.498 | 13 | |
| 1461 | -.576 | 13 | |
| 1462 | .708 | 13 | |
| 1463 | -.164 | 13 | |
| 1464 | -.602 | 13 | |
| 1465 | .096 | 13 | |
| 1466 | -.639 | 13 | |
| 1467 | -.738 | 13 | |
| 1468 | -.017 | 13 | |
| 1469 | 1.385 | 13 | |
| 1470 | .426 | 13 | |
| 1471 | .260 | 13 | |
| 1472 | -.324 | 14 | |
| 1473 | -.220 | 14 | |
| 1474 | .142 | 14 | |
| 1475 | .730 | 14 | |
| 1476 | .198 | 14 | |
| 1477 | -.044 | 14 | |
| 1478 | .619 | 14 | |
| 1479 | -.818 | 14 | |

| Year | Value | No | Ab |
|---|---|---|---|
| 1500 | -.225 | 15 | |
| 1501 | -.003 | 15 | |
| 1502 | -.164 | 15 | |
| 1503 | .982 | 15 | |
| 1504 | .120 | 15 | |
| 1505 | -2.055 | 15 | |
| 1506 | .599 | 15 | |
| 1507 | 1.177 | 15 | |
| 1508 | .148 | 15 | |
| 1509 | 1.365 | 15 | |
| 1510 | -.402 | 15 | |
| 1511 | .909 | 15 | |
| 1512 | .172 | 15 | |
| 1513 | -.888 | 15 | |
| 1514 | .746 | 15 | |
| 1515 | -1.150 | 15 | |
| 1516 | -.982 | 15 | |
| 1517 | .270 | 15 | |
| 1518 | -.322 | 16 | |
| 1519 | -.421 | 16 | |
| 1520 | -1.213 | 16 | |
| 1521 | -1.660 | 16 | |
| 1522 | -1.397 | 16 | |
| 1523 | -.095 | 16 | |
| 1524 | 1.555 | 16 | |
| 1525 | 2.111 | 17 | |
| 1526 | .104 | 18 | |
| 1527 | -.069 | 19 | |
| 1528 | 1.711 | 19 | |
| 1529 | -3.536 | 19 | 2 |

| Year | Value | No | Ab |
|---|---|---|---|
| 1550 | -3.514 | 22 | |
| 1551 | -.168 | 22 | |
| 1552 | -.900 | 22 | |
| 1553 | .162 | 22 | |
| 1554 | -.876 | 22 | |
| 1555 | -.214 | 22 | |
| 1556 | -.774 | 22 | |
| 1557 | .214 | 22 | |
| 1558 | .600 | 23 | |
| 1559 | 1.048 | 23 | |
| 1560 | 1.782 | 23 | |
| 1561 | .296 | 23 | |
| 1562 | -.643 | 23 | |
| 1563 | .524 | 24 | |
| 1564 | 1.345 | 24 | |
| 1565 | -1.035 | 24 | |
| 1566 | -.271 | 24 | |
| 1567 | -1.219 | 24 | |
| 1568 | -.802 | 24 | |
| 1569 | -.729 | 24 | |
| 1570 | -.179 | 24 | |
| 1571 | -1.003 | 24 | |
| 1572 | .213 | 24 | |
| 1573 | -.322 | 24 | |
| 1574 | .631 | 24 | |
| 1575 | 1.385 | 24 | |
| 1576 | -.097 | 24 | |
| 1577 | .898 | 24 | |
| 1578 | .974 | 24 | |
| 1579 | .379 | 24 | |

| Year | Value | No | Ab |
|---|---|---|---|
| 1600 | -1.684 | 25 | |
| 1601 | -.177 | 25 | |
| 1602 | .611 | 25 | |
| 1603 | -1.670 | 25 | |
| 1604 | .212 | 25 | |
| 1605 | .326 | 25 | |
| 1606 | .587 | 25 | |
| 1607 | -.247 | 25 | |
| 1608 | .263 | 25 | |
| 1609 | -.222 | 25 | |
| 1610 | 1.255 | 26 | |
| 1611 | .847 | 26 | |
| 1612 | -.043 | 26 | |
| 1613 | 1.277 | 26 | |
| 1614 | .829 | 27 | |
| 1615 | -.144 | 27 | |
| 1616 | .190 | 27 | |
| 1617 | 1.670 | 27 | |
| 1618 | 1.848 | 27 | |
| 1619 | -.871 | 27 | |
| 1620 | .295 | 28 | |
| 1621 | -.655 | 28 | |
| 1622 | -1.624 | 28 | |
| 1623 | -2.211 | 28 | |
| 1624 | -.382 | 28 | |
| 1625 | .318 | 28 | |
| 1626 | .061 | 28 | |
| 1627 | .815 | 28 | |
| 1628 | .748 | 28 | |
| 1629 | -2.133 | 28 | |

| Year | Value | No | Ab |
|---|---|---|---|
| 1650 | .539 | 27 | |
| 1651 | -.568 | 27 | |
| 1652 | -4.794 | 27 | 2 |
| 1653 | -.761 | 27 | |
| 1654 | -.018 | 27 | |
| 1655 | .131 | 27 | |
| 1656 | .499 | 27 | |
| 1657 | -.570 | 27 | |
| 1658 | .846 | 28 | |
| 1659 | .336 | 28 | |
| 1660 | .592 | 28 | |
| 1661 | -1.211 | 28 | |
| 1662 | -1.301 | 28 | |
| 1663 | -.635 | 28 | |
| 1664 | -.890 | 28 | |
| 1665 | -1.476 | 28 | |
| 1666 | -.333 | 28 | |
| 1667 | .101 | 28 | |
| 1668 | .153 | 28 | |
| 1669 | .479 | 29 | |
| 1670 | .784 | 29 | |
| 1671 | .558 | 29 | |
| 1672 | 1.416 | 29 | |
| 1673 | 1.776 | 29 | |
| 1674 | 1.327 | 29 | |
| 1675 | 1.103 | 29 | |
| 1676 | 1.259 | 29 | |
| 1677 | -1.005 | 30 | |
| 1678 | .012 | 30 | |
| 1679 | -.188 | 30 | |

| Year | Index | Depth | | Year | Index | Depth | | Year | Index | Depth | | Year | Index | Depth | | Year | Index | Depth | | Year | Index | Depth |
|---|---|---|---|---|---|---|---|---|---|---|---|---|---|---|---|---|---|---|---|---|---|---|
| 1430 | .164 | 11 | | 1480 | -.584 | 15 | | 1530 | 1.308 | 19 | | 1580 | .726 | 24 | | 1630 | -.078 | 28 | | 1680 | -.742 | 31 |
| 1431 | -.149 | 12 | | 1481 | -2.285 | 15 | | 1531 | .801 | 19 | | 1581 | -2.729 | 24 | | 1631 | -1.552 | 28 | | 1681 | -.062 | 32 |
| 1432 | -1.410 | 12 | | 1482 | -1.997 | 15 | | 1532 | -.286 | 19 | | 1582 | .046 | 24 | | 1632 | -1.684 | 28 | | 1682 | -1.640 | 32 |
| 1433 | -1.331 | 12 | | 1483 | -1.373 | 15 | | 1533 | .274 | 19 | | 1583 | -.705 | 24 | | 1633 | -.480 | 28 | | 1683 | -1.511 | 32 |
| 1434 | -.033 | 12 | | 1484 | -.575 | 15 | | 1534 | .063 | 19 | | 1584 | .196 | 24 | | 1634 | -.532 | 28 | | 1684 | -.574 | 32 |
| 1435 | .395 | 12 | | 1485 | 1.130 | 15 | | 1535 | .374 | 19 | | 1585 | .110 | 24 | | 1635 | -.692 | 28 | | 1685 | -.839 | 32 |
| 1436 | -2.388 | 12 | | 1486 | .265 | 15 | | 1536 | 1.608 | 19 | | 1586 | -1.293 | 24 | | 1636 | .172 | 28 | | 1686 | -.217 | 32 |
| 1437 | .296 | 12 | | 1487 | -.414 | 15 | | 1537 | -1.245 | 19 | | 1587 | -.483 | 24 | | 1637 | .516 | 28 | | 1687 | .160 | 32 |
| 1438 | .519 | 12 | | 1488 | -.010 | 15 | | 1538 | -.091 | 19 | | 1588 | 1.463 | 25 | | 1638 | .265 | 28 | | 1688 | -.453 | 32 |
| 1439 | -.068 | 12 | | 1489 | -1.251 | 15 | | 1539 | .917 | 20 | | 1589 | .826 | 25 | | 1639 | -.578 | 28 | | 1689 | .538 | 33 |
| 1440 | -.206 | 12 | | 1490 | 1.477 | 15 | | 1540 | -1.059 | 20 | | 1590 | .791 | 25 | | 1640 | .967 | 28 | | 1690 | 1.565 | 33 |
| 1441 | .404 | 12 | | 1491 | .776 | 15 | | 1541 | -.800 | 20 | | 1591 | -.219 | 25 | | 1641 | 2.530 | 28 | | 1691 | .507 | 33 |
| 1442 | 1.002 | 12 | | 1492 | .871 | 15 | | 1542 | -.084 | 20 | | 1592 | -.908 | 25 | | 1642 | 1.391 | 28 | | 1692 | 1.131 | 33 |
| 1443 | -.034 | 12 | | 1493 | .516 | 15 | | 1543 | .828 | 20 | | 1593 | .699 | 25 | | 1643 | .334 | 28 | | 1693 | .094 | 33 |
| 1444 | .028 | 12 | | 1494 | .354 | 15 | | 1544 | .793 | 20 | | 1594 | -.994 | 25 | | 1644 | -.348 | 28 | | 1694 | 1.325 | 33 |
| 1445 | .185 | 12 | | 1495 | -.002 | 15 | | 1545 | -.055 | 20 | | 1595 | .476 | 25 | | 1645 | .843 | 28 | | 1695 | -3.277 | 33 |
| 1446 | -.140 | 12 | | 1496 | 2.205 | 15 | | 1546 | -.162 | 21 | | 1596 | -.090 | 25 | | 1646 | -.141 | 28 | | 1696 | .656 | 33 |
| 1447 | 1.923 | 12 | | 1497 | .317 | 15 | | 1547 | 1.688 | 21 | | 1597 | .457 | 25 | | 1647 | .341 | 28 | | 1697 | .903 | 33 |
| 1448 | .197 | 12 | | 1498 | -.095 | 15 | | 1548 | .011 | 22 | | 1598 | -1.530 | 25 | | 1648 | 1.328 | 27 | | 1698 | .006 | 33 |
| 1449 | .473 | 12 | | 1499 | -1.360 | 15 | | 1549 | .222 | 22 | | 1599 | -.538 | 25 | | 1649 | 1.213 | 27 | | 1699 | .174 | 33 |

**Figure 6.14** Part 3 of COFECHA shows the index values and sample depth for the master chronology.

```
Year Rel value  Year Rel value  Year Rel value
1600g           1610--------E   1620------A
1601----a       1611------C     1621--C
1602------B     1612----@       1622f
1603g           1613--------E   1623i
1604----a       1614------C     1624--b
1605------A     1615----a       1625------A
1606------B     1616------A     1626----@
1607----a       1617--------G   1627------C
1608------A     1618--------G   1628------C
1609----a       1619-c          1629i

Year Rel value  Year Rel value  Year Rel value
1650------B     1660------B     1670------C
1651--b         1661-e          1671------B
1652s           1662-e          1672------F
1653--C         1663--C         1673------G
1654----@       1664-d          1674------E
1655------A     1665f           1675------D
1656------B     1666----a       1676------E
1657--b         1667----@       1677-d
1658------C     1668------A     1678----@
1659------A     1669------C     1679----a

Year Rel value  Year Rel value  Year Rel value
1700------D     1710--b         1720------@
1701------@     1711--b         1721i
1702------D     1712----a       1722--c
1703----@       1713------C     1723----a
1704--b         1714-d          1724--b
1705-e         1715------H      1725------A
1706--c        1716------F      1726------D
1707------A     1717----@       1727------E
1708g          1718----@       1728------B
1709------B     1719------C     1729----a

Year Rel value  Year Rel value  Year Rel value
1750--------G   1760----@       1770j
1751------D     1761------D     1771-d
1752------D     1762------B     1772----@
1753------D     1763----a       1773------D
1754------A     1764--c         1774------A
1755------C     1765------C     1775------D
1756-f         1766------A      1776-e
1757h          1767------D      1777f
1758--b        1768------D      1778----@
1759----c       1769------A     1779------A

Year Rel value  Year Rel value  Year Rel value
1800--b         1810----B       1820------C
1801------A     1811----@       1821--c
1802------B     1812--------F   1822----a
1803-e         1813------E      1823-f
1804j          1814------E      1824----@
1805g          1815------A      1825------B
1806----a       1816------A     1826------E
1807-d         1817------A      1827----@
1808-d         1818------D      1828--c
1809------C     1819------C     1829g

Year Rel value  Year Rel value  Year Rel value
1850----@       1860------D     1870----@
1851--b         1861------E     1871----a
1852--b         1862------C     1872--b
1853----a       1863------E     1873------A
1854------C     1864--c         1874----@
1855--------F   1865-e          1875----a
1856------B     1866------B     1876--b
1857------C     1867------A     1877------C
1858----a       1868----@       1878------B
1859----a       1869----a       1879--------F

Year Rel value  Year Rel value  Year Rel value
1900----a       1910------C     1920----a
1901----@       1911------C     1921------C
1902--c         1912----@       1922------C
1903----a       1913--------F   1923------C
1904------A     1914----@       1924h
1905----@       1915--b         1925------B
1906----a       1916------C     1926--b
1907------B     1917------B     1927------B
1908------B     1918----a       1928--------F
1909------C     1919------C     1929g

Year Rel value  Year Rel value  Year Rel value
1950------C     1960------A     1970--C
1951------E     1961-e          1971--C
1952------C     1962------A     1972----a
1953----a       1963--------D   1973-e
1954------C     1964----@       1974-f
1955------A     1965-e          1975--c
1956--------F   1966------C     1976-d
1957------E     1967----@       1977f
1958------A     1968j           1978------C
1959------C     1969----a       1979------B
```

```
1630-----@      1680--c          1730---------D    1780-------D     1830---a         1880--b          1930-e          1980-----B
1631f           1681-----@       1731---------C    1781--b          1831----@        1881----@        1931f           1981-d
1632g           1682g            1732---------G    1782-------A     1832------D      1882----@        1932------A     1982------D
1633---b        1683f            1733------E       1783--c          1833----@        1883----B        1933------A     1983------C
1634--b         1684--b          1734-----@        1784------D      1834--c          1884------B      1934-d          1984------D
1635--c         1685--c          1735------A       1785--c          1835----@        1885----A        1935g           1985------E
1636-----A      1686---a         1736h             1786-c           1836------D      1886--a          1936-e          1986------G
1637-------B    1687------A      1737f             1787--c          1837------G      1887----A        1937----@       1987----B
1638-------A    1688---b         1738-e            1788-----C       1838------G      1888-------D     1938----@       1988------F
1639--b         1689-------B     1739-e            1789------F      1839-e           1889---b         1939-e          1989------B
----            ----                               ----             ----                                              ----
1640---------D  1690--------F    1740--b           1790------C      1840--f          1890m            1940--c         1990----@
1641---------J  1691-------B     1741g             1791------E      1841----C        1891--c          1941h           1991----B
1642-------F    1692------E      1742--@           1792----B        1842-----D       1892--b          1942--------F   1992-e
1643-------A    1693---@         1743--------C     1793--b          1843------C      1893---a         1943------D     1993--c
1644--a         1694-----E       1744--c           1794--b          1844--b          1894------G      1944------A     1994h
1645----C       1695m            1745----A         1795----@        1845----@        1895----C        1945----B       1995---b
1646----a       1696------C      1746----@         1796----D        1846i            1896---b         1946----C
1647------A     1697--------D    1747-------C      1797-----@       1847f            1897-------G      1947----C
1648----------E 1698-----@       1748----@         1798---a         1848--c          1898--b           1948----@
1649----------E 1699------A      1749------B       1799------B      1849-d           1899j             1949-d
```

**Figure 6.15** Part 4 of COFECHA provides a graphical representation of the master chronology. The @ symbol is an average ring, uppercase letters represent larger than average rings, and lowercase letters represent smaller than average rings. The further up the alphabet, the larger or smaller the ring.

Correlations of  50-year dated segments, lagged  25 years
Flags:  A = correlation under  .3281 but highest as dated;   B = correlation higher at other than dated position

| Seq | Series | Time_span | 1375 1424 | 1400 1449 | 1425 1474 | 1450 1499 | 1475 1524 | 1500 1549 | 1525 1574 | 1550 1599 | 1575 1624 | 1600 1649 | 1625 1674 | 1650 1699 | 1675 1724 | 1700 1749 | 1725 1774 | 1750 1799 | 1775 1824 | 1800 1849 | 1825 1874 | 1850 1899 |
|---|---|---|---|---|---|---|---|---|---|---|---|---|---|---|---|---|---|---|---|---|---|---|
| 1 | LCW01A | 1689 1995 | | | | | | | | | | | | | .52 | .52 | .55 | .51 | .51 | .79 | .72 | .60 |
| 2 | LCW01B | 1676 1995 | | | | | | | | | | | | | .58 | .70 | .68 | .46 | .43 | .69 | .73 | .43 |
| 3 | LCW02A | 1399 1995 | | .65 | .48 | .29A | .53 | .60 | .64 | .73 | .71 | .53 | .57 | .55 | .58 | .80 | .52 | .48 | .57 | .57 | .60 | .61 |
| 4 | LCW02B | 1399 1995 | | .56 | .55 | .39 | .30A | .46 | .72 | .71 | .61 | .51 | .51 | .63 | .46 | .35 | .36 | .51 | .16B | .23B | .21B | .25B |
| 5 | LCW03A | 1414 1937 | | .47 | .48 | .36B | .32B | .34 | .52 | .44 | .50 | .65 | .75 | .72 | .63 | .49 | .39 | .51 | .46 | .63 | .53 | .38 |
| 6 | LCW03B | 1431 1930 | | | .49 | .53 | .48 | .47 | .52 | .59 | .78 | .72 | .68 | .64 | .63 | .53 | .66 | .51 | .41B | .51 | .37 | .56 |
| 7 | LCW04A | 1527 1995 | | | | | | | .55 | .52 | .79 | .78 | .68 | .64 | .63 | .53 | .60 | .55 | .46 | .51 | .54 | .47 |
| 8 | LCW04B | 1563 1995 | | | | | | | | .65 | .69 | .72 | .77 | .83 | .81 | .66 | .68 | .46 | .53 | .64 | .54 | .59 |
| 9 | LCW05A | 1558 1995 | | | | | | | | .41 | .50 | .68 | .72 | .81 | .81 | .66 | .44 | .32A | .53 | .76 | .66 | .49 |
| 10 | LCW06A | 1744 1995 | | | | | | | | | | | | | | | .36 | .40 | .26A | .43 | .62 | .53 |
| 11 | LCW06B | 1767 1995 | | | | | | | | | | | | | | | | .39 | .50 | .43 | .48 | .44 |
| 12 | LCW08A | 1417 1995 | | .47 | .44 | .40 | .62 | .71 | .48 | .60 | .32A | .37B | .70 | .81 | .57 | .30A | .39B | .50 | .27A | .57 | .53 | .59 |
| 13 | LCW08B | 1397 1995 | .59 | .61 | .50 | .47 | .61 | .65 | .75 | .60 | .46 | .58 | .59 | .52 | .59 | .39 | .56 | .42 | .59 | .64 | .55 | .65 |
| 14 | LCW09A | 1751 1995 | | | | | | | | | | | | | | | | .44 | .59 | .64 | .53 | .50 |
| 15 | LCW09B | 1721 1995 | | | | | | | | | | | | | | .50 | .47 | .59 | .53 | .69 | .66 | .60 |
| 16 | LCW10B | 1788 1995 | | | | | | | | | | | | | | | | | .16B | .25B | .15B | .41 |
| 17 | LCW10C | 1526 1647 | | | | | | | .50 | .37 | .43 | .45 | | | | | | | | | | |
| 18 | LCW11A | 1539 1995 | | | | | | | .41 | .42 | .56 | .62 | .82 | .73 | .66 | .69 | .67 | .61 | .54 | .65 | .59 | .67 |
| 19 | LCW11B | 1546 1995 | | | | | | | .43 | .40 | .52 | .58 | .74 | .63 | .47 | .56 | .75 | .70 | .61 | .67 | .56 | .56 |
| 20 | LCW12A | 1727 1995 | | | | | | | | | | | | | | .70 | .70 | .53 | .56 | .74 | .68 | .66 |
| 21 | LCW12B | 1681 1995 | | | | | | | | | | | | | .71 | .75 | .72 | .68 | .63 | .71 | .62 | .64 |
| 22 | LCW13A | 1669 1995 | | | | | | | | | | | | .68 | .75 | .72 | .66 | .70 | .24B | .38 | .40 | .21B |
| 23 | LCW13B | 1610 1995 | | | | | | | | | | .71 | .68 | .56 | .75 | .66 | .61 | .55 | .41 | .55 | .68 | .51 |
| 24 | LCW14A | 1614 1995 | | | | | | | | | | .61 | .72 | .67 | .64 | .58 | .62 | .62 | .62 | .57 | .42 | .53 |
| 25 | LCW14B | 1658 1995 | | | | | | | | | | | | .57 | .55 | .46 | .53 | .49 | .53 | .59 | .43 | .49 |
| 26 | LCW15A | 1417 1995 | | .30A | .25B | .28B | .61 | .49 | .69 | .68 | .70 | .59 | .53 | .60 | .68 | .65 | .48 | .62 | .33B | .54 | .59 | .48 |
| 27 | LCW15B | 1428 1970 | | | .25B | .49 | .58 | .72 | .56 | .74 | .59 | .47 | .63 | .78 | .59 | .68 | .62 | .47 | .47 | .53 | .56 | .34 |
| 28 | LCW16A | 1394 1995 | .60 | .52 | .19B | .25A | .58 | .78 | .73 | .74 | .69 | .79 | .55 | .50 | .57 | .66 | .66 | .54 | .22B | .44 | .59 | .27B |
| 29 | LCW16B | 1472 1995 | | | | .15B | .38 | .56 | .74 | .51 | .61 | .39 | .55 | .49 | .57 | .41 | .60 | .67 | .47 | .65 | .72 | .33 |
| 30 | LCW17A | 1451 1995 | | | | .38 | .56 | .85 | .74 | .51 | .61 | .39 | .55 | .51 | .41 | .37 | .42 | .45 | .57 | .71 | .62 | .49 |
| 31 | LCW17B | 1399 1995 | | .52 | .50 | .23B | .42 | .62 | .45 | .18B | .19B | .35 | .42B | .60 | .61 | .54 | .53 | .18B | .49 | .60 | .43 | .16B |
| 32 | LCW18A | 1680 1995 | | | | | | | | | | | | | .47 | .54 | .65 | .42 | .65 | .69 | .57 | .57 |
| 33 | LCW18B | 1712 1995 | | | | | | | | | | | | | | .48 | .40 | .44 | .71 | .69 | .57 | .60 |

| # | Series | First | Last | 1400 | 1450 | 1500 | 1550 | 1600 | 1650 | 1700 | 1750 | 1800 | 1850 | 1900 | 1950 |
|---|--------|-------|------|------|------|------|------|------|------|------|------|------|------|------|------|
| 34 | LCW19A | 1754 | 1995 | | | | | | | | .50 | .57 | .34B | .29B | .60 |
| 35 | LCW19B | 1764 | 1995 | | | | | | | | .52 | .48 | .43 | .36B | .46 |
| 36 | LCW19C | 1764 | 1995 | | | | | | | | .53 | .54 | .51 | .47 | .47 |
| 37 | LCW20A | 1548 | 1930 | | | | .61 | .62 | .54 | .55 | .61 | .59 | .53 | .32B | |
| 38 | LCW20B | 1518 | 1995 | | | .73 | .51 | .68 | .36 | | .42 | .49 | .61 | .58 | .46 |
| 39 | LCW21A | 1399 | 1995 | .35 | .36 | .26B | .20B | .24B | .29B | .69 | .34 | .10B | .07B | .35 | .58 |
| 40 | LCW21B | 1399 | 1995 | .37 | .35 | .27A | .34 | .54 | .29B | .50 | .28A | .31A | .53 | .58 | .53 |
| 41 | LCW22A | 1480 | 1995 | | | .66 | .74 | .39 | .61 | .55 | .65 | .64 | .63 | .64 | .65 |
| 42 | LCW22B | 1525 | 1995 | | | | .73 | .58 | .67 | .72 | .65 | .37 | .43 | .52 | .51 |
| 43 | LCW23A | 1588 | 1995 | | | | | .56 | .58 | .57 | .65 | .79 | .59 | .44 | .39 |
| 44 | LCW23B | 1620 | 1995 | | | | | | .53 | .46 | .60 | .48 | .46 | .30A | .25A |
| 45 | LCW38A | 1744 | 1920 | | | | | | | .57 | .55 | .44 | .39 | .41 | |
| 46 | LCW38B | 1743 | 1920 | | | | | | | .52 | .49 | .33 | .46 | .35B | .18B |

**Figure 6.16** Part 5 of COFECHA shows the correlation of each 50-year segment to the master. An A flag means that the series dated best where it was, but the correlation was below the critical level defined on page 1, and a B flag means that segment correlates better within a 20-year window of where it is currently dated.

For each series with potential problems the following diagnostics may appear:

[A] Correlations with master dating series of flagged 50-year segments of series filtered with 32-year spline, at every point from ten years earlier (-10) to ten years later (+10) than dated

[B] Effect of those data values which most lower or raise correlation with master series

[C] Year-to-year changes very different from the mean change in other series

[D] Absent rings (zero values)

[E] Values which are statistical outliers from mean for the year

```
================================================================================================================
LCW01A   1689 to 1995   307 years                                                                      Series   1

[B] Entire series, effect on correlation ( .622) is:
    Lower 1883 -.013  1731 -.007  1910 -.006  1738 -.006  Higher 1890  .017  1968  .013  1770  .012  1846  .010
================================================================================================================
LCW01B   1676 to 1995   320 years                                                                      Series   2

[A] Segment  High  -10   -9   -8   -7   -6   -5   -4   -3   -2   -1   +0   +1   +2   +3   +4   +5   +6   +7   +8   +9  +10
    -------  ----  ---  ---  ---  ---  ---  ---  ---  ---  ---  ---  ---  ---  ---  ---  ---  ---  ---  ---  ---  ---  ---
    1875 1924  -1  .05 -.07  .10  .15 -.20 -.11  .07 -.23 -.12 .35* .32| .16  .11 -.28 -.13  .04 -.09 -.14  .22  .16  .09

[B] Entire series, effect on correlation ( .560) is:
    Lower 1897 -.010  1776 -.007  1767 -.007  1994 -.006  Higher 1968  .011  1770  .011  1721  .010  1839  .006
1875 to 1924 segment:
    Lower 1897 -.057  1896 -.016  1906 -.015  1900 -.011  Higher 1890  .075  1879  .028  1880  .016  1913  .012
================================================================================================================
```

```
LCW02A    1399 to 1995    597 years                                                Series   3

[A] Segment  High   -10   -9   -8   -7   -6   -5   -4   -3   -2   -1   +0   +1   +2   +3   +4   +5   +6   +7   +8   +9  +10
    -------  ----   ---   ---  ---  ---  ---  ---  ---  ---  ---  ---  ---  ---  ---  ---  ---  ---  ---  ---  ---  ---  ---
    1450 1499   0   .06   .14  .10 -.09  .01 -.15 -.07 -.19  .04 -.03 .29* -.01 -.03 -.08 -.30  .19  .14  .18  .12 -.16 -.11

[B] Entire series, effect on correlation ( .558) is:
       Lower  1452 -.009  1817 -.007  1762 -.007  1544 -.006  Higher  1652  .017  1529  .007  1581  .006  1428  .005
    1450 to 1499 segment:
       Lower  1452 -.052  1492 -.036  1482 -.033  1483 -.030  Higher  1496  .088  1481  .084  1485  .031  1499  .018

=====================================================================================================================

LCW03B    1431 to 1930    500 years                                                Series   6

[B] Entire series, effect on correlation ( .524) is:
       Lower  1925 -.008  1711 -.005  1622 -.005  1463 -.005  Higher  1652  .018  1890  .014  1846  .007  1529  .006

[E] Outliers   1   3.0 SD above or -4.5 SD below mean for year
       1829 -5.0 SD

=====================================================================================================================
```

**Figure 6.17** Part 6 of COFECHA provides core-level analysis of how well each core dates against the master, the 20-year window of possible other dates for problem segments, the effect of the best and worst segments on the overall correlation, and any outliers that are more than three standard deviations from the mean so that those measurements can be checked for accuracy.

the top-left corner and a series number is assigned to each core based on its order in the file. These series numbers can be used to find the cores more easily in COFECHA or other dendrochronological programs such as EDT (also called EDRM). Section A in Part 6 is printed only when segments have a low correlation (as shown by an A flag in Part 5) or a better date somewhere else in the 20-year window around the present date for the segment (as shown by a B flag in Part 5). Section B is always presented showing the 5 years that added the most weight to the correlation, labeled "Higher," and the 5 years that lowered the correlation the most, labeled "Lower." This section also provides the correlation of each series to the master. Section C presents any interannual differences (such as an acute increase or decrease in growth from one year to the next) that were unexpected based on the master chronology. Any absent rings in a core are presented in section D, along with a comparison to what the master shows. Section E presents any ring-width measurements that are more than three standard deviations from the mean. Because environmental effects on the trees are likely to cause rings that are larger or smaller than the mean, we should be concerned mainly when rings are five or more standard deviations from the mean; then the measurements should be rechecked for human error.

The four cores presented in figure 6.17 all date well, although the middle two (LCW01B and LCW02A) have been flagged with a B flag and A flag, respectively, in Part 5. Core LCW01B correlates better at a −1 shift for the 1875–1924 segment. If the outside (bark side) is the known date of coring and should not be shifted, then the segment to be shifted falls in the middle of the series and necessitates not only a missing ring near the modern part of the segment, but also a false ring near the older part of the segment. Although the occurrence of both missing and false rings in a 50-year segment is certainly possible, note that the correction would only lead to a 0.03 increase in correlation (from 0.32 to 0.35), a small increase for a lot of change in dating. This kind of flag obliges the researcher to go back to the wood. In this case, after checking the sample, I ruled this a spurious correlation and left the core the way it was dated. Core LCW02A has an A flag because the segment from 1450–1499 correlated at 0.29 with the master, which is below the critical level. Again, after checking the growth on the sample and seeing nothing anomalous, I left this core alone with no correction.

The four cores shown on this page of Part 6 correlated with the master at 0.622, 0.560, 0.558, and 0.524, which are good correlations for this site. It is important to realize that there is no specific threshold that guarantees that a core is well dated. The correlation depends upon the species being analyzed and the site characteristics. Once a researcher has worked in a region and with a tree species for some time, he or she can learn what a good score is and use that for a benchmark.

In contrast to the case of LCW01B in figure 6.17, LCW10B in figure 6.18 has three segments in a row that suggest a clear −1 shift: they are at one end of the core and the correlation of each overlapping segment increases dramatically with the shift (for example, from 0.16 to 0.70 for 1788–1837). This type of pattern strongly suggests that there is a missing ring in the series and that ring is in the area around 1825–1850 because the 1850–1899 segment dated without any problems (check Part 5 to see this correlation). The other series on this page date well with the master chronology.

Part 7 summarizes all of the descriptive statistics for each core including its correlation with the master chronology and its mean sensitivity (fig. 6.19). At the bottom of the chart, we see again the average of all of the series intercorrelations (0.520) and the average of the mean sensitivities (0.254) that were reported in Part 1.

## Conclusions on COFECHA

COFECHA is one of the most useful programs in dendrochronology and it can provide standard statistics that enable researchers to compare between sites and species. It should not be used as the sole dating method for samples, but rather as a quality-control check on previously dated samples. The COFECHA program is designed to assist in dating and to develop individual series that are well dated. In a later section I describe ARSTAN, which is a much more powerful program that is used for chronology building. The tree-ring series that are vetted in COFECHA are input into ARSTAN for final chronology development. On the way to chronology development, COFECHA is used iteratively with EDRM to make corrections of problem segments that are identified in COFECHA and confirmed on the wood.

## EDRM

EDRM (standing for Edit Ring Measurements and formerly called EDT) enables the editing of ring-width measurements (fig. 6.20). This program is most often used after COFECHA has identified some sections of a core that need to be corrected or eliminated. EDRM and COFECHA are often run many times to correct a series. EDRM takes an input file name and accepts the standard dendrochronological file formats such as compact, measurement (with 0.01- or 0.001-mm precision), indices, Accurite measurements, meteorological data, spreadsheet data, or one- or two-column data. It asks for an output file name so that a new file is always created instead of overwriting old data. This is a good safety procedure so that original data files are not accidentally corrupted. The output file can be in compact, measurement at 0.01-mm precision, or measurement at 0.001-mm precision. The program asks if you want to use the first line of data as a header or title for the file. As with all DOS programs, the option in brackets is the default response. The program then takes one core at a time and allows the user to conduct various procedures on that core, such as copy as is, insert a value, eliminate a value, change the first year of the core, cut the core from the beginning or end, omit a series, or change the core ID.

## ARSTAN

ARSTAN is one of the main programs in dendrochronology that is used to build the final stand-level chronologies. ARSTAN differs from COFECHA in that it has a broader range of standardization techniques that can be used on individual series before a master chronology is compiled. This should not be confused with the master chronology that is developed in COFECHA. COFECHA also uses standardization (usually a 32-year cubic smoothing spline) to create a master chronology for the dating of other cores. This master chronology, however, was created specifically for dating purposes and is not the master chronology that should be used for the final analysis.

In ARSTAN, different standardization techniques can be used to maximize the signal of interest and remove noise from the final chronology. It was developed to be able to mathematically

```
LCW09A    1751 to 1995    245 years                                              Series 14

[B] Entire series, effect on correlation ( .562) is:
    Lower 1838 -.017  1869 -.011  1947 -.011  1864 -.007 Higher 1924 .015  1804 .014  1846 .012  1929 .009


LCW09B    1721 to 1995    275 years                                              Series 15

[B] Entire series, effect on correlation ( .530) is:
    Lower 1972 -.012  1721 -.010  1757 -.009  1755 -.009 Higher 1968 .020  1890 .019  1924 .013  1770 .013

[E] Outliers    1   3.0 SD above or -4.5 SD below mean for year
    1939 -4.8 SD


LCW10B    1788 to 1995    208 years                                              Series 16

[A] Segment  High  -10   -9   -8   -7   -6   -5   -4   -3   -2   -1   +0   +1   +2   +3   +4   +5   +6   +7   +8   +9  +10
    -------  ----  ---  ---  ---  ---  ---  ---  ---  ---  ---  ---  ---  ---  ---  ---  ---  ---  ---  ---  ---  ---  ---
    1788 1837  -1  -.12 -.15 -.11 -.08 -.17 -.07 -.13  .16  .24 .70*  .16| .01 -.05  .03  .05  .17 -.06 -.16 -.34 -.07  .05
    1800 1849  -1  -.21 -.22 -.04  .00 -.17 -.04 -.16 -.08  .18 .73*  .25| .01 -.02 -.04 -.04  .27  .00 -.12 -.35 -.14  .06
    1825 1874  -1  -.33 -.18 -.03 -.03 -.07 -.06 -.11 -.26  .17 .65*  .15| .08 -.01 -.22 -.03  .37  .00  .00 -.14 -.07 -.01

[B] Entire series, effect on correlation ( .428) is:
    Lower 1846 -.018  1818 -.015  1841 -.014  1860 -.014 Higher 1890 .028  1929 .019  1924 .017  1804 .009
1788 to 1837 segment:
    Lower 1818 -.051  1788 -.032  1823 -.031  1824 -.028 Higher 1804 .081  1805 .079  1837 .032  1812 .026
1800 to 1849 segment:
    Lower 1818 -.051  1846 -.050  1841 -.047  1824 -.035 Higher 1804 .046  1805 .042  1837 .028  1838 .025
1825 to 1874 segment:
    Lower 1841 -.052  1860 -.051  1863 -.043  1846 -.041 Higher 1847 .044  1837 .034  1861 .031  1838 .030
```

```
LCW10C    1526 to 1647    122 years                                          Series  17

[B] Entire series, effect on correlation ( .430) is:
    Lower 1596 -.023 1540 -.023 1631 -.013 1628 -.011  Higher 1600 .015 1622 .013 1530 .012 1550 .012

[E] Outliers   1   3.0 SD above or -4.5 SD below mean for year
    1540 +3.3 SD
================================================================================================
LCW11A    1539 to 1995    457 years                                          Series  18

[B] Entire series, effect on correlation ( .620) is:
    Lower 1550 -.010 1610 -.008 1865 -.007 1828 -.005  Higher 1652 .013 1846 .008 1770 .005 1890 .005

[D]  1 Absent rings:   Year   Master   N series Absent
                       1899   -2.592            45       1

[E] Outliers   2   3.0 SD above or -4.5 SD below mean for year
    1865 -5.3 SD;  1899 -4.8 SD
================================================================================================
LCW11B    1546 to 1995    450 years                                          Series  19
```

**Figure 6.18** A second page from COFECHA Part 6 showing when a core has a missing ring. Note that LCW10B, also called series 16 by COFECHA, has three inside segments that correlate better if they are shifted back one year in time. If we assume that the outsides of the core is anchored in time by the coring date, a negative shift usually means that a missing ring needs to be inserted, and a positive shift means that a false ring needs to be removed.

| | | | | | | Corr | //—————— Unfiltered ——————\\ | | | | | //—— Filtered ——\\ | | |
|---|---|---|---|---|---|---|---|---|---|---|---|---|---|---|---|
| | | | No. | No. | No. | with | Mean | Max | Std | Auto | Mean | Max | Std | Auto | AR |
| Seq | Series | Interval | Years | Segmt | Flags | Master | msmt | msmt | dev | corr | sens | value | dev | corr | () |
| 1 | LCW01A | 1689 1995 | 307 | 12 | 0 | .622 | .82 | 3.18 | .547 | .918 | .184 | 1.91 | .314 | -.036 | 1 |
| 2 | LCW01B | 1676 1995 | 320 | 12 | 1 | .560 | 1.13 | 4.96 | .856 | .884 | .230 | 2.00 | .347 | -.015 | 2 |
| 3 | LCW02A | 1399 1995 | 597 | 24 | 1 | .558 | .46 | 1.02 | .159 | .632 | .231 | 2.08 | .295 | -.012 | 1 |
| 4 | LCW02B | 1399 1995 | 597 | 24 | 7 | .452 | .40 | 1.06 | .175 | .715 | .264 | 2.21 | .336 | -.019 | 1 |
| 5 | LCW03A | 1414 1937 | 524 | 21 | 3 | .485 | .83 | 5.78 | .677 | .898 | .274 | 1.91 | .322 | -.005 | 1 |
| 6 | LCW03B | 1431 1930 | 500 | 20 | 0 | .524 | .83 | 2.77 | .427 | .810 | .249 | 1.87 | .253 | -.016 | 1 |
| 7 | LCW04A | 1527 1995 | 469 | 18 | 1 | .544 | .60 | 2.26 | .362 | .821 | .290 | 1.95 | .342 | -.014 | 2 |
| 8 | LCW04B | 1563 1995 | 433 | 17 | 0 | .646 | .73 | 2.26 | .383 | .833 | .253 | 2.02 | .284 | -.009 | 1 |
| 9 | LCW05A | 1558 1995 | 438 | 17 | 2 | .573 | .39 | .96 | .158 | .743 | .228 | 2.10 | .325 | -.022 | 1 |
| 10 | LCW06A | 1744 1995 | 252 | 10 | 1 | .428 | .30 | .73 | .129 | .516 | .368 | 1.99 | .353 | -.001 | 1 |
| 11 | LCW06B | 1767 1995 | 229 | 9 | 3 | .407 | .34 | .82 | .135 | .499 | .356 | 2.01 | .358 | -.031 | 1 |
| 12 | LCW08A | 1417 1995 | 579 | 23 | 4 | .534 | .34 | 1.54 | .221 | .870 | .275 | 1.93 | .234 | -.019 | 1 |
| 13 | LCW08B | 1397 1995 | 599 | 24 | 2 | .522 | .41 | 2.28 | .373 | .927 | .259 | 1.93 | .215 | -.014 | 1 |
| 14 | LCW09A | 1751 1995 | 245 | 9 | 0 | .562 | .51 | .95 | .147 | .522 | .234 | 1.97 | .366 | -.017 | 1 |
| 15 | LCW09B | 1721 1995 | 275 | 11 | 0 | .530 | .54 | 1.13 | .212 | .753 | .232 | 1.79 | .262 | -.001 | 1 |
| 16 | LCW10B | 1788 1995 | 208 | 8 | 3 | .428 | .56 | 1.27 | .177 | .569 | .240 | 2.01 | .412 | -.022 | 1 |
| 17 | LCW10C | 1526 1647 | 122 | 4 | 0 | .430 | .23 | .39 | .069 | .693 | .190 | 2.03 | .378 | -.007 | 2 |
| 18 | LCW11A | 1539 1995 | 457 | 18 | 0 | .620 | .71 | 1.67 | .318 | .772 | .245 | 1.86 | .244 | -.013 | 1 |
| 19 | LCW11B | 1546 1995 | 450 | 18 | 1 | .555 | .75 | 2.20 | .329 | .766 | .239 | 1.96 | .299 | -.006 | 1 |
| 20 | LCW12A | 1727 1995 | 269 | 10 | 0 | .667 | .95 | 2.85 | .611 | .917 | .187 | 2.04 | .366 | -.010 | 2 |
| 21 | LCW12B | 1681 1995 | 315 | 12 | 0 | .686 | .88 | 2.26 | .419 | .890 | .179 | 1.91 | .292 | -.023 | 1 |
| 22 | LCW13A | 1669 1995 | 327 | 13 | 2 | .515 | .82 | 2.57 | .525 | .852 | .279 | 2.15 | .309 | -.020 | 2 |
| 23 | LCW13B | 1610 1995 | 386 | 15 | 0 | .557 | .72 | 1.95 | .335 | .763 | .276 | 2.17 | .307 | -.020 | 1 |
| 24 | LCW14A | 1614 1995 | 382 | 15 | 0 | .588 | .32 | .85 | .130 | .622 | .267 | 1.97 | .269 | -.010 | 1 |
| 25 | LCW14B | 1658 1995 | 338 | 13 | 0 | .536 | .41 | 1.01 | .166 | .596 | .311 | 2.08 | .338 | -.009 | 1 |
| 26 | LCW15A | 1417 1995 | 579 | 23 | 3 | .538 | .60 | 1.58 | .211 | .504 | .295 | 1.85 | .253 | -.004 | 1 |
| 27 | LCW15B | 1428 1970 | 543 | 21 | 3 | .533 | .47 | 1.53 | .228 | .738 | .279 | 1.95 | .298 | -.018 | 1 |
| 28 | LCW16A | 1394 1995 | 602 | 24 | 5 | .539 | .39 | 1.33 | .166 | .739 | .268 | 1.84 | .217 | -.011 | 2 |
| 29 | LCW16B | 1472 1995 | 524 | 21 | 1 | .584 | .43 | 1.96 | .246 | .793 | .319 | 1.92 | .266 | -.025 | 1 |
| 30 | LCW17A | 1451 1995 | 545 | 21 | 3 | .458 | .40 | 2.55 | .244 | .813 | .299 | 1.92 | .252 | -.011 | 1 |
| 31 | LCW17B | 1399 1995 | 597 | 24 | 8 | .412 | .42 | 1.46 | .223 | .824 | .234 | 1.89 | .248 | -.000 | 1 |
| 32 | LCW18A | 1680 1995 | 316 | 12 | 0 | .569 | .97 | 2.57 | .490 | .819 | .226 | 1.83 | .231 | -.045 | 1 |
| 33 | LCW18B | 1712 1995 | 284 | 11 | 0 | .575 | .94 | 2.32 | .462 | .788 | .247 | 1.91 | .280 | -.020 | 2 |
| 34 | LCW19A | 1754 1995 | 242 | 9 | 3 | .462 | .44 | .76 | .140 | .642 | .225 | 2.04 | .304 | .005 | 2 |

| | | | | | | | | | | | | | | | |
|---|---|---|---|---|---|---|---|---|---|---|---|---|---|---|---|
| 35 | LCW19B | 1764 | 1995 | 232 | 9 | 3 | .456 | .44 | 1.14 | .177 | .579 | .311 | 2.04 | .362 | -.011 | 1 |
| 36 | LCW19C | 1764 | 1995 | 232 | 9 | 1 | .480 | .63 | 1.36 | .226 | .650 | .241 | 1.95 | .319 | -.011 | 2 |
| 37 | LCW20A | 1548 | 1930 | 383 | 16 | 1 | .515 | .56 | 1.38 | .259 | .826 | .226 | 1.80 | .227 | -.003 | 1 |
| 38 | LCW20B | 1518 | 1995 | 478 | 19 | 1 | .529 | .57 | 1.64 | .278 | .873 | .204 | 1.86 | .265 | -.013 | 2 |
| 39 | LCW21A | 1399 | 1995 | 597 | 24 | 11 | .333 | .35 | 1.01 | .146 | .696 | .252 | 1.85 | .232 | -.007 | 1 |
| 40 | LCW21B | 1399 | 1995 | 597 | 24 | 5 | .416 | .30 | .93 | .132 | .750 | .248 | 2.02 | .309 | -.027 | 1 |
| 41 | LCW22A | 1480 | 1995 | 516 | 20 | 1 | .592 | .76 | 2.83 | .391 | .795 | .243 | 1.91 | .277 | -.019 | 1 |
| 42 | LCW22B | 1525 | 1995 | 471 | 18 | 2 | .539 | .75 | 1.92 | .269 | .494 | .271 | 1.93 | .267 | .002 | 2 |
| 43 | LCW23A | 1588 | 1995 | 408 | 16 | 1 | .529 | .48 | 1.31 | .223 | .834 | .207 | 2.03 | .325 | -.002 | 2 |
| 44 | LCW23B | 1620 | 1995 | 376 | 15 | 2 | .420 | .53 | 1.09 | .177 | .723 | .199 | 1.94 | .281 | -.011 | 1 |
| 45 | LCW38A | 1744 | 1920 | 177 | 7 | 0 | .449 | .33 | .59 | .082 | .413 | .210 | 2.03 | .328 | .045 | 1 |
| 46 | LCW38B | 1743 | 1920 | 178 | 7 | 3 | .353 | .43 | .75 | .100 | .599 | .181 | 1.91 | .321 | -.003 | 1 |
| Total or mean: | | | | 18495 | 727 | 88 | .520 | .56 | 5.78 | .283 | .748 | .254 | 2.21 | .287 | -.010 | |

- = [ COFECHA LCWEXCOF ] = -

**Figure 6.19** Part 7 of COFECHA provides a table of the descriptive statistics for each core including the sequence number, sample ID, start and end dates, number of years, number of segments, number of segments with flags, and then statistics on each core for the ring-width series before and after filtering. This last part shows the autocorrelation and how it was removed from the series.

```
cs  C:\Documents and Settings\jim speer\My Documents\Research\Rubino Archaeological Work\...  - □ ×
   -: Not data
   \: Close file
      Enter code for FORMAT of file => m

EDITED MEASUREMENTS
   ... Name   of   NEW   OUTPUT  file => test1.txt

Format for new edited data file:
      <C>  Compact format
       M:  Measurement .01  precision
       L:  Measurement .001 precision
FORMAT for edited file => m

Line from original file:
BUR01A   1717   1240   1030    870

Copy as title or header on new file? Y/<N> =>
No   1   BUR01A   Interval 1717  1866   150 years

C: COPY as is           F: new FIRST year        U: new LAST year
I: INSERT value         E: ELIMINATE value       R: REPLACE value
<: Cut from BEGINNING    >: Cut from END          P: DISPLAY data
T: Take remaining series 0: OMIT series          N: New identification
X: Exit program         Q: Re-edit series        K: COPY and re-edit
S: Copy all until ..    Select =>
```

**Figure 6.20** EDRM showing the options for editing a file.

standardize tree-ring series and to remove or control the autocorrelation component in the time series (Cook 1985, Cook and Holmes 1986). The program fits a curve to the measurements from each core, divides the ring width by the modeled curve value, averages together the resultant index for each core to create a tree-level index, and then averages together the tree indices to develop a stand-level chronology (fig. 6.21; Fritts and Swetnam 1989).

Historically, a negative exponential curve was considered a conservative standardization technique because it removed a known age-related geometric curve from the ring-width series. A negative exponential curve describes the decreasing thickness of rings from pith to bark that can develop in open-grown pine trees putting the same volume of wood each year on an ever-increasing cylinder. More recently, dendrochronologists have come to realize that this curve works best where the trees are open grown and do not experience many disturbance events. Cook (1985) demonstrated the need for more complex standardization techniques in closed-canopy forests that have more stand dynamic signal than open-grown forests. Cubic smoothing splines take into consideration autocorrelation (the effect of previous growth or climate on the current year's growth), and Cook (1985) suggested the use of cubic smoothing splines as an empirical fit to the growth of the trees (fig. 6.22). Today these spline fits are commonly used, but too often they are applied with little rigor; it is essential that the researcher know what signal is being removed and what signal is being kept in the resultant chronology (see chapter 2 for more about standardization and spline length choice).

ARSTAN was first developed for the Macintosh operating system and continues to have the most features among the available dendrochronology programs. It has been made available in two different formats for the personal computer. The DOS version of ARSTAN is a black box where the researcher chooses the standardization procedure that is then applied to all cores. This technique assumes that the researcher understands the choice of standardization

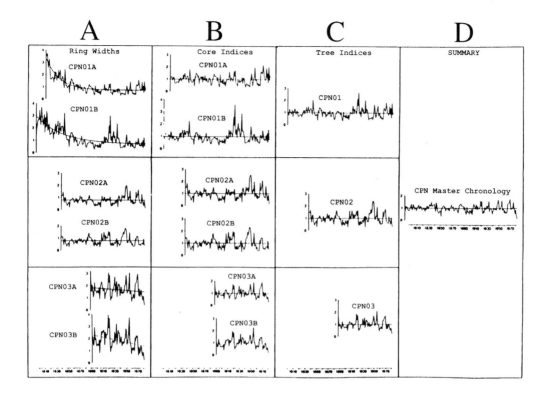

**Figure 6.21** Standardization and tree-level index series. ARSTAN matches a curve to the individual series, as seen in column A, with a negative exponential curve used for cores CPN01A and CPN01B, a straight line fit for cores CPN02A and CPN02B, and a decreasing trend for cores CPN03A and CPN03B. Note that in this case the site ID is CPN the tree ID is tree number 01, 02, and 03 respectively, and the last digit (A or B) stands for the first and second core from the same tree. ARSTAN then takes the ring width and divides it by the model fit (from column A) and the resultant series is plotted in column B as a dimensionless index value with the average of the series drawn as a straight line of value 1. ARSTAN then averages the index series from the two cores from each tree together to create a tree-level index series in column C. Finally, the tree-level series are averaged together to produce the stand-level master chronology in column D. The intermediate step of the development of a tree-level series avoids the circumstance of overrepresentation of one tree in the master chronology from which multiple cores may have been taken. (Modified from Fritts and Swetnam 1989: 126)

and is manually plotting out the ring-width chronologies, standardization curve fits, and the resultant index series to ensure the correct standardization technique is chosen for keeping the signal being pursued. A version of ARSTAN for Windows was recently developed that enables the researcher to interactively detrend the series, showing the curve fit and the resultant index series for each core. Users can choose to fit different standardization curves to the data and see how well the curve fits (fig. 6.23). This procedure is a good way to visualize the data and to see how standardization affects the process.

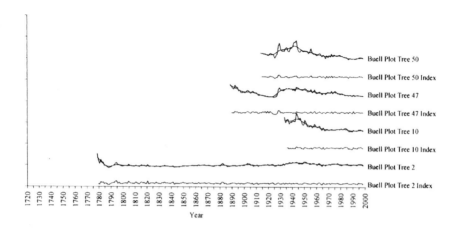

**Figure 6.22** Examples of four tree-ring chronologies that have been standardized using a 15-year cubic smoothing spline. This was a very flexible spline that was used to remove as much climate as possible to enhance a mast (synchronous fruiting) signal in oak trees from the southeastern United States. This graph shows the original ring-width chronology, with the model fit on top of that chronology, followed by the resultant index chronology for four trees (Buell Plot Trees 50, 47, 10, and 2). (From Speer 2001)

## Keystroke Tutorial for ARSTAN for Windows

To begin, the ring-width file (from a measuring program, checked with COFECHA, and edited in EDRM) should be placed in the ARSTAN directory and the ARS37win_5f.exe file should be executed. Enlarge the windows so that they fill the entire screen. Next, press Enter twice to get past the introduction to the program. At this point the user is prompted for the name of the data file. Following that, the user can identify a second file to include in this run or press Enter to use only the first file. Enter a descriptive title for the run that will allow for the identification of this run at a later date. The next option allows the user to run ARSTAN in batch mode, enabling the program to be run on many file sets. The default response is No.

The main menu in ARSTAN that controls the whole program appears next (fig. 6.24). There are more than 20 options that can be accessed. The options that I find most useful are 4, first detrending; 7, interactive detrending; 15, site-tree-core mask; and 19, summary plots. ARSTAN provides the most powerful standardization options of any of the dendrochronological programs.

With option 4, the user can choose to fit a negative exponential, linear trend, or various cubic smoothing splines. Option 5 allows for a second detrending, but I am personally opposed to adjusting the data more than necessary, and a second detrending is rarely warranted. Some researchers use second detrending when a deterministic model such as a negative exponential or regression line is used first to remove noise from a known cause, such as an age-related growth trend. Many of the standard detrending methods, for example, most cubic smoothing splines, remove noise such as a negative exponential curve so that two runs at detrending the series are not necessary. Also, two separate detrending curves move the data farther from the raw ring widths that were measured on the actual wood. I suggest using the interactive detrending option 7, as seen in figure 6.24, because this is the best way to visualize the data.

Option 15 allows the site, tree, and core mask to be changed to fit the identification tags, but the tags have to be consistent with the same number of characters for the site ID and tree number. The mask fits the tree identification code so that the program can differentiate separate cores from the same tree. In figure 6.24 option 15, the site-tree-core mask, is sssttcc where sss allows three letters for the site ID, tt allows two numbers for the tree ID, and cc allows two letters or numbers for the core ID. Option 19 provides summary plots so that the final chronologies can be visualized. Option 20 is also useful for some disturbance quantification techniques.

## Reading the Output of ARSTAN

When ARSTAN is run in interactive mode, it plots the ring-width measurements, curve fits, and resultant indices so that the user can see how well each curve fits the data (fig. 6.25). These curves are not saved, so it is useful to do a screen capture (press Fn + Prnt Scrn) of the plots and then paste them into another document such as Word or PowerPoint.

The output from ARSTAN summarizes all of the descriptive statistics for the raw ring widths and then goes through the same descriptive statistics for the standard, residual, and arstan chronologies (explained below). These statistics include the start and end dates, mean, standard deviation, skewness, kurtosis, mean sensitivity, and first-order autocorrelation for each core. The ARSTAN output also lists the detrending curve for each core so that any changes that have been made in the interactive detrending part of the analysis are recorded for later reference.

Four chronologies are produced by ARSTAN. The raw chronology is a simple average of the raw ring widths, in other words, no standardization was done on these series. The standard chronology is an average of the index values from the standardization process chosen by the user (see chapter 2 for more details on standardization). This chronology still has all autocorrelation included in the final chronology, which may be an issue when conducting regression analyses later, as one of the assumptions of regression analyses is that the series are not autocorrelated. The residual chronology has had all autocorrelation stripped from the series, making it a more suitable chronology for regression analysis, but not necessarily the most sensitive to the signal of interest. The arstan chronology has been calculated by removing the autocorrelation, modeling it, and reintroducing a stand-level autocorrelation back into the chronology. All four chronologies are output in the .crns file (meaning chronologies file). A benefit of using the interactive mode is that these chronologies are also plotted on the screen along with a sample depth curve for all of the chronologies (fig. 6.25). Chronology statistics such as the running $\bar{r}$ and EPS value (described above) are also graphically presented to help the researcher determine when the sample depth is so low that the stand-level signal is degraded (fig. 6.2).

## Regional Curve Standardization

The **regional curve standardization** technique was developed as an alternative standardization procedure that can maintain low-frequency variability in tree-ring chronologies while

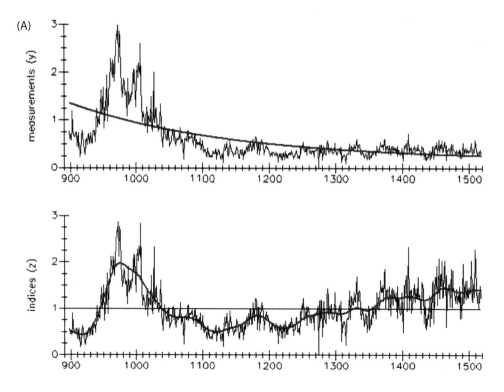

**Figure 6.23** Comparison of standardization with a negative exponential curve (A) versus a 100-year cubic smoothing spline (B) on a 600-year chronology. Notice the greater flexibility of the 100-year cubic smoothing spline for removing the slow growth when the tree is establishing followed by the spurt of juvenile growth and then the age-related growth trend. (From P. Clark and J. Speer, unpublished data)

removing the age-related growth trend that is unique to each site (Cook et al. 1995, Esper et al. 2002, Esper et al. 2003a). This is now a standardization option in ARSTAN. Low-frequency signal in climate reconstructions would be useful to determine long-term trends in past climate. Short-term cubic smoothing splines remove this low-frequency signal, making the reconstruction of the Medieval Warm Period and Little Ice Age impossible in 1000-year-long climate reconstructions (Cook et al. 1995).

In the regional curve standardization method, the pith for each individual tree-ring series is set to zero, regardless of the actual calendar year (fig. 6.26). It is important to note that because this technique is based on the biological age of each ring, obtaining the pith while coring is especially important. Esper et al. (2003a) demonstrated that this method was relatively robust for differing pith offsets and sample depths, but it was very sensitive to the calculation method used to obtain the regional curve standardization. The regional curve represents the average growth for that stand, which can be removed from each core by either calculating the difference from the mean growth curve (fig. 6.26) or as a ratio to the growth curve, as is done in the classical method of standardization. Esper et al. (2003a) indicated that

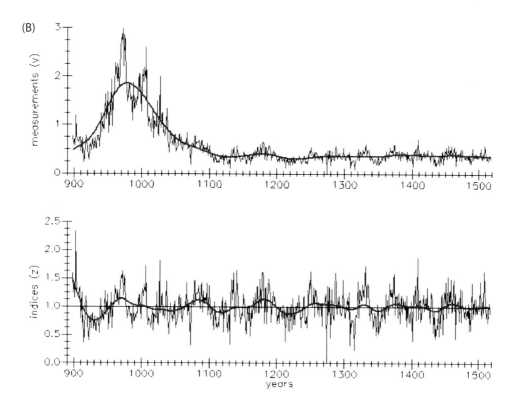

**Figure 6.23** (*Continued*)

a minimum sample depth of 5 series for any section of the curve is required and 40 series should be achieved at some point along the curve for the best results. This standardization technique has been programmed into ARSTAN for Windows, which also presents the standardization curves so that its validity can be examined on a site-level basis.

## YUX

YUX is a useful program that enables the user to convert a file with many chronologies to a spreadsheet in which each chronology is in a separate column. This spreadsheet file can then be read into Excel as tab, comma, or space delimited, based on user specification in the program. It is the most efficient way to convert output chronology files from ARSTAN (such as the .crns file) or to convert raw ring-width measurement files into a format that Excel can read.

## Climate Analysis Packages

Two stand-alone programs called PRECON (Fritts and Dean 1992) and DENDROCLIM 2002 (Biondi and Waikul 2004) have been developed to facilitate climate analysis. Similar

```
 File   Edit   Format   Window
                        ***                          ***
                        *************************************
                        *************************************

                        maximum tree-ring chronology length:   5000
                        maximum number of tree-ring series:    1500

<ret> to run, / to exit, h for more info:

open the file listing the data file names
type h for help or <ret> to enter them      ==>

okay, so enter your data file name(s)
which will be stored in the new file: arstan.files
when done, hit <ret> to process the data file(s).

file name # 1: hanover15.txt
file name # 2:

number of files to be processed:       1

okay, enter your overall run title:
==>

run in batch mode from log file? y/<n>/h    ==>

|************** arstan run time menu and current options settings **************|

                          opt          plt
     [1] tree-ring data type    1               !tucson ring-width format
     [2] missing data in gap   -9           0   !missing values estimated (no plots)
     [3] data transformation    0           0   !no data transformation (no plots)
     [4] first detrending       1           0   !1st-neg expon curve (k>0), no = opt 4
     [5] second detrending      0           0   !2nd-no detrending performed
     [6] robust detrending      1               !non-robust detrending methods used
     [7] interactive detrend    0               !no interactive detrending
     [8] index calculation      1               !tree-ring indices or ratios (rt/gt)
     [9] ar modeling method     1           0   !non-robust autoregressive modeling
    [10] pooled ar order        0           0   !minimum aic pooled ar model order fit
    [11] series ar order        0               !pooled ar order fit to all series
    [12] mean chronology        2    0    0  0  !robust chronology (w/ biweight plots)
    [13] stabilize variance     0               !no variance stabilization performed
    [14] common period years         0    0     !no common period analysis performed
    [15] site-tree-core mask        sssttcc     !site-tree-core separation mask
    [16] running rbar               50   25  0  !running rbar window/overlap (no plots)
    [17] printout option        2               !summary & series statistics printed
    [18] core series save       0               !no individual core series saved
    [19] summary plots          0               !no spaghetti and mean chronology plots
    [20] stand dynamics stuff   0           0   !no stand dynamics analyses done
         running mean window    0               !running mean window width
         percent growth change  0               !percent growth change threshold
         std error threshold    0               !standard error limit threshold

enter the option to change (<ret> = go)     ==>
```

**Figure 6.24** Main menu for ARSTAN.

analyses can also be conducted in Excel or SAS, but PRECON and DENDROCLIM 2002 were written specifically for dendrochronological applications, making it easier to enter tree-ring and meteorological data and incorporate more advanced **principal component analysis** (PCA) along with bootstrap techniques (Guiot 1991). Bootstrapping is a statistical technique that can be used to determine the significance of any statistic of interest even when the data are autocorrelated, not normally distributed, or when the data set is small. This technique creates pseudo–data sets by randomly sampling the original data with replacement (which means that a data point can be selected again) and then calculating statistical parameters for this new data set that can then be compared to the actual data. The result is a set of confidence intervals for any regression or correlation analysis that enables tests of significance (Guiot 1990).

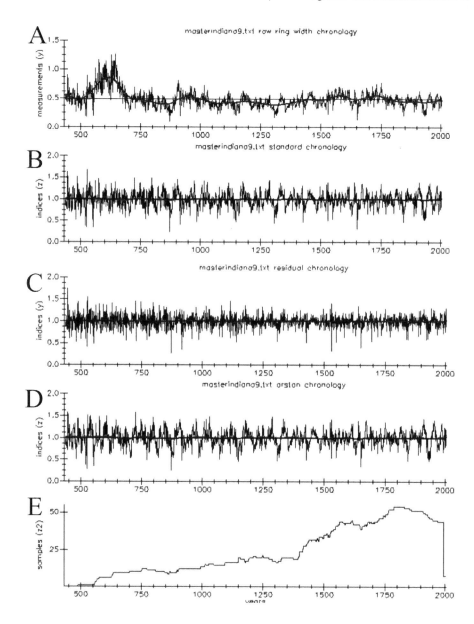

**Figure 6.25** Master chronologies for the Mokst Butte Lava Flow ponderosa pine chronology. (A) raw ring-width chronology, (B) standard chronology, (C) residual chronology, (D) arstan chronology, and (E) sample depth curve. (From P. Clark and J. Speer, unpublished data)

## PRECON

PRECON is a program written by Harold Fritts that is "an empirical model of climatic and prior growth factors preconditioning annual ring growth in trees" (fig. 6.27; Fritts and Dean 1992). PRECON 5.17B is the latest version, written in April 1999, and is a DOS program that

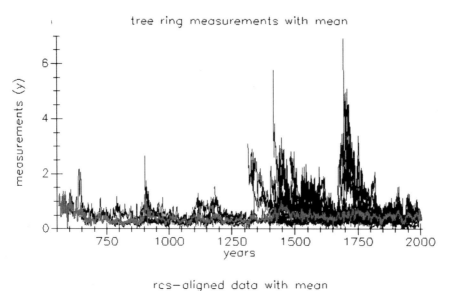

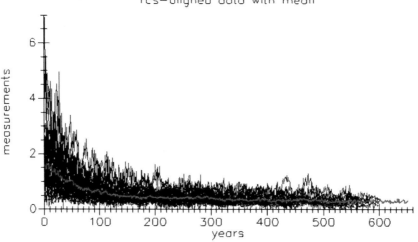

**Figure 6.26** Example of series lined up by pith date (top) versus establishment time for the regional curve standardization method (bottom). (From P. Clark and J. Speer, unpublished data)

allows the user to enter a tree-ring chronology file and climatic data sets. The program runs correlation matrices and PCA, resulting in response functions for each variable, which are then displayed in graphical form. PRECON uses a bootstrapping method to determine significance of the response function analysis (Guiot 1991).

## DENDROCLIM 2002

DENDROCLIM 2002 is a C++ computer program with a graphical user interface that also conducts correlation and response function analysis (fig. 6.28), but it uses a bootstrapping

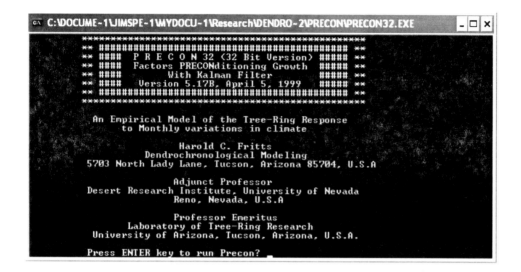

**Figure 6.27** The opening page of PRECON, a program used to determine the response function of how tree-ring chronologies respond to monthly climate data.

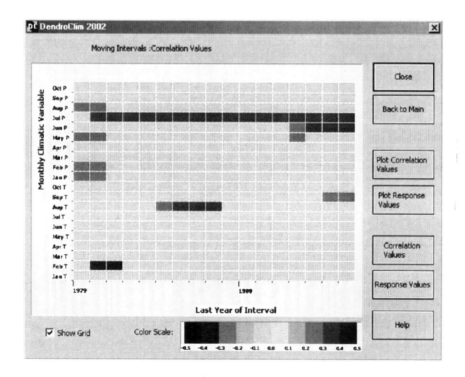

**Figure 6.28** Correlation results comparing tree rings to climate in DENDROCLIM 2002. (From Biondi and Waikul 2004)

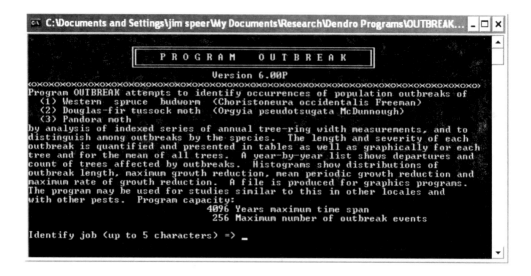

**Figure 6.29** The opening page of the program OUTBREAK.

technique to determine significance levels for both types of analysis, whereas PRECON uses bootstrapping for only the response function analysis (Biondi and Waikul 2004). This program also calculates the correlation and response function analyses in moving intervals through time to determine if the climatic response is stable or if it changes through time.

## OUTBREAK

The program OUTBREAK was written by Richard Holmes in consultation with Tom Swetnam (Holmes and Swetnam 1994a) for the purpose of quantifying and differentiating spruce budworm and tussock moth outbreaks as recorded in tree rings (fig. 6.29; for application of the program, see Swetnam et al. 1985, 1995, Swetnam and Lynch 1989, 1993, Speer et al. 2001, Ryerson et al. 2003). OUTBREAK allows for data from host trees to be entered into the program along with a nonhost chronology to control for climate. The program runs on tree-level ring-width indices that can be obtained from the DOS version of the ARSTAN program. Tree-level index chronologies are developed by averaging together the standardized A and B cores from the same tree, and the results are output as the .tre file. The tree-level chronologies give a better representation of growth in the tree than a single core and assure that individual trees are not overrepresented in the final chronology in the case that more cores were taken from one tree than another. The nonhost chronology is usually a master chronology from a site similar to the host sample site but of a different tree species that is not affected by the insect or pathogen that the researcher is studying. In 1996 this program was modified and calibrated for pandora moth outbreaks, which allowed for host chronologies to be entered but did not require the nonhost control (Speer et al. 2001). This modification was necessary in a ponderosa pine system where no long-lived nonhost species were available growing in the same climate conditions. In a case such as this, other efforts should be made to control for climate, such as determination of the climate response of the host trees based on modern climate or use of a regional climate reconstruction.

There are two questionable assumptions made with the host/nonhost comparison. First, it is assumed that the nonhost trees, usually of a different genus, have a similar climatic response as that of the host trees. The climate response can be tested for each genus and the reliability of this assumption can be determined. The second assumption is that the nonhost trees are not affected by the outbreak. Nonhost trees that are growing in the same stand as the host trees may change growth due to a reduction in competition, nutrient cycling, or possibly by some damage to the trees associated with the outbreak. If a nonhost species of a different genus is lacking, it may be tempting to use a host species for climate control that seems to be spatially separated from the outbreak. Spatial arguments are tenuous, however, because the spatial distribution of outbreaks is likely to have been different in the past. Therefore, a lack of modern outbreaks in a stand of host trees does not validate that stand as a long-term climate control site.

OUTBREAK should be calibrated in an iterative process on the specific site of interest in each new study. It was intended to quantify the effects of insect or pathogen outbreaks and to automate the process of identifying past outbreaks. OUTBREAK is preprogrammed with three insect types (western spruce budworm, Douglas-fir tussock moth, or pandora moth) that have default values for outbreak duration, severity, and onset rate. This program can be used to quantify the growth reduction of any insect or pathogen, but it should be calibrated with known outbreak occurrences. Characteristics of the wood should be the primary indicator that an outbreak occurred. Once the signature of the outbreak has been identified in the wood, then the program OUTBREAK can be run in an iterative process until it records the start and end dates of historically known outbreaks. Once the program is accurately representing known outbreaks, then it can be used to infer outbreaks in the past and to quantify the outbreak characteristics.

Four main parameters control the ability of OUTBREAK to recognize events in ringwidth measurement: the standard deviation of the maximum growth reduction, the shortest length of an outbreak, the longest length of an outbreak, and amount of the growth reduction at the beginning of the outbreak. The duration variables enable researchers to tease apart the effect of multiple insects in the same host tree, such as spruce budworm and tussock moth (Swetnam et al. 1995).

## Spectral Analysis

The maximum entropy method (Burg 1978, Dettinger et al. 1995), singular spectrum analysis (Vautard and Ghil 1989), and wavelet analysis (Torrence and Compo 1998) are all types of spectral analysis that can be used to examine cyclicity in time series (Villalba et al. 1998a, Speer et al. 2001). This is a common technique in insect outbreak studies to document the return interval of periodic outbreaks (Speer et al. 2001, Zhang and Alfaro 2002, Ryerson et al. 2003).

## EVENT

The program EVENT runs a superposed epoch analysis that overlays an event year (such as the occurrence of a fire or insect outbreak) every time it occurs in the chronology to examine

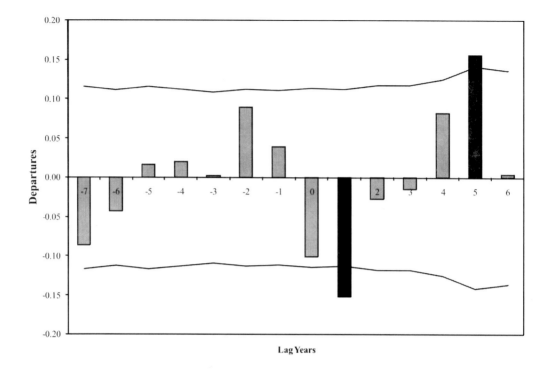

**Figure 6.30** A superposed epoch analysis showing the growth departure in pin oak (*Quercus palustris*) ring growth associated with periodical cicada emergences. Year 0 is the overlay of four emergence events back through time (every 17 years) and the analysis shows growth before and after the emergence, with the horizontal lines indicating 95% confidence intervals. This analysis shows a decrease in tree growth the year after emergence, presumably from damage to these trees from oviposition scarring. A significant increase in growth occurs five years after emergence, which could be related to nutrient cycling from the decay of dead cicadas at the base of the trees. (J. Speer, unpublished data)

previous and subsequent years of some variable such as climate or tree growth (Holmes and Swetnam 1994b). The inputs for the program are either a time series of the comparison variable, such as a climate variable like the Palmer drought severity index (PDSI), to see the effect of climate on the event, or a tree-ring chronology to see the effect of the event on tree growth combined with a list of event dates. An event window in time is identified by the user to look at a number of years prior and subsequent to the event. Each event year is taken as year 0 for that event, and then the lag years are taken from the chronology and averaged for all of the events. A bootstrap technique is then employed that uses a large number of random simulations (default of 1000) with randomly selected event years to produce confidence intervals to determine if any lag year has a significant response or correlation to the event. This analysis enables the researcher to determine if climate is forcing fire or insect outbreaks and can also be used to examine the effect of known repeated insect outbreak emergences (such as periodical cicadas, *Magicicada* spp.) on tree growth (fig. 6.30).

## Conclusion

Most of these programs and statistics are the basic tools of dendrochronologists. Other programs and statistics are used by researchers in the various subdisciplines, but they are more specialized and will either be described in subsequent chapters on the various applications of dendrochronology or in the references cited in each chapter. Each of the following chapters will expand on a different subdiscipline and provide some of the specific methods that are involved in each application, along with citations of many of the main works in that subdiscipline.

# 7
# Dendroarchaeology

Dendrochronology has gained recognition among archaeologists as an accurate tool for chronological control. Tree rings have been used to date the construction of archaeological structures (Douglass 1929, Haury 1962, Dean 1978, Dean et al. 1985, Billamboz 1992, Cufar 2007), to date scars from Native American use of the inner bark of pine trees (Kaye and Swetnam 1999), and to verify the dating of historical works of art (Lavier and Lambert 1996, Jansma et al. 2004, Cufar 2007), such as the panels in paintings (Bauch and Eckstein 1970, Eckstein et al. 1986) or the wood in violins (Grissino-Mayer et al. 2002). Tree rings also can be used to **dendro-provenance** archaeological or historical wood (Eckstein and Wrobel 2007) using wood anatomy and correlation to regional master chronologies to determine the origin of and trade routes for wood that has been incorporated into artifacts.

The first contribution of dendrochronology to archaeology was made by A. E. Douglass, who determined the exact occupation dates of 45 archaeological sites in the southwestern United States (fig. 7.1; Douglass 1929, Haury 1962, Nash 1999). This work started in 1914, when Clark Wissler (fig. 7.2), curator of anthropology with the American Museum of Natural History, suggested that Douglass use tree rings to date the Native American structures in the American Southwest. Douglass began to examine samples that were submitted from archaeological sites in New Mexico. In 1921 Neil Judd of the U.S. National Museum (fig. 7.3) approached Douglass about continuing his dating efforts in the Southwest and suggested applying for funds from the National Geographic Society, which provided funds for Douglass' research from 1923 to 1930.

Douglass' efforts to build a long chronology in the southwestern United States to date the archaeological ruins and to build a climate chronology for himself is a classic story in dendrochronology and also demonstrates many of the basic principles of the field. The foundation for Douglass' chronology came from living trees that he sampled throughout the Flagstaff and Prescott areas. Funding from the National Geographic Society for the first two beam expeditions in 1923 and 1928 resulted in a 700-year modern chronology that was anchored in time by living trees with known sampling dates and extended further back in time with archaeological wood that had been submitted by Clark Wissler, Neil Judd, and Earl Morris (fig. 7.4). Samples from the beam expeditions and from previous work enabled Douglass to build a 585-year floating chronology that provided relative dates for several of the archaeological ruins in the southwestern United States but that did not date against the modern chronology.

Douglass acquired funding from the National Geographic Society to conduct a third beam expedition in 1929 to search for wood from archaeological sites that would bridge the gap between the modern and floating chronologies. This expedition was led by Lyndon Hargrave (fig. 7.5) and Emil Haury (fig. 7.6), with intermittent visits by Douglass himself.

**Figure 7.1**  A. E. Douglass (1867–1962) coring a ponderosa pine in the Forestdale Valley in Arizona in 1928. Douglass' first major project was to date 45 archaeological ruins in the southwestern United States. (Laboratory of Tree-Ring Research, University of Arizona; from Webb 1983, Nash 1999)

On June 22, 1929, Hargrave and Haury were leading an expedition at Whipple Ruin in Show Low, Arizona. With the help of the Whipple family, they excavated a beam that was labeled HH-39 (fig. 7.7). That same day, Douglass visited the ruin and spent the evening examining the sample in the local hotel. After his analysis, he was able to announce that sample HH-39 bridged the gap between his modern chronology and his floating chronology. In truth, there was no gap at all, but the overlap was so small that it had not been noticed. HH-39 bridged the gap with enough rings covering the chronologies on either end that it made Douglass

**Figure 7.2** Clark Wissler (1870–1947) (left) and W. Sidney Stallings (1910–1989) (right) with specimens from Pueblo Bonito and Aztec Ruins in 1932. Wissler attended a Carnegie lecture by Douglass in 1914 and realized the value of tree-ring dating for obtaining dates on archaeological wood in the southwestern United States. He was the first to send Douglass archaeological samples to date. (Negative number 280306, by Clyde Fisher, Department of Library Services, American Museum of Natural History, reprinted in Nash 1999)

confident of the date of the floating chronology (Haury 1962, Nash 1999). The work of Douglass, Haury, and the beam expeditions resulted in the creation of a 1200-year-long chronology that extended back to 700 (Douglass 1929, Nash 1999) and revolutionized southwestern archaeology by anchoring cultural traditions in time with great accuracy long before the advent of radiocarbon and other dating techniques.

## Archaeological Methods

Many of the methods used in dendroarchaeology are similar to those employed in basic dendrochronology, such as crossdating, sample preparation, and standardization. Methods such as site selection cannot be employed, because the site is determined by the location of the archaeological dwelling, and the original locations of the trees were chosen by the residents of the dwelling. Dendroarchaeology also has some unique field methods of its own.

### Sample Collection

Samples are often taken from structural beams in houses or wood that is in place and has been in position and drying for hundreds of years. To reduce the damage to the original structure and to be able to get a sample from dry wood, a special archaeological borer is used (fig. 7.8). A drill guide can be used to hold the drill bit steady as the researcher begins to core the beam. This drill guide is a plastic or metal plate with a hole in the center of it, just larger than the diameter of the drill bit. It is affixed to the beam with two short nails and is removed once

**Figure 7.3** Neil Merton Judd (1887–1976), who was enthusiastic about dendrochronological dating of dwellings and sent Douglass many samples. He also suggested that Douglass pursue funding from the National Geographic Society for his work in developing a long chronology in the Southwest, which began three major beam expeditions to complete the long master chronology for this region. This photograph was taken at Alkali Ridge, Utah, in 1908. (Photo from the Peabody Museum, Harvard University, PMAE 2004.24.33345)

the core is taken. The archaeological borer is driven by an electric drill and uses a specially made extralong hole-saw to cut the wood away from around a 10- to 12-mm-diameter core. The core is then removed from the hole with a bent wire that is inserted down the side of the hole and twisted to break the core off at the center of the beam. The most difficult part of this type of coring is that the dust and wood chips from drilling can clog the borer. To remove this debris from the drill hole, the drill bit can be frequently run in and out of the hole or the core can be taken up into the beam so that the dust falls out with gravity. However, the best surface of the beam is seldom in a convenient coring location. The dust and wood chips can also be removed by spraying a stream of air into the cut from a can of compressed air.

The coring hole is often plugged with a cork to obscure the fact that core samples have been removed and to keep insects from making the core hole a home (fig. 7.9). Plugging the hole in archaeological samples differs from leaving the bore hole open in live samples because the live tree has mechanisms to defend itself, while the dead archaeological sample

**Figure 7.4** Earl Halstead Morris (1889–1957) with a charred beam at Broken Flute Cave, Arizona, in 1931. (From the American Museum of Natural History)

**Figure 7.5** Lyndon Lane Hargrave (1896–1978) examining a conifer cross section. Note the end of the beam cut by a stone axe to the right of the cross section that Hargrave is examining. (Courtesy of the Museum of Northern Arizona Photo Archives, MS-122-73)

does not. The sample ID can then be written on the cork so that any dendroarchaeologist can refer back to a sample that was previously removed.

Archaeologists must collect the outer surface of a beam to be able to get the cutting date of a tree. That is the most important date for a dendroarchaeologist. This outer surface can be

**Figure 7.6** Emil W. Haury (1904–1992) examining a buried beam at Pinedale Ruin, Arizona, during the Third Beam Expedition in 1929. (Photo from the Laboratory of Tree-Ring Research, Arizona, reprinted in Nash 1999)

*Beam HH-39, the specimen which "closed the gap" in 1929. A workman is shown securing the charcoal fragment for removal and analysis.* By Neil M. Judd © National Geographic Society

**Figure 7.7** Farmer Whipple removing sample HH-39 from an archaeological site in Show Low, Arizona. This is the famous sample that bridged the gap between Douglass' modern chronology and his floating chronology, allowing Douglass to provide absolute dates to the archaeological ruins in the Southwest. (Courtesy of the Laboratory of Tree-Ring Research, University of Arizona, reprinted in Nash 1999)

**Figure 7.8** A drill with an archaeological borer can be used to cut a 12-mm core from dry wood. This borer uses a hollow bit that cuts away the wood around the core as the bit is drilled into the beam. A starter plate can be used to hold the bit in place while the core is taken. A long piece of metal is inserted along the side of the core, and then twisted to break the core off on the inside of the beam. This tool is being demonstrated by Dr. Darin Rubino. (Photo provided by Darin Rubino)

identified by bark, a smooth outer surface that may gain a patina with age, or by bark beetle galleries on the outer surface of the stem. Bark beetles feed in the cambium layer while the tree is still alive and leave a small indentation in the xylem of the tree. Other wood-boring insects, however, leave galleries in the xylem, which should not be mistaken for an indication of the outer wood surface.

Cross sections can also be obtained from wooden beams and artifacts. This process is more destructive, but it provides a larger amount of wood for analysis when searching for micro or locally absent rings. Cross sections also give the researcher a greater chance to find more rings toward the outside of the tree, and thus get closer to a cutting date. One test for a cutting date on a tree sample is the continuity of the outer ring around the circumference of the section. A full section can provide this data, whereas a core cannot. Collecting a cross

**Figure 7.9** Although smaller than primary beams, window lintels can also be used for dendro-chronological dating of structures as long as the cores have enough rings from bark to pith of the tree. The core holes in archaeological samples are often plugged with cork to protect the beams from insect invasion into these spaces and also for aesthetic reasons (note the cork plug on the right side of the front-most lintel beam). (Photo by the author)

section from the end of a beam in a door frame or window frame can also reduce the visibility of sampling. The amount of wood available and the integrity of the artifact may constrain how much wood one is allowed to sample.

In the southwestern United States, the Pueblo cultures used large primary beams and smaller crossing secondary beams to support multiple stories in their structures (figs. 7.10 and 7.11). These structures have provided extensive samples for the development of local chronologies from which cutting dates have been determined. Archaeological samples such

**Figure 7.10** Native Americans in the southwestern United States constructed complex above ground dwellings and incorporated large beams to support multiple stories. The major beams (in the wall on the left) making up the support for the floor are called primary beams and the smaller poles (in the wall on the right) making up the floor are called secondary beams. (Photo by the author)

as cross sections and cores taken from these beams can be surfaced with sandpaper using the methods discussed in chapter 5.

Charcoal can also be used to date archaeological structures (fig. 7.12). Once the wood is carbonized, it is relatively inert and can last on a site for hundreds or even thousands of years without any biological decay. The cell structure is preserved in carbon, but it is extremely fragile, and may be mechanically broken down over time. The surface of carbonized wood cannot be prepared in the same way as other dendrochronological samples; instead of sanding, the wood must be snapped to produce a freshly broken surface along the cross-sectional view or can be cut with a very sharp blade. A freshly broken surface is perfect for dating because all of the wood structure is visible in reflected light. Snapping carbonized wood is a delicate procedure and takes some practice. The dendrochronologist is also effectively breaking an archaeological artifact or ecofact (a natural object found at an archaeological site) in this type of sample preparation, and therefore should proceed conservatively.

Dean (1978) developed a key to inside and outside dates that are identified in archaeological samples (table 7.1). This key can really be used on any tree-ring sample and helps researchers determine the quality of the dates. This nomenclature can be used for any application of dendrochronology where the inside or outside date of the sample is important.

**Figure 7.11** Cross sections from the main support beams can be sampled to collect a complete series of years. Cutting dates can be obtained by crossdating the ring series of these dead trees against a master chronology of the area to assign exact felling dates, demonstrating when the trees were cut for incorporation into the architecture. (Photo by the author)

## Chronologies Used in Dendroarchaeology

Long-term tree-ring series have been constructed that have application for archaeological regions worldwide (Cufar 2007). Excellent preservation of wooden beams in arid environments has made dendrochronology prominent in archaeology in the American southwest. This preservation has enabled the creation of pine (*Pinus* spp.), fir (*Abies* spp.), spruce (*Picea* spp.), Douglas-fir (*Pseudotsuga menziesii*), and juniper (*Juniperus* spp.) chronologies that extend as far back as 2300 years (Kuniholm 2001). The bristlecone pine (*Pinus longaeva*) chronology is more than 8700 years long (Ferguson et al. 1985) and provides important dates for volcanic events (LaMarche and Hirschboeck 1984) and climate reconstruction (LaMarche 1974); it also has been used in the calibration of the radiocarbon curve (Becker 1991, Friedrich et al. 2004). Long oak chronologies extending back 11,000 years have been developed in Ireland and Germany, providing the master chronologies needed for obtaining construction dates on structures throughout the region (Pilcher et al. 1984, Becker 1993, Baillie 1995, Jansma 1996, Cufar 2007). The eastern Mediterranean chronology has wood that goes back 9000 years but has a number of gaps left to be filled (Kuniholm 2003). These chronologies have been developed from modern specimens, samples taken from consecutively deeper layers of oaks in bogs, and from archaeological structures themselves. Many other long-term

**Figure 7.12** Charcoal samples can also be used for archaeological dating. Because the charcoal is inert, it is well preserved in the soil so that the wood does not decay through time. Charcoal is very fragile, and care must be taken when collecting these samples. Unlike green wood or old beams, charcoal samples should not be sanded. These samples can be broken to expose a clean surface of the cross-sectional view. (From Stokes and Smiley 1968)

chronologies have been developed around the world that might be used as master chronologies for archaeological dating (table 7.2).

## Applications of Dendrochronology to Archaeology

Dean (1997) categorized the use of dendrochronological evidence in archaeology under three separate applications: chronological control, behavioral information, and environmental information. Chronological control has been the standard use of dendrochronology in archaeology, although in Bannister's (1963) article summarizing the state of dendroarchaeology, the

**Table 7.1**    Symbols used to mark archaeological samples. Dendroarchaeologists working on wood use a series of codes to demonstrate the quality of the outside dates. The presence of beetle galleries, patina, smoothness of the outer surface, and presence of a complete ring around the circumference of the section can all indicate whether an accurate death date can be determined for the tree.

| Symbols used | |
| --- | --- |
| **With the inside date** | |
| Year | No pith ring is present. |
| p | Pith ring is present. |
| fp | The curvature of the inside ring indicates that it is far from the pith. |
| ± p | Pith ring is present, but because of the difficult nature of the ring series near the center of the specimen, an exact date cannot be assigned to it. The date is obtained by counting back from the earliest dated ring. |
| **With the outside date** | |
| B | Bark is present. |
| G | Beetle galleries are present on the surface of the specimen. |
| L | A characteristic surface patina and smoothness, which develops on beams stripped of bark, is present. |
| c | The outermost ring is continuous around the full circumference of the specimen. |
| r | Less than a full section is present, but the outermost ring is continuous around the available circumference. |
| v | A subjective assessment that, although there is no direct evidence of the true outside of the specimen, the date is within a very few years of being a cutting date. |
| vv | There is no way of estimating how far the last ring is from the true outside. |
| + | One or more rings may be missing from the end of the ring series, whose presence or absence cannot be determined because the specimen does not extend far enough to provide an adequate check. |
| ++ | A ring count is necessary because, beyond a certain point, the specimen could not be dated. |

*Source*: From Nash (1997, 1999)

*Note*: The symbols B, G, L, c, and r indicate cutting dates in order of decreasing confidence. The + and ++ symbols are mutually exclusive but may be used in combination with all other symbols.

useful chronologies were confined to Western Europe, Russia, and the Southwest and Great Plains in the United States. Since that time, the application of dendrochronology has become more popular around the globe, making master chronologies available in many more regions than previously realized. Dendrochronological dates are useful in archaeology because they are accurate to the year without any error. Because of this accuracy, tree rings have been used to calibrate the radiocarbon curve and have, on occasion, upset previously determined archaeological chronologies (Baillie 1995). Dean (1997) noted that tree-ring dating of artifacts provides a suite of behavioral information ". . . including treatment of trees as natural resources, use of wood as raw material, seasonal timing of tree felling, sources of wood, tools and techniques

**Table 7.2**  Long-term chronologies from around the world. The length indicates how far back in time these chronologies extend. There are gaps in some of these chronologies, and some of the archaeological chronologies do not extend to the present.

| Species | Location | Inside Date | Length (years) | Reference |
|---|---|---|---|---|
| Combined *Pinus* and *Quercus* | Germany | 10,461 BC | 12,460 | Friedrich et al. (2004) |
| *Pinus* sp. | Germany | 9494 BC | 11,370 | Becker (1993) |
| *Quercus petraea, Quercus robur* | Germany | 8021 BC | 10,076 | Becker (1993) |
| *Juniperus* sp. | eastern Mediterranean | 7020 BC | 9000 | Kuniholm (2003) |
| *Pinus longaeva* | White Mountains, California | 6716 BC | 8700 | Ferguson et al. (1985) |
| *Quercus petraea, Quercus robur* | Ireland | 5218 BC | 7272 | Pilcher et al. (1984) |
| Various species | Switzerland | 4086 BC | 6086 | Egger et al. (1985) |
| *Quercus petraea, Quercus robur* | France | 3659 BC | 5659 | Girardclos et al. (1996), Lambert et al. (1996) |
| *Quercus* sp. | Netherlands (floating chronology) | 2258 BC | 1100 | Jansma (1996) |
| *Fitzroya cuppressoides* | Chile | 1634 BC | 3622 | Lara and Villalba (1993) |
| *Sabina przewalskii* | China | 1580 BC | 3585 | Shao et al. (2007) |
| *Sequoiadendron giganteum* | California, United States | 1229 BC | 3220 | Brown et al. (1992) |
| *Pinus aristata* | Arizona, United States | 662 BC | 2262 | Salzer (2000) |
| *Quercus petraea, Quercus robur* | Poland | 474 BC | 2474 | Krapiec (1996) |
| *Pinus* sp., *Pseudotsuga* sp. | southwestern United States | 322 BC | 2327 | Dean (1997) |
| *Taxodium distichum* | southeastern United States | AD 372 | 1600 | Stahle et al. (1988) |
| *Pinus sylvestris* | Fennoscandia | AD 443 | 1555 | Briffa et al. (1990) |
| *Lagarostrobos franklinii* | Tasmania | AD 900 | 1210 | Cook et al. (1992) |
| *Larix sibirica* | polar Urals | AD 961 | 1008 | Graybill and Shiyatov (1992) |

of tree felling and wood modification, differential use of species, use of dead wood, reuse of timbers salvaged from older structures, stockpiling, structure remodeling and repair." Also, the expansion of new applications of dendrochronology has produced environmental records of climate and possible resource availability that can be used in archaeological interpretation (Speer and Hansen-Speer 2007). Dendroecological records are becoming more available around the world and are not dependent upon preservation conditions in archaeological sites.

**Figure 7.13** A log cabin in the southern Appalachian Mountains. Log cabins from the eastern United States are a great resource for old chronologies, and a dendroarchaeologist can provide construction dates for these dwellings. (Photo by the author)

The prevalence of dendroecological studies can extend the benefit of dendrochronology to archaeologists who do not have preserved wood on their particular sites.

## Construction Dates

Construction dates are the most common application of dendrochronology to archaeology (Bannister and Robinson 1975, Billamboz 1992). This is the information that Douglass (1929) provided for the archaeological ruins throughout the southwestern United States. Additional work has been done since that time, providing initial construction dates as well as expansion and repair dates, enabling the archaeologist to interpret human behavior and habitation periods.

Archaeological dates from the southeastern United States are becoming more common as cabins and other historical structures from the settlement of North America are dated (figs. 7.13 and 7.14). Stahle (1979) successfully dated 24 cabins from Arkansas that had cutting dates that ranged from 1825 to 1911. This work helped to extend the living chronologies for yellow pine (*Pinus* spp.), eastern red cedar (*Juniperus virginiana*), white oak (*Quercus* spp.), and bald cypress (*Taxodium distichum*) further back in time, providing a resource for future

**Figure 7.14** Cross section of a beam from a log cabin. Many pioneer log cabins have very old wood incorporated in their structures. Some of these beams can prove problematic in determining accurate outside dates because the outer rings were often removed as the timbers were shaped for construction. Care must be taken to sample through an area that has complete outer rings, as observed in the cross section. (Photo by the author)

dating attempts. Bonzani et al. (1991) were able to use wooden planks from a lock system on the Main Line Canal in Pittsburg, Pennsylvania, to extend a white pine (*Pinus* spp.) chronology back to 1658. Dendrochronology provides the ability to verify or reject previously held beliefs for construction dates of historical homes. Bortolot et al. (2001) dated a cabin that was thought to have been constructed in 1814 but was actually constructed in 1876. It has often been the case that these homes have been built later than previously thought.

The wood in historical structures throughout Europe is an important resource that has been extensively used to obtain dates of construction and to develop long chronologies (Eckstein 1972, Becker and Delmore 1978, Becker 1979, Baillie 1982, Laxton and Litton 1988, Billamboz 1992). Extensive archaeological collections now enable broad-scale analysis of towns in Europe and allow researchers to compare construction dates to the earliest historical documentation of the towns. Westphal (2003) used 5002 beam samples from 87 towns that were constructed between 800 and 1300 between the Elbe and Lower Oder Rivers in Germany. On average, the towns were constructed 40 years prior to any written comment of them and 50–60 years prior to them being called towns. In some cases, 250 years passed before there was any written mention of the town. Work in Finland has dated wooden causeways that both provide behavioral information on past cultures and a large quantity of wood for extending chronologies (Zetterberg 1990).

## Dating Artifacts

Lavier and Lambert (1996) reported on research conducted at the Laboratoire de Chrono-Ecologie in France, where they frequently date wood from paintings, furniture, sculptures, and covers of books. They take this work further by examining where the wood came from, how the artwork was made, how wood was chosen, and the time between felling trees for the artwork and when the work was completed. All of this work demonstrates some of the unique contributions that dendrochronology and wood anatomy can make to archaeological research, specifically dealing with the behavioral information to which Dean (1997) referred.

Wooden panels were used in the Netherlands and England as the medium for paintings of the 14th through 16th centuries (Fletcher 1976, 1977, Eckstein et al. 1986). These panels can be dated to determine when the paintings were actually completed and to verify their authenticity. Also, if the date of the painting is known from historical records, dendrochronological dates can be used to determine behavioral aspects of how the wooden panels were processed. Exact dating on wooden panels is hampered by the practice of cutting away the outer surface of the wood, possibly in an attempt to remove damage by wood boring insects (Baillie 1982).

Dating musical instruments using dendrochronology is also possible if there are enough rings in the instrument and the proper master chronology can be found for comparison (fig. 7.15). Wood from exotic locations is often used in the construction of artifacts. This foreign wood makes finding the proper master chronology a challenge in dating art and artifacts. Besides dating the Messiah violin of Stradivari (Grissino-Mayer et al. 2004) as related in chapter 1, Grissino-Mayer et al. (2005) dated the Karr-Koussevitzky double bass (fig. 7.16). With this analysis they found that the instrument had 317 rings on its face plate (the most rings ever recovered from a musical instrument) but the last rings grew in 1761, demonstrating that the instrument was not made in 1611 by the Amati Brothers as was originally thought.

## Climate Reconstructions

Archaeologists have made good use of dendroclimatic reconstructions of temperature and precipitation to explain environmental resource limitations and subsequent migration

**Figure 7.15** Rings on the face of a cello. Tree rings are clearly evident on the face plates of musical instruments and can be crossdated against master chronologies from the region where the wood for the instrument was harvested. (Photo from Topham and McCormick 1997)

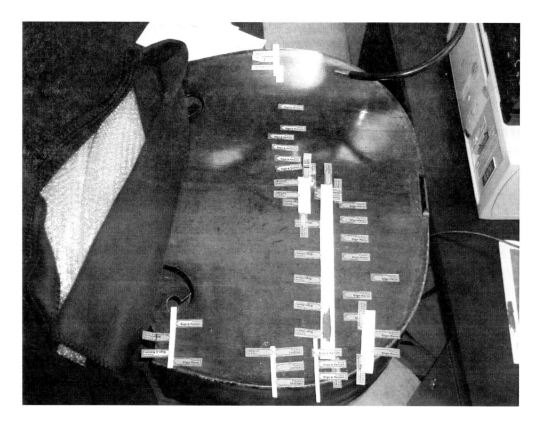

**Figure 7.16** The Karr-Koussevitzky double bass marked up for measurement. (From Grissino-Mayer et al. 2005)

patterns (Dean et al. 1985, Grissino-Mayer 1995, Ahlstrom et al. 1995, Kaye and Swetnam 1999, van West and Dean 2000) and have used streamflow reconstructions to provide paleoenvironmental information for an area (Nials et al. 1989). Stahle et al. (1998a) reconstructed the last 800 years of climate variability from bald cypress in the southeastern United States. This chronology helped to elucidate the climate during the establishment of the Roanoke and Jamestown colonies along the east coast of the United States. The Roanoke colony was established during the most extreme drought recorded in the 800-year chronology, and the Jamestown colony was established during one of the driest 7-year stretches during that same time period. Such climatic data can assist interpretation of the archaeological record in the context of the past climate of the area.

## Ecological Reconstructions and Anthropogenic Ecology

Dendroecology is a recent branch in the field of dendrochronology (starting in the 1970s) that uses tree rings to reconstruct environmental records other than climate (Fritts 1971, Fritts and Swetnam 1989). This field has not been used to its full capacity in archaeological research. Dendroecology can be used to develop records of fire history (Swetnam and

Baisan 1996), insect outbreaks (Swetnam et al. 1985, Speer et al. 2001), and acorn production (Speer 2001). Researchers are developing long records of these variables that can be useful to archaeologists interested in anthropogenic ecology and resource availability (Speer and Hansen-Speer 2007).

Billamboz (1992) used the cutting dates for timbers in two lake dwellings in southwestern Germany and found some distinct periods of forest clearance in 1767–1730 BC and 1511–1480 BC. These clearance events were associated with settlement phases and were documented by the gradual shift to smaller timbers and a change in the tree species that were used for structural timbers over time. This use of archaeological timbers to understand silvicultural practices of past cultures has been termed **dendrotypology** and demonstrates another set of information that can be obtained from archaeological wood (Billamboz 1992, 2003).

*Fire in the Southwestern United States.* Native American use of fire is an issue that has been debated for the last half century (Pyne 1982, Swetnam 1990, Agee 1993, Vale 2002, Wagner 2003). Native Americans may have used fire to aid in hunting, to improve grasslands, and in warfare (Stewart 1936, Shinn 1978, Pyne 1982). Lightning ignition of fires is also very common in the southwestern United States and produces a natural background of fire occurrence (Swetnam and Baisan 1996). Swetnam and Baisan (1996) argued that ignition sources are not the limiting factor, but that the appropriate fuel and climatic conditions control the occurrence of fire.

Work by Wilkinson (1997) revealed some effect from Native American burning as demonstrated by an increase in fire occurrence during times of Spanish pressure on Native American encampments. In the Sacramento Mountains of New Mexico, she found that broad-scale disturbance from anthropogenic sources did not occur until the introduction of grazing in the 1880s and fire suppression in the early 1900s. This local effect on the fire regime was identified by comparing fire occurrence over a broad area and in a specific forest type to individual site's histories. Such an approach makes the broad-scale pattern the norm to which irregular fire histories can be compared and described.

*Fire in the Eastern United States.* In the eastern United States, the fire issue is not so clear. Many people believe that fire is a natural part of the oak woodlands (Abrams 1985, 1992, 2000). Recent work, however, has suggested that much of past fire occurrence is from the direct effect of Native American and Euro-American burning (Jenkins et al. 1997, Sutherland 1997, Guyette et al. 2002). In the eastern United States, few fire histories extend much before 1800. Most of fire history chronologies in the eastern United States are from oak trees, but the full suite of hardwood trees have not been examined for fire history. More regional work, use of other hardwood tree species, and a longer time perspective may help to answer questions of Native American burning in the eastern United States.

*Culturally Modified Trees.* Direct evidence of Native American use of trees can be found on culturally modified trees (fig. 7.17; Swetnam 1984, Mobley and Eldridge 1992, Wilkinson 1997, Towner et al. 1999, Lewis 2002). These trees provide the year and season of Native American occupation and can be related to social forcing factors of the time. Culturally modified trees are found throughout the ponderosa pine zone from Mexico into Canada. Native Americans

**Figure 7.17** Peel bark trees or culturally modified trees can provide a date when Native Americans were active on a site. These trees have axe marks in the wood at about knee height and again above head height. The bark was then peeled from the tree and most likely used as a starvation food source. In Canada these are considered artifacts and are protected by law whether they are living or dead trees in the forest. (Photo by the author)

were thought to peel the bark from these trees in the spring and eat the inner cambium as a starvation food. Peeled trees generally occur in clusters of about 20 individuals (personal observation), and the scar left on the trees can easily be dated to the year of damage and sometimes the season.

Mobley and Eldridge (1992) conducted a systematic examination of culturally modified trees, reporting on 967 peeled trees in the Pacific Northwest, with the oldest scarred tree dating back to 1467 (error approximately ± 10 years, based on a ring count). While this work demonstrates the use of tree rings to determine the use of culturally modified trees, it would be much improved if crossdating was used so that the exact year of Native American activity could be determined.

Slash pine (*Pinus elliotii*) and longleaf pine (*Pinus palustris*) have been modified in the southeastern United States by Euro-Americans since the mid-1700s for the production of turpentine as part of the naval stores industry (Grissino-Mayer et al. 2001). Workers cut through the bark and into the wood of these pines, a process called chipping, and collect the sap that came from these wounds. Grissino-Mayer et al. (2001) found a concentration of chipping events in two southern Georgia sites in 1925, 1947–1948, and 1954–1956. These studies show that any preserved evidence of tree modification can be used to interpret the timing of past human behavior. Culturally modified trees are now protected as archaeological artifacts in Canada, and many management agencies in the United States are also starting to protect these trees.

*Insect Outbreaks.* Speer et al. (2001) developed a record of pandora moth outbreaks that extends back 622 years in south-central Oregon (see fig. 9.11). Pandora moth is a phytophagous (leaf-eating) insect that defoliates ponderosa pine, Jeffrey pine, and lodgepole pine in the western United States. The Klamath and Piute Indians used the pandora moth larvae and pupae as a traditional food source when it was available, indicating they had knowledge of its life cycle (Blake and Wagner 1987). This led early forest entomologists to speculate that pandora moth outbreaks recurred often in the past (Aldrich 1912, 1921, Patterson 1929). These types of reconstructions can be used to demonstrate resource availability for native peoples.

*Mast.* Recent work in dendroecology has produced a new technique for developing mast (massive fruit production in trees) reconstructions from tree rings (fig. 7.18; Speer 2001). Native American groups have been present in the southern Appalachians for at least the past 12,000 years (Yarnell 1998) and have been using acorns as a food source throughout much of their history in North America. One use of a mast reconstruction is determining the dependability of mast as a human food source in prehistoric times and as a livestock feed in historic times.

*Dendrogeomorphology in Archaeology.* Geological applications of dendrochronology can also be used to inform archaeological interpretation. One of the better examples of this is the reconstruction of the eruption of the volcano that produced Sunset Crater in 1064 in northern Arizona by dating a growth reduction due to projectile damage from the eruption (Smiley 1958). On a broader scale, researchers have identified short-term global or regional temperature changes that were caused by major volcanic eruptions (LaMarche and

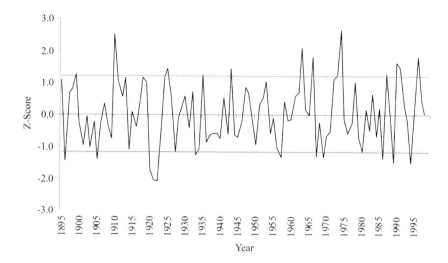

**Figure 7.18** White oak (*Quercus alba*) regional mast reconstruction from the southern Appalachian region. The reconstruction is based on 165 white oak trees from Tennessee, North Carolina, and northern Georgia. Mast years are shown as Z-scores, with numbers larger than 1.2 and less than −1.2 considered extremely good or poor mast years, respectively. (From Speer 2001)

Hirschboeck 1984, Baillie 1995). Tree rings can also be used to determine bounding dates on land surfaces and some archaeological earthworks, helping to determine the chronology of archaeological sites.

## Future of Dendroarchaeology

Dendroarchaeologists will continue to find new applications for the chronological control that dendrochronology provides. The use of dendrochronology to determine construction dates has long been used to great benefit in archaeology. I recommend that archaeologists look more to climatic and ecological reconstructions from the various subfields of dendrochronology to develop a richer data set for the interpretation of the archaeological record.

# 8
# Dendroclimatology

One of the first and most publicly debated applications in dendrochronology has been the ability to reconstruct climate from tree rings. Because trees respond to their surroundings, they are subject to climatic stresses such as variations in temperature, rainfall, soil moisture, cloudy days (number of days with clouds, which reduces photosynthesis), and wind stress. In fact, climate seems to be one of the main controlling factors of most tree-ring growth across all spatial and temporal scales. The basic steps in a climate reconstruction are relatively simple and are often normal procedures that are done even before ecological reconstructions. But the statistical analyses of tree-ring chronologies for dendroclimatic reconstructions have become increasingly sophisticated.

Dendroclimatologists are interested in past climate so that the variation and trend of modern climate can be put into perspective. The natural range of variation of the climate system can be reconstructed from examination of the past through tree rings (Morgan et al. 1994). From various types of climate reconstructions (based on ice cores, marine and lake sediments, and dendrochronology), we have documented the glacial–interglacial cycle (100,000 years), the shorter-term Holocene climate variation (past 10,000 years), and recent warming in the modern era (fig. 8.1). Mann et al. (1998) reconstructed climate variation from multiple proxies, including tree rings, for the past six centuries; the data showed an abrupt increase in temperature associated with the industrial revolution (fig. 8.1). This reconstruction has been questioned from many quarters, with the most constructive criticism stating that it does not take low-frequency climate variability into consideration as shown by lack of evidence for the Medieval Warm Period and the Little Ice Age (Moberg et al. 2005).

Climate phenomena, such as hurricanes, can be reconstructed from tree rings because of the specific signal recorded in ring width and in the isotopic chemistry of the rings. Climatic reconstruction, therefore, can be used to examine the proximal cause of ring width, such as changes in temperature or rainfall, or it can be used to examine broader scale patterns and phenomena that are recorded along with changes in temperature and rainfall. In the case of hurricanes, an isotopic signature can be identified in the fluctuations of wood chemistry through time due to hurricane water being depleted of $^{18}O$ relative to normal rainwater (Mora et al. 2006). Another powerful tool is use of tree-ring networks to examine climate variability on a broad spatial scale such that inferences can be drawn about long-term changes in synoptic climatology (the flow in the climate system including pressure differences; Hirschboeck et al. 1996).

Tree growth is one example of a proxy, or a natural phenomenon that indirectly records an event of interest, such as a hurricane or flood. Other examples of proxies that record climate are coral growth, ice deposition, sediment deposition, and cave dripstone. By studying the dynamics of a region with multiple proxies, we can better understand the vegetation

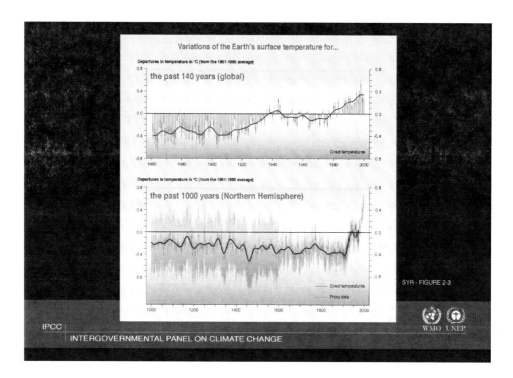

**Figure 8.1** Tree-ring climate reconstruction for the past 1000 years. The Mann et al. (1998) "hockey stick" graph (below), which was used by the Intergovernmental Panel on Climate Change, was built from long tree-ring chronologies from around the world. The solid black line is a running average to smooth the data. Many more recent papers have discussed improvements for this curve, because while tree rings are excellent at capturing short-frequency variability, they are not very good at capturing long-term variability.

response to changes in climate. For example, tree-ring reconstructions of climate can be examined alongside pollen reconstructions of vegetation change to see how ecological systems respond and interact with climate change (Friedrich et al. 2001). Given fine enough resolution in the proxy records, a long-term record of climate and vegetation change can inform us about the mechanisms involved in vegetation change and reveal possible feedback loops through microclimatic effects.

## Methods of Dendroclimatology

Climate reconstruction starts with a site-level analysis of a tree species' climate response. Standard dendrochronological methods are used, such as site selection, coring at breast height, crossdating, and measuring the samples (see chapters 2 and 5 for a full description). Trees are chosen from climate-sensitive sites (fig. 8.2), such as steep rocky slopes or northern treeline. A variety of tree ages can be used in climate reconstructions because trees may change in their climatic response with age. The oldest trees are chosen to obtain the longest

**Figure 8.2** Trees struggling to grow in harsh conditions, such as this lava flow in Oregon, tend to be the oldest individuals in the species and also can be good recorders of past climate (especially precipitation records). Preservation on these sites is also very good because of the lack of soil microbes, leading to the potential for very long chronologies. (Photo by Tom Swetnam)

chronologies, but older trees may have a weakened climate signal due to senescence (deterioration due to old age). Trees with obvious injuries or subdominant canopy position are avoided because of possible complication of the climate signal with other microenvironmental factors. The climate signal in the growth of very young trees may similarly be distorted by such factors.

Sample depth is always an important issue in dendrochronology, but it is of paramount importance in climate reconstruction. Sample depth is simply the number of samples that represent a phenomenon back through time. The ring-width measurements are corrected for an age-related growth trend (see standardization in chapter 2) and the resultant index values are averaged together to create a chronology with a stand-level signal that is analyzed for its climate response. The goal is to create a robust climate reconstruction that maintains a consistent climate signal whether sample depth is increased or the ring-width series are standardized in a different fashion. Because living trees are often used for climate reconstructions, at least 30 living trees (two cores per tree) can be sampled for a robust sample depth in the modern era. Not all of those trees, however, established at the same time, so they fall from the record at different times as it goes back into the past. When the chronology falls below 10 or 20 trees, growth variations of individual trees may overwhelm the common growth signal that conceptually represents the response to climate; a statistical side effect can be the increase in variance at the beginning of the chronology.

An important part of the **standardization** procedure in the processing of tree-ring measurements for dendroclimatology is the removal of nonclimatic trends from the ring widths. A sensible strategy in standardization is to retain as much variance as possible at the low frequencies or long wavelengths. Such variance represents the gradual fluctuations in growth over periods of decades and longer. A negative exponential or linear trend line can be used to remove the age-related growth trend from the time series. How well these lines fit the data should be examined on an individual core basis to ensure that the curve accurately represents the ring-width series. Chronologies can also be truncated after the irregular juvenile growth and the steep curve from an age-related growth trend have leveled out. Such truncation removes many years from the beginning of each tree, but it can sometimes simplify the standardization curve that is required to process a site. **Cubic smoothing splines** are used in many dendrochronological applications because they produce a flexible curve that fits the data fairly closely. Splines, however, should be used with caution and with full knowledge about the variance that is being removed. LaMarche (1974) argued that the use of raw ring widths can sometimes provide a more accurate climate reconstruction because real climatic trends in the data may be removed during the standardization process. He was working in a unique circumstance with bristlecone pine (*Pinus longaeva* and *Pinus aristata*) trees from above treeline. His chronologies were longer than 1000 years, so that he could omit the juvenile growth from the trees and still examine long-term climate changes.

The first step in a climate reconstruction (and most dendrochronological studies) is to examine the **climate response** of the chronology, which can be accomplished with a simple correlation matrix or a **response function analysis**. Climate variables such as monthly temperature, precipitation, and PDSI should be gathered for each research area and entered into a spreadsheet. Data from individual climate stations can be obtained from the Historical Climate Network, and climate division data can be obtained from the National Climate Data Center for the entire United States back to 1895. Another recently developed data set is the PRISM data set (see appendix E for Web address), which was developed at Oregon State University and takes data from individual climate stations and models the signal over the landscape based on a physiological model. This data set provides accurate climatological information for locations that have not been previously monitored. Other historical data have been used to calibrate dendroclimatic reconstructions, such as grape harvest data in France (Guiot et al. 2005).

Climate division data are often preferred to individual site data for many reasons. First, it may be difficult to find an individual climate station that is near to a sampling site and similar in microenvironmental condition. Second, most individual stations have some data gaps in their records, while the climate division data draws on many climate stations and has been corrected for changes in the location of individual stations and for these data gaps. A correlation matrix can be created in almost any statistical package, including Excel, to compare the master chronologies to every month of climate data. This analysis reveals which months of climate data are correlated with ring width. The significant months can then be aggregated into seasons that are appropriate for each tree species being examined. Such a posteriori determination of the effective climate window for a particular site and species enables researchers to document the climate response of the chronology rather than forcing a hypothetical climate window onto a species for a given location (Fritts 1976: 34).

**Simple linear regression** can be used to develop a model for reconstructing one climate variable (Duvick and Blasing 1981). With 100 years or more of climate data from the local climate division, a model can be built from half of the data (the calibration set) and verified using the other half (Fritts 1976). If the calibration and verification procedures meet the statistical requirements of the study, a significant climate reconstruction can be completed for the length of the chronology by repeating the calibration on the full length of overlap of climate and tree-ring data and substituting the long-term tree-ring data into the regression equation. Sometimes the model is extended to multiple linear regression by including more than one tree-ring series as predictor variables or by including tree-ring series that are lagged relative to the climate series (Meko et al. 1980). More sophisticated models can also be used to examine the response of trees to climate. Graumlich (1993) used response surfaces, Woodhouse (1999) used neural networks, and Meko and Baisan (2001) used binary classification trees to find the most accurate way to identify the climate signal in tree-ring chronologies.

Some research in climate reconstruction has used PCA to reduce the number of climate variables, produce orthogonal factors (completely independent variables), and create variables that represent similar climate measures (LaMarche and Fritts 1971, Mann et al. 1998). PCA plots a cloud of climate variables in as many dimensions as there are variables, and then creates a best-fit line through the data that represents most of the variance of all of the climate factors. This first line is called the first eigenvector. Then a second eigenvector is fit to the data so that it is orthogonal (or completely perpendicular and independent) to the first eigenvector. This process continues until all of the variance in the original data set is captured. PCA generally produces two to five eigenvectors that represent a large part of the variance in the original data set (often some 70 variables). In climatic reconstruction, PCA can be used to reduce the number of climate variables, the tree-ring variables, or both. Regression analysis can then be used to model the relationship between the eigenvectors of transformed climate data and transformed tree-ring variables. The process of combining PCA and regression analysis usually explains more variance in the tree-ring chronology than simple linear regression could with untransformed climate variables.

Cook et al. (1994) reviewed spatial regression methods using PCA in dendroclimatology. A novel approach using PCA on the tree-ring chronologies in a moving spatial window was developed by Cook et al. (1999) to combine a dense network of tree-ring sites and create a regular grid of PDSI reconstructions throughout the United States. This use of PCA, which will be discussed more in the next section, reduces chronologies to modes of tree-ring variation for geographic regions centered on gridpoints. PCA is a powerful tool for reducing a complex set of variables to the common signal and is likely to have more application in dendroclimatology in the future.

## Applications of Dendroclimatology

Tree response to climate from many sites in a region or across a continent can be used to map the climate variables that affect tree growth in different regions (Fritts 1976: 35). With a **network of chronologies**, spatial patterns of effective climate variables can be determined. Furthermore, with the time depth provided by dendrochronology, the spatial patterns can be studied to determine the size and distribution of climate events such as droughts through time. Brubaker (1980) conducted one of the earlier dendrochronological network analyses to examine climate response across the Pacific Northwest using PCA. She found that the first eigenvector responded to spring and summer rainfall, and the second to summer temperature and winter rainfall. This signal remained constant over her 400-year chronology.

LaMarche and Fritts (1971) started collecting a climate network of tree-ring chronologies to reconstruct broad-scale drought throughout the United States and Canada. A reconstruction of PDSI from the network established a long-term context for the Dust Bowl drought of the 1930s in western North America (Stockton and Meko 1975) and revealed a bidecadal drought rhythm with a weak statistical link to the Hale Sunspot Cycle (Mitchell et al. 1979). Expansion of the geographical coverage of tree-ring collections, especially in the eastern United States, resulted in a climatically screened network of chronologies whose statistical properties and drought signal were analyzed by Meko et al. (1993). This initial network was further developed by Cook et al. (1999), who examined tree response to PDSI in order to map drought reconstructions for the continental United States on a 2° latitude by 3° longitude grid for 1700 to 1978. Their landmark paper provided long-term drought reconstructions for the entire United States that were then used to examine the intensity of the Dust Bowl drought and other climatic phenomena in comparison to this long climate window. Stahle et al. (2000) used a similar network with a broader spatial coverage and expanded temporal depth to examine drought across western North America, including Mexico, and found a mega-drought in the 1600s that was a much more extreme event than the 1930s Dust Bowl. Cook et al. (2009) later enhanced the resolution of their grid to 0.5 degrees latitude by 0.5 degrees longitude to examine the effects of past megadroughts across North America and to compare them to IPCC predictions of moisture variability in the future.

Broad-scale tree-ring networks, such as those used in the PDSI reconstructions, can be more generally applied in **synoptic climatology**, the study of climate from the perspective of atmospheric circulation. Circulation patterns can be inferred from reconstructed patterns of precipitation, temperature, and pressure (see, for example, Fritts et al. 1971, Blasing and Fritts 1976, Fritts 1976, Fritts and Shao 1992, Hirschboeck et al. 1996, Barber et al. 2004, Girardin et al. 2006).

The compiling of **hemispheric climate reconstructions**, begun in the 1970s, brought to light standardization issues that arise when different species and age chronologies are compared across different regions. Researchers from around the globe standardize their tree-ring chronologies differently depending upon the expected signal in the chronology and the goal of the research. When many chronologies are combined for broad-scale analysis, the raw ring-width measurements have to be standardized with one technique across all sites, even though the sites are likely to be affected by different climatic forces. Briffa et al. (2001) reconstructed mean summer temperature from wood density of tree rings from 387 sites in the Northern Hemisphere for the past 600 years. They used a new technique called **age band decomposition** in which the tree-ring series are decomposed into predetermined age bands, averaged together, scaled for equal mean and variance, then recombined into a master series of relative growth changes. This technique may better preserve the low-frequency (multidecade to century) signal in long chronologies.

Dendrochronological records of global climate variability must contain a widely distributed network of climate reconstructions from around the world. Outside of North America and Europe, much explorative dendrochronological research was conducted by LaMarche et al.

(1979a, 1979b, 1979c, 1979d, 1979e) in the Southern Hemisphere in Australia, New Zealand, South Africa, Argentina, and Chile. Much more work was accomplished in South America as a dendrochronology laboratory was established in Argentina and local researchers undertook tree-ring investigations (Villalba et al. 1985, Roig et al. 1988, Villalba and Boninsegna 1989, Lara and Villalba 1993).

Natural climate variability in northern Africa and the eastern Mediterranean region is becoming of great interest as general circulation models are projecting severe drying in the region associated with increased greenhouse gases (Seager et al. 2007). Several recent tree-ring studies have been advancing dendroclimatology in the region and have developed a broad network of tree-ring chronologies (for example, Touchan et al. 2003, 2007).

Recent work in India has reconstructed the Indian monsoon back to 1835 using teak (*Tectona grandis*; Shah et al. 2007). Work in China is examining the climate response of natural forests that are stressed by the proximity of the Loess Plateau (Du et al. 2007), and a 680-year reconstruction has examined the strength of the Asian monsoon and the effect of the Little Ice Age on the Qinghai-Tibetan Plateau (Huang and Zhang 2007). Work in Siberia has continued to develop long chronologies from high latitudes that are useful in examining modern climate changes (Vaganov et al. 1996, Hantemirov et al. 2004). Cook et al. (1992, 2000) reconstructed warm season temperature for Tasmania from Huon pine (*Lagarostrobos franklinii*) back to 1600 BC. This reconstruction showed a weak signal representing the Medieval Warm Period in the 1100s and the Little Ice Age in the 1600s, suggesting that these events were stronger in the Northern Hemisphere than in the Southern. Their record also showed higher temperatures over the last 25-year period than any other time during their 1090-year reconstruction (Cook et al. 1992). Although this finding is not conclusive proof of global warming, it does support the theory. Climate reconstructions from New Zealand also show that tree growth since 1950 has been significantly higher than any prior period since 1500, when the oldest chronologies start (D'Arrigo et al. 1998).

Beyond simple reconstructions of temperature and precipitation, researchers are exploring correlations with other natural variables and strengthening our understanding of the connectivity of the global circulation system. The location of the Cook et al. (2000) reconstruction on the relatively small landmass of Tasmania enabled a **sea-surface temperature** reconstruction for the southern Indian Ocean between 30°S and 40°S. This **teleconnection** (that is, the interconnection of physical parameters over long distances, such as sea-level pressure in the Pacific Ocean affecting weather around the world) between marine and terrestrial systems can help us understand the climate system with its fully complex interactions. Work in West Africa in a variety of tree species has also revealed a relationship between tree growth and sea-surface temperature (Schöngart et al. 2006). Villalba et al. (1998b) examined the connection between tree growth in South America and **sea-level pressure** over the Pacific to explain long-term precipitation changes. These connections with the climate system are providing a better grasp of the complexity of broad-scale atmospheric circulation patterns and interconnectedness of the global system.

## Climate Indices

The **El Niño–Southern Oscillation** is a prominent example of teleconnections in our climate system that has raised popular as well as scientific awareness of broad-scale climatic processes. El Niño is a phenomenon first noted in the Peruvian fisheries in which the waters became warm around Christmastime and the fisheries failed. Later investigation discovered that this change was the same phenomena as the **Southern Oscillation index** (SOI), which is quantified as the variability in the pressure difference between the town of Darwin on the northern tip of Australia and the island of Tahiti. The scientific community first took note of El Niño–Southern Oscillation as a global phenomenon during the 1972–1973 event. The 1982–1983 event drove greater scientific interest in this phenomenon. Finally, the 1997–1998 event was strong enough and public media was active enough that El Niño became a household word.

The escalating interest in teleconnections has led scientists to look for other long-term oscillations in the climate system that may lead to climate prediction and a deeper understanding of the linked marine-terrestrial system. Stahle and Cleaveland (1993) used networks of chronologies from Mexico, Texas, and Oklahoma to reconstruct the SOI for the period from 1699 to 1971. They found that 41% of winter SOI was explained by tree-ring predictors and the reconstruction correlated significantly with an independent winter SOI measure. Stahle et al. (1998b) continued to examine the winter SOI effect on terrestrial chronologies from North America. They were able to explain 53% of the variance in the tree-ring chronologies for the period from 1706 to 1977. D'Arrigo and Jacoby (1991) examined millennial-length chronologies developed from archaeological wood samples from the northwestern corner of New Mexico. The American Southwest is a region that is strongly affected by El Niño, receiving drier conditions on either side of an event. Principal components from five of their six chronologies explained 30% of the variance of the SOI data for the period 1865–1970 (D'Arrigo and Jacoby 1991).

The **Pacific Decadal Oscillation** (PDO; Mantua et al. 1997, Gedalof et al. 2002, MacDonald and Case 2005), **North Atlantic Oscillation** (NAO; Barnston and Livezey 1987), and the **Atlantic Multidecadal Oscillation** (Gray et al. 2004) are three of the more important marine phenomena that affect climate in the Northern Hemisphere besides El Niño–Southern Oscillation. Warm phases of PDO occur when the eastern North Pacific is warm and the central North Pacific is cool; this temperature gradient switches during cool phases of PDO. Biondi et al. (2001) reconstructed PDO back to 1661 based on a network of chronologies of Jeffrey pine (*Pinus jeffreyi*) and big-cone Douglas-fir (*Pseudotsuga macrocarpa*) in a transect from northern Baja California to southern California. MacDonald and Case (2005) were able to develop a millennial-length record of PDO from limber pine in California that demonstrated that PDO had a strong 50- to 70-year period, but that it was not consistent through time. Over the past 1000 years, this signal was only evident for about half of the time.

On the eastern coast of North America, NAO is measured by the height of the 500-mb isobar, with a positive phase representing below-normal heights in the high latitudes of the North Atlantic and above-normal heights over the central North Atlantic. The phase of the NAO affects both the North Atlantic jet stream and the meridionality of the Rossby Waves (meanders in high-altitude winds associated with the polar-front jet stream; Hurrell 1995). The NAO has a 1.7- to 7.5-year periodicity that creates alternately cold or warm conditions in Europe associated with this pressure variation. D'Arrigo et al. (1993) demonstrated a tree-ring response to NAO from Scots pine (*Pinus sylvestris*) chronologies located in Scandinavia and successfully reconstructed sea-surface temperature for the North Atlantic back to 1713.

Gray et al. (2004) found that the Atlantic Multidecadal Oscillation, which is a 60- to 100-year variation in Atlantic sea-surface temperature, was a consistent pattern throughout their record extending back to 1567.

## Climatic Gradient Studies

Dendrochronological studies along gradients can be useful to examine climatic and environmental changes. Because ecotones are by definition transition zones, they are particularly sensitive to climate change and rapidly bear evidence of shifting vegetation responses. High-latitude studies are likely to show the first evidence of global warming because these locations are likely to show greater increases in temperature than the middle latitudes. Elevational gradients show the same vegetation changes as latitudinal gradients but over a much shorter spatial scale. Both ecotones and high latitude sites are being studied to see if predicted changes to temperature are occurring and to determine the vegetational response to these changes.

### Latitudinal Gradient

Jacoby et al. (1996) examined climate response of trees for a north–south transect through Alaska covering from 62°N to 72°N latitude. In the 300-year record of their northern chronologies, they found that recent decades exhibited a warming trend. Their southern chronologies and those located along the coast with a strong maritime influence did not show this warming trend. This evidence fits with the predictions of general circulation models and our understanding of the importance of gradient studies.

Jacoby and D'Arrigo (1999) reviewed four climate reconstructions from northern latitudes and high elevation (in Mongolia, Siberia, Alaska, and a general Northern Hemisphere reconstruction) and found that all of these reconstructions showed unusual and persistent warming since the 1800s. They also noted other evidence such as glacial retreat and that trees once limited by low temperatures were instead becoming limited by moisture stress. D'Arrigo and Jacoby (1993) found that trees growing at their northern limit showed an increase in growth since the mid-1800s, which is consistent with expectations of global warming. The authors successfully modeled the observed increase in tree growth with projected changes in climatic parameters such as temperature and precipitation with little residual signal. Because other climatic parameters explained these changes, they concluded that there was no direct affect from carbon dioxide fertilization.

### Treeline Studies

Trees growing at treeline are often limited by cold temperature and can be useful for long-term temperature reconstructions (for example, Esper et al. 2003b). Treeline studies are an alternate use of dendrochronology to reconstruct climate through its effect on establishment of trees at the cold-limited high-elevation extent of the species (Nicolussi et al. 2005), and treeline studies can be reveal broad-scale climate changes. Esper and Schweingruber (2004) reported on a recent broad-scale treeline advance throughout the northern Arctic

**Figure 8.3** Bristlecone pine trees in the White Mountains of California. For climate reconstructions, dendrochronologists go to high latitude or high elevation (as in this photo) to get tree-ring chronologies that are sensitive to temperature. The old age of these trees, combined with cross-dated samples of the subfossil wood on the ground, allow the reconstruction of long chronologies of temperature fluctuations extending back approximately 8000 years before present. (Photo by the author)

region, suggesting that this present trend is associated with the reported Northern Hemisphere warming. LaMarche and Mooney (1967) and LaMarche (1973) examined remnant bristlecone pine (*Pinus longaeva*; fig. 8.3) wood from above treeline and found that warmer conditions lasted from the beginning of their record at 5300 BC to 2200 BC and extended the treeline to higher elevations. Cooler and wetter conditions lasted from 1500 BC to 500 BC, and then a cool dry period dominated from AD 1100 to AD 1500, resulting in the lowering of treeline.

Treeline sites can also exhibit stressful conditions in which trees in tropical environments produce annual rings, even though excess moisture prevents annual ring formation at lower elevations in the tropics (Speer et al. 2004). In the Dominican Republic at 19.5°N latitude, heavy rain in the lowlands makes West Indian pine (*Pinus occidentalis*) trees produce three or four rings per year (Food and Agriculture Organization 1973, van der Burgt 1997). At the highest elevation on the island and along the margin of an area of loose rocks without much soil development, the trees are stressed enough by the lack of moisture that the January–March dry season forces them to systematically shut down, producing reliable annual rings (fig. 8.4).

**Figure 8.4** Old *Pinus occidentalis* growing on a high-elevation site in the Dominican Republic. Annual dating of tree rings in the tropics is possible on unique sites where the tree growth shuts down for some part of the year. This site is called Conuco del Diablo (Cornfield of the Devil) and is located on the flank of one of the highest peaks in the Dominican Republic. Trees stop growing in the dry season from January to March in part because the rocky earth prevents much soil development or water retention. These trees have been used to build a chronology for the region (see Speer et al. 2004).

## Dendrohydrology: Water Table Height and Flood Events

Water table changes, land subsidence, flood height and energy, and streamflow can all be reconstructed using tree-ring data. **Dendrohydrology** is the subfield of dendrochronology that uses tree rings to reconstruct these phenomena (Schweingruber 1996). Dendrohydrological records can be reconstructed through suppression or release events in trees associated with water table changes and land subsidence, scars and growth changes associated with flood events, establishment of trees on newly deposited surfaces (fig. 8.5), and changes in growth as a response to climatic phenomena that drive river discharge.

Stream behavior can be documented by a variety of effects on tree growth that include flood scarring, tree leaning from undercutting, and establishment of trees on new sediment surfaces (fig. 8.6; Gottesfeld and Gottesfeld 1990). For example, a flood history of the Potomac River in Washington, D.C., was determined using tree rings to date flood scars (Sigafoos 1964). The height of the scars can also be used to document the height of flood waters in the

**Figure 8.5** The age of a delta or any sedimentary deposit can be determined from trees growing on that sediment. In this photo, four different age surfaces are discernable based on the structure of the vegetation, with the youngest being the bare sediment in the delta, the second oldest is the low vegetation in the left of the image, the third oldest is just above that and inland from the road, the oldest vegetation is on the hill slope at the top of the image. (Photo by the author)

past. Bégin (2000) recorded ice scarring on the trees surrounding lakes in Quebec, Canada, to record lake flood events. Yanosky and Jarrett (2001) found distinct variations in the wood anatomy of oak trees; they identified white rings that were formed from open fibers when a tree's root were submerged in water and earlywood vessels when a tree was submerged and stripped of leaves at the end of the growing season. These distinct anatomical changes are excellent indicators of past flood damage.

Information about long-term patterns of streamflow, flooding, and water level in reservoirs is relevant to anyone who makes decisions about water allocation (Woodhouse and Meko 2009). Streamflow reconstructions, for example, can help municipal water managers plan for the natural variability in water resources (Woodhouse 2001). For example, correlations of ring width to streamflow data from the Colorado Front Range was used to reconstruct streamflow along the South Platte River and Middle Boulder Creek back to 1703 (Woodhouse 2001).

Stockton and Jacoby (1976) reconstructed streamflow for 12 stream-gauge stations in the Upper Colorado River Basin and found that flow was at record high levels in the early 1900s based on their 450-year reconstruction. This meant that the water allocation for the Colorado River based on the early 1900s levels could not be met during a normal year of streamflow. This was actually known at the time of the allocation decision based on research done by Douglass and Schulman (Schulman 1938). The region's water commission reduced the amounts that were allocated because of this higher growth shown in the tree-ring chronologies, but they did not adjust it enough (for published reconstructions, see Schulman 1938).

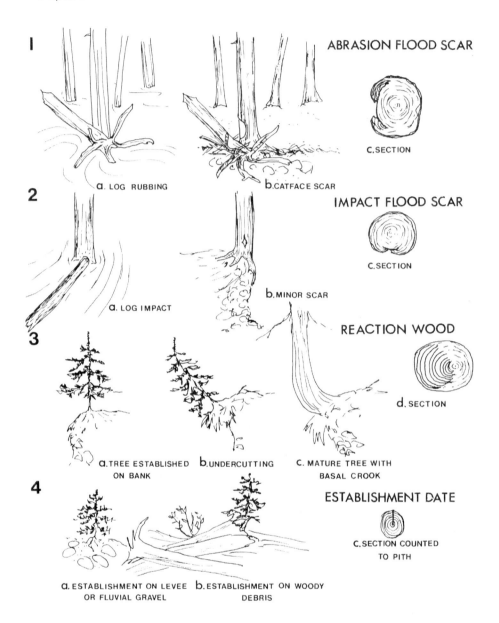

**Figure 8.6** Flood events can damage trees in many ways, providing dendrochronologists with different approaches to reconstruct flood activity. Establishment dates can also provide timing for these events. (From Gottesfeld and Gottesfeld 1990)

Cook and Jacoby (1977) used standard climate reconstruction techniques to document drought frequency in the past as it relates to water supplies in the Hudson River Valley of New York. Other work has demonstrated the direct connection between frequency of drought events and the reliability of water reserves in various reservoirs (Stockton and Jacoby 1976, Jain et al. 2002, Woodhouse et al. 2006).

Another application of dendrohydrology is to provide information about the timing and extent of ecological changes as water levels rise or fall. Phipps et al. (1979) used the growth of loblolly pine (*Pinus taeda*) near the margin of the Great Dismal Swamp to document anthropogenic ditching and subsequent drainage of the swamp. Schweingruber (1996) observed a similar phenomenon with spruce trees growing along the margin of a bog in the Swiss Jura Mountains. The marked release in growth made dating the drainage events readily observable. Changes in hydrology can also be related to landslide events, broadly called mass movement events.

## Segment-Length Curse

The ability to obtain a low-frequency climate signal from a chronology is dependent in part upon the length of the individual ring-width series that contribute to the chronology. The limitation is imposed by the detrending of individual ring-width series in tree-ring standardization and becomes a problem when trying to reconstruct climate over a long period of time from a chronology that has been formed by splicing together relatively short tree-ring segments. This phenomenon, called the **segment-length curse**, was originally proposed by Cook et al. (1995), who demonstrated the issue with modeled chronologies composed of sine waves with 1000-, 500-, and 250-year wavelengths and supplied illustrations with real chronologies from the bristlecone pines in the White Mountains of California.

The segment-length curse must be considered when examining long chronologies that have been constructed from shorter series. Cook et al. (1995) used a very conservative spline of a horizontal line fit through the mean of the series and, for the bristlecone pine, a negative exponential curve fit through the series. They suggested that the regional curve standardization (Briffa et al. 1992) technique may better preserve the low-frequency information of long chronologies composed of many short series, such as the European oak (*Quercus* spp.; Pilcher et al. 1984) chronology or Scots pine (*Pinus sylvestris*) chronology from Fennoscandia (Briffa et al. 1990). St. George and Nielson (2002) applied this technique to oak trees in southern Manitoba to reconstruct hydroclimatic events while maintaining the long-term variability in their chronology.

## Archaeological Uses of Climate Reconstructions

Climate reconstructions have long been used to provide an environmental backdrop to the settlement patterns of native populations (Dean et al. 1985, Dean 1997). Grissino-Mayer (1996) developed a climate reconstruction for El Malpais, New Mexico, that extends back to 100 BC. This 2000-year long precipitation record delineates drought and moisture episodes for much of the southwestern United States. He compared this climate reconstruction to major changes in Native American settlement patterns and found that settlement patterns changed during periods of high variability in climate. Stahle et al. (1998a) examined bald cypress (*Taxodium distichum*) growth in southern Virginia and found that the Roanoke and Jamestown colonies were established during two of the most severe droughts recorded in their 800-year record. Both of these colonies struggled, and Roanoke failed soon after it was established, which demonstrated the communities' reliance upon the resources provided by a temperate climate (see chapter 7 for additional discussion).

## Use of Climate Reconstructions for Future Prediction

Policymakers and laypeople are interested in discerning the future climate of the Earth. Studies of past climate can give us an idea about climatic variability and the causal mechanisms that should hold true in the future (Vaganov et al. 1999, Briffa 2000). For example, Cook et al. (2004) examined climate variability for the past 1200 years in the western United States and found that instances of higher temperature (such as the Medieval Warm Period, here reconstructed as 900–1300) corresponded to drought, suggesting that future climatic warming may result in an increase in aridity in this area. Other tree-ring studies have examined the effects on past streamflow and water supplies, changes in tree response to climate, and changes in landforms (see chapter 10). Studying the past provides researchers with an understanding of the natural range of variability so that we can prepare to adapt to climatic changes in the future.

# 9
# Dendroecology

Dendroecology uses dated tree rings to study ecological events such as fire and insect out-breaks. Dendroecology was developed as a field of study by Theodor Hartig and Robert Hartig in the late 1800s in Germany, with Bruno Huber continuing the tradition from 1940 to 1960 (Schweingruber 1996). In the United States, dendroecology did not develop until the 1970s with early work proposed by Hal Fritts (1971). Since the 1970s, dendroecology has greatly expanded (Fritts and Swetnam 1989) to include the study of fire history (Dieterich and Swetnam 1984), insect outbreaks (Swetnam et al. 1985), masting (synchronous fruiting in trees; Speer 2001), stand-age structure (Lorimer and Frelich 1989), pathogen outbreaks (Welsh 2007), and endogenous disturbance history (Abrams and Nowacki 1992).

I exclude from dendroecology the subfields of dendroclimatology and geological applications of dendrochronology, which are included in the definition given for dendroecology in the *Multilingual Glossary of Dendrochronology* (Kaennel and Schweingruber 1995). All three of these subfields of dendrochronology have a sufficient amount of research, refined methods, and techniques to be addressed independently. For this work, I define dendroecology as analysis of ecological issues such as fire, insect outbreaks, and stand-age structure with tree rings. Therefore, dendrohydrology, dendroclimatology, and dendrogeomorphology are described in chapters 8 and 10. Furthermore, some research tools used in dendroecology such as stable isotopes, dendrochemistry, and x-ray densitometry are treated in greater depth in chapter 11.

## Methods of Dendroecology

General methods of dendroecology usually involve the standard field and laboratory analyses described in chapter 5, with particular emphasis on establishment dates for succession studies, scarring from fires, or suppression and release events to document insect outbreaks or episodes of logging. Some methods are specific to dendroecology; for example, in order to determine exact tree establishment dates, cores are often taken at ground level and special care is directed toward obtaining pith.

### Stand-Age Structure

A stand-age structure analysis is a useful technique for many of the studies that follow. Stand-age structures require that all living and dead trees be sampled in a plot to quantify the current forest composition and past conditions (Lorimer and Frelich 1989, Abrams et al. 1995, Bergeron 2000, Daniels 2003). Exact age dating is important to provide a complete picture of the establishment and mortality of all tree species on the plot (Gutsell and Johnson 2002).

This method can be used as the basis for a study on succession dynamics (Abrams et al. 1995, Bergeron 2000), endogenous disturbances such as gap dynamics (Kneeshaw and Bergeron 1998), or for fire history in a stand-replacing fire regime (Bergeron 2000).

A stand-age structure analysis can be conducted in a circular plot, in a square plot, or along a transect. One preferred technique is to use a band transect. In this method, a tape measure is laid out for the length of the transect (50 m, for example) and all living and dead trees within a designated distance (1 m, for example) of either side of the tape are sampled. Although sampling along the transect is very intensive, the larger size classes are often not well represented because larger trees tend to grow at lower densities than smaller trees. Subsequent bands can be added to the outside of the base transect, in which trees of large DBH are sampled. For example, in addition to the complete sample within 1 m of either side of the tape, all trees greater than 20 cm DBH within 2 m of either side of the tape can be sampled, and all trees greater than 40 cm DBH within 3 m of either side of the tape can be sampled. This sampling technique results in a 100% sample of trees of all ages in a 2 × 50 m transect and all larger trees within a 4- or 6-m swath, increasing the sample depth of the larger trees. Only the data from the inner transect is used when estimating the number of trees in each age class or when quantifying the percentage of each species recorded. Careful field notes should be kept during sampling that record the location of each tree that is cored, the species, DBH, and sample ID of each tree (see Appendix D for sample note cards). With this data, one can examine the interaction among trees and plot out the distribution of different tree species along the transect. Transects are particularly useful for crossing boundaries or ecotones, such as examining vegetation patterns on either side of a stream channel or across an edge from woodland to forest interior. Transects can also be run along contours to maintain a similar sampling pool of trees that are growing at the same elevation and aspect.

Selective and opportunistic sampling can be used to achieve a stand-age structure study that would otherwise be too difficult to sample or be untenable due to a lack of permission to sample extensively. Cross sections were taken from stumps in a clear-cut forest in coastal British Columbia to analyze the regeneration and growth characteristics of western red cedar (*Thuja plicata*; Daniels 2003). Western red cedar develops heartwood decay and can grow to diameters of 160 cm, making accurate sampling of pith dates difficult with an increment borer. Daniels (2003) was able to determine that tree size was a poor indicator of tree age, recruitment was continuous and most likely affected by light gaps more than broad-scale disturbance, and mortality events were gradual and continuous through time. She concluded that current regeneration rates were sufficient to maintain the species on these sites. Daniels' research demonstrates the usefulness of opportunistic sampling when cross sections or intensive sampling are required.

## Ring-Width Analysis

Analysis of ring widths can be used to deduce disturbance events such as suppression from insect outbreaks, decline in growth associated with atmospheric pollution, trade-off between incremental growth and reproductive effort (masting), and release events associated with growth into canopy gaps. These applications use the same basic techniques as a dendroclimatic study, except that climate is often noise in these chronologies and should be controlled or removed so that the effect of the disturbance agent can be isolated. If a disturbance is expected to be recorded throughout the entire stand, such as an insect outbreak, older trees are often targeted for sampling because they provide a greater temporal depth. Sometimes, complete stand inventories are conducted and ring widths are examined on trees throughout the stand, such as for a stand-age structure study (Filion et al. 1998). Individual disturbances can also be targeted, for example trees growing in or around a light gap, to document the timing of and response to such a disturbance (Thompson et al. 2007).

## Tree Scars

Various types of ecological phenomena may leave scars on trees that provide a record of events for the dendrochronologist. A commonly studied disturbance is fire, which causes scars in the trunk when part of the cambium is killed by excessive heat during a surface fire (Swetnam and Baisan 1996). Animal herbivory and damage to roots by migrating caribou on trees also leaves behind a record of their effect and can even be used to estimate population levels of the herbivores (Spencer 1964, McLaren and Peterson 1994, Payette et al. 2004).

## Basal Area Increment

Basal area increment can be used as a type of standardization (see chapter 2 for more on standardization) in which annual growth increments are calculated by subtracting the area of a cross section in year $t - 1$ from that in year $t$. The result is an estimation of the two-dimensional growth increment added to the cross-sectional area of the tree. This calculation is useful because it removes any age-related growth trend resulting from adding the same volume of wood on an ever-increasing cylinder, while maintaining suppression and release events that may be due to forest disturbances (LeBlanc 1990, Phipps 2005).

## Applications of Dendroecology

### Gap-Phase Dynamics

Intensive sampling coupled with a detailed analysis of tree growth histories and stand-age structure can result in a chronology of gap-phase dynamics in which trees respond to openings in the canopy due to mortality of dominant trees. Tree-level ring-width series record suppression and release events, enabling dendrochronologists to document major disturbances that affect the growth of mature and understory trees (Lorimer and Frelich 1989). Gap-phase dynamics are the most common disturbances in many closed-canopy forest sites including the tropical and temperate forests, such as the eastern deciduous forest in the United States (Pickett and White 1985) and old-growth forests of the Pacific Northwest (Lertzman et al. 1996). Gaps provide resources that are limited, sunlight and growing space, to the lower levels in a dense forest and may provide the chance for suppressed understory trees to recruit into the canopy.

Kneeshaw and Bergeron (1998) examined gap dynamics in the southern boreal forest near Quebec. They found that aspen (*Populus tremuloides*) established soon after fire, and as the forest aged it became dominated by individual tree gap dynamics. Over time, balsam fir (*Abies balsamea*) replaced aspen, and larger gaps occurred as a result of spruce budworm defoliation. As gap size increased, shade-intolerant species were preferred and eastern white cedar (*Thuja occidentalis*) dominated. Daniels (2003) found a similarly complex establishment pattern in coastal British Columbia, where western red cedar (*Thuja plicata*), western hemlock (*Tsuga heterophylla*), and Pacific silver fir (*Abies amabilis*) competed for dominance. Western hemlock and Pacific silver fir depended on gaps to recruit into the canopy, whereas western red cedar did not require gaps and could regenerate under the closed canopy.

## Forest Productivity and Succession

Ring-width analysis can be used to examine forest health and productivity over time (Kienast 1982, Eckstein et al. 1984, Greve et al. 1986, Graumlich et al. 1989, Biondi 1999). For example, Biondi (1999) examined the growth of ponderosa pine (*Pinus ponderosa*) in the Gus Pearson Research Natural Area near Flagstaff, Arizona. The stand did not experience wildfires during the 20th century, and Biondi (1999) documented a decline in growth since 1920 associated with increased forest density. These changes were compared to the past 400 years of tree growth to determine if this was a unique pattern in the history of the stand, which made this decrease in growth even more pronounced. In another project, Graumlich et al. (1989) examined changes in net primary productivity of forests by measuring ring widths, demonstrating that trees in the Cascade Mountain Range in western Washington State were showing increased growth rates. They attributed this recent increase to warming summer temperatures and increased absorbed solar radiation rather than any carbon dioxide fertilization effect.

Cook et al. (1987) took a different approach to examine forest decline in red spruce (*Picea rubens*) in the southern Appalachians. They examined the relationship between climate and tree growth and found that the trees stopped responding to climate after 1967 and started to decline. They suggested that this response, not related to climatic forcing, could be due to anthropogenic pollution. **Fir waves** are another phenomenon in the eastern United States in which large swaths of fir trees die synchronously, but the agent for this mortality was unknown until the 1980s. Marchand (1984) examined tree growth and age structure in these fir stands and found that wind abrasion on the windward side of the stand caused these trees to die back while new fir trees established on the leeward side of the stand. The fir wave phenomena did not kill the stand but created a banded pattern of different stand ages. All of these specific studies are examples of how dendrochronologists can reconstruct the past to determine if modern growth of trees is similar to growth in the past, providing temporal perspective to current forest health issues.

**Dendromastecology** is a new subdiscipline devoted to developing mast (synchronous and massive fruit production in trees) reconstructions from tree rings (Speer 2001). Mast reconstructions require the researcher to consider multiple variables in a tree's signal, peeling apart one layer of signal after the other, until a large percentage of the overall pattern can be explained by climate and biological factors that control tree growth. The aggregate tree growth model discussed in chapter 2 is a conceptual model of this approach, where the age-related growth trend can be standardized out of the series, and then climate can be removed through regression analysis with significant correlates in the climate variables. Finally, the signal that is left may be a biological signal such as masting in the tree (Speer 2001). Mast reconstruction is a new technique that still has to be tested in multiple species and locations around the world.

Speer (2001) demonstrated that mast reconstructions were achievable on oak species in the eastern United States. However, good climate data and a long calibration data set of masting in the tree species of interest are necessary for this type of work. Speer (2001) also found that there was not a strict trade-off between incremental growth and reproductive effort as was suggested by ecological theory. Instead, the oaks in his study had the ability to store carbon as carbohydrate and starches (most likely in their roots) so that the carbon drain for acorns in one year was actually carried by energy production over multiple years. This suggests that mast reconstructions will not be evident on all sites, and Speer (2001) found only 25% success in mast reconstructions in his site-species chronologies. Mast fruiting may be a strong control on seed predator populations and also affect the ability of masting species to compete in a diverse forest.

Dendrochronologists can add information to larger ecological theories through exact dating of establishment and growth of trees in complex forested ecosystems. **Forest succession**, the development of the forest community through time on a site following a stand-replacing disturbance such as glacial retreat, volcanic eruptions, or farming, can be assessed by examination of establishment dates of different tree species on one or multiple sites (Abrams and Nowacki 1992). Fastie (1995) explored primary succession dynamics in Glacier Bay, Alaska, after the glacier had retreated. He used historical records of glacier retreat for the past 250 years to document the age of his plots located at increasing distances from the present foot of the glacier. His findings indicated that in this area primary forest succession was accelerated because of proximity to seed sources along the trimline of the glacier, which is the highest elevation that the edge of the glacier ice reaches. Mature trees left above the trimline produced seed that repopulated the newly exposed ground.

Abrams and Nowacki (1992) demonstrated variable mechanisms of succession by documenting a case of accelerated succession in the deciduous forests of Pennsylvania that was due to an exclusion of fire followed by thinning of the overstory trees in multiple logging operations. This management practice removed fire-tolerant oak and pine trees from the site and encouraged late-successional red maple (*Acer rubra*), sugar maple (*Acer saccharum*), and black cherry (*Prunus serotina*) to gain dominance in a forest that was formerly maintained by frequent fire.

## Old Forests

Dendrochronologists tend to find old trees in surprising locations. The concept of "longevity under adversity," first published by Schulman (1954), has led dendrochronologists to find extremely old trees on lava flows, cliff faces, and high mountain peaks. Stahle (1996) documented old trees throughout the eastern United States in locations that were previously assumed to have been completely logged around the 1900s. Most eastern states still have living trees that established prior to the founding of the United States (Stahle 1996). Orwig et al. (2001) documented four sites within 80 km (50 miles) of Boston that have trees in excess of 250 years old. Kelly et al. (1992) recorded eastern white cedars (*Thuja occidentalis*) growing on the Niagara Escarpment in southern Ontario that are more than 1000 years old. In the western United States, Grissino-Mayer et al. (1997) developed a 2000-year climate reconstruction from trees growing on the El Malpais lava flow in northwestern New Mexico and from dead trees that were well preserved on the rocks of the lava flow. They found some of the oldest documented Douglas-fir (*Pseudotsuga menziesii*) and ponderosa pine (*Pinus ponderosa*) trees growing in this extremely harsh environment with roots delving into the volcanic rock under a thin film of soil.

Bristlecone pine trees (*Pinus longaeva*), the oldest living nonclonal organisms (Currey 1965, Ferguson 1968), epitomize the principle of longevity under adversity. Found in the White Mountains of eastern California in cold, arid conditions at elevations of more than 10,000 feet, these trees grow so slowly that more than 100 rings may be contained in less than an inch of a wood cross section. As in many areas where long-lived trees are found, bristlecone pine forests have very little understory, usually only a few tundra herbs. The oldest trees studied by dendrochronologists are often not found in classic old-growth forests with complex understory vegetation, but are instead discovered in sites with sparse tree density on harsh sites (Orwig et al. 2001).

Dendrochronologists have been documenting the age of the oldest trees in each species that produces tree rings, providing an understanding of the maximum age attainable by each species (Brown 1996). By recognizing the maximum age attainable, managers can formulate strategies that take into account the temporal scale of the trees they manage. Documentation of the maximum age of trees and the sites on which they grow enable researchers to better understand the concept of old-growth forests and even provide insight into how organisms age and survive to extreme old age (appendix B; see the Web for an updated OLDLIST and Eastern OLDLIST).

## Dendropyrochronology

Reconstruction of fire histories is one of the major applications of dendrochronology for use in management of forests and the reestablishment of fire as a disturbance agent. Any prescribed fire policy in the United States must be supported with scientific evidence for that tract of land. These federal and state laws have motivated fire reconstructions on many parcels of land, which, in turn, have generated a comprehensive view of the role that fire plays in these fire-prone landscapes. The goal of the dendrochronologist is to determine the natural range of variability for fire on a particular site (Landres et al. 1999), which describes the past occurrence of fire, how frequently it affected a site, and the area that it has covered in the past. From this information, forest managers can determine how fire has behaved on their land in the past and how fire regimes have changed in the 20th century, when fire suppression was a common policy (Heyerdahl and Card 2000).

Three main fire types occur around the world. A **surface fire** is one that burns over the ground surface, consuming duff and fine fuels. These fires usually move through an area fairly quickly and burn at a low to moderate severity. Many forest types, such as ponderosa pine (fig. 9.1), red pine, and giant sequoia (fig. 9.2) depend on these frequent low-severity surface fires to remove competitors and to burn off the duff layer, allowing seedlings access

**Figure 9.1** A ponderosa pine stand in Oregon that has received multiple thinning and prescribed fire treatments. Note the triangular catface (fire scar wound) at the base of the closest tree on the left. The trees record multiple fires that burned through the site at low intensity. (Photo by the author)

to mineral soil. Oak woodlands also seem to be dependent upon frequent fire to maintain this forest type. **Stand-replacing fires** occur less frequently when fuels have built up to a critical level and often cause high tree mortality. These fires often burn through the canopy of the trees and, therefore, are also called **crown fires** (fig. 9.3). Some pine forests, such as lodgepole pine, are adapted to this type of fire. Stand-replacing fires burn through a forest and kill the mature trees. Many of the trees that are adapted to a stand-replacing fire regime have **serotinous cones** that only open to spread their seed when they are heated, as a coating of resin or woody layer is burned off. Stand-replacing fires occur frequently in the boreal forest, where dry summers in a continental climate combined with little topographic relief, warm winds, and convective storms result in fire that can burn a large area of the landscape. The third type of fire is a **ground fire** that actually burns underground in the organic-rich soils of histosols. These fires are common in Alaska, where they can burn for more than 30 years as they smolder through the thick organic layers of plant material in the ground.

*Surface Fire.* Each type of fire requires a different sampling method to accurately record the occurrence of fire in the past. Surface fire regimes burn frequently on a site but leave live mature trees that record the fire. Pine ecosystems seem to be the most adapted to surface fires and are most frequently sampled for long-term fire history. Fire histories in this type of forest are most productively accomplished by cutting fire-scarred samples from stumps, downed

**Figure 9.2** A catface can be a huge scar when it occurs in giant sequoia. Giant sequoia is a fire-adapted tree species that needs fire to regenerate. (Photo by the author)

**Figure 9.3** Stand-replacing fire in *Pinus sylvestris*. This crown fire burned through most of the stand, killing the mature trees. (Photo by Tom Swetnam)

logs, and living trees from these sites. Surface fires are often pushed by the wind and move uphill as they consume fuels. Fire can burn more intensively on the uphill sides of the trees because the fire can eddy there in a vortex from the rising air currents. Also, pine needles and cones collect on the uphill side of the tree and provide more fuels for the fire to burn hotter at this location.

The first time a tree is scarred, the fire does not usually damage the xylem of the tree. The cambium is killed because the fire heats it through the bark, later causing the bark to slough off. The scarred part of the tree will have an area of thinner bark and, if a pine tree, pitch will collect in it. Once the tree is initially scarred, it is more likely to scar along the exposed portion of the cambium when subsequent fires burn. Repeated fires create a triangular scar, called a **catface**, at the base of the tree (fig. 9.4).

Repeated fire scars in a catface can be sampled by taking a partial section from living or dead standing (snags) trees (Arno and Sneck 1973, Cochrane and Daniels 2008). This sampling technique involves two cuts with a chainsaw along the cross-sectional surface through a cat face followed by two plunge cuts along the edges of the sample to break it loose (fig. 9.5). The resultant sections have all of the fire history information from bark to pith (fig. 9.6), while leaving most of the base of the tree for stability and transport of substances through the xylem. Heyerdahl and McKay (2001) reexamined 138 trees six years after sampling partial

**Figure 9.4** A catface scar on a living ponderosa pine tree with a partial section removed from the left base of the tree. Subsequent fires kill off the living cambium and leave behind a scar that the tree tries to heal over. By tracing the vertical fissures in the wood that follow the ring boundaries, one can count the number of these scars on the face of the wound to get an estimate of the number of fire scars preserved on the sample. Then a decision is made about which trees to sample based on the number of scars recorded and on the preservation of the sample (whether there is much rot). (Photo by the author)

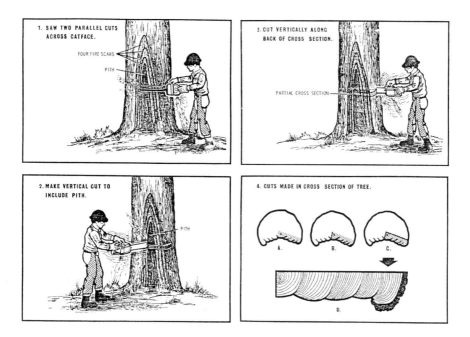

**Figure 9.5** Partial sections are taken from living trees to get a complete history of fire through the modern era, while the trees are left standing and healthy. In this process, the fieldworker uses a chainsaw to take two horizontal cuts and two plunge cuts to remove the fire-scarred section while leaving most of the tree behind for support and conduction of fluids. (From Arno and Sneck 1973)

sections for a fire history reconstruction in order to investigate the impact of fire scar sampling on the health of the trees. They estimated that only 8% of the cross-sectional area was removed in sampling and that these trees did not have greater mortality than a control group of 386 similar-sized trees that were not sampled for fire history. They conclude that partial sampling from the catface of pine trees is a nonlethal sampling technique that provides needed information for land management.

Hardwood trees can also scar from surface fires. This has most frequently been recorded in oak trees growing in open woodland settings (Abrams 1985, Smith and Sutherland 1999, 2001). In this case, the trees tend to grow on flat ground and fire scars are not recorded in a catface, but on multiple sides of the stem wherever a fissure in the bark allows the cambium to heat up to a temperature that can kill it. Therefore, old oak trees can record multiple fire scars, but a full cross section is needed to document past fires. Some hardwood trees develop catfaces due to successive fires, but these are not common as most hardwood trees develop rot, although the fire scars are usually still evident (Speer, unpublished data).

*Stand-Replacing Fire.* Past fire occurrence of a stand-replacing fire type can be documented by stand-age structure recording the time since the last fire (Heinselman 1973). This technique uses a stand-age structure in areas that have been identified as locations of different fire events

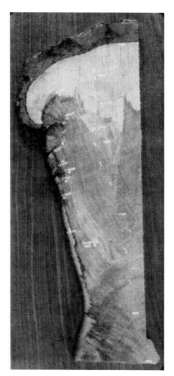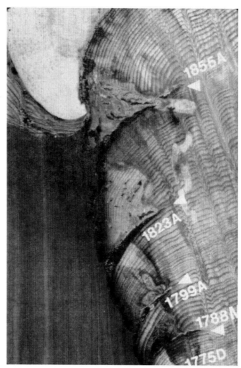

**Figure 9.6** A partial section from ponderosa pine with a close-up showing the fire scar dates. This partial section only removed a small portion of the living cambium and the rest of the tree was left for support and growth. The individual scars are obvious from the bark to the inside of the tree, where it started to record fires. By looking closely at the fire-scarred samples, the season of the fire can be determined based on the position of the scar on the earlywood or latewood within the ring. (Photo by the author)

based on aerial photos or a stratified random sampling protocol across the landscape to determine where the age-breaks occur (Johnson and Gutsell 1994). Within the bounds of each area, a plot can be established and a stand-age structure analysis conducted. This stand-age structure is likely to demonstrate that all of the trees in each patch are a single cohort with similar establishment dates controlled by the time since the last fire. This type of study requires the researcher to take a core near the ground surface and hit pith to get the most exact age estimate for each tree (see stand-age structure methodology above). Extensive landscape studies that examine fires scars along with establishment dates and survivorship curves can be used to interpret the entire fire history of a landscape, which can include surface and stand-replacing fires in lodgepole pine and subalpine fir forests (Sibold et al. 2006, 2007).

*Ground Fire.* Ground fires might be documented from root damage or scarring to living trees, although I am unaware of any dendrochronological studies that have examined these types of fire regimes. Most ground fires burn in regions with a rich organic peat layer that formed from an old bog. These areas usually do not support many trees, and any trees that were able to grow there may be killed by the passing of the fire. As long as the mortality of the tree can be attributed to the fire, the death dates of those trees can be used to determine the time of the event.

*Seasonal Resolution of Fire Scars.* Just as the year in which a fire occurred can be ascertained through crossdating, the season of burn can be determined from the position of fire scars in the earlywood or latewood of some trees (fig. 9.7; Swetnam and Baisan 1996). For example, if a few cells of earlywood were formed before the cambium was killed and seasonal growth was stopped in that part of the tree, researchers can infer that the fire occurred early in the tree's growing season, often in the spring. A latewood scar indicates a fire burned the tree late in its growing season, and a scar between two fully formed rings signifies a fire during the dormant season.

Knowledge of the season of past fires enables land managers to reintroduce fire to the landscape in a natural way. If fires are forced on the landscape in a different season than occurred naturally, different plant species will be favored by affecting sprouting, fruiting, and flowering. Native American use of fire can also potentially be determined by looking for a change in the fire season from the natural fire regime.

*Fire in the Southwestern United States.* Studies of fire effects on trees have been conducted since the early 1900s (Clements 1910, Anonymous 1923, Show and Kotok 1924, Presnall 1933). In the 1980s, crossdated fire histories became much more common in the southwestern United States, leading to a better understanding of the spatial and temporal patterns of fire in many pine ecosystems (Madany et al. 1982, Dieterich and Swetnam 1984, Swetnam et al. 1999). Forest managers can use prescribed burning to return the forests to a more natural condition and improve forest health (Morgan et al. 1994, Swanson et al. 1994, Fule et al. 1997, Landres et al. 1999, Swetnam et al. 1999). Fire history records extend before the late 1800s, which was a time of heavy grazing by sheep and cattle that was followed by fire suppression by the U.S. Forest Service (Savage and Swetnam 1990).

Swetnam and Baisan (1996) demonstrated how dendrochronological records can be used to examine fire across multiple spatial scales (fig. 9.8). Fire history data are collected on the individual tree basis. Researchers can also examine whether fires are recorded on multiple trees, and thus reconstruct a fire's spread through a site. Then multiple sites can be examined in a watershed to see how the fire spread across the watershed. Finally, sites throughout a region can be examined to identify those years when fires occurred in many separate watersheds because of the appropriate climatic factors. The result is a reconstruction of fire on multiple spatial scales, and different driving factors can influence fire events at each scale. For example, Swetnam and Betancourt (1990) showed that fire occurrence in the Southwest can often be explained by climate patterns, especially at the broad scale. Swetnam et al. (1999) examined fire histories that extended back to the 1600s from 55 sites throughout the southwestern United States (fig. 9.9) and found that regional fire occurrence was driven by long-term climate fluctuations, such as El Niño.

*Fire in Scandinavia.* New methods to examine the spatial dimension of fire are being conducted in Sweden. Dendropyrochronology has had great success in documenting the temporal component of past fires but has until recently lacked a rigorous systematic sampling across space

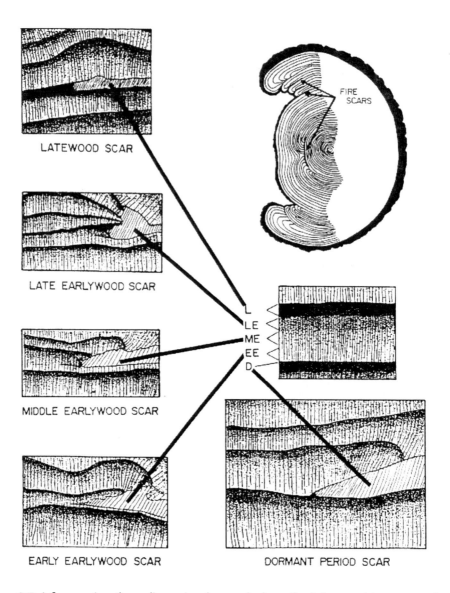

LATEWOOD SCAR

LATE EARLYWOOD SCAR

MIDDLE EARLYWOOD SCAR

EARLY EARLYWOOD SCAR

DORMANT PERIOD SCAR

FIRE SCARS

L
LE
ME
EE
D

**Figure 9.7** A fire scar is a three-dimensional wound where the living cambium meets the dead cambium. Right at that point, the year and the season in which the fire occurred can be determined based on the position of the scar in the ring. If a few earlywood cells formed before the cambium was killed, then it is termed an early earlywood scar. If the scar appears in the middle of the early-wood, then it is named a middle earlywood scar, and if late in the earlywood then a late earlywood fire scar. When the scar appears only in the latewood, it is called a latewood scar. If the scar appears right on the ring boundary with neither earlywood formed before it or latewood formed around it, it is called a dormant season fire. The season of the dormant fire scars can generally be assigned to spring or autumn by the dominance of other scars in the earlywood or latewood from that site. (From Swetnam and Baisan 1996)

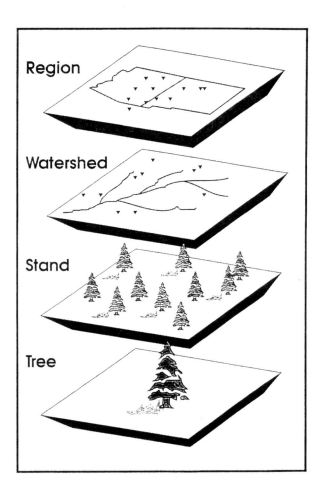

**Figure 9.8** Fire-history data can be collected on multiple spatial scales to understand the driving factors of this natural disturbance. Fire scars are collected from an individual tree, but are usually analyzed at the stand level to examine spreading fires. Multiple stands can be sampled in a watershed to look at fire spread across the landscape. Many such watersheds can be sampled on a regional basis to understand how climate can drive fire occurrence at this broadest scale. (From Swetnam and Baisan 1996)

that would enable the reconstruction of the spatial aspect of surface fires. Niklasson and Granström (2000) collected 1133 samples from 203 points that were spaced approximately 2 km apart across an area covering 19 × 32 km. This network of sampling points enabled them to examine the area burned by past fires in a *Pinus sylvestris* chronology extending into the 1100s, which successfully documented the spread of fires across the landscape so that spatial and temporal patterns could be compared. Researchers also found a signal from human-caused ignitions in Scandinavia by early settlers around the 1600s, probably for the purpose of improving cattle grazing conditions and for slash-and-burn agriculture (Lehtonen and Huttunen 1997, Groven and Niklasson 2005). Fires tended to cease around the late 1700s

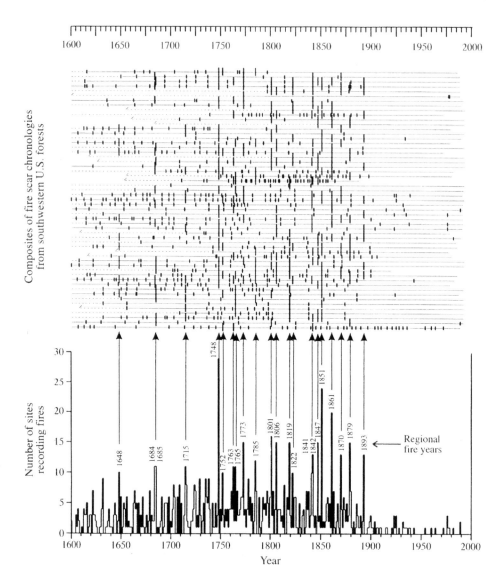

**Figure 9.9** A fire history chart for a network of 55 site-level chronologies extending back to 1600 throughout the southwestern United States. Each horizontal line in the top graph represents an individual site, and each tic mark on that line represents a separate fire event that affected many trees on the site. The bottom graph is a composite of fire charts throughout the western United States and Northern Mexico. (From Swetnam et al. 1999)

because of increased value of timber and a likely resultant attention to conservation of this resource (Groven and Niklasson 2005).

*Fire in Canada.* Considerable fire history research has been performed in Canada, from the mixed hardwood forests of south-central Ontario (Dey and Guyette 2000) to the boreal forest

(Bergeron 1991) and even at the latitudinal treeline at 58°N (Payette et al. 1989). Bergeron (1991) examined fire occurrence on mainland versus island sites to determine the driving factors that control fire frequency. He documented more frequent/less intense fires on the rocky islands dominated by red pine (*Pinus resinosa*) and common juniper (*Juniperus communis*) because of fuel limitation, in contrast to less frequent/stand-replacing fires on the mainland that was dominated by balsam fir (*Abies balsamea*), black spruce (*Picea mariana*), and paper birch (*Betula papyrifera*) on a site that was moister and had greater fuel accumulation. A decrease in fire frequency over the past 120 years was found in this study and attributed to a decrease in long-term droughts associated with warming since the Little Ice Age (Bergeron 1991, Bergeron and Archambault 1993). Studies from 55°N to 59°N latitude have examined the variability of fire rotation periods across biomes from boreal forest through the forest tundra and into the shrub tundra (Payette et al. 1989). It was estimated that the northern boreal forest fire rotation period was 100 years, while shrub tundra fire rotation period was greater than 7800 years.

## Dendroentomology

The study of insect outbreaks has become a major subfield of dendrochronology because forest managers are interested in the historical effects of insects on their managed lands. Dendroentomology documents past occurrence of insect outbreaks and gives an understanding of insect population dynamics, including duration of outbreaks, interval between outbreaks, and the spread of insect outbreaks (Swetnam et al. 1985). As with all dendrochronological applications, dendroentomology provides a long-term perspective for ecological dynamics in a forest system.

The earliest study of insect outbreaks using tree rings was conducted by the German botanist Julius Ratzeburg, who dated outbreaks of a defoliating caterpillar with annual resolution (Ratzeburg 1866, as cited in Wimmer 2001 and Studhalter 1955). In an introductory textbook on forestry, Hough (1882) illustrated the reduced growth of tree rings related to the defoliation of insects in the eastern United States. The presence of this illustration and statement in a forestry textbook in the late 1800s demonstrates the general knowledge of tree growth, the ability to date ecological phenomena with tree rings, and the effect of insects on trees and their growth. The field of insect outbreak reconstructions started in earnest in the 1950s and 1960s, when a series of publications made this discipline more accessible to researchers (Blais 1954, 1957, 1958a, 1958b, 1961, 1962, 1965, Hildahl and Reeks 1960).

Blais (1958a) documented a decrease in ring width of balsam fir and white spruce due to the effects of eastern spruce budworm (*Choristoneura fumiferana*). Hildahl and Reeks (1960) published a study on the effect of forest tent caterpillar (*Malacosoma disstria*) on quaking aspen in Manitoba and Saskatchewan. Blais (1962) did much to establish the techniques for studying insect outbreak dynamics in his study of eastern spruce budworm in Canada. Long-term reconstructions covering the past 200–300 years have demonstrated that spruce budworm outbreaks have increased in frequency, extent, and severity caused by human changes in the forest ecosystems (Blais 1983). Swetnam et al. (1985) published a manual on how to approach insect outbreak studies that became a standard in the field. This manual helped to codify an approach to insect outbreak reconstruction that was quickly followed from the

**Table 9.1**    Insects that have been studied using dendrochronology

| Common Name | Scientific Name | Type | Reference |
|---|---|---|---|
| Spruce beetle | *Dendroctonus rufipennis* | cambium feeder | Eisenhart and Veblen (2000) |
| Mountain pine beetle | *Dendroctonus ponderosae* | cambium feeder | Shore et al. (2006), Campbell et al. (2007) |
| Forest tent caterpillar | *Malacosoma disstria* | defoliator | Hildahl and Reeks (1960) |
| Gypsy moth | *Lymantria dispar* | defoliator | Asshof et al. (1999) |
| Larch sawfly | *Pristiphora erichsonii* | defoliator | Case and MacDonald (2003) |
| Pandora moth | *Coloradia pandora* | defoliator | Speer et al. (2001) |
| Western spruce budworm | *Choristoneura occidentalis* | defoliator | Blais (1962), Swetnam and Lynch (1993) |
| Tussock moth | *Orgyia* sp. | defoliator | Mason et al. (1997) |
| Two-year spruce budworm | *Choristoneura biennis* | defoliator | Zhang and Alfaro (2002) |
| Periodical cicadas | *Magicicada* sp. | root parasite | Speer unpublished data |

1990s to the present with a flurry of dendrochronological insect outbreak publications. Canada is one of the more active areas in insect outbreak reconstruction, with work by Krause and Morin (1999), Zhang and Alfaro (2002), and Campbell et al. (2007).

Insect outbreak studies come in many different forms depending upon how the insects affect the trees. Insects may be defoliators, cambium feeders, or root parasites. The defoliators focus on one type of tree and consume leaves or needles from those tree species. Examples of these types of insects include western spruce budworm (*Choristoneura occidentalis*; Swetnam and Lynch 1993), Douglas-fir tussock moth (*Orgyia pseudotsugata*; Swetnam et al. 1995, Mason et al. 1997), and pandora moth (*Coloradia pandora*; Speer et al. 2001); see table 9.1 for a more comprehensive list. Insects that feed on the cambium, usually killing the tree, include bark beetle larvae (*Dendroctonus* and *Ips* spp.; Eisenhart and Veblen 2000). Finally, an example of a root parasite is the periodical cicada (*Magicicada* spp.), a group of insects that are restricted to the eastern United States and spend 99% of their life cycle feeding on the xylem fluid in the roots of trees. Recent research has demonstrated that they do not greatly affect the trees but may cause a reduction in growth when they lay eggs in the branches of the trees. They may also increase the growth of the trees by providing a nutrient pulse when their carcasses decompose after a massive emergence (Speer, unpublished data).

Researchers can also document the spread of invasive species such as the hemlock wooly adelgid (*Adelges tsugae*), gypsy moth (*Lymantria dispar*), and the emerald ash borer (*Agrilus planipennis*) and use the techniques of dendroentomology to reconstruct the effects of fungus on tree populations such as the chestnut blight (*Cryphonectria parasitica*) and the Dothistroma needle blight (*Dothistroma septosporum*; Welsh 2007). Insects that cause mortality of the host trees, such as wooly adelgid, emerald ash borer, and many bark beetles, are more difficult to reconstruct because a mortality event could be caused by many different factors and that ends the record for those particular trees. Repeated outbreaks of these insects may be recorded by the response of other trees in the stand whose growth increases due to the mortality of the host species.

Among the different groups, dendroentomologists have reconstructed a greater variety of defoliating insects outbreaks than any other type. Calibration of the tree-ring record with historical documentation of past insect outbreaks has been very helpful in determining the insects' effects on the trees (Brubaker and Greene 1979, Swetnam et al. 1985, Wickman et al. 1994). Comparisons of ring patterns during periods of known outbreaks in a study area can identify a tree-ring signature specific to that insect species. By examining the defoliation effects of tussock moth and spruce budworm in the same tree, in some cases researchers have been able to differentiate between the signature of the two species and subsequently document past outbreaks of each species (Brubaker and Greene 1979, Mason and Torgerson 1987, Wickman et al. 1994). Douglas-fir tussock moth produces a four- to five-year signature of sharply reduced growth, while the western spruce budworm has more gradual but longer outbreak periods (often 10 years), leaving a signature of less abrupt but more persistent growth reduction (Wickman 1963, Brubaker and Greene 1979). The differentiation of outbreak patterns aptly demonstrated the effectiveness of dendrochronology in identifying specific **ring signatures** for phytophagous insects throughout the length of the tree-ring chronologies. However, when western spruce budworm and Douglas-fir tussock moth outbreaks occurred simultaneously or were closely spaced in time, they cannot always be differentiated in trees or stands that were defoliated by both species (Swetnam et al. 1995).

Reduction in tree growth reflects the period when defoliation significantly impacts tree health and does not usually begin precisely with the onset of the insect population's increased growth (Swetnam and Lynch 1993). Stored food reserves can delay defoliation-induced growth loss by one or more growing seasons (O'Neill 1963, Kulman 1971, Brubaker and Greene 1979). Because a tree requires time to replace lost foliage following severe defoliation, its growth may be inhibited for several years after the insect populations have crashed (Duff and Nolan 1953, Mott et al. 1957, Wickman 1963, Brubaker and Greene 1979, Alfaro et al. 1985, Lynch and Swetnam 1992).

Researchers have developed techniques for differentiating climate-related ring-width suppressions in the host trees from those produced by insect outbreaks (Wickman 1963, Koerber and Wickman 1970, Brubaker and Greene 1979, Swetnam et al. 1985). Climate subtraction techniques have been developed and widely tested in studies of the western spruce budworm (Brubaker and Greene 1979, Swetnam et al. 1985, Swetnam and Lynch 1993, Wickman et al. 1994, Swetnam et al. 1995, Weber and Schweingruber 1995). In the approach used by Swetnam et al. (1985), a nonhost control tree species is collected from a site adjacent to that of the host species and its tree-ring chronology is compared to the host series. The common climate signal then can be subtracted from the host chronology, thereby isolating the species-specific factors for further study. However, some error or noise may be introduced into the analysis due to differing responses to climate between the host and nonhost tree species (Swetnam et al. 1985).

Pandora moth is a phytophagous insect that defoliates ponderosa pine, Jeffrey pine, and lodgepole pine in the western United States (fig. 9.10). The Klamath and Piute Indians used the pandora moth larvae and pupae as a traditional food source when it was available, indicating they had knowledge of its life cycle (Blake and Wagner 1987). This led early forest entomologists

**Figure 9.10** A ponderosa pine forest denuded of needles by pandora moth larvae (inset). (From Speer et al. 2001)

to speculate that pandora moth outbreaks had often occurred in the past (Aldrich 1912, 1921, Patterson 1929). Pandora moth and ponderosa pine trees are well adapted to each other so that only 2% tree mortality occurs with the outbreaks (Patterson 1929, Massey 1940, Bennett et al. 1987).

Speer et al. (2001) developed a record of pandora moth outbreaks in south-central Oregon that extends back 622 years (fig. 9.11). They were able to identify a distinct ring-width pattern or signature that is associated with an outbreak of this insect in ponderosa pine forests (fig. 9.12). This signature was calibrated from sites with historically documented outbreaks and was applied to reconstructing outbreaks in the past. Further analysis demonstrated that pandora moth was recorded on multiple trees within a site and in multiple sites (fig. 9.13).

Mountain pine beetle (*Dendroctonus ponderosae*) has become a major influence in the western United States and Canada, with an outbreak from 1999 to 2006 affecting more than 7 million hectares in Canada alone (Taylor et al. 2006). Bark beetle outbreaks can be reconstructed by documenting the mortality of host trees and occasionally from scars that are

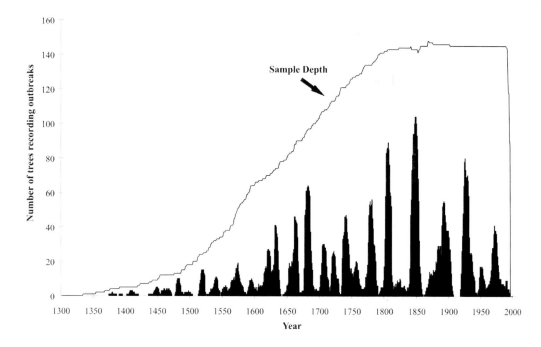

**Figure 9.11** A 622-year pandora moth reconstruction from south-central Oregon. The top line represents the number of trees recording through time. The sample depth decreases further back in time, with 20 trees still recording outbreaks at 1500. The dark area shows the number of trees recording outbreaks through time across the entire south-central region of Oregon. (From Speer et al. 2001)

preserved on trees that live through the outbreak. Tree death is recorded indirectly as release in trees that survive the outbreak (Taylor et al. 2006). These types of reconstructions are more difficult because a distinct signature for cambium-feeding insects does not exist like it does for most defoliating insects. The economic impact of the recent mountain pine beetle outbreak in Colorado and neighboring states and the large outbreak in British Columbia has brought more attention to this insect to try to understand if these events are natural or triggered by other factors, such as forest management practices and/or climate change.

*Stem Analysis.* Potential wood volume increases of a forest stand can be reduced during insect outbreaks either through mortality of the host trees or suppression of radial growth, and this reduction has implications for forest management policies. For example, while pandora moth outbreaks typically cause almost no loss due to mortality, the amount of volume reduction due to the effects of defoliation can be quite substantial (Massey 1940, Wickman 1963, Koerber and Wickman 1970, Speer and Holmes 2004). Growth loss during outbreaks may be offset by a growth increase after the insect population has crashed, a phenomenon observed with spruce budworm and Douglas-fir tussock moth outbreaks (Wickman 1980, Alfaro et al. 1985, Swetnam and Lynch 1993). This effect may be attributable to factors such as reduced competition among trees for resources and nutrient cycling associated with frass (excrement) accumulation.

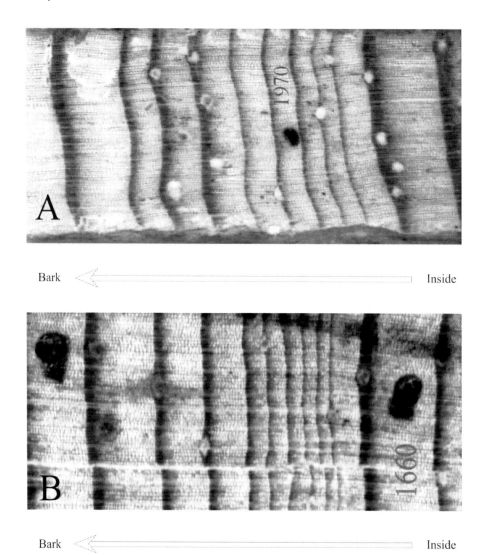

Bark ⟵ ———————————————————————————————— ⊐ Inside

Bark ⟵ ———————————————————————————————— ⊐ Inside

**Figure 9.12** A tree-ring signature has been identified for pandora moth in which the first year is half the size of normal, the next two years are the smallest in the series, and subsequent years gradually return to normal growth. Thin latewood throughout the outbreak is another characteristic of the signal. (A) A tree affected by a documented pandora moth outbreak in the 1960s, which was used as a calibration for inferred pandora moth outbreaks with the signature starting in 1661, as seen in (B). (From Speer 1997)

Stem analysis has been used extensively to investigate the effects of insect defoliation on growth allocation (fig. 9.14). The standard technique, with refinements by Duff and Nolan (1953, 1957), involves taking multiple cross sections along the stem of the tree. The ring widths are then measured from each cross section and used to estimate three-dimensional growth throughout the entire tree (fig. 9.15). Duff and Nolan (1957) and LeBlanc (1990) suggested

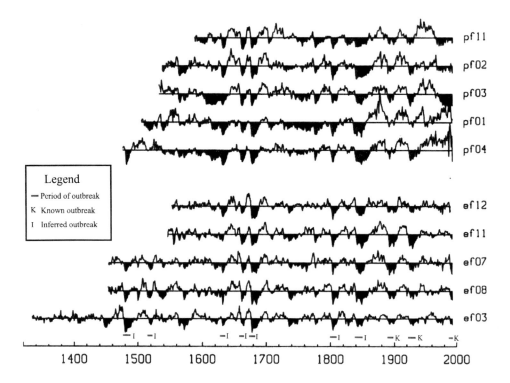

**Figure 9.13** Insect outbreaks often affect many trees both on an individual site and on multiple sites. In this graphic, each horizontal line represents an individual tree with its ring-width index plotted through time, and two sites (pf and ef) are illustrated. Dashes at the bottom of the graphic indicate known (K) outbreaks and inferred (I) outbreaks. Each outbreak event is recorded not only by all trees from the same site, but by trees on different sites, demonstrating that pandora moth outbreaks occurred on a broad scale and affected multiple sites. (From Speer 1997)

sampling a section midway between each internode to allow for quantification of height and radial growth in every year. Yet for trees a few centuries in age, it is very difficult or impossible to identify internodes on the external surfaces of the main stem. Thus, with increasing age it becomes impractical to determine all of the annual height increments; however, cross sections can be taken at regular intervals along the trunk instead (fig. 9.15). LeBlanc et al. (1987) noted that stem analysis affords increased accuracy in determining the overall tree response to disturbance, but mentioned the added effort might preclude its widespread application. They also noted the additional difficulty when studying older and larger trees because of the obscurity of the internodes as trees age. The effort of conducting a stem analysis is worthwhile, however, if the researcher wants to visualize the changes in wood volume due to defoliation and loss of photosynthetic potential (fig. 9.16).

*Conclusions of Dendroentomology.* The tools developed from dendroentomology are now being used for other forest disease agents such as fungal pathogens (Welsh 2007) and to address complex disturbance systems involving multiple agents (for example, Thompson

**Figure 9.14** The author takes samples from a 600-year-old ponderosa pine tree for a stem analysis to examine the wood volume lost due to pandora moth defoliation. This is also an example of opportunistic sampling, because this tree was killed by a winter storm in 1993, enabling easy sampling in 1996 without having to cut down a living tree. (Photo by Tom Swetnam)

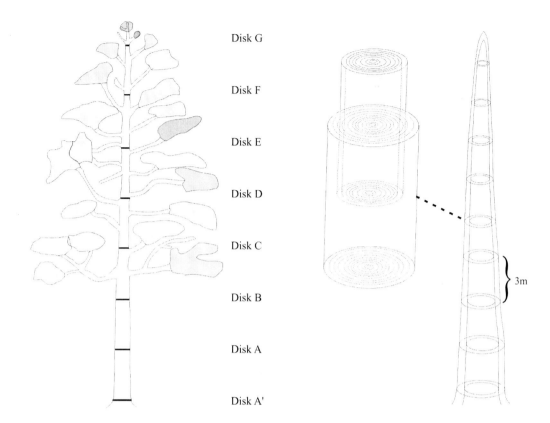

**Figure 9.15** Diagram showing how samples taken every 3 m up a tree can be used to calculate wood volume for the whole tree. (From Speer and Holmes 2004)

2005). These concepts take advantage of the aggregate tree growth model, limiting factors, site selection, and replication, just to name a few of the main principles of dendrochronology that are applied and honed through insect outbreak studies. These techniques continue to be refined as research expands to new insect systems, such as periodical cicadas and mountain pine beetle. The management concerns of foresters affect the research agendas of many scientists as we react to public concern and governmental interest.

## Wildlife Populations and Herbivory

Dendrochronology can be used to determine the dates of herbivory on trees, to estimate wildlife populations through resource availability linkages, and even to study fishery populations based on covariance with sea-surface temperature measures (Spencer 1964, Schweingruber 1996, Speer 2001, Drake et al. 2002). Past fluctuations in animal populations can be documented through scars left on trees such as those from porcupine (*Erethizon epixanthum*) feeding on small branches of pinyon pine in Mesa Verde, Colorado (Spencer 1964), or porcupine populations expanding into northern treeline in Quebec (Payette 1987). A study on Isle

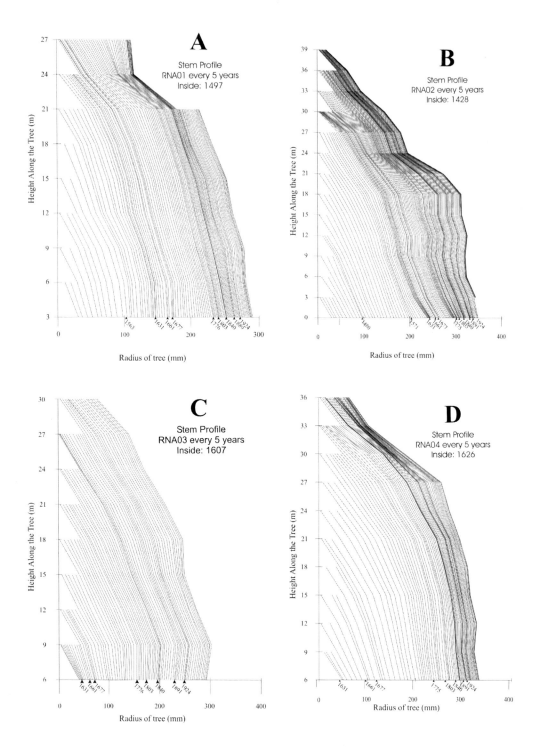

**Figure 9.16** Examples of four trees showing changes in wood volume with height of the tree. The dates and arrows along the x-axis show where pandora moth outbreaks resulted in a decrease in wood volume. (From Speer and Holmes 2004)

Royale National Park in Michigan demonstrated how the removal of wolves (*Canis lupus*) resulted in an increase in moose (*Alces alces*) populations, which then overgrazed balsam fir trees (McLaren and Peterson 1994). Hessl and Graumlich (2002) examined the effects of an elk herd on aspen regeneration in Wyoming, and found that high elk populations reduce the recruitment of aspen trees. Speer (2001) was able to reconstruct masting and found a significant correlation between the regional white oak mast reconstruction in the southern Appalachians and black bear population estimates. Wildlife population reconstructions and examination of ecological interactions help zoologists study wildlife population fluctuations and increase understanding of complex food-web interactions. The long-term perspective of dendrochronology provides the time depth needed to examine the behavior of animals over multiple generations.

Dendrochronology can also provide valuable information for the management of fisheries. Drake et al. (2002) documented a significant correlation between Sitka spruce (*Picea sitchensis*) tree growth and Northeast Pacific salmon stocks, suggesting that both tree and fish responded to, or were tracking, the same environmental variable such as sea-surface temperature. They were able to take this relationship further by reconstructing salmon populations that were verified against other known salmon stock data. Clark et al. (1975) documented fluctuations in albacore tuna (*Thunnus alalunga*) populations by examining tree growth response to broad-scale atmospheric flow patterns that affected sea-surface temperature in the North Pacific, influencing both tree growth and tuna populations. This technique of examining synoptic climate linkages between terrestrial records from trees and sea-surface temperature or circulation patterns has enabled dendrochronologists to shed light on broad-scale circulation and temperature phenomena that also affect fish populations. This type of analysis effectively extends the usable range of dendrochronological reconstructions and, in these examples, aids fishery managers.

## Distributional Limits of Species

Biogeographers have long been interested in the factors that control the range limits of different tree species. Range limits may also mark the ecotone boundaries between different biomes. An **ecotone** is a zone of change from one vegetation type to another that often results in high plant and animal diversity. Ecotones are interesting to study because they are the first place that demonstrates a response to climate change and because of their inherently high level of biodiversity.

Some of the main variables controlling tree species distribution seem to be temperature, precipitation, and disturbance. In a study at the northern range limit of red pine (*Pinus resinosa*), Bergeron and Brisson (1990) found that the species is restricted to island sites that have more frequent fires (a disturbance process), which may limit the competitive ability of boreal forest species, enabling red pine populations to be maintained at 48°N latitude. Conkey et al. (1995) documented growth of jack pine (*Pinus banksiana*) in a marginal location at the eastern edge of its range limit in Acadia National Park, Maine. Jack pine is an early successional species that is fire adapted, but the species was able to survive in a marginal habitat because of the thin soil that prevented later successional species from outcompeting it. Copenheaver et al. (2004) studied a prominent ecotone at Buffalo Mountain, Virginia, between dense forest and mountaintop balds (grassy openings on a mountaintop that are not above treeline). They used transects and stand-age structure analyses, finding that some of these balds are stable while others are being invaded by the surrounding forests. In a study across an elevational gradient in northern Arizona, Fritts et al. (1965) documented that trees growing on the semiarid lower forest border were more sensitive to climatic variability. This lower treeline is controlled by a lack of soil moisture and produces sensitive tree-ring chronologies. Fine-scale analyses of the factors that control a species' range help biogeographers better understand the distribution of species. This understanding of the controlling mechanisms also helps scientists predict future range limits under a changing environment.

## Treeline and Subarctic Studies

High-elevation treeline (the elevational limit to which trees can grow because of temperature or moisture limitations) is another interesting ecotone where trees may take on a shrub-like form, called krumholz. Krumholz growth can occur in response to harsh winter weather, where conditions under the snow pack are more conducive to survival over the winter. Historically, treeline has been studied as a proxy for temperature fluctuations, with the understanding that elevational treeline is limited by cold temperatures (LaMarche and Mooney 1967, LaMarche 1973, LaMarche and Stockton 1974).

Daniels and Veblen (2003) found that precipitation controlled the local elevation of treeline in northern Patagonia and that disturbance locally lowered treeline. They also documented that treeline in Chile and Argentina was limited by lower precipitation as well as low temperatures and predicted that treeline advance may be restricted in a warming climate because of a lack of precipitation (Daniels and Veblen 2003, 2004). Lloyd and Graumlich (1997) also found that treeline is dependent upon moisture as well as temperature, suggesting that treeline response to future warming may depend heavily on water supply. Similar studies have been conducted in high latitudes at the transition to arctic tundra. Au and Tardif (2007) examined tree rings in the shrub dryas (*Dryas integrifolia*) in subarctic Manitoba, Canada. They found that these shrubs produced datable annual rings and could demonstrate that the shrubs were sensitive to previous October precipitation and current year's May temperature. As dendrochronological methods advance, we can now begin to see the complex interactions of the effect of climate as well as disturbances in controlling factors of altitudinal and latitudinal treeline.

## Interactions of Multiple Disturbances

Dendrochronologists have separately studied disturbances such as fire, insect outbreaks, blown down trees, avalanches, and herbivory. In the mid-1990s, researchers started to examine the interaction of multiple disturbances on the same site, giving managers a more complete idea of the how processes affect one another on a given landscape (Hadley 1994, Veblen et al. 1994, Kulakowski and Veblen 2002, Kulakowski et al. 2003, Thompson 2005). Veblen et al. (1994) found that snow avalanches create fire breaks that result in smaller fires, while fires and avalanches kill mature trees, which delays the onset of bark beetle outbreaks because the remaining trees are not large enough for selection by bark beetles. Kulakowski et al. (2003)

found that spruce beetle outbreaks in Colorado also affected the fire regime, resulting in fewer occurrences of surface fires. They suggested a mechanism of the bark beetle outbreaks resulting in higher moisture on the forest floor, which agreed with Reid's (1989) observation of a proliferation of mesic understory herbs in Colorado. Similar observations have been made after mountain pine beetle outbreaks in British Columbia, where an increase in soil moisture was documented due to a decrease in transpiration (Kathy Lewis, personal communication).

Kulakowski et al.'s (2003) finding of fewer surface fires following bark beetle infestation was contrary to previous research that suggested bark beetle outbreaks resulted in an increase in forest fires due to an increase in available fuels (Stuart et al. 1989, McCullough et al. 1998). Buildup of fuels usually occurs after stand-replacing fires, so a difference in the scale of the fire effect might have resulted in these opposite findings. Kulakowski et al. (2003) stated, however, that their observation also holds for stand-replacing fires.

The time since defoliation can also be an issue in fire occurrence, where extensive needle fall occurs a few years after defoliation, which could increase the spread of fire. Those fine fuels decompose quickly and the stand is left with much standing fuel, but it may not have the fine fuel necessary to carry a fire, resulting in a decrease in fire occurrence. Controversial issues such as these remain to be examined with further dendroecological research.

Researchers have found that natural disturbances regenerate forests and make them less susceptible to subsequent disturbances until the forest matures (Kulakowski and Veblen 2002). After the 1997 blowdown event in the Routt National Forest, Colorado, which took down more than 10,000 hectares of subalpine forest, Kulakowski and Veblen (2002) found that forests that had experienced stand-replacing fire within the last 120 years were less susceptible to wind damage because of their vigor. Anderson et al. (1987) found that fire suppression in a ponderosa pine forest in western Montana enabled Douglas-fir to proliferate over the last 100 years, providing more host trees, which resulted in an increase in duration and intensity of western spruce budworm outbreaks. As a way to control the outbreaks, they suggest that fire be reintroduced to maintain the ponderosa pine forest and reduce Douglas-fir density, bringing this forest back into its historical condition. Only after forest managers understand the complex interactions among natural disturbances will they be able to manage their forests tracts in an ecologically sustainable fashion.

## Other Applications of Dendroecology

Schweingruber (1996) developed a program of ecological examination in Switzerland that focuses on the growth and adaptation of plants to environmental stressors. He is also expanding his work to tropical and tundra environments by studying wood anatomy and rings in perennial herbs and shrubs. Tree rings have been used to determine the factors that drive wet heartwood occurrence in forest trees, which is heartwood that has unusually high water content. Krause and Gagnon (2006) found trees growing in an area of a high water table were more likely to have wet heartwood as well as suppressed growth due to the stress of growing in a frequently saturated soil.

Root age can be determined from tree-ring analysis, which provides an understanding of how roots develop in different tree species (Krause and Morin 2005). Studies of black spruce and balsam fir in Quebec demonstrated that adventitious roots grew more than 60% of their length in the first year of development, whereas lateral roots produced 93% of their elongation in their first 10 years (Krause and Morin 2005). This work is useful for our understanding of how roots grow and suggests that the major structure of a root develops fairly quickly. Other research in root wood anatomy will be presented in the chapter on dendrogeomorphology (chapter 10) because this can be a useful tool in examining soil erosion.

Maximum latewood density of annual rings has been found to correlate with normalized-difference vegetation indices, which provide an estimate of vegetation productivity or net primary productivity based on satellite imagery (Malmstrom et al. 1997, D'Arrigo et al. 2000). This correlation is useful for broad-scale estimates of forest productivity and change associated with global climate change, which is an area likely to take on greater importance in the presence of global warming. This work demonstrates that interesting frontiers still exist to be studied with dendrochronology. More of these new directions of research will be discussed in chapter 12.

## Conclusion

Dendroecology has been and is becoming more useful for exploring a wide range of research topics that can provide important information to wildlife, fisheries, and forest resource managers. Combining the study of tree rings and ecology can help us understand the dynamics of natural processes such as disturbance and the interactions between multiple natural phenomena. Trees can provide long-term records on many phenomena at different spatial scales, enabling dendroecologists to contribute to important discussions on scaling laws that could aid management in a changing environment.

# 10
# Dendrogeomorphology

Geomorphology is the study of landforms and the earth surface processes that form and modify them (Gärtner 2007a). **Dendrogeomorphology** uses tree rings to date geological processes that affect tree growth, such as landslides, river deposits, or glacial activity. I consider dendrogeomorphology to include the subfields of **dendroglaciology**, the study of the movement or mass balance of glaciers; **dendrovolcanology**, the study of past volcanic eruptions; and **dendroseismology**, the study of past earthquake events and fault movements through the use of tree rings (table 10.1).

The use of dendrochronology to reconstruct geological phenomena was pioneered in North America more than a century ago. Sherzer (1905) used the growth of spruce trees to estimate the ages of glacial moraines in the Canadian Rockies and Selkirk Mountains in Canada as one of the first dendrogeomorphological applications. In another early application, dendrochronology helped resolve a boundary line dispute between Texas and Oklahoma (Sellards et al. 1923). The Red River marked the boundary between the two states, but because its stream channel meandered over time, the relative location of the state line changed. By examining the age of trees on different land surfaces, the researchers were able to determine the location of the historical boundary. Dendrogeomorphology really became established as a subfield in the United States in the 1970s, and its applications have expanded since this time (Alestalo 1971, Shroder 1978, 1980, Butler 1987, Shroder and Butler 1987, Schweingruber 1996, Wiles et al. 1996).

Shroder (1980: 165) outlined a process-event-response system for the analysis of dendrogeomorphological phenomena. He identified seven basic events: inclination, shear of rootwood or stemwood, corrasion (abrasion or some removal of wood through contact), burial of stemwood, exposure of rootwood, inundation, and denudation (or the removal of vegetation); and he categorized seven responses to these events (Shroder 1980: 165): reaction wood growth, growth suppression, growth release, ring termination and new callous growth, sprouting, succession, and miscellaneous structural or morphological changes in external or internal wood character. This systemic approach is still useful today for dating possible events and responses of trees to geomorphic phenomena.

Most tree-ring sampling for geomorphological research needs to involve targeted sampling in which the direct effects of landslides, earthquakes, glaciers, or soil creep can be identified. Because of the variety of phenomena that can cause reaction wood or scarring in a tree, samples must be selected from areas that have been affected by the process of interest (Shroder 1980, Butler 1987). Targeted or directed sampling uses the basic dendrochronological principle of site selection discussed in chapter 2. Random sampling on the landscape is likely to miss these geomorphological events or require a huge amount of sampling to detect such localized events.

**Table 10.1**   Geomorphic events and how they can be reconstructed using tree rings

| Process | Event | Possible responses | Citation |
|---|---|---|---|
| Volcanic | loss of photosynthesis | suppression | Smiley (1958), Yamaguchi (1983) |
| | lava flow and temperature stress | suppression | |
| | atmospheric cooling | suppression | LaMarche and Hirschboeck (1984) |
| | crown defoliation from tephra fallout | suppression | Smiley (1958), Yamaguchi (1983) |
| | eluviation of leachates harmful/favorable to growth | suppression, release | |
| | reduced aeration of soils due to burial | suppression | |
| | direct encounter with flow | scarring | |
| | denudation of surface | tree establishment | Yamaguchi and Hoblitt (1995) |
| | gas release | suppression | |
| Floodplain dynamics | debris impact during floods | scarring | Gottsfeld and Gottsfeld (1990), McCord (1996) |
| | accretion of point bars | tree establishment | Gottsfeld and Gottsfeld (1990) |
| | erosion of banks | tilting, mortality | Gottsfeld and Gottsfeld (1990) |
| | inundation by sediment | mortality and burial | Sigafoos (1964) |
| | flow dynamics | ring-width variability | Woodhouse (2001) |
| Lake ice dynamics | direct ice push | scarring | Bégin (2000) |
| Glacial | physical impact from glacial ice | scarring | Lawrence (1950), Luckman (1988) |
| | inundation by glacial sediment | suppression, sprouting | Wiles et al. (1999) |
| | temperature stress from proximity of ice | suppression | Lawrence (1950), Wiles et al. (1996) |
| | advance/retreat | missing rings, mortality, establishment | Smith and Laroque (1996), Wiles et al. (1999) |
| | denudation of surface | tree establishment | Sigafoos and Hendricks (1961, 1972), Wiles et al. (1999) |
| | mass balance change | suppression, release | Laroque and Smith (2005) |
| | isostatic adjustment | tree encroachment | Bégin et al. (1993) |

*(Continued)*

**Table 10.1**   (*Continued*)

| Process | Event | Possible responses | Citation |
|---|---|---|---|
| Mass movement | inclination | reaction wood | Corominas and Moya (1999), Fantucci and Sorriso-Valvo (1999) |
| | shear | suppression | Shroder (1978) |
| | corrasion | scarring | Corominas and Moya (1999), Shroder (1978) |
| | exposure of roots | suppression, root mortality, change in cell thickness of roots | Danzer (1996), Gärtner et al. (2001) |
| | inundation | suppression, sprouting, mortality | Hupp (1984), Bégin and Filion (1988), Corominas and Moya (1999) |
| | denudation of surface | tree establishment | Hupp (1984), Hupp et al. (1987) |
| | change in hydrology | release, suppression | Fantucci and Sorriso-Valvo (1999) |
| Earthquake | shear | suppression, missing rings | Jacoby et al. (1988) |
| | inclination | reaction wood | Sheppard and Jacoby (1989) |
| | change in water table | suppression, release | Atwater and Yamaguchi (1991), Sheppard and Jacoby (1989) |
| | extreme ground shaking | suppression, missing rings | Sheppard and Jacoby (1989) |
| | broken tree tops | suppression, mortality | Jacoby (1997) |
| | root system or major limb damage | suppression | Jacoby (1997), Bekker (2004) |

*Source:* Modified from Shroder (1978), Sheppard and Jacoby (1989), and Wiles et al. (1996)

## Sources of Information

### Reaction Wood

Trees react structurally to being tilted by producing reaction wood. In an attempt to straighten the tree, gymnosperms (conifers) thicken cell walls and produce more cells on the downhill side of the tree, whereas angiosperms (flowering trees such as the hardwoods) thicken the tracheids on the uphill side of the tree (called tension wood; see fig. 4.18). This reaction wood can be used to determine the timing of events that tilted the tree trunk, such as landslides or earthquakes (Gärtner 2007a). Changes in the circularity of stem growth can record geomorphic changes through time. To sample for these events, a full cross section of the stem of the tree is preferred, although one can core on the downhill and uphill side of the tree through the reaction wood in an attempt to date such a tilting event. Note that this coring location is contrary to previous sampling protocols discussed in chapter 5, because it is targeting reaction wood, whereas such studies as climate reconstruction try to avoid this irregular growth. By examining the reaction wood of trees in an area of the eastern Pyrenees in Spain that experienced frequent landslides, researchers were able to reconstruct landslide activity there (Corominas and Moya 1999). The reaction wood documented slope instability over the prior 70 years, revealing that landslide activity had increased in recent times compared to the early portion of the chronology from 1926–1959.

## Death Dates

Death dates can be obtained by crossdating dead wood samples against a living tree-ring chronology to determine the advance of a glacier, when landslides occurred, or any other natural event that results in the death of a tree. Preservation of the sample and its outermost rings then determines how far back in time one can crossdate the event that caused tree mortality. Factors that contribute to the quality of wood preservation include climatic conditions (for example, hot and humid or dry and cold), where the tree is located (whether the tree is a standing snag, sitting on soil, suspended in the air, buried in sediment, or buried in a lake in anoxic conditions), and innate resistance of the wood itself to weathering and decay (for example, sequoia and cedar wood).

Death dates can also be used to determine the sedimentation rates on a slope. When a tree dies and falls across a slope, it will remain there for some period of time, catching sediment that comes down the slope in overland flow of water (fig. 10.1). The sedimentation rate can be determined from the amount of sediment present and the time since death of the tree (Hart 2002). Various factors complicate this process. If the tree died and stayed standing for 10 years, and then fell to become a sediment trap, the accumulation rate would be underestimated because of the 10 years that the tree remained standing.

## Establishment Dates

**Ecesis** is the process of vegetation becoming established on previously bare ground that was denuded by flooding or glacial activity (McCarthy and Luckman 1993). Establishment dates of trees can be used to provide a bounding date on when that material was deposited or wiped clean, but there is often a lag (from ecesis) between the time when the event occurred and when trees first establish on the site.

Estimates for this time period can be made on local sites of known disturbance to calibrate a local record. When determining the bounding date for a surface and estimating time of ecesis, the oldest tree on that surface should be sampled (Wiles et al. 1996). The techniques used for this process are the same as those for a stand-age structure employed by dendroecologists (see chapter 9). The goal is to document a cohort of tree establishment on a surface that was cleared or deposited by some geomorphic agent such as a volcanic eruption, landslide, or debris flow. One of the main problems with determining the age of a land surface with tree rings is the lag time between when the surface formed and how long it took trees to establish on the site (successional dynamics). This lag time can be driven by climate, the

**Figure 10.1** Coarse woody debris is composed of logs that fall in the forest. When they may fall across a slope, they catch sediment during overland flow of water. These trees are very important for sediment retention. If death dates can be established in the trees and the amount of sediment can be measured that accumulates behind the log, then sedimentation rates can be determined. (Photo from LaMarche 1968)

biology of the trees, distance to a seed source, and presence of seed dispersers (Fastie 1995). All of these factors combine, leaving some doubt as to the exact age of the surface, but establishment dates do provide a bounding date of the earliest possible time that the surface could have been formed.

## Wound Events

Trees can be damaged during geomorphic events, and these wounds can be dated to reconstruct rock falls or other damaging occurrences. For example, debris flow events were reconstructed near the Valais region of the Swiss Alps using tree scars and eccentric growth from trees being dislodged in past debris flows (Stoffel et al. 2005). The researchers were able to extend the debris flow records from 80 years of historical data to 397 years from tree-ring records and found that the peak of debris flow occurrence was in the 1800s. Scars can be caused by many sources, so location of the scar and clustering of scar events is important for documenting past geomorphic phenomena. Other possible geomorphic causes of tree scars include landslides, avalanches, flood waters, and ice flows.

## Coarse Woody Debris

Coarse woody debris is an important component of the dead wood in any forest because it acts as a sediment trap, nutrient source, and increases habitat (fig. 10.1; Daniels et al. 1997, Hart 2003, Rubino and McCarthy 2003, Campbell and Laroque 2005, 2007). Foresters and geomorphologists have defined stages of wood decay from recent (decay class I) to old (decay class VI). In a dendrochronological study on the southwestern coast of British Columbia, researchers successfully calibrated the decay classes of cedar by determining the time since death of the trees (Daniels et al. 1997), enabling foresters to more accurately assess how long logs had remained on the ground as a sediment trap. The authors also noted that no classification system was appropriate for snags because of their slower decay rate while they are standing above the ground surface. Gore et al. (1985) developed a model based on empirical evidence to estimate the maximum likelihood estimate of the average number of years that a bole would stand before it fell; however, their model does not take tree species or site conditions into consideration. An understanding of coarse woody debris and its dynamics through time help in stream restoration and provides information on habitat changes in riparian areas.

## Roots

Root analysis can be used as part of a whole-tree analysis, as demonstrated in the study conducted by Krause and Eckstein (1993), who found that root increment was significantly correlated with temperature. Gärtner (2007b) discussed the usefulness and difficulties of using roots to determine the rate of soil erosion, deposition, and other damages to trees through geomorphic agents. He noted that little work to date has been successful in the use of roots, but current work with anatomical features of roots have promise in providing information in the future. Gärtner et al. (2001) and Gärtner (2007b) demonstrated different anatomical characteristics for roots at different depths in the soil (fig. 10.2) and showed that this change in root wood anatomy can be used to determine the year and even the season of subaerial exposure of roots through erosion.

## Subfields of Dendrogeomorphology

### Dendrovolcanology

Volcanic eruptions can be documented with tree rings through the direct effect on tree stems from the shock wave, ash fall, or debris from the eruption; mortality of trees on a site; or a

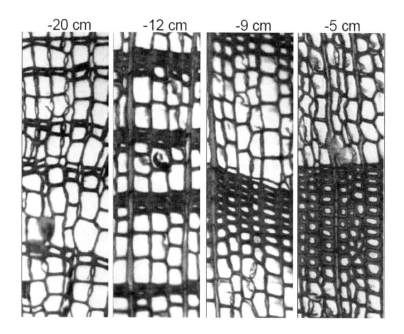

**Figure 10.2** Wood structure for roots of *Larix decidua* at four different depths in the soil (20, 12, 9, 5 cm; from Gärtner 2003). Note the lack of latewood thickening for roots from deeper locations in the soil.

global cooling event from the injection of gases and aerosols into the atmosphere. Several fascinating studies have linked trees to notable volcanic eruptions (Smiley 1958, LaMarche and Hirschboeck 1984, Yamaguchi and Hoblitt 1995, Briffa et al. 1998, Jacoby et al. 1999). Yamaguchi (1983) was able to use suppression events in Douglas-fir to document major eruptions from Mount St. Helens. In a subsequent collaborative effort, Yamaguchi and Hoblitt (1995) used establishment of trees to determine bounding dates on a series of lava flows since 870 and determined that Mount St. Helens has had dormant periods that have lasted from 123 to 600 years during their record. In Arizona, an eruption date of 1064 was determined for Sunset Crater (Smiley 1958) by the presence of narrow rings in archaeological wood collected from nearby Wupatki ruin, an Ancestral Pueblo site occupied from approximately 900 to 1275.

Large eruptions near the equator can put enough sulfur dioxide and aerosols into the stratosphere to reduce global temperatures for one to three years. If temperatures get cool enough during the growing season of the trees, then a frost ring can be produced. LaMarche and Hirschboeck (1984) identified frost rings in the bristlecone pine chronology at 3000-m elevation in the White Mountains of California that were related to major volcanic eruptions such as Krakatau in 1680, Vesuvius in 1785, and Tambora in 1815, among others. Jacoby et al. (1999) documented an extremely low density ring in 1783 in Alaska and northern Canada. They were able to compare this date to historical accounts of Inuits in the area that document a population decrease. They also found that the Inuit oral traditions speak of a great disaster around that time. This extremely cold summer apparently caused extensive mortality in the Inuit in 1783. Further discussion of volcanic effects on trees and how they can be used to date events can be found in Schweingruber (1996).

Volcanic events may affect a broader spatial scale than normal climatic fluctuations, as suggested by the work of LaMarche and Hirschboeck (1984). For example, in a study of ring-width density chronologies from both North America and Europe, Jones et al. (1995) documented consistent years of low density in 1601, 1641, 1669, 1699, and 1912. Four of these years coincide with known volcanic eruptions. Decreased density of tree rings means that individual cell walls are less lignified, which in the case of volcanic eruptions could be due to an increase in aerosols in the atmosphere resulting in cooler temperatures and thus reducing lignification in late summer. Jones et al.'s (1995) study is also a good example of the use of spatial scale to tease apart different signals in tree-ring chronologies. They only wanted to record extreme broad-scale events, so they examined years with low tree-ring density on both the European and North American continents.

## Dendroglaciology

Early work in dendroglaciology set the precedent for the variety of information that can be obtained from tree-ring studies as they apply to glacial research (Tarr and Martin 1914, Lawrence 1950, Sigafoos and Hendricks 1961, 1972). Glacial advance can be documented by dating mortality events of sheared trees that are deposited in outwash till, and glacial retreat can be documented by the establishment of trees on newly exposed glacial till (Wiles et al. 1999). Dating mortality events from glacial advance is more precise because the death of the trees can occur in a year or less, while it may take decades for trees to establish on newly exposed rock and till after glacial retreat (McCarthy and Luckman 1993). Through connections with climatic forcing factors, **glacial mass balance** (periods of growth and ablation) can also be reconstructed from tree rings (Matthews 1977, Laroque and Smith 2005). Trees that grow at the trimline (fig. 10.3) where the ice is directly next to the trees, can record fine-scale glacial fluctuation in time (Lawrence 1950, Wiles et al. 1996). Hard work over the past few decades has produced evidence for many alpine and continental glacial changes over the past 2000 years that have been combined into broad-scale interpretation of glacial dynamics (Wiles et al. 2008). Such dendroglacial reconstructions as these extend many centuries into the past and clarify the mechanisms that drive glacial activity. For further reading, Smith and Lewis (2007) document the history of the field of dendroglaciology and outline the various techniques that can be used to glean information on glacial activity.

The rate of **isostatic adjustment** (the rise of land) after the retreat of glaciers has been documented using the downslope establishment of trees toward present-day sea level (Bégin et al. 1993). Once the weight of ice from a major glacier is removed from the terrain, the land begins to adjust to that lack of weight and to rise, sitting higher on the mantle. New land surfaces are exposed upon which trees can establish. During the last glacial maximum at 21,000 calendar years ago, there were approximately 6 km of ice above the Canadian Shield. In a research project located on the margins of Hudson Bay in Quebec, Bégin et al. (1993) dated tree establishment along transects to current sea level parallel to the slope, documenting the progressive advancement of this lower treeline. A similar pattern was identified from land

**Figure 10.3** A glacier may kill trees as it advances and incorporate those trees in the till. Massive glacial advances can then be dated from the mortality events of the trees. The glacier leaves the trees alive above the trimline (the highest position of the glacier upslope on the canyon-valley walls). Trees at the trimline may survive, but their growth is stunted by the proximity of the glacier. Their suppressed growth can then be used to determine the ice accumulation of the glacier, and fine-scale fluctuations of the glacier can be tracked through time. (Photo by the author)

adjustment after Little Ice Age glacial retreat in Glacier Bay, Alaska, where Motyka (2003) documented 3.2 m of uplift since the late 18th century.

## Mass Movement

Tree rings can also be used to examine any mass movement such as rockslides (fig. 10.4), landslides (Corominas and Moya 1999), rock glaciers (Giardino et al. 1984), debris flow (Hupp 1984, Hupp et al. 1987), or volcanic mudflow (also known as a lahar; Yamaguchi and Hoblitt 1995). Just as with flooding, trees can be scarred by mass movements of earth, they can be killed, or fresh earth surfaces can be deposited or exposed on which trees can establish (Hupp 1984, Hupp et al. 1987, Corominas and Moya 1999, Fantucci and Sorriso-Valvo 1999). Soil creep can cause curvature of stems, although it can be difficult to differentiate from curvature due to wintertime snow pressure (Shroder 1980). Soil erosion can expose roots and cause root mortality (LaMarche 1968, Danzer 1996) or producing cells with different cell-wall thicknesses depending upon their depth in the soil (fig. 10.2 and 10.5; Gärtner and Schweingruber 2001, Gärtner 2007b).

**Figure 10.4** Frequent rockfall down a landslide shoot may accumulate a large amount of sediment. As the trees growing on the slope are killed and fall downslope to be incorporated in the sediment pile (and in this case the lake) at the base of the slope, the wood is well preserved and can be sampled to determine the landslide frequency for the area. Landslide debris piles are also a great source of old deadwood that may have been accumulating for some time and could result in a very long chronology. (Photo by the author)

## Dendroseismology: Plate Boundaries, Faults, and Earthquakes

Any earthquake could cause damage by breaking fine and even large roots for the locally affected trees. Jacoby (1997) provided a complete review of paleoseismology from tree-ring analysis, noting that trees can be damaged directly from shaking, elevation changes, and

**Figure 10.5** These trees around Yellowstone Lake have been subject to soil erosion; the roots can be sampled to determine when they died to date this past event. (Photo by the author)

liquefaction or indirectly through earthquakes that induce landslides and tsunamis. A massive earthquake that triggered a tsunami and landslide killed thousands of trees sometime between 894 and 897 and was documented by studying submerged logs from Lake Washington near Seattle (Jacoby et al. 1992). This work combined dendrochronology with $^{14}$C dating to determine a window of dates for a floating chronology (a chronology not anchored in time) composed of trees that had been killed in the same season of the same year by a tsunami triggered by this earthquake. Atwater and Yamaguchi (1991) also found evidence for a major coastal event that submerged trees in the Seattle area in 1700. In addition to tree mortality and damage, suppression of ring width over several years may be another indicator of seismological events. For example, an 1887 earthquake in Kazakhstan resulted in ring-width reduction for 4 to 15 years in most sampled trees (Yadov and Kulieshius 1992).

Considerable research has been conducted to study specific types of plate movement associated with plate tectonics and fault types, such as transform plate boundaries (Page 1970, LaMarche and Wallace 1972, Wallace and LaMarche 1979, Meisling and Sieh 1980, Jacoby et al. 1988, Sheppard and Jacoby 1989, Lin and Lin 1998, Wells et al. 1998, Vittoz et al. 2001), convergent plate boundaries (Jacoby and Ulan 1983, Sheppard and Jacoby 1989, Atwater and Yamaguchi 1991, Veblen et al. 1992, Yadav and Kulieshius 1992, Kitzberger et al. 1995,

Jacoby et al. 1997), strike-slip faults (Stahle et al. 1992, Van Arsdale et al. 1998), reverse faults (Ruzhich et al. 1982, Stahle et al. 1992, Van Arsdale et al. 1998), and normal faults (Sheppard and White 1995, Bekker 2004). Because earthquakes are the results of plate tectonics, the study of geological faults with dendrochronology uses the same techniques as earthquake reconstructions. It is important that the researcher take into account damage to trees and the spatial distribution of sampling when determining whether suppression of tree rings is directly related to the seismic events under study (Jacoby 1997, Bekker 2004).

## Limitations of Dendrogeomorphology

As with all tree-ring work, accurate crossdating of samples is paramount for producing a solid dendrogeomorphological study. Reduced tree growth due to proximity of ice or damage from an earthquake can cause trees to have micro or missing rings for a number of years. Only crossdating can detect these locally absent rings and provide accurate dates for geomorphic events. There are other restrictions on the application of dendrogeomorphology that are more difficult to correct (McCarthy et al. 1991, McCarthy and Luckman 1993). A lag can occur between the deposition of a surface and the establishment of trees on that surface. This lag can be affected by the climate, proximity to a seed source, and the substrate itself making it difficult to accurately determine the timing of some event. Other potential sources of error include sampling above the root collar, which can underestimate the age of a surface and missing the pith of the tree (McCarthy et al. 1991). Also when dealing with suppression events, it is difficult to assign the cause of such an event definitely, so climate and other confounding factors must be thoroughly examined. Being aware of these possible sources of error and working to minimize them can result in accurate dating of past geomorphic events.

## Conclusion

Dendrogeomorphology has greatly expanded in the last 20 years, with a wealth of applications and studies documenting past geologic events. The researcher has to think creatively about how a past event may have been recorded by the trees in the area. The variety of sampling techniques and sources of data used in this subfield of dendrochronology are probably more diverse than in any of the other applications. As with all of dendrochronology, these studies rely on the accuracy provided by crossdating. Without it, researchers would not be able to definitely determine the timing of events or to assign a specific event to a growth response. In the next chapter, I will describe the use of chemical and isotopic analysis of tree rings, which is one of the newest forms of data being drawn from tree rings.

# 11
# Dendrochemistry

Dendrochemistry is the measurement of element concentrations within tree rings to make spatial and historical estimates of element availabilities and to understand the physiological processes that control the uptake, transport, and sequestration of elements in secondary xylem. This field also broadly includes stable isotope dendrochronology (the measurement of stable isotopes such as $^{12}C$, $^{13}C$, $^{16}O$, and $^{18}O$ in tree rings for climate and ecological applications) and calibration of the radiocarbon dating curve. All of these applications involve the chemical analysis of tree rings and share some similar issues in sampling and analysis.

Dendrochemistry is the use of tree rings as indicators of past chemical fluctuations in the environment (Cutter and Guyette 1993). Trees take up nutrients and elements through the bark, directly from the atmosphere through their leaves, and through their roots along with absorbed soil moisture (Donnelly et al. 1990, Leavitt 1992). Most chemical analysis deals with the examination of the uptake of heavy metals because they are one of the main contaminants of soil and water. Trees take up heavy metals that often travel as part of soluble organic compounds (**ligands**) and usually become fixed as part of cell walls. Wood rays can transport the ligands from the outer rings to the inside of the sapwood. Essential elements (most commonly phosphorous) also can be transported from interior to outer rings to meet the metabolic needs of the cambium. This process is called **radial translocation** and is one of the major complicating factors of dendrochemistry, which are discussed in greater detail below.

## Methods of Elemental Analysis

When sampling in the field for a dendrochemistry project, the researcher must take precautions to avoid contaminating the sample with materials like WD-40 and metals from jewelry. Cross-contamination between trees, cores, and even individual tree rings should also be prevented. New borers (before the Teflon coating is worn off) can be used to reduce contamination from the metal of the borer, and the borer should be cleaned with acetone to ensure that no industrial lubricant is contaminating the samples. In the field, I wear latex gloves to avoid contaminating the core and rinse the increment borer with isopropyl alcohol or acetone between each core.

Two cores can be taken from the same side of the tree separated by a vertical inch so that one core can be sanded for dating and the other can be sectioned for dendrochemical analysis based on the dating of the first core. The cores are packed in paper straws in the field for drying in an oven (at about 60°C) for 24 hours in the laboratory. If volatile elements, such as mercury, are being studied, air drying the samples for a longer period of time rather than oven drying is preferable because these elements may be lost through vaporization.

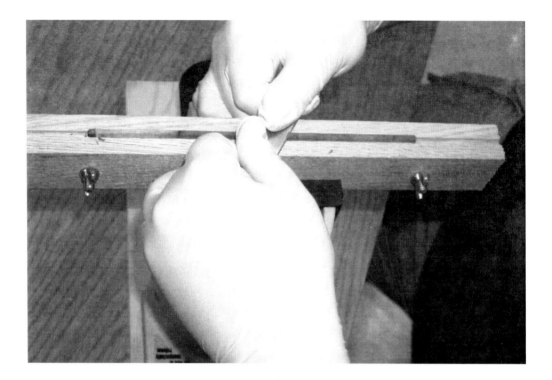

**Figure 11.1** A dendrochemistry sample in a core clamp. The clamp is constructed from two pieces of wood that are grooved on the top center to hold the core. The center of the two boards is drilled through in three places and a bolt with a wing nut is inserted through each hole to clamp down the core. In this picture, note that the researcher wears gloves to avoid contamination of the sample and uses a stainless steel scalpel instead of sandpaper to surface the sample prior to dating. (Photo by the author)

Normal dendrochronological preparation in which cores are glued to a core mount and their surfaces are sanded with a belt sander cannot be used in dendrochemical research for a number of reasons. First, while the core samples do need to be surfaced and dated, they also need to be removed from the core mount for the subsequent chemical analysis. Not only does gluing make removal difficult, but glue may carry contaminants. Second, sanding with a belt sander creates a lot of dust from the often-metallic components of the sandpaper that fills the surface of the cells.

In addition to sampling a pair of cores, a good finishing technique is to use a temporary vise clamp made of wood to hold the core (fig. 11.1) and surface the core with a stainless steel scalpel so that the ring structure can be observed for dating of the sample. Normal razor blades should be avoided because they are likely to leave metal flakes that can contaminate the wood. In some cases where the composition of the steel itself may cause contamination, alternate cutting methods such as the use of a laser may be required (Sheppard and Witten 2005). The core samples are often cut into annual segments or blocks of rings (3–20 years) for analysis using wet chemistry, depending upon the minimum amount of wood needed for accurate analysis of the element(s) of interest. The precision of new chemical analysis techniques and instruments enable sampling at annual and even subannual resolution if needed. Many instruments have been used for elemental analysis of tree rings. Inductively coupled plasma mass spectrometry (Guyette et al. 1991), neutron activation analysis (Guyette et al. 1989), proton-induced X-ray emission (Hall 1987), and proton-induced gamma-ray emission (Hall 1987) are some of the more commonly used methods of elemental analysis in tree rings.

In the past, analysis would be conducted on clusters of tree rings because enough wood could not be extracted from a single year of growth when sampled with a standard Swedish increment borer with 5.15 mm diameter. Instrument detection levels are consistently improving, thereby enabling researchers to use smaller samples for analysis. Also, some tools, such as a 12-mm borer, have been used to obtain a larger wood sample for each year. Because of radial transport within the sapwood, however, annual resolution is not always possible.

## Radial Translocation

The movement of elements across ring boundaries is known as radial translocation. This transfer is problematic for dendrochronologists because the resultant signal of an element does not necessarily relate to the time that it was taken up. Whether a given element is translocated seems to be a function of both species and environment (Cutter and Guyette 1993). Tom Yanosky (personal communication) has suggested that translocation may act as a pressure valve that helps maintain physiologically favorable element concentrations within living parenchyma, especially near the cambium. When concentrations exceed some threshold, an element may be translocated away from the cambium, whereas at more typical concentrations the same element may not be particularly mobile (Vroblesky et al. 2005). Trees growing over parts of an aquifer contaminated by large concentrations of potassium (from chemical munitions) showed large heartwood concentrations of potassium and sapwood concentrations that increased from outer to inner rings, whereas trees growing over uncontaminated reaches showed smaller concentrations of potassium in heartwood and an increasing gradient from inner to outer sapwood rings (Vroblesky et al. 2005). Translocation is an issue for some species and for many elements, but the salient issue is whether there remains a usable environmental signal (Yanosky, personal communication).

Hall (1987) examined translocation of 90 elements in pitch pine from New Jersey and found that calcium, sodium, and potassium were all translocated, whereas titanium, manganese, iron, copper, zinc, phosphorous, nitrogen, fluorine, magnesium, aluminum, strontium, and rubidium were not. Lead is a toxic but common contaminant in which many researchers, public health inspectors, and politicians have reason to be interested. Some studies have indicated that lead is an element that trees translocate across ring boundaries, complicating any conclusions about the timing of lead contamination in the past (Ault et al. 1970, Bindler et al. 2004), while others have shown that lead can be accurately recorded in the heartwood of trees with dry heartwood (Guyette et al. 1991). By studying $^{206}Pb/^{207}Pb$ (Pb, lead) in Scots pine in Sweden, Bindler et al. (2004) found that the tree-ring records did not match the timing of other natural records of lead, such as peat sequences or soil lead contamination. In one of the first studies of lead uptake by trees in the United States, Ault et al. (1970) looked at lead concentrations in tree rings around the New Jersey Turnpike and found that the amount of lead contained in the rings greatly increased toward the outside of the tree. They demonstrated almost a doubling of lead concentration in the rings over a 30-year period, which was greater than the atmospheric increase of lead over the same time. They speculated that the trees might be excluding lead from the inner xylem and therefore are not an accurate record of the environment.

However, some tree species with dry heartwood were shown to be excellent long-term records of changes in lead concentrations in the soil (Guyette et al. 1991). This research was able to reconstruct lead for the past 300 years from the heartwood of eastern red cedar (*Juniperus virginiana*) in southeastern Missouri and showed an increase in lead after mining operations started close to the study site in the late 1800s. Guyette et al. (1991) also identified that sites need to have acidic soils for efficient uptake of lead, and samples have to be taken from heartwood that is relatively dry. Without these conditions, lead may not be brought into the tree from the soils and it may be translocated in the sapwood.

A tree often accumulates metabolic wastes and unneeded elements in the heartwood, making it resistant to decay and avoided by insects. Baldcypress (*Taxodium distichum*) in North Carolina was found to compartmentalize excess chloride in its heartwood as a response to saltwater intrusion due to dredging and sea-level rise (Yanosky et al. 1995). The researchers could estimate the timing of saltwater intrusion because the trees seemed to transport the chloride from the oldest part of the sapwood to the innermost sapwood, which then became irrevocably sequestered as the heartwood boundary progressed toward the outside of the tree. From elevated levels of chloride in the heartwood and an estimate of the location of the heartwood/sapwood boundary in the past, they were able to estimate that this contamination started around 1850 (Yanosky et al. 1995).

## Other Confounding Factors

The solubility of elements is often controlled by other environmental conditions such as pH. Guyette et al. (1992) used manganese concentrations in tree rings as a measure of soil pH in eastern red cedar (*Juniperus virginiana*) on four sites in the eastern Missouri Ozark Mountains. They were able to document changes in soil pH back to 1700 and to use soil chemistry and historical records to demonstrate the validity of their record. They suggested that this technique may be useful on other sites to document changes in soil pH due to acid deposition, climate change, or ecological disturbances. Elemental concentrations in trees may be dependent on more factors than the simple levels of that element in the environment, so that soil pH needs to be considered in dendrochemical reconstructions. This also means that, under the right circumstances, soil pH itself can be measured from tree rings.

## Event Reconstructions

Ring width is often adversely affected by the availability of toxic or highly concentrated metals. A suppression in ring width has been observed when certain elements in the surrounding area reach toxic levels. For example, a decrease in the size of tree rings of shortleaf pine (*Pinus echinata*) at Cades Cove, Tennessee, in the early 1900s corresponded with peak levels of iron and titanium in those same rings (Baes and McLaughlin 1984). Further research showed that the probable source of the metal was the nearby Copperhill smelter that was active at the turn of the century. In another example, Yanosky et al. (2001) found an increase in chloride in the rings of oak trees that had access to water contaminated with chlorinated hydrocarbons; they also observed a decrease in ring width in these same affected trees, demonstrating the timing of contamination. This use of multiple lines of information from the same cores helps to corroborate the timing and cause of injury in dendrochronological records.

### Elements That Are Useful in Dendrochemistry

Guyette and McGinnes (1987) found elevated levels of aluminum, iron, zinc, copper, strontium, boron, and manganese in eastern red cedar trees in Missouri that matched smelting activity in nearby mining areas. Aluminum, iron, and zinc showed the greatest change in concentration in conjunction with smelting, and these elements are suggested as possible indicators to track the timing and influence of smelting on sites with unknown exposure. As mentioned earlier, Hall (1987) found that titanium, manganese, iron, copper, zinc, phosphorous, nitrogen, fluorine, magnesium, aluminum, strontium, and rubidium did not translocate in pitch pine from New Jersey, suggesting that these elements may be reliable measures of the timing of their introduction to the environment. Vroblesky and Yanosky (1990) measured iron and chloride on the Aberdeen Proving Grounds in Maryland and found that both elements demonstrated an increase in concentration in the tree rings of tulip poplar (*Liriodendro tulipifera*) when historical activity would have caused an increase in deposition or mobilization of these elements.

## Conclusions on Dendrochemistry

Trees can be used as environmental indicators that provide the timing and spatial extent of contamination events (Vroblesky et al. 2005). An excellent knowledge of soil chemistry is required in dendrochemistry because most metals enter the tree through root uptake. Dendrochemical work is complicated by translocation of elements and how well the trees take up certain elements, but it shows potential for future work in dendrochronology. The tree-species being selected for analysis is an important consideration in dendrochemistry. The ability of a tree to become a recorder of environmental chemistry is based on habitat-based, xylem-based, and element-based factors, all of which need to be carefully considered when choosing where and how to conduct a dendrochemical analysis (Cutter and Guyette 1993).

## Radiometric Isotopes

One of the earliest applications of dendrochronology involving isotopes was the calibration of the $^{14}$C dating curve. Radiocarbon, like all radiometric isotopes, decays at a regular rate known as its half-life. This decay rate enables researchers to determine how much time has passed since the isotope was incorporated in the organism. With $^{14}$C, plants take in carbon from the atmosphere as long as they are alive, remaining in equilibrium with atmospheric levels of carbon. However, the natural production of $^{14}$C in the atmosphere varies slightly through time as affected by solar activity and the Earth's magnetic field, which contribute to variable differences in calendar and radiocarbon ages in the past. Thus, $^{14}$C dates needed to be calibrated to account for these differences and to ensure the most reliable ages on samples. Wood samples from giant sequoia (*Sequoiadendron giganteum*) and bristlecone pine (*Pinus longaeva*) were taken for the length of each chronology and submitted to various radiocarbon labs (Ferguson 1968). The labs were able to verify each other's dates and the measurements from the two species also confirmed the temporal drift in the radiocarbon record, so that at 10,000 years before present the radiocarbon curve is off by 2000 years. This means that a 10,000-year BP radiocarbon date has a true age of 12,000 calendar years. This distinction is important when comparing $^{14}$C production in the atmosphere to absolutely dated sunspot records for the purpose of determining what drives $^{14}$C production.

The current, widely accepted radiocarbon calibration curve is based on the European oak tree-ring chronology (from Ireland and Germany) going back about 10,000 calendar years, which has been extended back nearly an additional 2000 years with a European preboreal pine chronology (Becker 1993, Friedrich et al. 1999).

## Stable Isotopes

Stable isotope analysis of tree rings is becoming one of the fastest growing applications of dendrochronology (table 11.1; Long 1982, Epstein and Krishnamurthy 1990, Leavitt 1992, McCarroll and Loader 2004). This technique analyzes isotope ratios (usually $^{2}$H/$^{1}$H, $^{13}$C/$^{12}$C, and $^{18}$O/$^{16}$O), with the carbon coming from carbon dioxide ($CO_2$) in the atmosphere and the hydrogen and oxygen signatures deriving from soil moisture (McCarroll and Loader 2004). Other stable isotope ratios such as $^{15}$N/$^{14}$N (Bukata and Kyser 2005), $^{34}$S/$^{32}$S (Yang et al. 1996), and $^{87}$Sr/$^{86}$Sr (English et al. 2001) have been examined but not as extensively as those of hydrogen, carbon, and oxygen. The biological pathways that control how trees fractionate stable isotopes and then incorporate them into their rings are fairly well understood, enabling researchers to reconstruct atmospheric temperature, humidity, and water source from which precipitation came (McCarroll and Loader 2004). Most trees take up surface water, which comes directly from precipitation. If a tree is taking up a significant amount of groundwater from deeper underground (such as mesquite trees in the American Southwest, which can have a 60-m-deep tap root), the isotopic composition could be much different. Uncertainties arise because of the variety of factors that control the concentration of these isotopes in the atmosphere and how the plant incorporates them. Oxygen isotopes are controlled by the amount and source of precipitation, temperature, atmospheric humidity, and transpiration of the plant, whereas carbon isotopes are controlled by the carbon dioxide source, water stress, temperature, humidity, transpiration, and abundance of the isotopes (fig. 11.2).

For example, $\delta^{18}$O analysis was used to develop a 1000-year-long precipitation reconstruction from juniper trees in the Karakorum Mountains of northern Pakistan (Treydte et al. 2006). $\delta^{18}$O was used instead of ring width because the precipitation signal was enhanced due to the multiple effects of atmospheric humidity on tree physiology. The dendrochronologists demonstrated that the 20th century was the wettest period throughout the record and that this wet interval diverged from normal cycles but matched predictions associated with anthropogenic warming for this region. This research demonstrates the good replication of

**Table 11.1** A summary of the tree-ring isotope studies for paleoenvironmental research

| Reference | Species | Site | Age range | Wood component | Isotopes | Data treatment | Environmental or other signal |
|---|---|---|---|---|---|---|---|
| Anderson et al. (1998) | 4 *Abies alba* | central Switzerland | 1913–1995 | pooled WW α-cellulose | $\delta^{13}C$, $\delta^{18}O$ | first difference | temp., prec., and RH |
| Anderson et al. (2002) | 4 fir *Abies alba* | central Switzerland | 1913–1995 | pooled WW α- cellulose | $\delta^{18}O$ | none | prec. and RH |
| Becker et al. (1991) | *Quercus* sp. and *Pinus sylvestris* | south-central Europe | Late glacial–Holocene | 10-year blocks, cellulose | $\delta^{13}C$, $\delta D$ | none | qualitative to Late glacial–Holocene |
| Bert et al. (1997) | 10 *Abies alba* | France | 1860–1980 | 5-year blocks, holocellulose | $\delta^{13}C$ | D | possible age-related trend |
| Buhay and Edwards (1995) | elm, pine, maple | Ontario, Canada | 1610–1990 | 10-year blocks, cellulose | $\delta^{18}O$, $\delta D$ | none | modeled $\delta^{18}O$ of prec. and air RH |
| Burk and Stuiver (1981) | various | North America | spatial | 3 years + blocks, cellulose | $\delta^{18}O$ | none | RH and temp. |
| Craig (1954) | *Sequoiadendron giganteum* | North America | 1027 BC–AD 1649 | WW | $\delta^{13}C$ | none | link to $^{13}C$ in wood and the atmosphere |
| Dubois (1984) | *Pinus sylvestris* | United Kingdom | Recent and ancient | bulk cellulose | $\delta D$ | none | prec. and RH |
| Dupouey et al. (1993) | *Fagus sylvatica* | France | 1950–1990 | cellulose annual | $\delta^{13}C$ | $C_i$ calculated | extractable soil moisture (July) and $CO_2$ |
| Duquesnay et al. (1998) | *Fagus sylvatica* | northeastern France | 1850–1990 | pooled 10-year cellulose | $\delta^{13}C$ | D, $C_i$, and WUE | age effects and long-term trends |
| Edwards et al. (2000) | 19 fir *Abies alba* | southern Germany | 1004–1980 | LW cellulose | $\delta^{13}C$, $\delta D$ | detrended and shifted | RH and temp. |
| Epstein and Krishnamurthy (1990) | 1 *Pinus aristata* (+22 sp.) | California and global | 990–1990 | 3– to 5-year blocks, cellulose | $\delta^{13}C$, $\delta D$ | 25-year moving average | qualitative link to temp. |

*(Continued)*

**Table 11.1** (Continued)

| Reference | Species | Site | Age range | Wood component | Isotopes | Data treatment | Environmental or other signal |
|---|---|---|---|---|---|---|---|
| Epstein and Yapp (1976) | various (incl. *Pinus aristata*) | Scotland and North America | 1841–1970, 970–1974 | WW 10-year blocks | δD | 40-year running mean | winter temp. |
| Farmer and Baxter (1974) | *Quercus robur, Larix decidua* | United Kingdom | 1892–1972 | WW | δ¹³C | 10-year running mean | atmospheric C |
| February and Stock (1999) | 6 *Widdringtonia cedarb* | South Africa | 1900–1976 | whole ring cellulose | δ¹³C | corrected not detrended | Air δ¹³C, not prec. |
| Feng et al. (1999) | 2 *Picea* | northeastern China | 1967–1996, 10,040 BP | 5-year blocks, cellulose | δD | none | monsoon influence |
| Feng and Epstein (1995a) | pine, juniper, oak | North America | 1840–1990 | 5-year blocks, cellulose | δ¹³C | polynomial, 15-year running average | high frequency, prec. low frequency, atmospheric C |
| Feng and Epstein (1995b) | 7 various | North America | 1840–1990 | 5-year blocks, cellulose | δD | 25-year running average | +5.3%/°C to +17%/°C |
| Freyer (1979a) | 26 various | Northern Hemisphere | 1850–1975 | 2- to 5-year blocks, cellulose | δ¹³C | none | trends in atmospheric C |
| Freyer (1979b) | 10 various | Germany | 1890–1975 | 2-year blocks | δ¹³C | none | influence of pollution on δ¹³C |
| Freyer and Belacy (1983) | 12 *Quercus robur* and *Pinus sylvestris* | Germany and Sweden | 1480–1979 | 1- and 10-year blocks, cellulose | δ¹³C | first difference | "industrial effect", temp., prec. |
| Gray and Se (1984) | 3 *Picea glauca* | Canada | 1883–1975 | 5-year blocks, cellulose | δD | none | temp. and source water |
| Gray and Thompson (1976) | 1 *Picea glauca* | Canada | 1880–1969 | 5-year blocks, cellulose | δ¹⁸O | none | 1.3 ± 0.1%/°C |
| Gray and Thompson (1977) | *Picea glauca* | Canada | 1882–1969 | 5-yr blocks WW, cellulose, lignin | δ¹⁸O | none | signal strength with temp. |

| Reference | Species | Location | Years | Blocks | Isotopes | Correction | Climate signal |
|---|---|---|---|---|---|---|---|
| Hemming et al. (1998) | *Fagus sylvatica, Pinus sylvestris, Quercus robur* | United Kingdom | 1900–1994 | various | $\delta^{13}C$, $\delta^{18}O$, $\delta D$ | corrected and first difference | RH>temp.> prec.>sunshine |
| Jedrysek et al. (1998) | 2 *Quercus* + fragments | Poland | 1850–1970, 10th–20th c. | 1- and 5-year LW cellulose | $\delta^{13}C$, $\delta D$ | 5-year running average | $^{13}C$ May–July prec. |
| Kitagawa and Matsumoto (1995) | 12 *Cryptomeria japonica* | southern Japan | 1862–1991 | 5- and 10-year blocks, α-cellulose | $\delta^{13}C$ | none | temp. MWP and LIA |
| Krishnamurthy (1996) | 1 *Juniperus phoenica* | Sinai Peninsula | 1550–1950 | 5-year wood blocks | $\delta^{13}C$ | ratio internal to ambient $CO_2$ | air $\delta^{13}C$ and climate, possible moisture |
| Krishnamurthy and Epstein (1985) | 1 *Juniperus procera* | Kenya | 1834–1979 | 5-year blocks, cellulose | $\delta D$ | none | lake levels and water stress |
| Lawrence and White (1984) | 2 *Pinus strobus* | North America | 1960–1980 | annual (C-bound H) | $\delta D$ | none | May–August prec. amount |
| Leavitt (1993) | 56 *Pinus edulis* | North America | 1780–1990 | 5-year blocks | $\delta^{13}C$ | none | moisture stress |
| Leavitt and Lara (1994) | 5 *Fitzroya cupressoides* | Chile | 1700–1900 | 5-year block, holocellulose | $\delta^{13}C$ | corrected and $C_i$, $C_a$ | "anthropogenic effect" in Southern Hemisphere |
| Leavitt and Long (1985) | 10 *Juniperus* sp. | North America | 1930–1979 | 5-year blocks, cellulose | $\delta^{13}C$ | none | temp. and prec. |
| Libby and Pandolfi (1974) | *Quercus petraea* | Germany | 1712–1954, 1530–1800 | 3- to 4-year blocks, WW | $\delta^{13}C$, $\delta^{18}O$, $\delta D$ | $^{13}C$ corrected for Suess, 9-year running average | temp. |
| Libby et al. (1976) | *Quercus petraea, Abies alba, Cryptomeria japonica* | Germany, Japan | 1350–1950, 1660–1950, 137–1950 | 5-year blocks | $\delta^{18}O$, $\delta D$ | smoothed by eye | temp. |

(Continued)

**Table 11.1** (Continued)

| Reference | Species | Site | Age range | Wood component | Isotopes | Data treatment | Environmental or other signal |
|---|---|---|---|---|---|---|---|
| Lipp and Trimborn (1991) | *Picea abies, Abies alba* | southern Germany | 1004–1980 | LW cellulose | $\delta^{13}C$, $\delta D$ | unclear | $\delta^{13}C$ 0.48%/°C $\delta D$ 2.2%/°C |
| Lipp et al. (1991) | *Abies alba* | Germany | 1004–1980 | LW cellulose nitrate | $\delta^{13}C$, $\delta D$ | detrended and shifted | $\delta^{13}C$ August temp., $\delta D$ no signal |
| Liu et al. (1996) | 4 *Pinus tabulaeformis* | northern China | 1885–1990 | annual pooled multiple radii | $\delta^{13}C$ | D calculated | June temp. and May–June prec. |
| Loader and Switsur (1996) | 3 *Pinus sylvestris* | United Kingdom | 1760–1991 | 1– to 10-year blocks, cellulose | $\delta^{13}C$ | first difference | correlation with summer temp. |
| McCarroll and Pawellek (2001) | 36 *Pinus sylvestris* | northern Finland, 4 sites | 1961–1995 | LW cellulose | $\delta^{13}C$ | corrected and detrended | summer sun or prec. |
| McCormack et al. (1994) | 360 *Quercus robur* and *Q. petraea* | United Kingdom | 4890 BC–AD 1980 | 10- to 20-year, holocellulose | $\delta^{13}C$ | none | difference between land and bog oaks |
| Okada et al. (1995) | 3 *Chamaecyparis* | Japan | 1680–1989 | 4 radii, 5-year blocks, cellulose | $\delta^{13}C$ | none | no direct external forcing identified |
| Pearman et al. (1976) | *Athrotaxis selaginodies* | Australia | 1895–1970 | WW 5-year blocks | $\delta^{13}C$ | running mean | February max. temp. |
| Pendall (2000) | *Pinus edulis* | southwestern United States | 1989–1996 | EW and LW α-cellulose | $\delta D$ | none | RH dominates, LW more sensitive than EW |
| Ramesh et al. (1985) | *Abies pindrow* | India | 1903–1932 | cellulose and cellulose nitrate | $\delta^{13}C$, $\delta D$, $\delta^{18}O$ | none | identified common forcing between radii |
| Ramesh et al. (1986) | *Abies pindrow* | India | 1903–1932 | cellulose and cellulose nitrate | $\delta^{13}C$, $\delta D$, $\delta^{18}O$ | none | RH, temp., prec. |

| Reference | Species | Location | Years | Material | Isotope | Detrending | Climate relationship |
|---|---|---|---|---|---|---|---|
| Robertson et al. (1997a, 1997b) | 10 *Quercus robur* | southwestern Finland | 1895–1995 | LW α-cellulose | $\delta^{13}C$ | standardized by filtering | prec.>RH>temp. |
| Robertson et al. (2001) | 4 *Quercus robur* | eastern England | 1895–1994 | LW α-cellulose | $\delta^{18}O$ | no detrending | $\delta^{18}O$ of winter prec. and summer RH |
| Saurer and Siegenthaler (1989) | 4 *Fagus sylvatica* | central Switzerland | 1935–1986 | 3-year block, cellulose | $\delta^{13}C$ | none | $\delta^{13}C$ temp. and prec. |
| Saurer et al. (1995) | 12 *Fagus sylvatica* | central Switzerland | 1934–1989 | 3-year block, cellulose | $\delta^{13}C$ | none | $\delta^{13}C$ soil moisture status, total prec. |
| Saurer et al. (1998a, 1998b) | *Fagus sylvatica* | central Switzerland | 1935–1990 | 3-year block, cellulose | $\delta^{13}C$, $\delta^{18}O$ | standardized | $\delta^{13}C$ temp. and prec. $\delta^{18}O$ of source prec. |
| Saurer et al. (2002) | *Larix, Picea, Pinus* | Eurasia | 1861–1890, 1961–1990 | 30-year blocks, WW | $\delta^{18}O$ | none | prec. |
| Schiegl (1974) | *Picea* | Germany | 1785–1970 | 5-year blocks, WW | $\delta D$ | none | correlation with summer temp. |
| Schleser et al. (1999) | 5 *Picea abies* | Germany | 1957–1992 | EW and LW, cellulose and WW | $\delta^{13}C$ | none | July temp., mean annual temp. |
| Sheu et al. (1996) | *Abies kawakamii* | Taiwan | 1873–1992 | annual (cellulose) | $\delta^{13}C$ | none | May–October temp. |
| Sonninen and Jungner (1995) | 1 *Pinus sylvestris* | Finland | 1841–1990 | annual (cellulose) | $\delta^{13}C$ | none | July temp. 0.1%/°C |
| Stuiver and Braziunas (1987) | 19 conifers | North America | 1100–1850 | 10-year block, cellulose | $\delta^{13}C$ | standardized | latitudinal trend, RH>temp. (0.32%/°C) |
| Switsur et al. (1994) | *Quercus robur* | United Kingdom | 1890–1990 | annual, EW, and LW cellulose | $\delta^{13}C$, $\delta^{18}O$, $\delta D$ | none | $\delta^{13}C$ July temp. and RH, $\delta^{18}O$ July temp., July–August RH |
| Switsur et al. (1996) | 1 *Quercus robur* | eastern England | 1869–1993 | LW α-cellulose | $\delta^{13}C$, $\delta^{18}O$, $\delta D$ | none | temp. (D, $^{13}C$, $^{18}O$), RH ($^{13}C$, $^{18}O$), prec. ($^{18}O$) |

*(Continued)*

**Table 11.1** *(Continued)*

| Reference | Species | Site | Age range | Wood component | Isotopes | Data treatment | Environmental or other signal |
|---|---|---|---|---|---|---|---|
| Tang et al. (1999) | *Pinus longaeva* | California, United States | 1795–1993 | every 5th ring, cellulose | $\delta^{13}C$ | detrended, WUE | WUE increases with $CO_2$ |
| Tang et al. (2000) | *Pseudotsuga menziesii* | northwestern United States | 1934–1996 | annual cellulose nitrate | $\delta D$ | none | source-water signal |
| Tans and Mook (1980) | 3 oak, 1 beech | Netherlands | 1855–1977 | annual wood, cellulose | $\delta^{13}C$ | corrected for $\delta^{13}C$ | mean summer temp. and annual temp. |
| Treydte et al. (2001) | *Picea abies* | Swiss Alps | 1946–1995 | pooled LW α-cellulose | $\delta^{13}C$ | corrected for $\delta^{13}C$ | late summer temp., prec., and RH |
| Treydte et al. (2006) | *Juniperus* sp. | northern Pakistan | 950–2006 | annual wood, cellulose | $\delta^{18}O$ | corrected to VSMOW | prec. |
| Waterhouse et al. (2000) | 5 *Pinus sylvestris* | northern Russia | 1898–1990 | annual LW α-cellulose | $\delta^{13}C$ | 3-year running mean | correlation with flow of River Ob |
| Yapp and Epstein (1982) | 25 various | North America | 1961–1975 | cellulose nitrate | $\delta D$ | corrected for outliers | correlation with mean annual temp. |
| Zimmermann et al. (1997) | *Juniperus cf. tibetica* | Tibetan Plateau | 1200–1994 | 5-year blocks | $\delta^{13}C$ | corrected for $\delta^{13}C$ | inferred soil moisture status |

*Source:* Modified from McCarroll and Loader (2004)

*Abbreviations:* LW, latewood; EW, earlywood; WW, whole wood; D, discrimination; $C_i$, internal $CO_2$ concentration; $C_a$, ambient $CO_2$ concentration; WUE, water use efficiency; VSMOW, Vienna standard mean ocean water; temp., temperature; prec., precipitation; RH, relative humidity; MWP, Medieval Warm Period; LIA, Little Ice Age

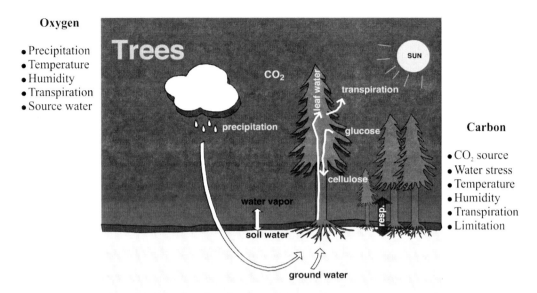

**Figure 11.2** Controls on the isotopic signature in plants. Oxygen and carbon isotopes in tree rings can vary due to the many factors listed here. (From Anderson et al. 2003)

stable isotopic records over long time periods with relatively few samples, and it highlights the relevance of the science of dendrochronology in helping to understand modern issues.

One of the more recent applications of stable isotopes in tree rings is reconstruction of past hurricane events by the variation of $\delta^{18}O$ in wood cellulose (Mora et al. 2006). During normal evaporation of ocean water, more $H_2{}^{16}O$ than $H_2{}^{18}O$ evaporates from the ocean surface, such that rainwater is relatively depleted in $^{18}O$. During hurricanes, a massive amount of water is evaporated from the ocean surface, resulting in even lower $^{18}O/^{16}O$ ratios in precipitation, which is conveyed to tree rings formed during these events.

## Limitations

One of the main limitations of isotopic analysis is that multiple environmental factors can cause a change in fractionation of the various stable isotopes (McCarroll and Pawellek 2001). To overcome this limitation, assumptions have to be made about the site from which a sample is collected and how the tree is interacting with the environment as it ages. These assumptions become more tenuous the further back in time the reconstructions run. The best solution for circumventing this problem is the use of multiple proxies, for example, using three stable isotopes (such as $^2H$, $^{13}C$, and $^{18}O$) from the same tree samples to constrain the possible temperature variation in a paleoclimatic study (McCarroll and Loader 2004) or using tree-ring width, density, and stable isotopes in combination as repeated measures of temperature variation (Gagen et al. 2006). When multiple proxies are used to make independent estimates of temperature, for example, those resultant estimates can be averaged together. As long as the signal (for example, atmospheric temperature) is the same between the multiple proxies, but the noise is from different sources, the noise averages out and leaves a clearer picture of past temperature fluctuations (McCarroll and Loader 2004).

## Standard Procedures

In angiosperms, the earlywood vessels may have some isotopic input from the previous year's stored photosynthates, although the overall affect of stored reserves from the previous year's growth is still a contested issue. Therefore, working only with the latewood from each year is likely to provide the best record of an individual year's isotopic composition (McCarroll and Loader 2004).

Most analysis of tree rings for stable isotopes starts with the extraction of holocellulose or cellulose. This is a useful starting point for stable isotopic analysis because cellulose has a well-defined composition compared to that of whole wood, it is structurally bound in each year, and it does not suffer from possible translocation (Leavitt and Danzer 1993). McCarroll and Loader (2004) suggested, however, that whole-wood analysis should be reexamined in greater detail because the time constraints of cellulose extraction slow the processing of multiple samples in automated analysis, and the isotopic variability in whole wood seems to be comparable to that in the cellulose.

**Holocellulose** is the total cellulose, including cellulose and hemicellulose (non-glucose celluloses), and is a product that is obtained after removal of lignin from the wood. **Cellulose** $(C_6H_{10}O_5)_n$ is a structural polymer of glucose $(C_6H_{12}O_6)$, which is the basic sugar produced during photosynthesis. The typical cellulose polymer is a linear chain consisting of thousands of glucose building blocks. Cellulose can naturally be found bundled together as microfibrils (a bundle of approximately 50 cellulose molecules). Cellulose can be broken down into three main components: alpha cellulose, beta cellulose, and gamma cellulose. The different types of cellulose are defined by how they behave during a sodium hydroxide extraction. **Alpha cellulose** is insoluble in strong sodium hydroxide (17.5%) and can be removed as a solid; **beta cellulose** is soluble in strong sodium hydroxide but precipitates after neutralization; **gamma cellulose** is soluble in strong sodium hydroxide and remains in solution after neutralization. **Hemicellulose** is another product from wood that is made up of polysaccharides that coat the surface of cellulose microfibrils, running parallel with their structure.

To isolate cellulose for analysis of carbon or oxygen stable isotopes, lignin is removed through oxidation in acidified sodium chlorite, yielding holocellulose. The hemicellulose is then removed by reaction with sodium hydroxide, producing alpha-cellulose (Leavitt and Danzer 1993, McCarroll and Loader 2004). Different procedures have been perfected for different tree species. For example, resins need to be removed from pine tree samples prior to cellulose extraction, which can be done with a Soxhlet apparatus and a solvent of toluene: ethanol in a 2:1 mixture (McCarroll and Loader 2004). See the papers cited in table 11.1 for specific methods for each stable isotope.

Once the appropriate wood extraction has been accomplished, the sample is usually converted to a gaseous form through combustion. The ionized particles are then driven down a flight tube by high-voltage electric charge and through a magnetic field of a mass spectrometer. The different isotopes are separated by the pull of the magnet and are collected in

Faraday cup detectors (I think of this like a prism separating out the different wavelengths of white light into a rainbow). The heavier ions follow an arc with a greater radius of curvature than the lighter ions. The Faraday cup detector is a series of metal cups that build up charge depending upon how many ions come in contact with the cups. Once this charge is measured, the mass spectrometer can report how many isotopes were in each weight category and therefore the isotopic composition of the sample.

Results from stable isotope analyses are reported as deviations from a known standard, which is why most stable isotopes are reported as a $\delta$ (delta) value. For example, analysis of stable carbon ratios might be reported as $-20‰$ $\delta^{13}C$, meaning the sample is 20 parts per 1000 more depleted in $^{13}C$ than the standard. Thus, the ‰ (permil) symbol means per 1000 units, just as a % (percent) symbol means per 100 units. Concentrations of many of these stable isotopes are fairly low so they are reported as the number of atoms of the stable isotopes for every 1000 atoms in the standard. The standard to which hydrogen and oxygen samples are compared is standard mean ocean water (SMOW). For carbon isotopes, the standard is a calcium carbonate fossil belemnite from the Pee Dee formation in South Carolina (or PDB, for Pee Dee belemnite; Leavitt 1992, McCarroll and Loader 2004). The fossil carbonate that was originally used as the PDB standard has since been used up and was replaced by the Vienna-PDB (VPDB) standard. Likewise, the standard mean ocean water has been replaced by the Vienna standard mean ocean water (VSMOW; Coplen 1995).

## Fractionation

The process of fractionation is how any ratio of stable isotopes changes from its source to where it is later sampled or stored. When examining $^{18}O/^{16}O$, standard mean ocean water is the standard or baseline and therefore $\delta^{18}O$ of standard sea water is 0‰. But when water evaporates from the ocean, more $^{16}O$ is likely to go into the atmosphere because it is lighter, producing a lighter fraction in the atmosphere compared to the standard (that is, $-13‰$ in the initial water vapor shown in fig. 11.3). As this water moves over land and rain precipitates out of the air mass, more $^{18}O$ is lost, creating an even lighter isotopic composition of the water remaining in atmospheric vapor. In this example, if everything else is held constant, one can tell the distance to the water source based on the $^{18}O/^{16}O$ in an air mass. The $^{18}O/^{16}O$ ratio in sea water also changes as a result of this evaporation and storage on land, so that marine sediments become enriched in $^{18}O$ at the same time that glaciers expand with the $^{18}O$-depleted water (snow) derived from ocean evaporation.

Further fractionation occurs in the plant itself. Diffusion of carbon isotopes from the atmosphere into the leaf of the plant causes a $-4.4‰$ reduction in $\delta^{13}C$, because the lighter $^{12}C$ isotope diffuses more rapidly into the leaves (fig. 11.4). The process of carboxylation (the addition of a -COOH group to a molecule) within the plant further fractionates the $\delta^{13}C$ of air, about $-27‰$ on average. Again, many things can control how carbon isotopes fractionate in the plant, such as leaf morphology, irradiance, air humidity, root-to-leaf distance, root depth, temperature, and amount and seasonality of precipitation (fig. 11.4; Lambers et al. 1998, Anderson et al. 2003).

Feedback mechanisms also exist, in which the plant changes its environment through taking up certain isotopes more so than others. By removing more $^{12}CO_2$ from the atmosphere

# Fractionation

### Example $^{18}O/^{16}O$ in Precipitation

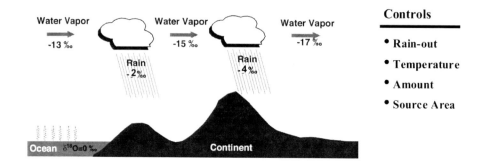

**Figure 11.3** An example of fractionation of $^{18}O/^{16}O$ from sea water to an inland site with two rain events. Evaporation from the ocean causes the main fractionation event, with more $^{16}O$ evaporating off of the ocean so that the ratio is −13‰. Each rain event removes more $^{18}O$ so that the isotopic ratio drops by −2‰ for each event. (From Anderson et al. 2003 after Siegenthaler 1979)

during photosynthesis, for example, the $^{13}CO_2$ concentration in ambient air increases, changing the chemistry of the air around the plant. Also, evaporation of water on the ground or in the atmosphere, temperature, humidity, and the amount of circulation in the atmosphere around the leaves all affect the availability of hydrogen and oxygen isotopes for assimilation into the plant (fig. 11.5; Lambers et al. 1998, Anderson et al. 2003).

Different tree species take up stable isotopes in different concentrations. Because conifer trees transport water much less efficiently than hardwoods, resulting in more fractionation from soil water, the gymnosperms have heavier fractionations of hydrogen and oxygen isotope values than angiosperms (McCarroll and Loader 2004). Leaf shape and size in angiosperms also controls how trees fractionate stable isotopes, as does the number of stomata on a leaf, which can change through time. One evolutionary consequence of broader leaves is more area for evaporative cooling, and therefore broadleaf trees are less coupled to atmospheric temperature than are the needles of a conifer. Rooting depth controls the source of water that trees take up. A shallow-rooted tree, for example, has a greater interannual variability in its isotopic composition because of its dependence on rainwater, as opposed to a tree with a deep taproot that can access groundwater. Canopy dominance also controls isotopic fractionation because dominant trees have more direct contact with moving air, which increases the coupling with open atmospheric temperature, humidity, and sunlight, which in turn increases rates of photosynthesis (McCarroll and Loader 2004). Trees growing in the understory of a forest experience lower temperatures, higher humidity, and less direct sunlight.

Because of isotopic variation within a single ring of a tree, Leavitt and Long (1984) suggested pooling the wood from four radii from four trees (for a total of 16 cores) to obtain accurate values of atmospheric $\delta^{13}C$ for the site. McCarroll and Pawellek (1998) argued against

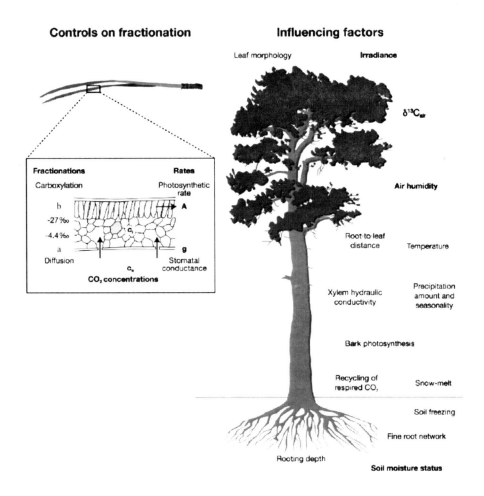

**Figure 11.4** Factors that control fractionation in a pine tree. Fractionation due to diffusion reduces the amount of $^{13}C$, resulting in a $-4.4‰$ decrease, while the photosynthetic enzyme and the process of carboxylation preferentially takes more $^{12}C$, reducing the relative amount of $^{13}C$ by $-27‰$. The rate of this process is controlled by the amount of photosynthesis and the size of the stomatal openings. (From McCarroll and Loader 2004)

this method, stating that it would be better to quantify the $\delta^{13}C$ differences from one core to another by keeping the individual samples separate. They noted that variability between trees was much greater than the variation within a ring, and therefore recommended taking samples from more trees rather than more cores from one tree to average for a more precise measure of the atmospheric isotopic concentrations. McCarroll and Pawellek (1998) also outlined statistical measures on latewood $\delta^{13}C$ to quantify the error within and between sites and suggested that developing individual tree isotope records was a better way to understand the noise in a chronology rather than pooling wood from multiple trees. The cost and time it takes to process samples in an isotopic study often constrains the number of replicate samples that can be obtained as well as the temporal and spatial resolution and extent.

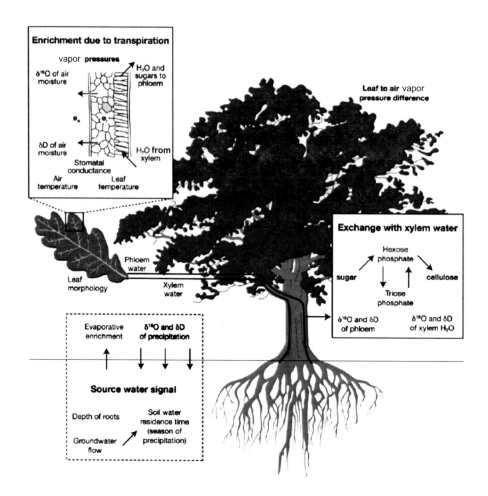

**Figure 11.5** Feedback mechanisms affecting fractionation in an oak tree. (From McCarroll and Loader 2004)

## Other Usable Elements

Trees can be used as a measure of change in the nitrogen cycle due to alteration of land-use by examining variations in ¹⁵N, according to a study by Bukata and Kyser (2005). They observed an increase in ¹⁵N in white and red oak trees growing on the margin of sites that were clearcut and experienced a permanent change in land-use. The timing and the magnitude of the events was recorded in the nitrogen signal in the trees, although the event seemed to last longer (19 years) than suggested by previous studies of disturbance to the nitrogen cycle when foliage alone was sampled. After 19 years, the nitrogen levels in the tree rings returned to predisturbance levels. The authors noted that transport of fluids in the sapwood tended to skew the signal, so that some minor translocation likely occurred.

Yang et al. (1996) found that trees and shrubs in Death Valley, California, accurately recorded variations in soil sulfur. The authors measured levels of ³⁴S in the wood of the plants and examined variations in growth rings of *Tamarix aphylla*. They found that sulfur levels in the plants varied along with sulfur levels in the source water and root growth.

English et al. (2001) used $^{87}Sr/^{86}Sr$ to determine the source area of wooden beams in structures from Chaco Canyon, New Mexico, that were built around 1000. They examined the $^{87}Sr/^{86}Sr$ ratio in spruce and fir logs from the archaeological site and examined the $^{87}Sr/^{86}Sr$ ratio in the soil from three surrounding mountains in the spruce-fir zone. The authors determined that the logs came from two of the mountains, both approximately 75 km away, while a third mountain source was avoided even though the mountain was the same distance. This example shows the use of stable isotopes as a marker to determine where wood has come from on the landscape.

## Conclusion

Stable isotopes provide another record that can be drawn from tree rings and give more information about the environment such as paleohumidity, summer rainfall, or drought frequency (McCarroll and Pawellek 1998). The application of dendrochronology to isotopic analysis is growing as the methodology becomes automated, reducing the time-consuming attention that was needed in the past by a geochemistry expert. Smaller sample sizes are being analyzed, which enables greater replication, finer sampling resolution, and longer time series. Among all dendrochronological applications, dendrochemistry and stable isotopes have grown the most recently, changing the face of contemporary tree-ring research. In the next chapter, I explore new applications, techniques, and methodologies of dendrochronology that are on the cutting edge of research questions today.

# 12
## Frontiers in Dendrochronology

Although people have long recognized the annual nature of temperate tree rings, dendrochronology as a discipline remains a young science, less than a century old, with its first laboratory founded in 1937 at the University of Arizona. The field is growing quickly, with 55 major laboratories located around the world today, according to Dr. Henri Grissino-Mayer's Ultimate Tree-Ring Web Pages. Four large laboratories exist in the United States (Laboratory of Tree-Ring Research in Tucson, Arizona; Tree-Ring Laboratory at the Lamont-Doherty Earth Observatory in Palisades, New Jersey; Tree-Ring Laboratory at the University of Arkansas; and Laboratory of Tree-Ring Science at the University of Tennessee), with many smaller ones scattered throughout the United States. Canada has many active laboratories, and almost every country in the European Union has at least one dendrochronology laboratory. Russia has many active researchers, and China, Australia, and Thailand all have active research programs. South America joined in dendrochronology research about 30 years ago, with some of the first research on that continent conducted by researchers at the Laboratory of Tree-Ring Research in Arizona in the 1970s (LaMarche et al. 1979c, 1979d). New applications of old techniques are being explored (such as the identification of different insect outbreak systems) and new techniques are being perfected (such as stable isotopic analysis and image analysis). Geographic frontiers still exist in dendrochronology with the use of wood anatomy to explore and examine tropical trees; a greater number of usable tropical species have been identified in the last 10 years than anyone had anticipated. Some researchers are also extending dendrochronological techniques to perennial weeds, shrubs, and even to other organisms, such as fish, clams, and turtles. Dendrochronology is a vibrant field with many active researchers contributing to important societal concerns (such as climate change) and pushing the frontiers of our knowledge of the natural world.

Dendrochronologists continue to explore interrelationships between different organisms and trees as they are recorded in tree rings, such as pandora moth (*Coloradia pandora*; Speer et al. 2001) or Dothistroma needle blight (*Dothistroma septosporum*; Welsh 2007). What used to be considered noise in a tree-ring signal is now understood to be additional biological information that can be isolated as data layers are peeled away. For example, patterns of synchronous fruiting history (masting; Speer 2001) have recently been identified in five oak species. Researchers such as Dean et al. (1985) continue to push the human behavioral interpretations that can be made from tree-ring data, resulting in the field of dendrochronology being more widely used with greater importance to human society. Along those lines, Speer and Hansen-Speer (2007) outlined the dendroecological records that can be applied to understand more about anthropogenic ecology and resource availability for native cultures through food resource reconstructions, such as mast and insects, and landscape modification, such as fire history and vegetation change.

## Stable Isotopes

Stable isotope analysis is probably the application in dendrochronology that is most quickly adding to our knowledge of past environments. In the last decade, isotope dendrochronologists have overcome many of the hurdles of the time-consuming sample preparation and wet chemical processing steps in their technique. Now, as these methods become streamlined and analytical equipment improves, isotopic dendrochronologists are able to process hundreds of samples a day in the laboratory, making annual resolution on long chronologies with good sample replication a readily achievable goal (McCarroll and Loader 2004).

New techniques are being developed, such as automated laser ablation of whole samples connected directly to an inductively coupled plasma mass spectrometer, so that sampling and whole core surveys can both be accomplished quickly. Furthermore, this technique removes small amounts of the wood such that cores are not completely destroyed, enabling researchers to archive their samples for future reanalysis if necessary (Watmough et al. 1998, Schulze et al. 2004). Another procedural advance has been the achievement of subannual resolution by using robotic micromilling to mill small sample aliquots from a core or slab (Wurster et al. 1999, Dodd et al. 2007). The masses needed for analysis have also decreased with improvements made to mass spectrometers. Previously, samples as small as 0.15–0.30 mg depending on the isotope system were routinely analyzed, and now the technology is pushing the useful sample size to only 0.02–0.06 mg, again depending on the isotope of interest (Bill Patterson, personal communication). By decreasing the size of samples and increasing our ability to isolate tiny aliquots of cellulose, dendrochronologists can achieve sample resolutions that represent a week or less for fast-growing trees. Newer laser-robotic coupled systems envisioned for the near future should reduce the time-resolution to days or less (Bill Patterson, personal communication). The quick processing of whole samples will move isotope dendrochronologists beyond single-tree analysis to the investigation of many trees, such that replication between years can be completed from stands of trees with good sample depth back through time.

Isotope dendrochronology truly remains one of the new frontiers in dendrochronology, as many environments have not been examined to determine the trees' response to climatic forcing factors that affect stable isotopic fractionation. For example, in the first stable $^{13}$C analysis from a subalpine zone, Treydte et al. (2001) found that the spruce trees were responding to late summer temperature, precipitation, and relative humidity. The study of climatic responses at extreme environments, such as mountaintop sites, is important in the current condition of global warming, because many of the mountaintop species may be stressed by warmer conditions yet restrained from moving to higher elevations because they are already located at the peaks of the mountains.

## Multiple Proxies

Stable isotopes provide a wonderful new set of information that have expanded the information dendrochronologists can extract from tree rings. But, as was discussed in chapter 11, isotopic studies are limited by the many mechanisms that can control the concentrations of a single isotope in the tree-ring record (McCarroll and Pawellek 2001). The use of multiple proxies such as ring width, density, and a variety of stable isotopes helps dendrochronologists narrow down the main driving factors that control these variables in tree rings, making climatic reconstructions more accurate (Gagen et al. 2006).

Beyond the use of multiple proxies to examine the climatic records of the past, we can use proxies of multiple disturbances to understand the interactions between climate, fire, and insect outbreaks (Kulakowski and Veblen 2002, Kulakowski et al. 2003). Historically, each disturbance was examined in isolation to determine its influence on tree growth. Now dendrochronologists are embracing the complexity of the natural system by examining all of the disturbances that may occur on a site and determining how they influence each other.

## Image Analysis of Reflected Light

Students new to the field often ask if there is an automated technique for measuring and dating dendrochronological samples. Many attempts have been made to automate the process, but in the end, none of them today are equal to manual observation of the tree rings through a good microscope, although a few tools have been developed that allow scanning and automated ring boundary detection. So far, these techniques are still limited to nonporous wood species (such as pine trees) that have clear ring boundaries and are not hindered by false and micro ring structures. Some of these automated instruments, such as Windendro (Guay et al. 1992, Sheppard and Graumlich 1996) and LignoVision (Rinntech, Heidelberg, Germany), can provide good results, but the automated systems are no substitution to quality-controlled crossdating and direct observation of the wood with a good-quality binocular microscope. These automated systems work from a scanned sample of wood and optical light reflectance to determine ring boundaries. Both Windendro and LignoVision are expensive and limited by the resolution of the image, but some laboratories have had regular success dating samples with these systems.

Potentially, image analysis from reflected light has the capability to quickly provide many different measures of a ring, such as whole ring width, earlywood width, latewood width, cell lumen area, double wall thickness, and circularity index (of individual cells). These latter measurements actually provide a measure of density throughout the tree rings, based on cell lumen area and cell wall thickness (Jagels and Telewski 1990). Image analysis of tree-ring samples started with the work of Telewski et al. (1983) and went through a series of advances with the work of Jagels and Telewski (1990), Park and Telewski (1993), Munro et al. (1996), Sheppard et al. (1996), and Sheppard and Wiedenhoeft (2007). Methodological issues such as removing variations in color that do not relate to ring boundaries have hindered the widespread applicability of this technique to tree-ring analysis. Recent advances, however, have been able to correct for this color difference in the pine heartwood-to-sapwood transition, moving the technique closer to general use (Sheppard and Wiedenhoeft 2007).

## Wood Anatomy

Wood anatomy has been studied for hundreds of years, but it is taking on new energy with regard to the applications of dendrochronology. Gärtner (2007b) demonstrated the usefulness of root wood anatomy to determine burial depth of roots and how geomorphological events change that burial depth. Dietz and Schweingruber (2001) examined root wood anatomy in dicotyledonous perennial herbs of genera never before considered by dendrochronologists to determine the timing of past ecological events.

Efforts are being made to tease apart finer scale effects of climate on tree growth by examining different climate responses from weekly and daily climate records and determining the effect on the growth of individual cells in tree rings. Rossi et al. (2006) examined the effect of day length and temperature on weekly xylem cell production in *Picea*, *Pinus*, *Abies*, and *Larix*, finding that the trees were more likely to respond to day length than they were to temperature.

Vessel size in angiosperms is being used as another response to environmental factors. Fonti and Garcia-Gonzalez (2004) analyzed vessel size in a European chestnut (*Castanea sativa*) and found that, although variability was not great, earlywood vessel size responded to temperature at the end of the growing season when carbon reserves are put aside for the following year's growth and at the beginning of the growing season. These periods of time are not usually recorded in ring width or density and can provide a wider range of climatic data from a tree-ring series.

Fichtler et al. (2003) demonstrated the use of wood anatomy combined with radiocarbon dating to determine the oldest age of several tropical tree species from Costa Rica, finding the most ancient tree to be 530 years old based on a ring count. Close examination of the wood anatomy enables researchers to recognize cell types that can be used to identify ring boundaries, especially in angiosperm wood, that have complex wood structures. These early attempts at ring identification need to be cross checked with other methods to determine their accuracy; in this case radiocarbon dating was used to help verify the age of these trees. This study is the first step to recognizing the annual rings in some of these tropical tree species through wood anatomy, and further work should be able to crossdate these species to develop absolutely dated chronologies for more extensive regions of the tropics.

## Tropical Dendrochronology

Although dendrochronology in tropical environments had been conducted in the 19th century, it was avoided by dendrochronologists during the 20th century, because conventional wisdom said that there was not enough seasonality in temperature or precipitation to cause trees to shut down on a regular basis and force annual rings to form (Worbes 2002). Today, however, many locations have been found in the tropics where the annual seasonality is great enough or trees are sensitive enough to even slight climatic variations to cause the cambium to form different wood anatomical structures that become visible as rings. Many genera of trees are being investigated that do produce annual rings in the tropics (Worbes 1995, 2002, Fichtler et al. 2003, 2004). Through this work, dendrochronologists are pushing the geographic frontiers of dendrochronology and covering the globe with a more uniform distribution of tree-ring chronologies (fig. 12.1).

Early dendrochronological research in new geographic locations generally starts with a close examination of the wood anatomy of multiple species to demonstrate that these trees produce annual rings (for example, Villalba et al. 1985, Boninsegna et al. 1989). The next step is to test the annual nature of the chronology and the reliability of ring development through

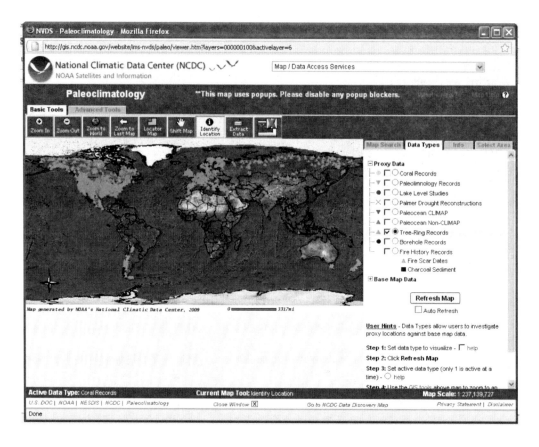

**Figure 12.1** The National Climatic Data Center runs the World Data Center for Paleoclimatology, which houses the tree-ring chronologies of the International Tree-Ring Data Bank. Note the prevalence of chronologies across North America, Europe, and Siberia, as represented by the grey triangles. There are a growing number of chronologies coming from South America and New Zealand, but a lack of chronologies from Africa and the tropics.

crossdating (Villalba and Boninsegna 1989, Stahle 1999, Speer et al. 2004). Stahle (1999) suggested a series of tests to determine if trees have annual rings, based on the ability to crossdate the samples between trees and across multiple sites, their correlation to climate, and through blind crossdating tests of samples with known ages. By following these methods, researchers have been able to document seasonal production of tree rings in Africa (Gourlay 1995, February and Stock 1998, Stahle 1999, Fichtler et al. 2004), India (Bhattacharyya et al. 1992), Indonesia (D'Arrigo et al. 1994), Java (Pumijumnong et al. 1995), Mexico (Stahle 1999), the Brazilian Amazon region (Vetter and Botosso 1989, Worbes 1989, Schöngart et al. 2004), Honduras (Johnson 1980), and the Dominican Republic (Speer et al. 2004).

Until the 21st century, the continent of Africa was largely unexplored for the occurrence of tree species that develop annual rings. Gourlay (1995) was able to demonstrate that trees in the genus *Acacia* did develop rings that were bounded by marginal parenchyma cells and that were highly correlated with annual rainfall. February and Stock (1998) examined the potential of two *Podocarpus* species in South Africa, but they were unable to date the rings due to poor circuit uniformity and locally absent rings. Stahle et al. (1999) developed chronologies from *Pterocarpus angolensis* in Zimbabwe at 18°S latitude, enabling the researchers to inform the forest managers about the growth rates for this valuable timber species in tropical Africa. Research throughout Africa continues to find older and datable species that can contribute to the data gap on this continent (Eshete and Stahl 1999, Trouet et al. 2001, Worbes et al. 2003, Fichtler et al. 2004, Schöngart et al. 2004, Verheyden et al. 2004, Couralet et al. 2005, Schöngart et al. 2005, Verheyden 2005, Therrell et al. 2006, Trouet et al. 2006).

Unique methods have also been used to determine the growth of tropical trees and to test for the annual nature of tree rings in some locations. The artificial increase in $^{14}C$ in the atmosphere from atomic weapons testing caused what is known as the Bomb Spike, which is an elevated level of $^{14}C$ that peaks in 1962 in all trees in the world (Worbes and Junk 1989). The Bomb Spike can be used to find the 1962 ring and determine how much growth has occurred in the intervening years. This information may be useful for forest managers so that they can determine, at least roughly, the growth rate of tropical trees that are being harvested. Mariaux (1981) developed an original way for determining the growth rate and ring production in tropical trees by wounding the cambium and returning to see if rings were produced annually.

## Unique Environments

Many forests in North America are limited in long-term tree-ring chronologies by extensive logging that occurred around 1900 and removed many of the old trees, especially in the eastern United States. Many areas have well-preserved old trees on sites, such as old lava flows, barrens, or swamps, that the loggers avoided because the wood was not merchantable. This can be overcome by finding unique sites to which loggers did not have access (Larson et al. 1999). For example, the Niagara Escarpment in southern Ontario has eastern white cedar (*Thuja occidentalis*) growing on cliffs that obtain ages in excess of 1000 years (Kelly et al. 1992). Research in an environment such as this requires a dendrochronologist who is also skilled at rock climbing.

Submerged logs in anoxic environments (without oxygen) can be preserved for centuries, millennia, and rarely even tens of millions of years. These trees have the potential to produce long tree-ring chronologies (Larson and Melville 1996). Places such as the Great Lakes, bog environments, lakes in Siberia, and debris piles at the bases of cliffs have all produced preserved logs. Sampling for submerged wood requires dendrochronologists that are interested in scuba diving or have connections with scuba professionals. Submerged environments are great preservation sites that have not yet been explored to their full potential.

Extremely long chronologies are now being developed from **subfossil wood** (usually buried wood that has been preserved but not yet fossilized by the replacement of cellulose by minerals) being mined from streambanks on tributaries of the Missouri River (Guyette and Stambaugh 2003). This wood has the potential to form the longest tree-ring chronology in the world, extending back some 15,000 years, but work is slow and expensive. Target dates for the samples are determined by radiocarbon dates and the density of the wood (because the longer a specimen is buried the more mass it loses, even in anoxic conditions). Once the sample is placed into a broad period of history, crossdating attempts can be more productive when trying to date the sample against floating chronologies from that time period. As in any tree-ring chronology, adequate sample depth throughout the series is necessary to reliably interpret the data; for this project, the task becomes significant because of the length of the chronology.

## Sclerochronology

**Sclerochronology** is the use of boney structures in a variety of organisms to determine the age of the organism and to develop long-term histories of the environment from those structures. Sclerochronology has been applied to fish otoliths (earstones in the head of fish used for balance and other sensory information), shells of clams, shells of turtles, and even in dinosaur bones. Counting these increments to estimate the age of the organisms has been done for some time. For example, Aristotle discussed determination of a fish's age by counting rings in an otolith. Sclerochronologists are now bringing the tool of crossdating to their field to provide quality control and verification of these ages. With the benefit of crossdating, longer chronologies with annual resolution can now be developed (Guyette and Rabeni 1995, Black et al. 2005, Helama et al. 2006).

During the 2006 North American Dendroecological Fieldweek held at the Hatfield Marine Science Center, Bryan Black led a group that dated geoduck clams from the Vancouver Island area. They found that the clams had better series intercorrelations than any other chronology developed during the fieldweek and also had a significant correlation with January–March sea-surface temperature (Black et al. 2006). Black et al. (2005) examined 50 rock fish (*Sebastes diploproa*) otoliths and found that they ranged from 30 to 84 years in age. The otoliths' growth was significantly correlated with the Northern Oscillation Index, an upwelling index, and the PDO. These results have implications for fisheries management, because many of these fish live much longer than previously expected, thereby reducing the understood rate of replacement. Perhaps the most tragic example of species depletion relates to the age estimate of orange roughy (*Hoplostethus atlanticus*) which was thought to be an average of 15 years of age; in reality, the fish being harvested were 150 years old. With longer lives and slower development rates, fish would have to be taken less frequently to maintain viable populations.

## Conclusion

Dendrochronology is a vibrant field of science that is growing quickly, with many frontiers remaining to be explored. Researchers throughout our discipline are investigating most areas of the natural sciences and touching on a wide variety of fields. Science as a whole is becoming more interdisciplinary, and dendrochronology is a tool that can be applied to questions in ecology, archaeology, climatology, geology, hydrology, atmospheric sciences, and resource management. These varied uses of the same basic skills make dendrochronology a useful field of study that contributes immensely to our knowledge of the natural world.

# Appendix A
## Tree and Shrub Species That Have Been Used by Dendrochronologists

### How to Use This List

The table has five columns: Crossdating Index (CDI), Species Code, Genus, Species, and Common Name(s). For the CDI, "0" indicates the species does not crossdate or no crossdating information is available; "1" indicates a species known to crossdate within and between trees (minor importance to dendrochronology); and "2" indicates a species known to crossdate across a region (major importance to dendrochronology). The species code is the standard four-letter abbreviation assigned by the International Tree-Ring Data Bank for archiving purposes. An asterisk (*) beside the four-letter code indicates this species has tree-ring measurements and chronologies held in the International Tree-Ring Data Bank. The common names are compiled from various sources. This data was originally published by Grissino-Mayer (1993) and is currently maintained on the Ultimate Tree-Ring Web Pages that he maintains.

| CDI | Species Code | Genus | Species | Common Name |
|---|---|---|---|---|
| 2 | ABAL* | *Abies* | *alba* | silver fir, European fir |
| 1 | ABAM* | *Abies* | *amabilis* | Pacific silver fir |
| 2 | ABBA | *Abies* | *balsamea* | balsam fir |
| 1 | ABBO* | *Abies* | *borisii-regis* | Bulgarian fir, King Boris fir |
| 0 | ABBN | *Abies* | *bornmuelleriana* | Bornmueller's fir |
| 0 | ABBR | *Abies* | *bracteata* | bristlecone fir |
| 1 | ABCE* | *Abies* | *cephalonica* | Greek fir |
| 0 | ABCH | *Abies* | *chensiensis* | Chensien fir |
| 1 | ABCI | *Abies* | *cilicica* | Cilician fir |
| 2 | ABCO* | *Abies* | *concolor* | white fir |
| 0 | ABEQ | *Abies* | *equi-trojani* | |
| 0 | ABFX | *Abies* | *faxoniana* | Faxon fir |
| 0 | ABFI | *Abies* | *firma* | Japanese fir, Momi fir |
| 1 | ABFO | *Abies* | *forestii* | Chinese fir |
| 1 | ABFR | *Abies* | *fraseri* | Fraser fir |
| 1 | ABGR | *Abies* | *grandis* | grand fir, giant fir |
| 0 | ABHO | *Abies* | *holophylla* | Manchurian fir |
| 1 | ABKA | *Abies* | *kawakamii* | Taiwan fir |
| 1 | ABKO | *Abies* | *koreana* | Korean fir |
| 2 | ABLA* | *Abies* | *lasiocarpa* | subalpine fir, corkbark fir |

*(Continued)*

| CDI | Species Code | Genus | Species | Common Name |
|-----|------|-------|---------|-------------|
| 1 | ABMA* | *Abies* | *magnifica* | California red fir |
| 1 | ABMR | *Abies* | *mariessi* | Marie's fir |
| 1 | ABMC | *Abies* | *marocana* | Moroccan fir |
| 0 | ABNB | *Abies* | *nebrodensis* | Sicilian fir |
| 0 | ABNE | *Abies* | *nephrolepis* | East Siberian fir |
| 1 | ABNO* | *Abies* | *nordmanniana* | Caucasian fir |
| 1 | ABNU | *Abies* | *numidica* | Algerian fir |
| 1 | ABPI* | *Abies* | *pindrow* | Himalayan silver fir |
| 1 | ABPN* | *Abies* | *pinsapo* | Spanish fir |
| 1 | ABPR* | *Abies* | *procera* | noble fir |
| 1 | ABRC | *Abies* | *recurvata* | Min fir |
| 0 | ABRE | *Abies* | *religiosa* | Mexican fir, sacred fir |
| 0 | ABSA | *Abies* | *sachalinensis* | Sachalin fir, todo |
| 0 | ABSI | *Abies* | *sibirica* | Siberian fir |
| 1 | ABSB* | *Abies* | *spectabilis* | silver fir, East Himalayan fir |
| 0 | ABSQ | *Abies* | *squamata* | flaky fir |
| 0 | ABVI | *Abies* | *vietchii* | Vietch's silver fir |
| 0 | ACAL | *Acacia* | *alpina* | |
| 0 | ACCA | *Acacia* | *catechu* | cutch, Indian acacia |
| 0 | ACGI | *Acacia* | *giraffae* | camel thorn |
| 0 | ACHO | *Acacia* | *hotwittii* | |
| 0 | ACME | *Acacia* | *melanoxylon* | blackwood |
| 0 | ACNI | *Acacia* | *nilotica* | gum arabic tree |
| 0 | ACRA | *Acacia* | *raddiana* | Israelian acacia |
| 1 | ACCA | *Acer* | *campestre* | hedge maple, field maple |
| 0 | ACMO | *Acer* | *mono* | maple |
| 0 | ACNE | *Acer* | *negundo* | boxelder, ash-leaved maple |
| 1 | ACOP | *Acer* | *opalus* | Italian maple |
| 0 | ACPE | *Acer* | *pensylvanicum* | striped maple |
| 1 | ACPL | *Acer* | *platanoides* | Norway maple |
| 1 | ACPS | *Acer* | *pseudoplatanus* | sycamore maple, plane tree |
| 1 | ACRU | *Acer* | *rubrum* | red maple |
| 0 | ACSA* | *Acer* | *saccharinum* | silver maple |
| 2 | ACSH* | *Acer* | *saccharum* | sugar maple |
| 0 | ACSC | *Acer* | *spicatum* | mountain maple |
| 0 | ACTU | *Acer* | *turkestanica* | |
| 0 | ADDI | *Adansonia* | *digitata* | baobab, monkey bread tree |
| 0 | ADFA | *Adenostoma* | *fasciculatum* | chamise, greasewood |
| 1 | ADHO* | *Adesmia* | *horrida* | |
| 1 | ADUS* | *Adesmia* | *uspallatensis* | |
| 0 | AEHI | *Aesculus* | *hippocastanum* | horse chestnut |
| 0 | AEPU | *Aextoxicon* | *punctatum* | olivillo, tique |

(*Continued*)

| CDI | Species Code | Genus | Species | Common Name |
|---|---|---|---|---|
| 0 | AFAF | *Afzelia* | *africana* | afzelia, apa, doussie, alinga, papao |
| 0 | AFQU | *Afzelia* | *quanzensis* | afzelia, mambokofi, chanfuta |
| 2 | AGAU* | *Agathis* | *australis* | kauri pine |
| 0 | AGMA | *Agathis* | *macrophylla* | Fijian kauri |
| 0 | AGMO | *Agathis* | *moorei* | kauri |
| 0 | AGOV | *Agathis* | *ovata* | kauri |
| 0 | AGPA | *Agathis* | *palmerstoni* | North Queensland kauri |
| 2 | AGRO | *Agathis* | *robusta* | kauri pine, Queensland kauri |
| 0 | AGVI | *Agathis* | *vitiensis* | |
| 0 | AIAL | *Ailanthus* | *altissima* | tree of heaven |
| 0 | ALVE | *Allocasuarina* | *verticillata* | |
| 1 | ALGL | *Alnus* | *glutinosa* | common alder, European alder |
| 0 | ALHI | *Alnus* | *hirsuta* | |
| 1 | ALIN | *Alnus* | *incana* | gray alder, white alder |
| 0 | ALMA | *Alnus* | *maximowiczii* | |
| 0 | ALRH | *Alnus* | *rhombifolia* | white alder |
| 0 | ALRU | *Alnus* | *rubra* | red alder |
| 0 | ALRG | *Alnus* | *rugosa* | speckled alder, rough alder |
| 0 | ALSE | *Alnus* | *serrulata* | hazel alder |
| 0 | ALSI | *Alnus* | *sinuata* | Sitka alder |
| 1 | ALVI | *Alnus* | *viridis* | green alder |
| 0 | ALCR | *Alnus* | *viridis* | American green alder |
| 1 | AMSP | *Amelanchier* | spp. | serviceberry |
| 0 | AMOV | *Amelanchier* | *ovalis* | snowy mespilus |
| 0 | AMLU | *Amomyrtus* | *luma* | luma |
| 0 | ANCO | *Andira* | *coriacea* | Saint Martin rouge |
| 1 | ANSP | *Annona* | *spraguei* | araucaria |
| 1 | ARAN | *Araucaria* | *angustifolia* | Parana araucaria, Parana pine |
| 2 | ARAR* | *Araucaria* | *araucana* | monkey puzzle, araucaria, pehuen |
| 0 | ARBI | *Araucaria* | *bidwilli* | bunya pine, bunya |
| 0 | ARCU | *Araucaria* | *cunninghamii* | hoop pine, Moreton bay pine |
| 0 | ARHE | *Araucaria* | *heterophylla* | Norfolk Island pine |
| 0 | ARHU | *Araucaria* | *hunsteinii* | pine |
| 0 | ARGL | *Arctostaphylos* | *glauca* | bigberry manzanita |
| 1 | ARTR | *Artemisia* | *tridentata* | big sagebrush |
| 2 | ATCU* | *Athrotaxis* | *cupressoides* | pencil pine, smooth Tasmanian cedar |
| 2 | ATSE* | *Athrotaxis* | *selaginoides* | King Billy pine |
| 0 | AUKL | *Aucoumea* | *klaineana* | okoume |
| 2 | AUCH* | *Austrocedrus* | *chilensis* | Chilean cedar, cipres de la cordillera |
| 0 | BAAE | *Balanites* | *aegyptiaca* | Jericho balsam, heglig |
| 0 | BLTA | *Beilschmiedia* | *tawa* | Kirk tawa |
| 0 | BBVU | *Berberis* | *vulgaria* | common barberry |

*(Continued)*

| CDI | Species Code | Genus | Species | Common Name |
|---|---|---|---|---|
| 0 | BTEX | *Bertholletia* | *excelsa* | Brazil nut, yuvia, turury, para nut tree |
| 0 | BEAB | *Betula* | *albosinensis* | Chinese birch |
| 1 | BEAL | *Betula* | *alleghaniensis* | yellow birch |
| 0 | BEER | *Betula* | *ermanii* | Japanese birch, dakekaba |
| 0 | BEGL | *Betula* | *glandulosa* | bog birch, dwarf birch |
| 1 | BEGR | *Betula* | *grossa* | Japanese cherry birch |
| 0 | BELE | *Betula* | *lenta* | sweet birch, black birch |
| 0 | BENI | *Betula* | *nigra* | river birch |
| 1 | BEPA | *Betula* | *papyrifera* | paper birch |
| 0 | BEAK | *Betula* | *papyrifera* var. *neoalaskana* | |
| 1 | BEPE | *Betula* | *pendula* | silver birch, European white birch |
| 0 | BEPL | *Betula* | *platyphylla* | jagjag-namu, Japanese birch |
| 0 | BEPO | *Betula* | *populifolia* | gray birch |
| 1 | BEPU | *Betula* | *pubescens* | downy birch, mountain birch |
| 1 | BEUT | *Betula* | *utilis* | Himalayan birch |
| 1 | BEVE | *Betula* | *verrucosa* | silver birch, European white birch |
| 0 | BOQU | *Bombacopsis* | *quinata* | |
| 0 | BOMA | *Bombax* | *malabaricum* | semul, ngiu, ngiew, gon run do |
| 1 | BUGR | *Bursera* | *graveolens* | palo santo |
| 0 | BUSI | *Bursera* | *simaruba* | gumbo-limbo, West-Indian birch |
| 1 | BUSE | *Buxus* | *sempervirens* | common box, boxwood |
| 0 | CACO | *Callitris* | *columellaris* | cypress pine |
| 0 | CAIN | *Callitris* | *intratropica* | cypress pine |
| 0 | CAMA | *Callitris* | *macleayana* | brush cypress pine |
| 1 | CAPR* | *Callitris* | *preissii* | Rottnest Island pine |
| 1 | CARO* | *Callitris* | *robusta* | |
| 1 | CADE | *Calocedrus* | *decurrens* | California incense cedar |
| 1 | CABU* | *Canthium* | *burttii* | canthium |
| 0 | CASC | *Capparis* | *scabrida* | sapote |
| 0 | CAPC | *Carapa* | *procera* | carapa |
| 0 | CPBE | *Carpinus* | *betulus* | hornbeam |
| 0 | CYCO | *Carya* | *cordoformis* | bitternut hickory |
| 1 | CYGL | *Carya* | *glabra* | pignut hickory |
| 1 | CYIL | *Carya* | *illinoensis* | pecan |
| 0 | CYOV | *Carya* | *ovata* | shagbark hickory |
| 0 | CYTO | *Carya* | *tomentosa* | mockernut hickory |
| 0 | CAGL | *Caryocar* | *glabrum* | chawari |
| 0 | CACR | *Castanea* | *crenata* | Japanese chestnut |
| 1 | CADN | *Castanea* | *dentata* | American chestnut |
| 1 | CASA | *Castanea* | *sativa* | sweet chestnut, European chestnut |

(*Continued*)

| CDI | Species Code | Genus | Species | Common Name |
|---|---|---|---|---|
| 0 | CSLI | *Casuarina* | *litoralis* | black she-oak |
| 0 | CTSP | *Catalpa* | *speciosa* | northern catalpa |
| 0 | CNCR | *Ceanothus* | *crassifolius* | hoaryleaf ceanothus |
| 1 | CEAN* | *Cedrela* | *angustifolia* | cedro salteno |
| 0 | CEFI | *Cedrela* | *fissilis* | central American cedar |
| 1 | CELI* | *Cedrela* | *lilloi* | cedro salteno |
| 0 | CEOD | Cedrela | odorata | |
| 0 | CETO | *Cedrela* | *toona* | Harms red cedar, Australian cedar |
| 2 | CDAT | *Cedrus* | *atlantica* | Atlantic cedar, Atlas cedar |
| 1 | CDBR* | *Cedrus* | *brevifolia* | |
| 1 | CDDE | *Cedrus* | *deodara* | deodar cedar, Himalayan cedar |
| 1 | CDLI* | *Cedrus* | *libani* | cedar of Lebanon |
| 1 | CLAU | *Celtis* | *australis* | southern nettle tree, hackberry |
| 0 | CLCA | *Celtis* | *caucasica* | Caucasian nettle tree |
| 0 | CLLA | *Celtis* | *laevigata* | sugarberry |
| 1 | CLOC | *Celtis* | *occidentalis* | hackberry |
| 1 | CLRE | *Celtis* | *reticulata* | netleaf hackberry |
| 0 | CEOC | *Cephalanthus* | *occidentalis* | buttonbush |
| 0 | CEMI | *Cercidium* | *microphyllum* | yellow paloverde |
| 0 | CRBE | *Cercocarpus* | *betuloides* | birchleaf mountain-mahogany |
| 0 | CRLE | *Cercocarpus* | *ledifolius* | curlleaf mountain-mahogany |
| 1 | CRMO | *Cercocarpus* | *montanus* | alderleaf cercocarpus |
| 1 | CHFO | *Chamaecyparis* | *formosensis* | Formosan false cypress |
| 2 | CHNO | *Chamaecyparis* | *nootkatensis* | Alaska yellow-cedar, Nootka cypress |
| 1 | CHOB | *Chamaecyparis* | *obtusa* | hinoki cypress, Formosan cypress |
| 1 | CHPI | *Chamaecyparis* | *pisifera* | sawara cypress |
| 0 | CHTH | *Chamaecyparis* | *thyoides* | Atlantic white-cedar |
| 0 | CLEX | *Chlorophora* | *excelsa* | iroko, kambala, mvule |
| 0 | CHSP | *Chorisia* | *speciosa* | paneira |
| 0 | CIFR | *Citharexylum* | *fruticosum* | Florida fiddlewood |
| 0 | COCO | *Copaifera* | *coleosperma* | Rhodesian copalwood, mehibi |
| 1 | COAL | *Cordia* | *alliodora* | laurel corriente, lauro amarillo, ajo ajo |
| 0 | COAP | *Cordia* | *apurensis* | |
| 0 | COBI | *Cordia* | *bicolor* | |
| 0 | COEL | Cordia | *elaeagnoides* | |
| 0 | COTR | *Cordia* | *trichotoma* | lauro pardo, peterebi |
| 0 | COFL | *Cornus* | *florida* | flowering dogwood |
| 0 | COSA | *Cornus* | *sanguinea* | |
| 0 | COAV | *Corylus* | *avellana* | common hazel |
| 0 | COSI | *Corylus* | *sieboldiana* | blume hazel |
| 0 | CTCO | *Cotinus* | *coggygria* | European smoketree |

(*Continued*)

| CDI | Species Code | Genus | Species | Common Name |
|---|---|---|---|---|
| 0 | CTSP | *Cotoneaster* | spp. | cotoneaster |
| 0 | CRAZ | *Crataegus* | *azarolus* | azarole |
| 0 | CRMO | *Crataegus* | *monogyna* | |
| 2 | CMJA* | *Cryptomeria* | *japonica* | Japanese cedar, sugi, cryptomeria |
| 1 | CUAZ | *Cupressus* | *arizonica* | Arizona cypress |
| 0 | CUAT | *Cupressus* | *atlantica* | Atlas cypress |
| 0 | CUDU | *Cupressus* | *dupreziana* | |
| 1 | CUGI | *Cupressus* | *gigantea* | |
| 0 | CUGL | *Cupressus* | *glabra* | smooth Arizona cypress |
| 0 | CULU | *Cupressus* | *lusitanica* | Mexican cypress |
| 2 | CUSE | *Cupressus* | *sempervirens* | Italian cypress, Mediterranean cypress |
| 0 | CYRA | *Cyrilla* | *racemiflora* | swamp cyrilla, leatherwood |
| 0 | DADA | *Dacrycarpus* | *dacrydioides* | kahikatea, white pine |
| 1 | DABD | *Dacrydium* | *bidwillii* | New Zealand mountain pine |
| 1 | DABI* | *Dacrydium* | *biforme* | |
| 1 | DACO* | *Dacrydium* | *colensoi* | |
| 2 | DACU | *Dacrydium* | *cupressinum* | rimu, red pine |
| 1 | DAFR | *Dacrydium* | *franklinii* | Huon pine |
| 0 | DIGU | *Dicorynia* | *guianensis* | angelique |
| 0 | DSVI | *Diospyros* | *virginiana* | common persimmon |
| 0 | DITO | *Discaria* | *toumatou* | matagouri, tumatu-kuru, wild Irishman |
| 1 | DITR | *Discaria* | *trinervis* | |
| 0 | DRLA | *Dracophyllum* | *latifolium* | neinei |
| 0 | DRWI | *Drimys* | *winteri* | canelo, winter bark |
| 1 | DUVI | *Duschenkia* | *viridis* | |
| 0 | DYMA | *Dysoxylum* | *malabaricum* | Bombay white cedar |
| 0 | ELGL | *Elaeoluma* | *glabrescens* | |
| 1 | EMRU | *Empetrum* | *rubrum* | murtilla |
| 1 | ENCA | *Enkianthus* | *campanulatus* | |
| 0 | ENAN | *Entandrophragma* | *angolense* | gedu nohor, kalungi, tiama, edinam |
| 0 | ENCA | *Entandrophragma* | *candollei* | kosipo, omu |
| 0 | ENCY | *Entandrophragma* | *cylindricum* | sapeli, sapele, sapelli, assi |
| 0 | ENUT | *Entandrophragma* | *utile* | sipo, utile |
| 0 | EUCA | *Eucalyptus* | *camaldulensis* | river red gum |
| 0 | EUDE | *Eucalyptus* | *delegatensis* | alpine ash |
| 0 | EUGL | *Eucalyptus* | *globulus* | Tasmanian bluegum |
| 0 | EUMA | *Eucalyptus* | *marginata* | jarrah |
| 0 | EUMI | *Eucalyptus* | *miniata* | Darwin woolybutt |
| 0 | EUNE | *Eucalyptus* | *nesophila* | Melville Island bloodwood |
| 0 | EUOR | *Eucalyptus* | *oreades* | Blue Mountains ash |
| 0 | EUPA | *Eucalyptus* | *pauciflora* | snow gum, cabbage gum |

*(Continued)*

| CDI | Species Code | Genus | Species | Common Name |
|-----|--------------|-------|---------|-------------|
| 0 | EUST | *Eucalyptus* | *stellulata* | black salee |
| 0 | EUTE | *Eucalyptus* | *tetradonta* | Darwin stringybark |
| 0 | EUVI | *Eucalyptus* | *viminalis* | ribbongum |
| 0 | EUCO | *Eucryphia* | *cordifolia* | ulmo, muermo |
| 0 | EUJA | *Eugenia* | *jambolana* | jaman, kelat eugenia |
| 0 | EXCU | *Exocarpus* | *cuppressiforme* | native cherry |
| 0 | FACR | *Fagus* | *crenata* | bunya beech |
| 1 | FAGR* | *Fagus* | *grandifolia* | American beech |
| 1 | FAOR | *Fagus* | *orientalis* | Oriental beech, eastern beech |
| 2 | FASY* | *Fagus* | *sylvatica* | European beech, common beech |
| 2 | FICU* | *Fitzroya* | *cupressoides* | alerce, Patagonian cypress |
| 1 | FRAM | *Fraxinus* | *americana* | white ash |
| 0 | FRCA | *Fraxinus* | *caroliniana* | Carolina ash |
| 1 | FREX* | *Fraxinus* | *excelsior* | European ash, common ash |
| 0 | FRMA | *Fraxinus* | *mandshurica* | Manchurian ash, yachidamo |
| 1 | FRNI* | *Fraxinus* | *nigra* | black ash |
| 0 | FRPE | *Fraxinus* | *pennsylvanica* | green ash, red ash |
| 1 | FRSP | *Fraxinus* | *spaethiana* | ash |
| 1 | FRVE | *Fraxinus* | *velutina* | velvet ash |
| 0 | GEAV | *Gevuina* | *avellana* | avellano |
| 0 | GIBI | *Gingko* | *biloba* | maidenhair tree, gingko |
| 0 | GLTR | *Gleditsia* | *triacanthos* | honey locust |
| 0 | GMAR | *Gmelina* | *arborea* | gumari, gumbar, yemane, gmelina |
| 0 | GOLA | *Gordonia* | *lasianthus* | loblolly-bay |
| 0 | GOGL | *Goupia* | *glabra* | goupia |
| 0 | GRVI | *Grevillea* | *victoriae* | |
| 0 | GUCE | *Guarea* | *cedrata* | bosse, guarea, white guarea |
| 0 | HABD | *Halocarpus* | *bidwillii* | bog pine |
| 1 | HABI* | *Halocarpus* | *biformis* | pink pine |
| 0 | HAKI | *Halocarpus* | *kirkii* | manoao |
| 0 | HAVI | *Hamamelis* | *virginiana* | witch hazel |
| 0 | HEAN | *Hedycaria* | *angustifolia* | native mulberry |
| 0 | HEAR | *Heteromeles* | *arbutifolia* | toyon |
| 1 | HEBR | *Hevea* | *brasiliensis* | |
| 0 | ILAQ | *Ilex* | *aquifolium* | English holly |
| 0 | ILCA | *Ilex* | *cassine* | dahoon, dahoon holly |
| 0 | ILCO | *Ilex* | *coriacea* | large gallberry, sweet gallberry |
| 0 | ILGL | *Ilex* | *glabra* | inkberry, gallberry |
| 0 | ILIN | *Ilex* | *inundata* | |
| 0 | ILOP | *Ilex* | *opaca* | American holly |
| 0 | JACO | *Jacaranda* | *copaia* | copaia, gobaja, futui, caroba |

*(Continued)*

| CDI | Species Code | Genus | Species | Common Name |
|---|---|---|---|---|
| 1 | JGAU* | *Juglans* | *australis* | Argentine walnut |
| 0 | JGCI | *Juglans* | *cinerea* | butternut |
| 0 | JGNI | *Juglans* | *nigra* | black walnut |
| 0 | JGRE | *Juglans* | *regia* | common walnut |
| 0 | JUCH | *Juniperus* | *chinensis* | Chinese juniper |
| 1 | JUCO | *Juniperus* | *communis* | common juniper |
| 0 | JUDE | *Juniperus* | *deppeana* | alligator juniper |
| 1 | JUDR | *Juniperus* | *drupacea* | Syrian juniper |
| 1 | JUEX | *Juniperus* | *excelsa* | Greek juniper, Grecian juniper |
| 1 | JUFO | *Juniperus* | *foetidissima* | stinking juniper |
| 0 | JUMA | *Juniperus* | *macropoda* | Himalayan pencil pine |
| 0 | JUMO | *Juniperus* | *monosperma* | one-seed juniper |
| 2 | JUOC* | *Juniperus* | *occidentalis* | western juniper |
| 1 | JUOS | *Juniperus* | *osteosperma* | Utah juniper |
| 1 | JUOX | *Juniperus* | *oxycedrus* | prickly juniper |
| 1 | JUPH | *Juniperus* | *phoenicea* | Phoenicean juniper |
| 0 | JUPI | *Juniperus* | *pinchotii* | redberry juniper, Pinchot juniper |
| 0 | JUPC | *Juniperus* | *procera* | Uganda juniper, African pencil cedar |
| 1 | JUPR | *Juniperus* | *przewalskii* | Qilianshan juniper |
| 1 | JURE | *Juniperus* | *recurva* | drooping juniper |
| 2 | JUSC* | *Juniperus* | *scopulorum* | Rocky Mountain juniper |
| 1 | JUSM | *Juniperus* | *semiglobosa* | |
| 1 | JUSE | *Juniperus* | *seravschanica* | |
| 0 | JUTH | *Juniperus* | *thurifera* | Spanish juniper |
| 1 | JUTU | *Juniperus* | *turkestanica* | Turkestan juniper |
| 2 | JUVI* | *Juniperus* | *virginiana* | eastern red cedar |
| 0 | KHGR | *Khaya* | *grandifolia* | acajou, Benin mahogany |
| 0 | KRDR | *Krenevaja* | *drevesina* | |
| 0 | KUER | *Kunzea* | *ericoides* | kanuka, white tea tree |
| 0 | LBGL | *Labatia* | *glomerata* | |
| 0 | LBAN | *Laburnum* | *anagyroides* | common laburnum |
| 1 | LGCO* | *Lagarostrobus* | *colensoi* | |
| 1 | LGFR | *Lagarostrobus* | *franklinii* | huon pine |
| 0 | LSFL | *Lagerstroemia* | *flos-reginae* | pyinma, banaba, banglang, jarul |
| 0 | LSLA | *Lagerstroemia* | *lanceolata* | benteak, nana |
| 0 | LSPA | *Lagerstroemia* | *parviflora* | lendia |
| 2 | LADE* | *Larix* | *decidua* | European larch |
| 1 | LAGM* | *Larix* | *gmelinii* | Dahurian larch |
| 1 | LAGR | *Larix* | *griffithiana* | Himalayan larch |
| 1 | LAJA | *Larix* | *japonica* | Japanese larch |
| 2 | LALA* | *Larix* | *laricina* | tamarack, eastern larch |

*(Continued)*

| CDI | Species Code | Genus | Species | Common Name |
|---|---|---|---|---|
| 2 | LALY* | *Larix* | *lyalli* | subalpine larch |
| 2 | LAOC* | *Larix* | *occidentalis* | western larch |
| 1 | LAPO | *Larix* | *potanini* | Chinese larch |
| 2 | LASI* | *Larix* | *sibirica* | Siberian larch |
| 0 | LAPH | *Laurelia* | *philippiana* | tepa |
| 0 | LASE | *Laurelia* | *sempervirens* | laurelia, Chilean laurel, huahuan |
| 0 | LAHU | *Laxopterigium* | *huasango* | haltaco |
| 0 | LECO | *Lecythis* | *corrugata* | angelique |
| 0 | LEIN | *Lepidothamnus* | *intermedius* | yellow-silver pine |
| 0 | LEFL | *Leptospermum* | *flavescens* | tea tree |
| 0 | LESC | *Leptospermum* | *scoparium* | manuka, red tea tree, black manuka |
| 2 | LIBI* | *Libocedrus* | *bidwillii* | New Zealand cedar, pahautea |
| 0 | LIPL | *Libocedrus* | *plumosa* | kawaka, plume incense cedar |
| 0 | LGVU | *Ligustrum* | *vulgare* | |
| 1 | LIST | *Liquidambar* | *styraciflua* | sweetgum |
| 1 | LITU* | *Liriodendron* | *tulipifera* | tuliptree, yellow-poplar, tulip-poplar |
| 0 | LOFR | *Lomatia* | *fraseri* | silky lomatia, tree lomatia |
| 0 | LOHI | *Lomatia* | *hitsuta* | radal |
| 0 | LOXY | *Lonicera* | *xylosteum* | |
| 0 | LOTR | *Lovoa* | *trichilioides* | dibetou |
| 0 | MAAC | *Magnolia* | *accuminata* | cucumbertree |
| 0 | MAGR | *Magnolia* | *grandiflora* | southern magnolia |
| 0 | MAVI | *Magnolia* | *virginiana* | sweetbay, swampbay |
| 0 | MASY | *Malus* | *sylvestris* | apple tree |
| 0 | MABI | *Manilkara* | *bidentata* | balata franc |
| 0 | MICH | *Michelia* | *champaca* | champak |
| 0 | MINI | *Michelia* | *niligirica* | pilachampa, champak |
| 0 | MOCO | *Moronobea* | *coccinea* | manil montagne, mountain manil |
| 0 | MOAL | *Morus* | *alba* | white mulberry |
| 0 | MORU | *Morus* | *rubra* | red mulberry |
| 0 | MYCE | *Myrica* | *cerifera* | southern bayberry, bayberry |
| 0 | MYGA | *Myrica* | *gale* | sweet gale, bog myrtle |
| 0 | NEAM | *Nectandra* | *amazonum* | |
| 0 | NTLO | *Notelaea* | *longifolia* | large mock-olive |
| 0 | NOAL | *Nothofagus* | *alpina* | rauli |
| 1 | NOAN | *Nothofagus* | *antarctica* | Antarctic beech, nirre |
| 1 | NOBE* | *Nothofagus* | *betuloides* | coihue de Magallanes, guindo |
| 0 | NOCU | *Nothofagus* | *cunninghamii* | Australian nothofagus, myrtle beech |
| 0 | NODO | *Nothofagus* | *dombeyi* | coihue, Dombey's southern beech |
| 0 | NOFU | *Nothofagus* | *fusca* | red beech, New Zealand red beech |
| 1 | NOGU* | *Nothofagus* | *gunnii* | tanglefoot beech |

*(Continued)*

| CDI | Species Code | Genus | Species | Common Name |
|---|---|---|---|---|
| 2 | NOME* | *Nothofagus* | *menziesii* | silver beech, Menzies's red beech |
| 0 | NONE | *Nothofagus* | *nervosa* | rauli |
| 0 | NONI | *Nothofagus* | *nitida* | roble chicote |
| 1 | NOOB | *Nothofagus* | *obliqua* | southern beech, roble |
| 1 | NOPU* | *Nothofagus* | *pumilio* | lenga |
| 2 | NOSO* | *Nothofagus* | *solandri* | mountain beech, black beech |
| 0 | NYOG | *Nyssa* | *ogechee* | Ogeechee tupelo |
| 0 | NYSY | *Nyssa* | *sylvatica* | black tupelo, blackgum |
| 0 | OCUS | *Ocotea* | *usambarensis* | ocotea, camphor |
| 0 | OSCA | *Ostrya* | *carpinifolia* | hop hornbeam |
| 0 | OXAR | *Oxydendrum* | *arboreum* | sourwood |
| 0 | PARI | *Parapiptadenia* | *rigida* | |
| 0 | PAAU | *Parkia* | *auriculata* | |
| 0 | PATO | *Paulownia* | *tomentosa* | empress tree |
| 0 | PECA | *Peronema* | *canescens* | sunkai, koeroes |
| 0 | PEBO | *Persea* | *borbonia* | redbay, shorebay |
| 0 | PELI | *Persea* | *lingue* | lingue |
| 0 | PELN | *Petrophile* | *linearis* | pixie mops |
| 0 | PBPO | *Phoebe* | *porfiria* | |
| 1 | PHAL* | *Phyllocladus* | *alpinus* | mountain toatoa, alpine celery top pine |
| 1 | PHAS* | *Phyllocladus* | *aspleniifolius* | |
| 1 | PHGL* | *Phyllocladus* | *glaucus* | toatoa |
| 1 | PHTR* | *Phyllocladus* | *trichomanoides* | tanekaha, celery pine |
| 2 | PCAB* | *Picea* | *abies* | Norway spruce |
| 0 | PCAS | *Picea* | *asperata* | dragon spruce |
| 1 | PCBA | *Picea* | *balfouriana* | |
| 1 | PCBR | *Picea* | *brachytyla* | |
| 1 | PCCA | *Picea* | *cajanensis* | |
| 1 | PCCH | *Picea* | *chihuahuana* | Chihuahua spruce |
| 2 | PCEN* | *Picea* | *engelmannii* | Engelmann spruce |
| 2 | PCGL* | *Picea* | *glauca* | white spruce |
| 1 | PCGN | *Picea* | *glehnii* | Sakhalin spruce |
| 0 | PCJE | *Picea* | *jezoensis* | Yezo spruce, Hondo spruce |
| 1 | PCLI | *Picea* | *likiangensis* | Likiang spruce |
| 2 | PCMA* | *Picea* | *mariana* | |
| 1 | PCOM* | *Picea* | *omorika* | Serbian spruce, Pancic spruce |
| 1 | PCOR* | *Picea* | *orientalis* | eastern spruce, Oriental spruce |
| 2 | PCPU* | *Picea* | *pungens* | blue spruce, Colorado spruce |
| 1 | PCPR | *Picea* | *purpurea* | |
| 2 | PCRU* | *Picea* | *rubens* | red spruce |

(Continued)

| CDI | Species Code | Genus | Species | Common Name |
|-----|-------------|-------|---------|-------------|
| 1 | PCSH | *Picea* | *shrenkiana* | Shrenk's spruce |
| 2 | PCSI* | *Picea* | *sitchensis* | Sitka spruce |
| 1 | PCSM | *Picea* | *smithiana* | Himalayan spruce |
| 1 | PCTI | *Picea* | *tienschanica* | Tien-shan spruce |
| 2 | PLUV* | *Pilgerodendron* | *uviferum* | cipres de las Guaytecas |
| 2 | PIAL* | *Pinus* | *albicaulis* | whitebark pine |
| 2 | PIAR* | *Pinus* | *aristata* | Rocky Mountain bristlecone pine |
| 1 | PIAM* | *Pinus* | *armandii* | David's pine, Armand's pine |
| 2 | PIBA* | *Pinus* | *balfouriana* | foxtail pine |
| 2 | PIBN* | *Pinus* | *banksiana* | jack pine |
| 1 | PIBR* | *Pinus* | *brutia* | Calabrian pine, brutia pine, see kiefer |
| 0 | PIBU | *Pinus* | *bungeana* | lacebark pine |
| 0 | PICN | *Pinus* | *canariensis* | Canary Island pine |
| 0 | PICA | *Pinus* | *caribaea* | Caribbean pine, Cuban pine |
| 2 | PICE* | *Pinus* | *cembra* | Swiss stone pine, Arolla pine |
| 2 | PICM* | *Pinus* | *cembroides* | Mexican pinyon, Mexican nut pine |
| 1 | PICH | *Pinus* | *chihuahuana* | Chihuahua pine |
| 2 | PICO* | *Pinus* | *contorta* | lodgepole pine |
| 0 | PICL | *Pinus* | *coulteri* | Coulter pine, bigcone pine |
| 1 | PIDN | *Pinus* | *densata* | |
| 1 | PIDE* | *Pinus* | *densiflora* | Japanese red pine |
| 2 | PIEC* | *Pinus* | *echinata* | shortleaf pine |
| 2 | PIED* | *Pinus* | *edulis* | pinyon, Colorado pinyon |
| 1 | PIEL | *Pinus* | *elliottii* | slash pine |
| 1 | PIEN | *Pinus* | *engelmannii* | Apache pine |
| 2 | PIFL* | *Pinus* | *flexilis* | |
| 1 | PIGE | *Pinus* | *gerardiana* | chilgoza pine, Gerard's pine |
| 2 | PIHA* | *Pinus* | *halepensis* | Aleppo pine, Jerusalem pine |
| 1 | PIHE | *Pinus* | *heldreichii* | Heldreich's pine, panzer fohre |
| 2 | PIJE* | *Pinus* | *jeffreyi* | Jeffrey pine |
| 1 | PIKE | *Pinus* | *kesiya* | Khasi pine |
| 1 | PIKO | *Pinus* | *koraiensis* | Korean pine |
| 1 | PILG | *Pinus* | *lagunae* | laguna pinyon |
| 2 | PILA* | *Pinus* | *lambertiana* | sugar pine |
| 2 | PILE* | *Pinus* | *leucodermis* | Bosnian pine, graybark pine |
| 2 | PILO* | *Pinus* | *longaeva* | intermountain bristlecone pine |
| 1 | PIMA | *Pinus* | *massoniana* | Masson pine |
| 1 | PIMK | *Pinus* | *merkusii* | Merkus pine, mindoro pine |
| 1 | PIME | *Pinus* | *mesogeensis* | cluster pine |
| 2 | PIMO* | *Pinus* | *monophylla* | singleleaf pinyon |
| 1 | PIMZ | *Pinus* | *montezumae* | Montezuma pine |

*(Continued)*

| CDI | Species Code | Genus | Species | Common Name |
|---|---|---|---|---|
| 1 | PIMC | *Pinus* | *monticola* | western white pine |
| 1 | PIMU* | *Pinus* | *mughus* | krumholz pine |
| 1 | PIMG | *Pinus* | *mugo* | mountain pine, stone pine |
| 0 | PIMR | *Pinus* | *muricata* | bishop pine |
| 2 | PINI* | *Pinus* | *nigra* | Austrian pine, black pine |
| 0 | PIOC* | *Pinus* | *occidentalis* | West Indian pine |
| 0 | PIOO | *Pinus* | *oocarpa* | Nicaraguan pitch pine, ocote pine |
| 1 | PIPA* | *Pinus* | *palustris* | longleaf pine |
| 0 | PIPT | *Pinus* | *patula* | Mexican weeping pine |
| 1 | PIPE* | *Pinus* | *peuce* | Macedonian pine, Balkan pine |
| 1 | PIPI* | *Pinus* | *pinaster* | maritime pine, cluster pine |
| 2 | PIPN* | *Pinus* | *pinea* | Italian stone pine, umbrella pine |
| 2 | PIPO* | *Pinus* | *ponderosa* | ponderosa pine, western yellow pine |
| 1 | PIPM | *Pinus* | *pumila* | dwarf Siberian pine |
| 1 | PIPU* | *Pinus* | *pungens* | Table Mountain pine |
| 1 | PIQU | *Pinus* | *quadrifolia* | Parry pinyon |
| 1 | PIRA | *Pinus* | *radiata* | Monterrey pine |
| 2 | PIRE* | *Pinus* | *resinosa* | red pine |
| 1 | PIRI* | *Pinus* | *rigida* | pitch pine |
| 1 | PIRO | *Pinus* | *roxburghii* | chir pine |
| 1 | PISI | *Pinus* | *sibirica* | Siberian stone pine |
| 2 | PISF* | *Pinus* | *strobiformis* | southwestern white pine |
| 2 | PIST* | *Pinus* | *strobus* | eastern white pine, Weymouth pine |
| 2 | PISY* | *Pinus* | *sylvestris* | Scots pine, Scotch pine |
| 1 | PITB | *Pinus* | *tabulaeformis* | Chinese pine |
| 2 | PITA* | *Pinus* | *taeda* | loblolly pine |
| 0 | PITH | *Pinus* | *thunbergii* | Japanese black pine |
| 1 | PITO | *Pinus* | *torreyana* | Torrey pine |
| 2 | PIUN | *Pinus* | *uncinata* | mountain pine |
| 1 | PIVI | *Pinus* | *virginiana* | Virginia pine, scrub pine |
| 1 | PIWA | *Pinus* | *wallichiana* | Himalayan pine, kail pine, blue pine |
| 0 | PSGR | *Pisonia* | *grandis* | |
| 0 | PTAT | *Pistacia* | *atlantica* | Atlas pistache, betoum |
| 0 | PTKH | *Pistacia* | *khinjuk* | kakkar |
| 0 | PTPA | *Pistacia* | *palaestina* | Israelian pistache |
| 0 | PTVE | *Pistacia* | *vera* | green mastic, real mastictree |
| 0 | PLAC | *Platanus* | *acerifolia* | London plane tree |
| 1 | PLOC | *Platanus* | *occidentalis* | American sycamore |
| 0 | PLOR | *Platanus* | *orientalis* | Oriental plane tree |
| 0 | PLIN | *Platonia* | *insignis* | parcouri |
| 1 | PLOR | *Platyeladus* | *orientalis* | Chinese pine |

*(Continued)*

| CDI | Species Code | Genus | Species | Common Name |
|---|---|---|---|---|
| 0 | POFA | *Podocarpus* | *falcatus* | yellowwood, oteniqua |
| 0 | POHA | *Podocarpus* | *hallii* | Hall's totara |
| 0 | POLA | *Podocarpus* | *lawrencei* | Tasmanian podocarpus |
| 1 | PONE | *Podocarpus* | *neriifolius* | thitmin |
| 0 | PONI | *Podocarpus* | *nivalis* | snow totara |
| 1 | PONU | *Podocarpus* | *nubigensus* | manio de hojas punzantes |
| 0 | POPA | *Podocarpus* | *parlatorei* | |
| 0 | POTO | *Podocarpus* | *totara* | totara |
| 0 | PYSA | *Polyscias* | *sambucifolius* | elderberry panax, elderberry ash |
| 1 | PPAL | *Populus* | *alba* | white poplar |
| 0 | PPAN | *Populus* | *angustifolia* | narrowleaf cottonwood |
| 1 | PPBA | *Populus* | *balsamifera* | balsam poplar |
| 0 | PPDE | *Populus* | *deltoides* | eastern cottonwood |
| 1 | PPEU | *Populus* | *euphratica* | charab poplar, Indian poplar |
| 0 | PPFA | *Populus* | *fastigiata* | |
| 1 | PPFR | *Populus* | *fremontii* | Fremont cottonwood |
| 1 | PPGR | *Populus* | *grandidentata* | bigtooth aspen |
| 1 | PPNI | *Populus* | *nigra* | lombardy poplar, black poplar |
| 1 | PPSI | *Populus* | *sieboldii* | Japanese aspen |
| 1 | PPTR | *Populus* | *tremuloides* | quaking aspen |
| 0 | PPTC | *Populus* | *trichocarpa* | black cottonwood |
| 1 | PRMX* | *Premna* | *maxima* | muchichio |
| 1 | PRFL | *Prosopis* | *flexuosa* | |
| 0 | PRGL | *Prosopis* | *glandulosa* | honey mesquite |
| 0 | PMAN | *Prumnopitys* | *andina* | lleuque |
| 0 | PMFE | *Prumnopitys* | *ferruginea* | miro |
| 0 | PMTA | *Prumnopitys* | *taxifolia* | matai, black pine |
| 0 | PNAM | *Prunus* | *americana* | American plum |
| 0 | PNAV | *Prunus* | *avium* | wild cherry |
| 0 | PNIL | *Prunus* | *ilicifolia* | |
| 0 | PNMA | *Prunus* | *mahaleb* | |
| 0 | PNPE | *Prunus* | *pennsylvanica* | pin cherry |
| 1 | PNSE | *Prunus* | *serotina* | black cherry |
| 0 | PNSP | *Prunus* | *spinosa* | |
| 0 | PSMU | *Pseudobombax* | *munguba* | muguba, huira |
| 1 | PSSE | *Pseudobombax* | *septenatum* | |
| 1 | PSJA | *Pseudotsuga* | *japonica* | Japanese Douglas-fir |
| 1 | PSMA* | *Pseudotsuga* | *macrocarpa* | bigcone Douglas-fir |
| 2 | PSME* | *Pseudotsuga* | *menziesii* | Douglas-fir |
| 0 | PSAX | *Pseudowintera* | *axillaris* | |
| 0 | PSCO | *Pseudowintera* | *colorata* | mountain horopito, pepper tree |

*(Continued)*

| CDI | Species Code | Genus | Species | Common Name |
|---|---|---|---|---|
| 0 | PSXA | *Pseudoxandra* | *polyphleba* | |
| 0 | PTAN* | *Pterocarpus* | *angolensis* | muninga, bloodwood |
| 0 | PTVE | *Pterocarpus* | *vernalis* | |
| 0 | PTRH | *Pterocarya* | *rhoifolia* | Japanese wing nut |
| 0 | PTPA | *Pteronia* | *pallens* | |
| 1 | PUTR | *Purshia* | *tridentata* | bitter brush |
| 0 | QUAC | *Quercus* | *acutissima* | |
| 0 | QUAF | *Quercus* | *afares* | |
| 2 | QUAL* | *Quercus* | *alba* | white oak |
| 0 | QUBI | *Quercus* | *bicolor* | swamp white oak |
| 0 | QUBO | *Quercus* | *boissieri* | Israelian oak |
| 1 | QUBR | *Quercus* | *brantii* | |
| 0 | QUCL | *Quercus* | *calliprinos* | Kermes oak, Israelian oak |
| 1 | QUCA | *Quercus* | *canariensis* | Mirbeck's oak, Algerian oak |
| 1 | QUCE | *Quercus* | *cerris* | Turkey oak, Austrian oak |
| 1 | QUCO | *Quercus* | *coccinea* | scarlet oak |
| 0 | QUCP | *Quercus* | *copeyensis* | |
| 0 | QUCR | *Quercus* | *costaricensis* | |
| 1 | QUDE | *Quercus* | *dentata* | kashiwa oak, Daimio oak |
| 1 | QUDG* | *Quercus* | *douglasii* | blue oak |
| 1 | QUDS | *Quercus* | *dschoruchensis* | |
| 1 | QUEL | *Quercus* | *ellipsoidalis* | northern pin oak |
| 0 | QUEM | *Quercus* | *emoryi* | Emory oak |
| 0 | QUEN | *Quercus* | *engelmannii* | Engelmann oak |
| 1 | QUFG | *Quercus* | *faginea* | Portuguese oak |
| 1 | QUFA | *Quercus* | *falcata* | southern red oak |
| 1* | QUFR | *Quercus* | *frainetto* | Hungarian oak |
| 2 | QUGA | *Quercus* | *gambelii* | Gambel oak |
| 0 | QUGY | *Quercus* | *garryana* | Oregon white oak |
| 1 | QUGR | *Quercus* | *grisea* | gray oak |
| 1 | QUHA | *Quercus* | *hartwissiana* | |
| 0 | QUIL | *Quercus* | *ilex* | holm oak, holly oak |
| 0 | QUIT | *Quercus* | *ithaburensis* | Mt. Tabor oak |
| 0 | QUKE | *Quercus* | *kelloggii* | California black oak |
| 1 | QULA | *Quercus* | *laurifolia* | laurel oak |
| 1 | QULO | *Quercus* | *lobata* | valley oak |
| 0 | QULU | *Quercus* | *lusitanica* | oak |
| 1 | QULY* | *Quercus* | *lyrata* | overcup oak |
| 1 | QUMA* | *Quercus* | *macrocarpa* | bur oak |
| 0 | QUMC | *Quercus* | *macrolepis* | Valonia oak |
| 0 | QUML | *Quercus* | *marilandica* | blackjack oak |

*(Continued)*

| CDI | Species Code | Genus | Species | Common Name |
|---|---|---|---|---|
| 0 | QUMI | *Quercus* | *michauxii* | swamp chestnut oak |
| 0 | QUMO | *Quercus* | *mongolica* | Mongolian oak |
| 0 | QUGS | *Quercus* | *mongolica* var. *grosseserrata* | |
| 0 | QUMU | *Quercus* | *muehlenbergii* | chinkapin oak |
| 1 | QUNI | *Quercus* | *nigra* | water oak |
| 0 | QUPA | *Quercus* | *palustris* | pin oak |
| 2 | QUPE* | *Quercus* | *petraea* | durmast oak, sessile oak |
| 1 | QUPO | *Quercus* | *pontica* | Armenian oak |
| 1 | QUPR* | *Quercus* | *prinus* | chestnut oak |
| 2 | QUPU | *Quercus* | *pubescens* | downy oak, pubescent oak |
| 0 | QUPY | *Quercus* | *pyrenaica* | Pyrenean oak |
| 2 | QURO* | *Quercus* | *robur* | English oak |
| 1 | QURU* | *Quercus* | *rubra* | red oak |
| 1 | QUSH | *Quercus* | *shumardii* | Shumard oak |
| 2 | QUST* | *Quercus* | *stellata* | post oak |
| 0 | QUSU | *Quercus* | *suber* | cork oak, cork tree |
| 1 | QUVE* | *Quercus* | *velutina* | black oak |
| 0 | QUAC | *Quintinia* | *acutifolia* | Westland quintinia |
| 0 | RAGU | *Rapanea* | *guianensis* | guiana rapanea |
| 0 | RESP | *Recordoxylon* | *speciosum* | wacapou guitin |
| 0 | RHCA | *Rhamnus* | *caroliniana* | Carolina buckthorn |
| 0 | RHCT | *Rhamnus* | *cathartica* | |
| 0 | RHCR | *Rhamnus* | *crocea* | hollyleaf buckthorn |
| 0 | RHOV | *Rhus* | *ovata* | sugar sumac |
| 1 | RONE | *Robinia* | *neomexicana* | New Mexico locust |
| 0 | ROPS | *Robinia* | *pseudoacacia* | black locust |
| 0 | SBPI | *Sabina* | *pingu* | |
| 0 | SBRE | *Sabina* | *recurva* | |
| 1 | SBSA | *Sabina* | *saltuaria* | |
| 1 | SBTI | *Sabina* | *tibetica* | |
| 1 | SBWA | *Sabina* | *wallichiana* | |
| 0 | SAAC | *Salix* | *acutifolia* | pointed-leaved willow |
| 1 | SAAL | *Salix* | *alba* | white willow |
| 0 | SAAM | *Salix* | *amygdalina* | almond-leaved willow |
| 0 | SAAD | *Salix* | *amygdaloides* | peachleaf willow |
| 0 | SAAR | *Salix* | *arbusculoides* | littletree willow |
| 0 | SAAT | *Salix* | *arctica* | Arctic willow |
| 0 | SABA | *Salix* | *babylonica* | weeping willow |
| 0 | SACN | *Salix* | *candida* | sage-leaf willow, silver willow |
| 0 | SACA | *Salix* | *caprea* | pussy willow, goat willow |

*(Continued)*

| CDI | Species Code | Genus | Species | Common Name |
|-----|--------------|-------|---------|-------------|
| 0 | SACR | *Salix* | *caroliniana* | Coastal Plain willow |
| 0 | SADI | *Salix* | *discolor* | pussy willow, glaucous willow |
| 0 | SAEL | *Salix* | *elaeagnos* | hoary willow |
| 0 | SAEX | *Salix* | *exigua* | sandbar willow |
| 0 | SAGL | *Salix* | *glauca* | grayleaf willow |
| 0 | SALA | *Salix* | *lanata* | Richardson's willow |
| 0 | SALS | *Salix* | *lasiolepis* | arroyo willow, white willow |
| 0 | SAMY | *Salix* | *myrsinifolia* | |
| 0 | SAPH | *Salix* | *phylicifolia* | tea-leaf willow |
| 0 | SAPL | *Salix* | *planifolia* | sandbar willow, lakeshore willow |
| 0 | SAPU | *Salix* | *purpurea* | purple willow, purple osier |
| 0 | SAVI | *Salix* | *viminalis* | basket willow, common osier |
| 0 | SNAL | *Santalum* | *album* | sandalwood, santalin, chandal |
| 0 | SAST | *Sapium* | *styllare* | |
| 0 | SAAL | *Sassafras* | *albinum* | sassafras |
| 1 | SACO | *Saxegothaea* | *conspicua* | Prince Albert's yew |
| 0 | SCTR | *Schleichera* | *trijuga* | ta-kro, kusum, kusamo |
| 0 | SCMI | *Schleronema* | *micranthum* | cordeiro, scleronema |
| 1 | SCVE | *Sciadopitys* | *verticillata* | |
| 1 | SESE | *Sequoia* | *sempervirens* | coast redwood |
| 2 | SEGI | *Sequoiadendron* | *giganteum* | giant sequoia |
| 0 | SHRO | *Shorea* | *robusta* | sal |
| 0 | SIAM | *Simarouba* | *amara* | simarouba |
| 0 | SOAM | *Sorbus* | *americana* | mountain ash |
| 0 | SOAR | *Sorbus* | *aria* | whitebeam |
| 0 | SOAU | *Sorbus* | *aucuparia* | mountain ash, rowan |
| 1 | SOTE | *Sorbus* | *torminalis* | chequer tree, wild service tree |
| 0 | SODU | *Sorocea* | *duckei* | |
| 0 | SWLA | *Swartzia* | *laevicarpa* | saboarana |
| 0 | SWMC | *Swietenia* | *macrophylla* | |
| 0 | SWMA | *Swietenia* | *mahagoni* | West Indies mahogany |
| 0 | SYGL | *Symphonia* | *globulifera* | manil |
| 0 | TABA | *Tabebuia* | *barbata* | Igapo-tree |
| 0 | TMAP | *Tamarix* | *aphylla* | dur |
| 1 | TMCH | *Tamarix* | *chinensis* | tamarisk, salt cedar |
| 0 | TMJO | *Tamarix* | *jordanis* | |
| 0 | TPGU | *Tapirira* | *guianensis* | tapirira, cedroi, jobo |
| 0 | TMXE | *Tasmannia* | *xerophila* | |
| 0 | TAAS | *Taxodium* | *ascendens* | pond cypress |
| 2 | TADI* | *Taxodium* | *distichum* | baldcypress |
| 2 | TAMU* | *Taxodium* | *mucronatum* | Montezuma cypress |
| 1 | TABA | *Taxus* | *baccata* | common yew, English yew |

(Continued)

| CDI | Species Code | Genus | Species | Common Name |
|-----|--------------|-------|---------|-------------|
| 1 | TACU | *Taxus* | *cuspidata* | Japanese yew |
| 1 | TEGR | *Tectona* | *grandis* | teak |
| 0 | TEBR | *Terminalia* | *brownii* | |
| 0 | TEGU | *Terminalia* | *guianensis* | |
| 0 | TETO | *Terminalia* | *tomentosa* | Indian laurel, taukkyan, sain |
| 1 | TEAR | *Tetraclinis* | *articulata* | Arar tree, African thuya |
| 2 | THOC* | *Thuja* | *occidentalis* | northern white-cedar |
| 0 | THOR | *Thuja* | *orientalis* | Chinese arborvitae, Oriental arborvitae |
| 1 | THPL* | *Thuja* | *plicata* | western red cedar, giant arborvitae |
| 1 | THST | *Thuja* | *standishii* | Japanese arborvitae |
| 1 | THDO | *Thujopsis* | *dolabrata* | hiba arborvitae |
| 1 | THHO | *Thujopsis* | *dolabrata* var. *hondai* | asunaro arborvitae |
| 1 | TIAM | *Tilia* | *americana* | American basswood |
| 1 | TICO | *Tilia* | *cordata* | littleleaf linden, winter linden, |
| 1 | TIPL | *Tilia* | *platyphyllos* | broad-leaved linden, summer linden |
| 1 | TOCA | *Torreya* | *californica* | California nutmeg |
| 0 | TRSC | *Triplochiton* | *schleroxylon* | abachi, obeche, wawa, arere |
| 0 | TRCO | *Tristania* | *conferta* | Queensland box tree |
| 2 | TSCA* | *Tsuga* | *canadensis* | eastern hemlock |
| 1 | TSCR* | *Tsuga* | *caroliniana* | Carolina hemlock |
| 0 | TSCH | *Tsuga* | *chinensis* | Chinese hemlock |
| 0 | TSDI | *Tsuga* | *diversifolia* | Japanese hemlock |
| 1 | TSDU | *Tsuga* | *dumosa* | East Himalayan hemlock |
| 2 | TSHE* | *Tsuga* | *heterophylla* | western hemlock |
| 2 | TSME* | *Tsuga* | *mertensiana* | mountain hemlock |
| 0 | TSSI | *Tsuga* | *sieboldii* | southern Japanese hemlock |
| 1 | ULGL | *Ulmus* | *glabra* | Wych elm, Scots elm, mountain elm |
| 1 | ULLA | *Ulmus* | *laevis* | European white elm |
| 1 | ULMI | *Ulmus* | *minor* | smooth-leaved elm, field elm |
| 0 | ULPU | *Ulmus* | *pumila* | Siberian elm |
| 1 | ULRU | *Ulmus* | *rubra* | slippery elm |
| 0 | VBLA | *Vibernum* | *lantana* | |
| 0 | VIME | *Virola* | *melinonii* | mountain yayamadou |
| 1 | VIKE* | *Vitex* | *keniensis* | moru, moru oak |
| 0 | VOAM | *Vouacapoua* | *americana* | wacapou |
| 0 | WERA | *Weinmannia* | *racemosa* | kamahi |
| 0 | WETR | *Weinmannia* | *trichosperma* | tineo, tenio, palo santo |
| 1 | WICE* | *Widdringtonia* | *cedarbergensis* | Clanwilliam cedar |
| 0 | ZISP | *Ziziphus* | *spina-christi* | Judas tree, Christ thorn |
| 0 | ZYDU | *Zygophyllum* | *dumosum* | |

From Ultimate Tree Ring Web Pages, http://web.utk.edu/~grissino/species.htm

# Appendix B
## Age of the Oldest Trees per Species

This list is a compilation of Peter Brown's OLDLIST (Brown 1996) and Neil Pederson's Eastern OLDLIST (http://people.eku.edu/pedersonn/OLDLISTeast/) for the eastern United States. Those two lists have been combined here, organized by the oldest age of the trees, and filtered so that only the oldest individual is represented for each species. The table includes genus, species, age, type (EX, extrapolations [based on ring measurements usually]; HI, historic record; RC, ring counted; XD, crossdated), sample identification number, location of the sample, and the collector's information or a reference where the tree is mentioned.

| Genus | Species | Age | Type | Sample ID | Location | Collector(s), Dater(s), Reference |
|-------|---------|-----|------|-----------|----------|-----------------------------------|
| Pinus | longaeva | 4844 | RC | WPN-114 | Wheeler Peak, Nevada, United States | Currey (1965) |
| Fitzroya | cupressoides | 3622 | XD | – | Chile | Lara and Villalba (1993) |
| Sequoiadendron | giganteum | 3266 | XD | CBR26 | Sierra Nevada, California, United States | M. Hughes, R. Touchan, E. Wright |
| Juniperus | occidentalis | 2675 | XD | Scofield juniper | Sierra Nevada, California, United States | Miles and Worthington (1998) |
| Pinus | aristata | 2435 | XD | CB-90-11 | central Colorado, United States | Brunstein and Yamaguchi (1992) |
| Ficus | religiosa | 2217 | HI | – | Sri Lanka | Anonymous |
| Sequoia | sempervirens | 2200 | RC | – | northern California, United States | E. Fritz |
| Pinus | balfouriana | 2110 | XD | SHP 7 | Sierra Nevada, California, United States | A. Caprio |
| Larix | lyalli | 1917 | EX | – | Kananaskis, Alberta, Canada | Worrall (1990) |

(*Continued*)

| Genus | Species | Age | Type | Sample ID | Location | Collector(s), Dater(s), Reference |
|-------|---------|-----|------|-----------|----------|-----------------------------------|
| *Juniperus* | *scopulorum* | 1889 | XD | CRE 175 | northern New Mexico, United States | H. Grissino-Mayer, R. Warren |
| *Pinus* | *flexilis* | 1670 | XD | ERE | northern New Mexico, United States | T. Swetnam, T. Harlan |
| *Pinus* | *balfouriana* | 1666 | XD | RCR 1 | Sierra Nevada, California, United States | A. Caprio |
| *Thuja* | *occidentalis* | 1653 | XD | FL117 | Ontario, Canada | Kelly and Larson (1997) |
| *Chamaecyparis* | *nootkatensis* | 1636 | RC? | – | Vancouver Island, Canada | L. Jozsa |
| *Taxodium* | *distichum* | 1622 | XD | BLK 69 | Bladen County, North Carolina, United States | Stahle et al. (1988) |
| *Pseudotsuga* | *menziesii* | 1275 | XD | BIC 63 | northern New Mexico, United States | H. Grissino-Mayer |
| *Pinus* | *albicaulis* | 1267 | XD | RRR15 | central Idaho, United States | Perkins and Swetnam (1996) |
| *Lagarostrobus* | *franklinii* | 1089 | XD | – | Tasmania, Australia | Cook et al. (1991) |
| *Pinus* | *edulis* | 973 | XD | SUN 2522 | northeastern Utah, United States | Schulman (1956) |
| *Pinus* | *ponderosa* | 929 | XD | – | Wah Wah Mountains, Utah, United States | S. Kitchen |
| *Picea* | *engelmannii* | 911 | XD | FCC 23 | central Colorado, United States | Brown et al. (1995) |
| *Pinus* | *monophylla* | 888 | XD | PGH-02 | Pine Grove Hills, Nevada, United States | F. Biondi, S. Strachan |
| *Juniperus* | *virginiana* | 860 | XD | – | Missouri | R. Guyette |
| *Larix* | *siberica* | 750 | XD | OVL-5N | Ovoont, Mongolia | B. Nachin, B. Buckley, N. Pederson |
| *Nyssa* | *sylvatica* | 679 | XD | – | New Hampshire, United States | D. Sperduto, P. Krusic |

(*Continued*)

| Genus | Species | Age | Type | Sample ID | Location | Collector(s), Dater(s), Reference |
|---|---|---|---|---|---|---|
| *Picea* | *glauca* | 668 | XD | – | Klauane Lake, Yukon, Canada | Luckman (2003) (B. Luckman, R. van Dorp, D. Youngblut, M. Masiokas) |
| *Pinus* | *siberica* | 629 | XD | TPX-16 | Tarvagatay Pass, Mongolia | G. Jacoby, B. Nachin, D. Frank |
| *Pinus* | *jeffreyi* | 626 | XD | TGS-02 | Truckee, California, United States | F. Biondi, S. Strachan |
| *Pinus* | *strobiformis* | 599 | XD | VPK02 | San Mateo Mountains, New Mexico, United States | H. Grissino-Mayer, J. Speer, K. Morino |
| *Tsuga* | *canadensis* | 555 | XD | 39021 | Tionesta, Pennsylvania, United States | E. Cook; Cook and Cole (1991) |
| *Fagus* | *sylvatica* | 503 | XD | 1012306F | Abruzzi National Park, Italy | Piovesan et al. (2005) |
| *Abies* | *lasiocarpa* | 501 | XD | – | southern Yukon, Canada | Luckman (2003) (B. Luckman, M. Kenigsberg) |
| *Pinus* | *resinosa* | 500 | RC | – | Granite Lake, Kenora, Ontario Canada | S. St. George; *Ontario's Old Trees* |
| *Picea* | *abies* | 468 | XD | LBG | Bavarian Forest, Germany | R. Wilson |
| *Quercus* | *alba* | 464 | XD | 85141 | Buena Vista, Virginia, United States | E. Cook; N. Pederson |
| *Torreya* | *californica* | 455 | XD | – | Sierra Nevada, California, United States | A. Caprio |
| *Picea* | *rubens* | 445 | RC | 05BCL901a | Fundy Escarpment, New Brunswick, Canada | B. Phillips |
| *Picea* | *rubens* | 445 | XD | 05BCL901a | Fundy Escarpment, New Brunswick, Canada | B. Phillips |

*(Continued)*

| Genus | Species | Age | Type | Sample ID | Location | Collector(s), Dater(s), Reference |
|-------|---------|-----|------|-----------|----------|-----------------------------------|
| *Liriodendron* | *tulipifera* | 434 | RC | – | Great Smoky Mountains National Park, Tennessee, United States | W. Blozan |
| *Quercus* | *muehlenbergii* | 429 | XD | PSC23 | Guadalupe Mountains National Park, Texas, United States | D. Stahle, M. Therrell, D. Griffin, D. (Daniel) Stahle |
| *Quercus* | *montana* | 427 | XD | LBC25 | Uttertown, New Jersey, United States | E. Cook; N. Pederson; Pederson et al. (2004) |
| *Platanus* | *occidentalis* | 412 | RC | BHY001 | Missouri, United States | R. Guyette, M. Stambaugh |
| *Pinus* | *strobus* | 408 | XD | sww51 | Swan Lake, Algonquin Park, Ontario, Canada | R. P. Guyette and B. Cole; ITRDB |
| *Quercus* | *gambelli* | 401 | XD | – | north-central Arizona, United States | F. Biondi |
| *Quercus* | *stellata* | 395 | XD | KEY13 | Osage County, Oklahoma, United States | D. Stahle; ITRDB |
| *Betula* | *alleghaniensis* | 387 | RC | – | Algonquin Park, Ontario, Canada | S. A. Vasiliauskas; *Ontario's Old Trees* |
| *Pinus* | *rigida* | 375 | XD | – | Mohonk Lake, New York, United States | E. Cook; ITRDB |
| *Betula* | *lenta* | 361 | XD | STE03 | New Paltz, New York, United States | E. Cook; N. Pederson and H. M. Hopton; Pederson et al. (2007) |
| *Carya* | *ovata* | 354 | XD | WFS08a | Fiddler's Green, Virginia, United States | N. Pederson; A. Curtis; Pederson et al. (2007) |

*(Continued)*

| Genus | Species | Age | Type | Sample ID | Location | Collector(s), Dater(s), Reference |
|-------|---------|-----|------|-----------|----------|-----------------------------------|
| *Pinus* | *palustris* | 354 | XD | SPB35 | Sprewell Bluff Wildlife Management Area, Meriwether County, Georgia, United States (on the Piedmont) | T. Knight |
| *Magnolia* | *acuminata* | 348 | XD | MDC02b | Fiddler's Green, Virginia, United States | N. Pederson; H. M. Hopton; Pederson et al. (2007) |
| *Quercus* | *macrocarpa* | 343 | XD | BHY002 | Missouri, United States | R. Guyette, M. Stambaugh |
| *Picea* | *mariana* | 330 | XD | – | Sleeping Giant Provincial Park, Ontario, Canada | Girardin et al. (2006) |
| *Quercus* | *rubra* | 326 | XD | hem79 | Wachusett Mountain, Massachusetts, United States | Orwig et al. (2001) |
| *Fraxinus* | *nigra* | 319 | XD | – | Lac Duparquet, Quebec, Canada | Tardif and Bergeron (1999) |
| *Pinus* | *echinata* | 315 | XD | LAW38 | Saline County, Arkansas, United States | D. Stahle |
| *Tsuga* | *caroliniana* | 307 | XD | 101231 | Kelsey Tract, North Carolina, United States | E. Cook; Cook and Cole (1991) |
| *Acer* | *rubrum* | 300 | XD | CATB142 | Catskill Mountains, New York, United States | P. Sheppard and C. Canham; P. Sheppard; Pederson et al. (2007) |
| *Quercus* | *bicolor* | 285 | XD | RHS01a | Catskill, New York, United States | D. Pederson, N. Pederson, M. Hopton |

(*Continued*)

| Genus | Species | Age | Type | Sample ID | Location | Collector(s), Dater(s), Reference |
|---|---|---|---|---|---|---|
| Acer | saccharum | 280 | RC | – | Peter's Woods, Ontario, Canada | Martin and Martin (2001); Ontario's Old Trees |
| Castanea | dentata | 270 | XD | GB204B | Greenbriar, Great Smoky Mountains, Tennessee, United States | J. Young, W. Blozan; ITRDB |
| Carya | glabra | 265 | XD | BCV16a | Mohonk Preserve, New York, United States | N. Pederson; Pederson et al. (2004) |
| Quercus | prinus | 265 | XD | GL18 | Pisgah National Forest, North Carolina, United States | Speer (2001) |
| Acer | nigrum | 247 | RC | BHY038 | Missouri, United States | R. Guyette, M. Stambaugh |
| Pinus | banksiana | 246 | XD | – | Blue Lake, Ontario, Canada | Girardin et al. (2006) |
| Abies | balsamea | 245 | XD | – | Lac Liberal, Canada | C. Krause, H. Morin; ITRDB |
| Pinus | taeda | 241 | XD | – | Congaree Swamp National Park, South Carolina, United States | N. Pederson; T. Doyle; Pederson et al. (1997) |
| Betula | papyrifera | 240 | XD | – | Rainbow Falls Provincial Park, Ontario, Canada | Girardin et al. (2006) |
| Quercus | margaretta | 234 | XD | RCP41 | Rambulette Creek, Taylor County, Georgia, United States | T. Knight |
| Pinus | pungens | 232 | XD | GKA111 | Griffith Knob, Virginia, United States | G. DeWeese, H. Grissino-Mayer, C. Lafon |

(Continued)

| Genus | Species | Age | Type | Sample ID | Location | Collector(s), Dater(s), Reference |
|---|---|---|---|---|---|---|
| *Ostrya* | *virginiana* | 230 | RC | – | Algonquin Park, Ontario, Canada | S. A. Vasiliauskas; *Ontario's Old Trees* |
| *Cotinus* | *obovatus* | 221 | RC | – | Arkansas, United States | R. Guyette |
| *Quercus* | *velutina* | 219 | XD | 293503 | Alley Spring, Shannon County, Missouri, United States | S. Voelker |
| *Quercus* | *lyrata* | 218 | XD | SNA7 | Desha County Arkansas, United States | D. Stahle |
| *Populus* | *tremuloides* | 213 | RC | – | Lake Abitibi Model Forest, Ontario, Canada | P. Lefort; *Ontario's Old Trees* |
| *Populus* | *balsamifera* | 207 | RC | – | Ontario, Canada | S. A. Vasiliauskas; *Ontario's Old Trees* |
| *Fagus* | *grandifolia* | 204 | RC | – | Backus Woods, Ontario, Canada | B. Larson; *Ontario's Old Trees* |
| *Xanthorrhoea* | *preissii* | 200 | XD | Tree 41 | Western Australia | D. Ward |
| *Fraxinus* | *quadrangulata* | 194 | RC | BHY012 | Missouri, United States | R. Guyette, M. Stambaugh |
| *Ulmus* | *alata* | 186 | RC | – | Rocky Creek, Shannon County, Missouri, United States | S. Voelker |
| *Carya* | *tomentosa* | 169 | XD | PCT2025 | Fentress County, Tennessee, United States | J. Hart |
| *Quercus* | *falcata* | 141 | XD | – | Knox County, Tennessee, United States | J. Hart and S. van de Gevel |
| *Fraxinus* | *americana* | 136 | XD | – | Coweeta Hydrologic Laboratory, North Carolina, United States | S. Butler |

*(Continued)*

| Genus | Species | Age | Type | Sample ID | Location | Collector(s), Dater(s), Reference |
|-------|---------|-----|------|-----------|----------|-----------------------------------|
| *Quercus* | *coccinea* | 124 | XD | 511068 | MOFEP Site 5, Shannon County, Missouri, United States | S. Voelker |
| *Populus* | *grandidentata* | 113 | XD | 83-2 | Good Harbor Plains, Michigan, United States | T. C. Wyse, P. C. Goebel; ITRDB |
| *Dirca* | *palustris* | 44 | RC | – | Missouri, United States | M. Stambaugh |

ITRDB, International Tree-Ring Data Bank

## Appendix C
Pith Indicators

# Appendix D
## Field Note Cards

Various note cards can be used for efficient data collection in the field. Note cards are useful because they remind the researcher of the variety of information that can be collected from a site for a particular project and enable uniform data collection for different research projects. The following pages present useful field note cards that can be photocopied or edited for personal use. I recommend printing these on card stock, so that they can stand up to hard use in the field and remain a more permanent record of that field data. These cards are meant to be the starting point for your own cards that hold the information needed for your particular project. The core collection note card and fire history sample cards are modified from formats used by the University of Arizona Laboratory of Tree-Ring Research, and the dendrogeomorphology sample card is modified from Shroder (1978) and was used at the University of Nebraska.

Core Collections

Site _____          Date _____          Page _____

Field Crew _____

| Site Description |
| --- |
| |
| |
| |
| |

| Sample ID | X Coordinate | Y Coordinate | Coring Height | Species | Notes |
| --- | --- | --- | --- | --- | --- |
| | | | | | |
| | | | | | |
| | | | | | |
| | | | | | |
| | | | | | |
| | | | | | |
| | | | | | |
| | | | | | |
| | | | | | |
| | | | | | |
| | | | | | |
| | | | | | |
| | | | | | |
| | | | | | |
| | | | | | |
| | | | | | |
| | | | | | |
| | | | | | |
| | | | | | |
| | | | | | |
| | | | | | |
| | | | | | |

Fire History Sample Card

| Site Name _____ | Date _____ |
|---|---|
| Researchers _____ | Species _____ |
| Number of External Scars _____ | Height of Sample _____ |
| Site Description | |
| Drawing of the Sample (include location of fire scars, pith, and breaks in the wood) | |

Dendrogeomorphology Sample Cards

Species _____

Collection Date _____

Crown Density _____

Lean Direction _____

Lean Degree _____

Lean Characteristics _____

Height of Samples above Base

A _____ B _____

C _____ D _____

Diameter at Sample Location

A _____ B _____

C _____ D _____

Section Orientation (azimuth, base side, crown side, etc.) _____

Drawing of Tree (show sample locations and height of measurements)

Specimen Number _____

Site ID _____

Field _____

Lab _____

Geomorphic Feature _____

Collector _____

Height of Tree _____

Species Density _____

Slope Direction _____

Slope Degree _____

Photo Data _____

_____

Core or Section Data

A

B

C

D

# Appendix E
## Web Resources

Please note that Web addresses change frequently. All attempts were made to ensure that all links in this appendix were operational when this book went to press. When encountering an incorrect address, please search the site name in a Web search engine to find the page.

| Site Name | Web Address (accessed 26 July 2009) |
| --- | --- |
| Bibliography of Dendrochronology | http://www.wsl.ch/dbdendro/ |
| DENDROCLIM 2002 Program | http://dendrolab.org/dendroclim2002.htm |
| Eastern OLDLIST | http://people.eku.edu/pedersonn/oldlisteast/ |
| Henri Grissino-Mayer's Ultimate Tree-Ring Web Pages | http://web.utk.edu/~grissino/ |
| International Dendroecological Fieldweek | http://www.wsl.ch/fieldevent/ |
| Measure J2X User's Guide | http://www.voortech.com/projectj2x/docs/userGuide.htm |
| North American Dendroecological Fieldweek | http://dendrolab.indstate.edu/nadef/index.htm |
| OLDLIST | http://www.rmtrr.org/oldlist.htm |
| PRECON Program | http://www.ltrr.arizona.edu/webhome/hal/precon.html |
| PRISM Data Set | http://www.prism.oregonstate.edu/ |

# References

Abbe, C. 1893. Notes by the editor. Monthly Weather Review 21:331–332.

Abrams, M.D. 1985. Fire history of oak gallery forests in a northeast Kansas tallgrass prairie. American Midland Naturalist 114:188–191.

Abrams, M.D. 1992. Fire and development of oak forests. Bioscience 42(5):346–353.

Abrams, M.D. 2000. Fire and the ecological history of oak forests in the Eastern United States. *In:* D.A. Yaussy, ed., Proceedings of the Workshop on Fire, People, and the Central Hardwoods Landscape. U.S. Department of Agriculture Forest Service, Northeastern Research Station. Gen. Tech. Rep. NE-274, Richmond, Kentucky. pp. 46–55.

Abrams, M.D., and Nowacki, G.J. 1992. Historical variation in fire, oak recruitment, and post-logging accelerated successions in central Pennsylvania. Bulletin of the Torrey Botanical Club 119(1):19–28.

Abrams, M.D., Orwig, D.A., and Demeo, T.E. 1995. Dendroecological analysis of successional dynamics for a presettlement-origin white-pine–mixed-oak forest in the southern Appalachians, U.S.A. Journal of Ecology 83(1):123–133.

Agee, J.K. 1993. Fire Ecology of the Pacific Northwest Forests. Island Press, Washington, D.C. 505 pp.

Ahlstrom, R.V.N., Van West, C.R., and Dean, J.S. 1995. Environmental and chronological factors in the Mesa Verde–Northern Rio Grande migration. Journal of Anthropological Archaeology 14:125–142.

Aldrich, J.M. 1912. Larvae of a Saturniid moth used as food by California Indians. Journal of the New York Entomological Society 20:28–31.

Aldrich, J.M. 1921. *Coloradia pandora* Blake, a moth of which the caterpillar is used as food by Mono Lake Indians. Annals of the Entomological Society of America 14:36–38.

Alestalo, J. 1971. Dendrogeomorphological interpretation of geomorphic processes. Fennia 105:1–140.

Alfaro, R.I., Thomson, A.J., and Van Sickle, G.A. 1985. Quantification of Douglas-fir growth losses caused by western spruce budworm defoliation using stem analysis. Canadian Journal of Forest Research 15:5–9.

Anderson, L., Carlson, C.E., and Wakimoto, R.H. 1987. Forest fire frequency and western spruce budworm outbreaks in western Montana. Forest Ecology and Management 22:251–260.

Anderson, W.T., Bernasconi, S.M., and McKenzie, J.A. 1998. Oxygen and carbon isotopic record of climatic variability in tree ring cellulose (*Picea abies*): an example from central Switzerland (1913–1995). Journal of Geophysical Research 103(D24):31625–31636.

Anderson, W.T., Bernasconi, S.M., McKenzie, J.A., Saurer, M., and Schweingruber, F. 2002. Model evaluation for reconstructing the oxygen isotopic composition in precipitation from tree ring cellulose over the last century. Chemical Geology 182:121–137.

Anderson, W.T., Evans, S.L., Hernadez, R., Pinzon, M.C., Kirby, M.E., Sternberg, L., and Grissino-Mayer, H.D. 2003. Oxygen isotopic records in tree rings as indicators of the climatic and atmospheric circulation changes from Europe, North America, and South America. Oral presentation at the Association of America Geographers Conference, New Orleans, 5–8 March 2003.

Anonymous. 1923. How a tree tells the story of forest fires. Scientific American 128(3):183.

Applequist, M.B. 1958. A simple pith locator for use with off-center increment cores. Journal of Forestry. 56: 141.

Arno, S.F., and Sneck, K.M. 1973. A Method for Determining Fire History in Conifer Forests of the Mountain West. U.S. Department of Agriculture Forest Service, GTR-INT-42. 26 pp.

Asshof, R., Schweingruber, F.H., and Wermelinger, B. 1999. Influence of a gypsy moth (*Lymantria dispar* L.) outbreak on radial growth and wood-anatomy of Spanish chestnut (*Castanea sativa* Mill.) in Ticino (Switzerland). Dendrochronologia 16–17:133–145.

Atwater, B.F., and Yamaguchi, D.K. 1991. Sudden, probably coseismic submergence of Holocene trees and grass in coastal Washington State. Geology 19:706–709.

Au, R., and Tardif, J.C. 2007. Allometric relationships and dendroecology of the dwarf shrub *Dryas integrifolia* near Churchill, subarctic Manitoba. Canadian Journal of Botany 85(6):585–597.

Ault, W.V., Senechal, R.G., and Erelebach, W.E. 1970. Isotopic composition as a natural tracer of lead in our environment. Environmental Science and Technology 4:305–313.

Babbage, C. 1838. Note M: On the age of strata, as inferred from the rings of trees embedded in them. *In:* The Ninth Bridgewater Treatise, a Fragment. 2nd ed. John Murray, London. pp. 256–264.

Baes, C.F., and McLaughlin, S.B. 1984. Trace elements in tree rings: evidence of recent and historical air pollution. Science 224:494–497.

Bailey, I.W. 1925a. The spruce budworm biocoenose. I. Frost rings as indicators of the chronology of specific biological events. Botanical Gazette 80:93–101.

Bailey, I.W. 1925b. Notes on the spruce budworm biocoenose. II. Structural abnormalities in *Abies balsamea*. Botanical Gazette 80:300–310.

Baillie, M.G.L. 1982. Tree-Ring Dating and Archaeology. University of Chicago Press, Chicago. 274 pp.

Baillie, M.G.L. 1995. A Slice through Time: Dendrochronology and Precision Dating. B.T. Batsford Ltd., London. 176 pp.

Bannister, B. 1963. Dendrochronology. *In:* D. Brothwell and E. Higgs, eds., Science in Archaeology. Basic Books, New York. pp. 161–176.

Bannister, B., and Robinson, W.J. 1975. Tree-ring dating in archaeology. World Archaeology 7(2):210–225.

Barber, V.A., Juday, G.P., Finney, B.P., and Wilmking, M. 2004. Reconstruction of summer temperatures in interior Alaska from tree-ring proxies: evidence for changing synoptic climate regimes. Climatic Change 63(1–2):91–120.

Barnston, A.G., and Livezey, R.E. 1987. Classification, seasonality and persistence of low-frequency atmospheric circulation patterns. Monthly Weather Review 115:1083–1126.

Bauch, J., and Eckstein, D. 1970. Dendrochronological dating of oak panels of Dutch seventeenth-century paintings. Studies in Conservation 15:45–50.

Becker, B. 1979. Holocene tree-ring series from southern central Europe for archaeological dating, radiocarbon calibration, and stable isotope analysis. *In:* R. Berger and H.E. Suess, eds., Radiocarbon Dating. University of California Press, Berkeley. pp. 554–565.

Becker, B. 1991. The history of dendrochronology and radiocarbon calibration. *In:* R.E. Taylor, A. Long, and R.S. Kra, eds., Radiocarbon after Four Decades: An Interdisciplinary Perspective. Springer Verlag, Heidelberg: pp. 34–39.

Becker, B. 1993. An 11,000-year German oak and pine dendrochronology for radiocarbon calibration. Radiocarbon 35:201–213.

Becker, B., and Delorme, A. 1978. Oak chronology for central Europe: the extension from medieval to prehistoric times. *In:* J. Fletcher, ed., Dendrochronology in Europe. British Archaeological Reports International Series, Vol. 51. Archaeopress, Oxford, U.K. pp. 59–64.

Becker, B., Kromer, B., and Trimborn, P. 1991. A stable isotope tree-ring timescale of the Late Glacial/Holocene boundary. Nature 353:647–649.

Bégin, Y. 2000. Ice-push disturbances in high-boreal and subarctic lakeshore ecosystems since A.D. 1830, northern Quebec, Canada. Holocene 10(2):179–189.

Bégin, Y., and Filion, L. 1988. Age of landslides along the Grande Rivière de la Baleine estuary, eastern coast of Hudson Bay, Quebec, Canada. Boreas 17:289–299.

Bégin, Y., Bérubé, D., and Grégoire, M. 1993. Downward migration of coastal conifers as a response to recent land emergence in eastern Hudson Bay, Québec. Quaternary Research 40:81–88.

Bekker, M.F. 2004. Spatial variation in the response of tree rings to normal faulting during the Hebgen Lake earthquake, southwestern Montana, U.S.A. Dendrochronologia 22(1):53–59.

Bennett, D.D., Schmid, J.M., Mata, S.A., and Edminster, C.B. 1987. Growth impact of the North Kaibab pandora moth outbreak. U.S. Dept. of Agriculture Forest Service, Research Note RM-474. pp. 1–4.

Bergeron, Y. 1991. The influence of island and mainland lakeshore landscapes on boreal forest fire regimes. Ecology 72(6):1980–1992.

Bergeron, Y. 2000. Species and stand dynamics in the mixed woods of Quebec's southern boreal forest. Ecology 81(6):1500–1516.

Bergeron, Y., and Archambault, S. 1993. Decreasing frequency of forest fires in the southern boreal zone of Québec and its relation to global warming since the end of the Little Ice Age. Holocene 3(3):255–259.

Bergeron, Y., and Brisson, J. 1990. Fire regime in red pine stands at the northern limit of the species range. Ecology 71(4):1352–1364.

Bert, D., Leavitt, S.W., and Dupouey, J.-L. 1997. Variations of wood d¹³C and water use efficiency of *Abies alba* during the last century. Ecology 78(5):1588–1596.

Bhattacharyya, A., Yadav, R.R., Borgaonkar, H.P., and Pant, G.B. 1992. Growth ring analysis on Indian tropical trees: dendroclimatic potential. Current Science 62:736–741.

Billamboz, A. 1992. Tree-ring analysis from an archaeodendrological perspective: the structural timber from the southwest German lake dwellings. *In:* T.S. Bartholin, B.E. Berglund, D. Eckstein, F.H. Schweingruber, and O. Eggertsson, eds., Tree Rings and Environment: Proceedings of the International Symposium, Ystad, Sweden, 3–9 September 1990. Lundqua Report (Department of Quaternary Geology, Lund University, Sweden) 34:34–40.

Billamboz, A. 2003. Tree rings and wetland occupation in southwest Germany between 2000 and 500 BC: dendrochronology beyond dating in tribute to F.H. Schweingruber. Tree-Ring Research 59(1):37–49.

Bindler, R., Renberg, I., Klaminder, J., and Emteryd, O. 2004. Tree rings as Pb pollution archives? A comparison of ²⁰⁶Pb/²⁰⁷Pb isotope ratios in pine and other environmental media. Science of the Total Environment 319:173–183.

Biondi, F. 1999. Comparing tree-ring chronologies and repeated timber inventories as forest monitoring tools. Ecological Applications 9(1):216–227.

Biondi, F., and Waikul, K. 2004. DENDROCLIM2002: A C++ program for statistical calibration of climate signals in tree-ring chronologies. Computers and Geosciences 30:303–311.

Biondi, F., Gershunov, A., and Cayan, D.R. 2001. North Pacific decadal climate variability since 1661. Journal of Climate 14(1):5–10.

Black, B.A., Boehlert, G.W., and Yoklavich, M.M. 2005. Using tree-ring crossdating techniques to validate annual growth increments in long-lived fishes. Canadian Journal of Fisheries and Aquatic Sciences 62(10):2277–2284.

Black, B.A., Allman, R., Campbell, B., Darbyshire, R., Klökler, D., Kormanyos, R., Munk, K., and Peterson, P. 2006. Application of dendrochronology techniques to a Pacific geoduck clam (*Panopea abrupta*) in northern British Columbia, Canada. Final Report of the 16th North American Dendroecological Fieldweek, 30 May–7 June, Hatfield Marine Science Center, Newport, Oregon. 13 pp.

Blais, J.R. 1954. The recurrence of spruce budworm infestations in the past century in the Lac Seul area of northwestern Ontario. Ecology 35:62–71.

Blais, J.R. 1957. Some relationships of the spruce budworm to black spruce. Forestry Chronicle 33:364–372.

Blais, J.R. 1958a. Effects of defoliation by spruce budworm (*Choristoneura fumiferana* Clem.) on radial growth at breast height of balsam fir (*Abies balsamea* (L.) Mill.) and white spruce (*Picea glauca* (Moench) Voss.). Forestry Chronicle 34:39–47.

Blais, J.R. 1958b. Effects of 1956 spring and summer temperatures on spruce budworm populations in the Gaspe Peninsula. Canadian Entomologist 90:354–361.

Blais, J.R. 1961. Spruce budworm outbreaks and the climate of the boreal forest in eastern North America. Report to the Quebec Society for the Protection of Plants 1959:69–75.

Blais, J.R. 1962. Collection and analysis of radial-growth data from trees for evidence of past spruce budworm outbreaks. Forestry Chronicle 38(4):474–484.

Blais, J.R. 1965. Spruce budworm outbreaks in the past three centuries in the Laurentide Park, Quebec. Forest Science 11:130–138.

Blais, J.R. 1983. Trends in the frequency, extent, and severity of spruce budworm outbreaks in eastern Canada. Canadian Journal of Forest Research 13:539–547.

Blake, E.A., and Wagner, M.R. 1987. Collection and consumption of pandora moth (*Coloradia pandora lindseyi*, Lepidoptera: Saturniidae) larvae by Owens Valley and Mono Lake Paiutes. Bulletin of the Entomological Society of America 33(1):5.

Blasing, T.J., and Fritts, H.C. 1976. Reconstructing past climatic anomalies in the North Pacific and western North America from tree-ring data. Quaternary Research 6:563–579.

Boninsegna, J.A., Villabla, R., Amarilla, L., and Ocampo, J. 1989. Studies of tree rings, growth rates, and age-size relationships of tropical tree species in Misiones, Argentina. International Association of Wood Anatomists Bulletin 10(2):161–169.

Bonzani, R.M., Carlisle, R.C., and King, F.B. 1991. Dendrochronology of the Pennsylvania Main Line Canal lock number four, Pittsburgh. North American Archaeologist 12(1):61–73.

Bortolot, Z.J., Copenheaver, C.A., Longe, R.L., and Van Aardt, J.A.N. 2001. Development of a white oak chronology using live trees and a post–Civil War cabin in south-central Virginia. Tree-Ring Research 57(2):197–203.

Bradley, R.S. 1999. Paleoclimatology: Reconstructing Climates of the Quaternary. Harcourt Academic Press, Amsterdam. 613 pp.

Briffa, K.R. 2000. Annual climate variability in the Holocene: interpreting the message of ancient trees. Quaternary Science Reviews 19:87–105.

Briffa, K., and Jones, P.D. 1990. Basic chronology statistics and assessment. *In*: E.R. Cook and L.A. Kairiukstis, eds., Methods of Dendrochronology: Applications in the Environmental Sciences. Kluwer Academic Publishers, Dordrecht, the Netherlands. pp. 137–162.

Briffa, K.R., Bartholin, T.S., Eckstein, D. Jones, P.D., Karlen, W., Schweingruber, F.H., and Zetterberg, P. 1990. A 1400-year tree-ring record of summer temperatures in Fennoscandia. Nature 346:434–439.

Briffa, K.R., Jones, P.D., Bartholin, T.S., Eckstein, D., Schweingruber, F.H., Karlen, W., Zetterberg, P., and Eronen, M. 1992. Fennoscandian summers from AD 500: temperature changes on short and long timescales. Climate Dynamics 7:111–119.

Briffa, K.R., Jones, P.D., Schweingruber, F.H., and Osborn, T.J. 1998. Influence of volcanic eruptions on Northern Hemisphere summer temperature over the past 600 years. Nature 393:450–455.

Briffa, K.R., Osborn, T.J., Schweingruber, F.H., Harris, I.C., Jones, P.D., Shiyatov, S.G., and Vaganov, E.A. 2001. Low-frequency temperature variations from a northern tree ring density network. Journal of Geophysical Research 106(D3):2929–2941.

Brown, P.M. 1996. OLDLIST: A database of maximum tree ages. *In*: J.S. Dean, D.M. Meko, and T.W. Swetnam, eds., Tree Rings, Environment, and Humanity: Proceedings of the International Conference, Tucson, Arizona, 17–21 May 1994. Radiocarbon, Tucson. pp. 727–731.

Brown, P.M. 2007. A modified increment borer handle for coring in locations with obstructions. Tree-Ring Research 63(1):61–62.

Brown, P.M., Hughes, M.K., Baisan, C.H., Swetnam, T.H., and Caprio, A.C. 1992. Giant sequoia ring-width chronologies from the central Sierra Nevada, California. Tree-Ring Bulletin 52:1–14.

Brown, P.M., Shepperd, W.D., Brown, C.C., Mata, S.A., and McClain, D.L. 1995. Oldest Known Engelmann Spruce. U.S. Department of Agriculture Forest Service, Rocky Mountain Forest and Range Experiment Station Research Note RM-RN-534. 6 pp.

Brubaker, L.B. 1980. Spatial patterns of tree growth anomalies in the Pacific Northwest. Ecology 61(4):798–807.

Brubaker, L.B., and Greene, S.K. 1979. Differential effects of Douglas-fir tussock moth and western spruce budworm on radial growth of grand fir and Douglas-fir. Canadian Journal of Forest Research 9:95–105.

Brunstein, F.C., and Yamaguchi, D.K. 1992. The oldest known Rocky Mountain bristlecone pines (*Pinus aristata* Engelm.). Arctic and Alpine Research 24:253–256.

Buhay, W.M., and Edwards, T.W.D. 1995. Climate in southwestern Ontario, Canada, between AD 1610 and 1885 inferred from oxygen and hydrogen isotopic measurements of wood cellulose from trees in different hydrologic settings. Quaternary Research 44:438–446.

Bukata, A.R., and Kyser, T.K. 2005. Response of the nitrogen isotopic composition of tree-rings following tree-clearing and land-use change. Environmental Science and Technology 39:7777–7783.

Burg, J.P. 1978. A new technique for time series data. *In:* D.G. Childers, ed., Modern Spectrum Analysis. IEEE Press, New York. pp. 42–48.

Burk, R.L., and Stuiver, M. 1981. Oxygen isotope ratios in trees reflect mean annual temperature and humidity. Science 211:1417–1419.

Butler, D.R. 1987. Teaching general principles and applications of dendrogeomorphology. Journal of Geological Education 35:64–70.

Campbell, E.M., Alfaro, R.I., and Hawkes, B. 2007. Spatial distribution of mountain pine beetle outbreaks in relation to climate and stand characteristics: a dendroecological analysis. Journal of Integrative Plant Biology 49(2):168–178.

Campbell, L.J., and Laroque, C.P. 2005. Dendrochronological Analysis of Endangered Newfoundland Pine Marten Habitat: Decay Classification of Coarse Woody Debris in Western Newfoundland. Mount Allison Dendrochronology Laboratory Report 2005–07. 33 pp.

Campbell, L.J., and Laroque, C.P. 2007. Decay progression and classification in two old-growth forests in Atlantic Canada. Forest Ecology and Managemnt 238(1–3):293–301.

Case, R.A., and MacDonald, G.M. 2003. Dendrochronological analysis of the response of tamarack (*Larix laricina*) to climate and larch sawfly (*Pristiphora erichsonii*) infestations in central Saskatchewan. Ecoscience 10(3):380–388.

Chaloner, W.G., and Creber, G.T. 1973. Growth rings in fossil woods as evidence of past climates. *In:* D.H. Tarling and S.K. Runcorn, eds., Implications of Continental Drift to the Earth Sciences. Academic Press, London. pp. 425–437.

Clark, N.E., Blasing, T.J., and Fritts, H.C. 1975. Influence of interannual climatic fluctuations on biological systems. Nature 256(5515):302–305.

Clements, F.E. 1910. The life history of lodgepole burn forests. U.S. Department of Agriculture Forest Service Bulletin 79:1–56.

Cochrane, J., and Daniels, L.D. 2008. Striking a balance: safe sampling of partial stem cross-sections in British Columbia. BC Journal of Ecosystems and Management 9(1):38–46.

Conkey, L.E., Keifer, M., and Lloyd, A.H. 1995. Disjunct jack pine (*Pinus banksiana* Lamb) structure and dynamics, Acadia National Park, Maine. Ecoscience 2(2):168–176.

Cook, E.R. 1985. A time series analysis approach to tree ring standardization. Dissertation, University of Arizona, Tucson. 171 pp.

Cook, E.R. 1992. A conceptual linear aggregate model for tree rings. *In:* E.R. Cook and L.A. Kairiukstis, eds., Methods of Dendrochronology: Applications in the Environmental Sciences. Kluwer Academic Publishers, Dordrecht, the Netherlands. pp. 98–104.

Cook, E.R., and Cole, J. 1991. On predicting the response of forests in eastern North America to future climatic change. Climatic Change 19:271–282.

Cook, E.R., and Holmes, R.L. 1986. Users manual for program ARSTAN. *In:* R.L. Holmes, R.K. Adams, and H.C. Fritts, eds., Tree-Ring Chronologies of Western North America: California, Eastern Oregon, and Northern Great Basin. Chronology Series Vol. 6. Laboratory of Tree-Ring Research, University of Arizona, Tucson. pp. 50–56.

Cook, E.R., and Jacoby, G.C., Jr. 1977. Tree-ring-drought relationships in the Hudson Valley, New York. Science 198:399–401.

Cook, E.R., and Kairiukstis, L.A. 1990. Methods of Dendrochronology: Applications in the Environmental Sciences. Kluwer Academic Publishers, Dordrecht, the Netherlands. 414 pp.

Cook, E.R., Johnson, A.H., and Blasing, T.J. 1987. Forest decline: modeling the effect of climate in tree rings. Tree Physiology 3:27–40.

Cook, E.R., Bird, T., Peterson, M., Barbetti, M., Buckley, B., D'Arrigo, R., Francey, R., and Tans, P. 1991. Climatic change in Tasmania inferred from a 1089-year tree-ring chronology of huon pine. Science 253:1266–1268.

Cook, E.R., Bird, T., Peterson, M., Barbetti, M., Buckley, B., D'Arrigo, R., and Francey, R. 1992. Climatic change over the last millennium in Tasmania reconstructed from tree-rings. Holocene 2:205–217.

Cook, E.R., Briffa, K.R., and Jones, P.D. 1994. Spatial regression methods in dendroclimatology: a review and comparison of two techniques. International Journal of Climatology 14:379–402.

Cook, E.R., Briffa, K.R., Meko, D.M., Graybill, D.A., and Funkhouser, G. 1995. The 'segment length curse' in long tree-ring chronology development for paleoclimatic studies. Holocene 5(2):229–237.

Cook, E.R., Meko, D.M., Stahle, D.W., and Cleaveland, M.K. 1999. Drought reconstructions for the continental United States. Journal of Climate 12:1145–1162.

Cook, E.R., Buckley, B.M., D'Arrigo, R.D., and Peterson, M.J. 2000. Warm-season temperatures since 1600 B.C. reconstructed from Tasmanian tree rings and their relationship to large-scale sea surface temperature anomalies. Climate Dynamics 16(2–3):79–91.

Cook, E.R., Seager, R., Heim, R.R., Vose, R.S., Herweijer, C., and Woodhouse, C. 2009. Megadroughts in North America: placing IPCC projections of hydroclimatic change in a long-term palaeoclimate context. Journal of Quaternary Science. DOI: 10.1022/jqs.

Cook, E.R., Woodhouse, C.A., Eakin, C.M., Meko, D.M., and Stahle, D.W. 2004. Long-term aridity changes in the western United States. Science 306:1015–1018.

Copenheaver, C.A., Fuhrman, N.E., Gellerstedt, L.S., and Gellerstedt, P.A. 2004. Tree encroachment in forest openings: a case study from Buffalo Mountain, Virginia. Castanea 69(4):297–308.

Coplen, T.B. 1995. The discontinuance of SMOW and PDB. Nature 375:285.

Corominas, J., and Moya, J. 1999. Reconstructing recent landslide activity in relation to rainfall in the Llobregat River basin, eastern Pyrenees, Spain. Geomorphology 30:79–93.

Corona, E. 1986. Dendrocronologia: principi e applicazioni. *In:* Dendrocronologia: Principi e Applicazioni. Atti del Seminario a Verona nei giorni 14 e 15 Novembre 1984. Istituto Italiano di Dendrocronologia, Verona, Italy. pp. 7–32.

Couralet, C., Sass-Klaassen, U., Sterck, F., Bekele, T., and Zuidema, P.A. 2005. Combining dendrochronology and matrix modelling in demographic studies: an evaluation for *Juniperus procera* in Ethiopia. Forest Ecology and Management 216(1–3):317–330.

Craig, H. 1954. Carbon-13 variations in *Sequoia* rings and the atmosphere. Science 119:141–144.

Cronon, W. 1997. John Muir: Nature Writings. Library of America, New York. 888 pp.

Cropper, J.P. 1979. Tree-ring skeleton plotting by computer. Tree-Ring Bulletin 39:47–60.

Cufar, K. 2007. Dendrochronology and past human activity: a review of advances since 2000. Tree-Ring Research 63(1):47–60.

Currey, D.R. 1965. An ancient bristlecone pine stand in eastern Nevada. Ecology 46(4):564–566.

Cutter, B.E., and Guyette, R.P. 1993. Anatomical, chemical, and ecological factors affecting tree species choice in dendrochemistry studies. Journal of Environmental Quality 22(3):611–619.

Daniels, L.D. 2003. Western red cedar population dynamics in old-growth forests: contrasting ecological paradigms using tree rings. Forestry Chronicle 79(3):517–530.

Daniels, L.D., and Veblen, T.T. 2003. Regional and local effects of disturbance and climate on altitudinal treelines in northern Patagonia. Journal of Vegetation Science 14:733–742.

Daniels, L.D., and Veblen, T.T. 2004. Spatiotemporal influences of climate on atlitudinal treeline in northern Patagonia. Ecology 85(5):1284–1296.

Daniels, L.D., Dobry, J., Klinka, K., and Feller, M.C. 1997. Determining year of death of logs and snags of *Thuja plicata* in southwestern coastal British Columbia. Canadian Journal of Forest Research 27:1132–1141.

Danzer, S.R. 1996. Rates of slope erosion determined from exposed roots of ponderosa pine at Rose Canyon Lake, Arizona. *In:* J.S. Dean, D.M. Meko, and T.W. Swetnam, eds., Tree Rings, Environment, and Humanity: Proceedings of the International Conference, Tucson, Arizona, 17–21 May 1994. Radiocarbon, Tucson. pp. 671–678.

D'Arrigo, R.D., and Jacoby, G.C. 1991. A 1000-year record of winter precipitation from northwestern New Mexico, U.S.A.: a reconstruction from tree-rings and its relation to El Niño and the Southern Oscillation. Holocene 1(2):95–101.

D'Arrigo, R.D., and Jacoby, G.C. 1993. Tree growth-climate relationships at the northern boreal forest tree line of North America: evaluation of potential response to increasing carbon dioxide. Global Biogeochemical Cycles 7(3):525–535.

D'Arrigo, R.D., Cook, E.R., Jacoby, G.C., and Briffa, K.R. 1993. NAO and sea surface temperature signatures in tree-ring records from the North Atlantic sector. Quaternary Science Reviews 12:431–440.

D'Arrigo, R.D., Jacoby, G.C., and Krusic, P.J. 1994. Progress in dendroclimatic studies in Indonesia. Terrestrial, Atmospheric and Oceanic Sciences 5:349–363.

D'Arrigo, R.D., Cook, E.R., Salinger, M.J., Palmer, J., Krusic, P.J., Buckley, B.M., and Villalba, R. 1998. Tree-ring records from New Zealand: long-term context for recent warming trend. Climate Dynamics 14:191–199.

D'Arrigo, R.D., Malmstrom, C.M., Jacoby, G.C., Los, S.O., and Bunker, D.E. 2000. Correlation between maximum latewood density of annual tree rings and NDVI-based estimates of forest productivity. International Journal of Remote Sensing 21(11):2329–2336.

Dean, J.S. 1978. Tree-ring dating in archeology. University of Utah Miscellaneous Paper 24: 129–163.

Dean, J.S. 1997. Dendrochronology. *In:* R.E. Taylor and M.J. Aitken, eds., Chronometric Dating in Archaeology. Plenum Press, New York. pp. 31–64.

Dean, J.S., Euler, R.C., Gumerman, G.J., Plog, F., Hevly, R.H., and Karlstrom, T.N.V. 1985. Human behavior, demography, and paleoenvironment on the Colorado plateaus. American Antiquity 50:537–554.

Dettinger, M.D., Ghil, M., Strong, C.M., Weibel, W., and Yiou, P. 1995. Software expedites singular-spectrum analysis of noisy time series. EOS: Transactions of the American Geological Union 76(2):12, 14, 21.

Dey, D.C., and Guyette, R.P. 2000. Anthropogenic fire history and red oak forests in south-central Ontario. Forestry Chronicle 76(2):339–347.

Dieterich, J.H., and Swetnam, T.W. 1984. Dendrochronology of a fire-scarred pandora pine. Forest Science 30(1):238–247.

Dietz, H., and Schweingruber, F.H. 2001. Development of growth rings in roots of dicotyledonous perennial herbs: experimental analysis of ecological factors. Bulletin of the Geobotanical Institute ETH 67:97–105.

Dodd, J.P., Patterson, W.P., Holmden, C., and Brasseur, J.M. 2007. Robotic micromilling of tree-ring cellulose: a new tool for obtaining sub-seasonal environmental isotope records. Chemical Geology special publication for The Stable Isotope Session from the 7th International Conference on Dendrochronology, Beijing, China.

Donnelly, J.R., Shane, J.B., and Schaberg, P.C. 1990. Lead mobility within the xylem of red spruce seedlings: implications for the development of pollution histories. Journal of Environmental Quality 19:268–271.

Douglass, A.E. 1909. Weather cycles in the growth of big trees. Monthly Weather Review 37:225–237.

Douglass, A.E. 1914. A method of estimating rainfall by the growth of trees. Carnegie Institute of Washington Publication 192:101–121.

Douglass, A.E. 1917. Climatic records in the trunks of trees. American Forestry 23(288):732–735.

Douglass, A.E. 1920. Evidence of climatic effects in the annual rings of trees. Ecology 1(1):24–32.

Douglass, A.E. 1921. Dating our prehistoric ruins: how growth rings in trees aid in establishing the relative ages of the ruined pueblos of the Southwest. Natural History 21(1):27–30.

Douglass, A.E. 1929. The secret of the Southwest solved by talkative tree rings. National Geographic Magazine 56:736–770.

Douglass, A.E. 1941. Crossdating in dendrochronology. Journal of Forestry 39(10):825–831.

Drake, D.C., Naiman, R.J., and Helfield, J.M. 2002. Reconstructing salmon abundance in rivers: an initial dendrochronological evaluation. Ecology 83(11):2971–2977.

Du, S., Yamanaka, N., Yamamoto, F., Otsuki, K., Wang, S., and Hou, Q. 2007. The effect of climate on radial growth of *Quercus liaotungensis* forest trees in Loess Plateau, China. Dendrochronologia 25(1):29–36.

Dubois, A.D. 1984. On the climatic interpretation of the hydrogen isotope ratios in recent and fossil wood. Bulletin de la Societe Belge de Geologie 93:267–270.

Duff, G.H., and Nolan, N.J. 1953. Growth and morphogenesis in the Canadian forest species. I. The controls of cambial and apical activity in *Pinus resinosa* Ait. Canadian Journal of Botany 31:471–513.

Duff, G.H., and Nolan, N.J. 1957. Growth and morphogenesis in the Canadian forest species. II. Species increments and their relation to the quantity and activity of growth in *Pinus resinosa* Ait. Canadian Journal of Botany 35:527–572.

Dupouey, J.-L., Leavitt, S.W., Choisnel, E., and Jourdain, S. 1993. Modeling carbon isotope fractionation in tree-rings based upon effective evapotranspiration and soil-water status. Plant, Cell and Environment 16:939–947.

Duquesnay, A., Breda, N., Stievenard, M., and Dupouey, J.L. 1998. Changes of tree-ring d¹³C and water-use efficiency of beech (*Fagus sylvatica* L.) in north-eastern France during the past century. Plant, Cell and Environment 21:565–572.

Duvick, D.N., and Blasing, T.J. 1981. A dendroclimatic reconstruction of annual precipitation amounts in Iowa since 1680. Water Resources Research 17:1183–1189.

Eckstein, D. 1972. Tree-ring research in Europe. Tree-Ring Bulletin 32:1–18.

Eckstein, D., and Bauch, J. 1969. Beitrag zu Rationalisierung eines dendrochronologischen Verfahrens und zu Analyse seiner Aussagesicherheit. Forstwissenschaftliches Centralblatt 88:230–250.

Eckstein, D., and Pilcher, J.R. 1990. Dendrochronology in western Europe. *In:* E.R. Cook and L.A. Kairiukstis, eds., Methods of Dendrochronology: Applications in the Environmental Sciences. Kluwer Academic Publishers, Dordrecht, the Netherlands. pp. 11–13.

Eckstein, D., and Wrobel, S. 2007. Dendrochronological proof of origin of historic timber: retrospective and perspectives. *In:* K. Haneca, A. Verheyden, H. Beekman, H. Gärtner, G. Helle, and G. Schleser. TRACE: Tree Rings in Archaeology, Climatology and Ecology—Proceedings of the Dendrosymposium 2006, 20–22 April 2006, Tervuren, Belgium. Vol. 5:8–20.

Eckstein, D., Richter, K., Aniol, R.W., and Quiehl, F. 1984. Dendroclimatological investigations of the beech decline in the southwestern part of the Vogelsberg (West Germany). Forstwissenschaftliches Centralblatt 103:274–290. In German with English abstract.

Eckstein, D., Wazny, T., Bauch, K., and Klein, P. 1986. New evidence for the dendrochronological dating of Netherlandish paintings. Nature 320:465–466.

Edwards, T.W.D., Graf, W., Trimborn, P., Stichler, W., and Payer, H.D. 2000. $d^{13}C$ response surface resolves humidity and temperature signals in trees. Geochimica et Cosmochimica Acta 64:161–167.

Egger, H., Gassmann, P., and Burri, N. 1985. Situation actuelle du travail au laboratoire de dendrochronologie de Neuchatel. Dendrochronologia 3:177–192.

Eisenhart, K.S., and Veblen, T.T. 2000. Dendroecological detection of spruce bark beetle outbreaks in northwestern Colorado. Canadian Journal of Forest Research 30(11):1788–1798.

English, N.B., Betancourt, J.L., Dean, J.S., and Quade, J. 2001. Strontium isotopes reveal distant sources of architectural timber in Chaco Canyon, New Mexico. Proceedings of the National Academy of Science 98(21):11891–11896.

Epstein, S., and Krishnamurthy, R.V. 1990. Environmental information in the isotopic record in trees. Philosophical Transactions of the Royal Society 330A:427–439.

Epstein, S., and Yapp, C.J. 1976. Climatic implications of the D/H ratio of hydrogen in C-H groups in tree cellulose. Earth and Planetary Science Letters 30:252–261.

Eshete, G., and Stahl, G. 1999. Tree rings as indicators of growth periodicity of acacias in the Rift Valley of Ethiopia. Forest Ecology and Management 116(1–3):107–117.

Esper, J., and Schweingruber, F.H. 2004. Large-scale treeline changes recorded in Siberia. Geophysical Research Letters 31:1–5.

Esper, J., Cook, E.R., and Schweingruber, F.H. 2002. Low-frequency signals in long tree-ring chronologies and the reconstruction of past temperature variability. Science 295:2250–2253.

Esper, J., Cook, E.R., Krusic, P.J., Peters, K., and Schweingruber, F.H. 2003a. Tests of the RCS method for preserving low-frequency variability in long tree-ring chronologies. Tree-Ring Research 59:81–98.

Esper, J., Shiyatov, S.G., Mazepa, V.S., Wilson, R.J.S., Graybill, D.A., and Funkhouser, G. 2003b. Temperature-sensitive Tien Shan tree ring chronologies show multi-centennial growth trends. Climate Dynamics 21(7–8):699–706.

Falcon-Lang, H.J. 1999. The Early Carboniferous (Courceyan-Arundian) monsoonal climate of the British Isles: evidence from growth rings in fossil woods. Geological Magazine 136(2):177–187.

Falcon-Lang, H.J. 2005. Global climate analysis of growth rings in woods, and its implications for deep-time paleoclimate studies. Paleobiology 31(3):434–444.

Fantucci, R., and Sorriso-Valvo, M. 1999. Dendrogeomorphological analysis of a slope near Lago, Calabria (Italy). Geomorphology 30:165–174.

Farmer, J.G., and Baxter, M.S. 1974. Atmospheric carbon dioxide levels as indicated by the stable isotope record in wood. Nature 247:273–275.

Fastie, C.L. 1995. Causes and ecosystem consequences of multiple pathways of primary succession at Glacier Bay, Alaska. Ecology 76(6):1899–1916.

February, E.C., and Stock, W.D. 1998. An assessment of the dendrochronological potential of two *Podocarpus* species. Holocene 8(6):747–750.

February, E.C., and Stock, W.D. 1999. Declining trends in the $^{13}C/^{12}C$ ratio of atmospheric carbon dioxide from tree rings of South African *Widdringtonia cedarbergensis*. Quaternary Research 52:229–236.

Feng, X., Cui, H., Tang, K., and Conkey, L.E. 1999. Tree-ring delta-D as an indicator of Asian monsoon intensity. Quaternary Research 51:262–266.

Feng, X.H., and Epstein, S. 1995a. Carbon isotopes of trees from arid environments and implications for reconstructing atmospheric $CO_2$ concentration. Geochimica et Cosmochimica Acta 59:2599–2608.

Feng, X.H., and Epstein, S. 1995b. Climatic temperature records in dD data from tree rings. Geochimica et Cosmochimica Acta 59:3029–3037.

Ferguson, C.W. 1968. Bristlecone pine: science and esthetics. Science 159(3817):839–846.

Ferguson, C.W., Lawn, B., and Michael, H.N. 1985. Prospects for the extension of the bristlecone pine chronology: radiocarbon analysis of H-84-1. Meteoritics 20(2):415–421.

Fichtler, E., Clark, D.A., and Worbes, M. 2003. Age and long-term growth of trees in an old-growth tropical rain forest, based on analyses of tree rings and C-14. Biotropica 35(3):306–317.

Fichtler, E., Trouet, V., Beeckman, H., Coppin, P., and Worbes, M. 2004. Climatic signals in tree rings of *Burkea africana* and *Pterocarpus angolensis* from semiarid forests in Namibia. Trees: Structure and Function 18(4):442–451.

Filion, L., Payette, S., Delwaide, A., and Bhiry, N. 1998. Insect defoliators as major disturbance factors in the high-altitude balsam fir forest of Mount Mégantic, southern Quebec. Canadian Journal of Forest Research 28:1832–1842.

Fletcher, J.M. 1976. A group of English royal portraits painted soon after 1513: a dendrochronological study. Studies in Conservation 21(4):171–178.

Fletcher, J.M. 1977. Tree-ring chronologies for the 6th to 16th centuries for oaks of southern and eastern England. Journal of Archaeological Science 4(4):335–352.

Fonti, P., and Garcia-Gonzalez, I. 2004. Suitability of chestnut earlywood vessel chronologies for ecological studies. New Phytologist 163(1):77–86.

Food and Agriculture Organization. 1973. Inventario forestall. Inventario y fomento de los recursos forestales: Republica Dominicana. Technical Report No. 3 FO:SF/DOM 8. Rome: United Nations Food and Agriculture Organization.

Freyer, H.D. 1979a. On the $^{13}C$ record in tree rings. 1. $^{13}C$ variations in Northern Hemispheric trees during the last 150 years. Tellus 31:124–137.

Freyer, H.D. 1979b. On the $^{13}C$ record in tree rings. 2. Registration of microenvironmental $CO_2$ and anomalous pollution effect. Tellus 31:308–312.

Freyer, H.D., and Belacy, N. 1983. $^{12}C/^{13}C$ records in Northern Hemispheric trees during the past 500 years: anthropogenic impact and climatic superpositions. Journal of Geophysical Research 88:6844–6852.

Friedrich, M., Kromer, B., Spurk, M., Hofmann, J., and Kaiser, K.F. 1999. Paleo-environment and radiocarbon calibration as derived from Late Glacial/Early Holocene tree-ring chronologies. Quaternary International 61:27–39.

Friedrich, M., Kromer, B., Kaiser, K.F., Spurk, M., Hughen, K.A., and Johansen, S.J. 2001. High-resolution climate signals in the Bolling-Allerod Interstadial (Greenland Interstadial 1) as reflected in European tree-ring chronologies compared to marine varves and ice-core records. Quaternary Science Reviews 20(11):1223–1232.

Friedrich, M., Remmele, S., Kromer, B., Hofmann, J., Spurk, M., Kaiser, K.F., Orcel, C., and Kuppers, M. 2004. The 12,460-year Hohenheim oak and pine tree-ring chronology from central Europe: a unique annual record for radiocarbon calibration and paleoenvironment reconstructions. Radiocarbon 46(3):1111–1122.

Fritts, H.C. 1971. Dendroclimatology and dendroecology. Quaternary Research 1:419–449.

Fritts, H.C. 1976. Tree Rings and Climate. Academic Press, New York. 567 pp.

Fritts, H.C. 2001. Tree Rings and Climate. Blackburn Press, Caldwell, New Jersey. 567 pp.

Fritts, H.C., and Dean, J.S. 1992. Dendrochronological modeling of the effects of climatic change on tree-ring width chronologies from Chaco Canyon and environs. Tree Ring Bulletin 52:31–58.

Fritts, H.C., and Shao, X.M. 1992. Mapping climate using tree-rings from western North America. *In:* R.S. Bradley and P.D. Jones, eds., Climate since AD 1500. Routledge, London. pp. 269–295.

Fritts, H.C., and Swetnam, T.W. 1989. Dendroecology: a tool for evaluating variations in past and present forest environments. *In:* M. Begon, A.H. Fitter, E.D. Ford, and A. Macfadyen, eds., Advances in Ecological Research, Vol. 19. Academic Press, London. pp. 111–188.

Fritts, H.C., Smith, D.G., Cardis, J.W., and Budelsky, C.A. 1965. Tree-ring characteristics along a vegetation gradient in northern Arizona. Ecology 46(4):393–401.

Fritts, H.C., Blasing, T.J., Hayden, B.P., and Kutzbach, J.E. 1971. Multivariate techniques for specifying tree-growth and climate relationships and for reconstructing anomalies in paleoclimate. Journal of Applied Meteorology 10(5):845–864.

Fule, P.R., Covington, W.W., and Moore, M.M. 1997. Determining reference conditions for ecosystem management of southwestern ponderosa pine forests. Ecological Applications 7(3):895–908.

Gagen, M., McCarroll, D., and Edourard, J.L. 2006. Combining ring width, density, and stable carbon isotope proxies to enhance the climate signal in tree-rings: an example from the southern French Alps. Climatic Change 78:363–379.

Gärtner, H. 2003. The applicability of roots in dendrogeomorphology. *In:* G. Schleser, M. Winiger, A. Bräuning, H. Gärtner, G. Helle, E. Jansma, B. Neuwirth, and K. Treydte, eds., Tree Rings in Archaeology, Climatology and Ecology, Vol. 1. Proceedings of the Dendrosymposium 2002. Schriften des Forschungszentrum Jülich, Reihe Umwelt 33:120–124.

Gärtner, H. 2007a. Glacial landforms, tree rings: dendrogeomorphology. *In:* S.A. Elias, ed., Encyclopedia of Quaternary Sciences, Vol. 2. Elsevier, Amsterdam. pp. 979–988.

Gärtner, H. 2007b. Tree roots: methodological review and new development in dating and quantifying erosive processes. Geomorphology 86:243–251.

Gärtner, H., Schweingruber, F.H., and Dikau, R. 2001. Determination of erosion rates by analyzing structural changes in the growth pattern of exposed roots. Dendrochronologia 19(1):81–91.

Gedalof, Z., Mantua, N.J., and Peterson, D.L. 2002. A multi-century perspective of variability in the Pacific Decadal Oscillation: new insights from tree rings and coral. Geophysical Research Letters 29(24), 2204, doi:10.1029/2002GL015824.

Giardino, J.R., Shroder, J.F., and Lawson, M.P. 1984. Tree-ring analysis of movement of a rock-glacier complex on Mount Mestas, Colorado, U.S.A. Arctic and Alpine Research 16(3):299–309.

Girardclos, O., Lambert, G., and Lavier, C. 1996. Oak tree-ring series from France between 4000 B.C. and 8000 B.C. *In:* J.S. Dean, D.M. Meko, and T.W. Swetnam, eds., Tree Rings, Environment, and Humanity: Proceedings of the International Conference, Tucson, Arizona, 17–21 May 1994. Radiocarbon, Tucson. pp. 751–768.

Girardin, M.P., Tardif, J.C., Flannigan, M.D., and Bergeron, Y. 2006. Synoptic-scale atmospheric circulation and boreal Canada summer drought variability of the past three centuries. Journal of Climate 19(10):1922–1947.

Glock, W.S. 1941. Growth rings and climate. Botanical Review 7(12):649–713.

Glock, W.S. 1951. Cambial frost injuries and multiple growth layers at Lubbock, Texas. Ecology 32(1):28–36.

Gore, A.P., Johnson, E.A., and Lo, H.P. 1985. Estimating the time a dead tree has been on the ground. Ecology 66(6):1981–1983.

Gottesfeld, A.S., and Gottesfeld, L.M.J. 1990. Floodplain dynamics of a wandering river, dendrochronology of the Morice River, British Columbia, Canada. Geomorphology 3:159–179.

Gourlay, I.D. 1995. Growth ring characteristics of some African acacia species. Journal of Tropical Ecology 11(1):121–140.

Graumlich, L. 1993. A 1000-year record of temperature and precipitation in the Sierra Nevada. Quaternary Research 39:249–255.

Graumlich, L.J., Brubaker, L.B., and Grier, C.C. 1989. Long-term trends in forest net primary productivity: Cascade Mountains, Washington. Ecology 70(2):405–410.

Gray, J., and Se, J.S. 1984. Climatic implications of the natural variation of D/H ratios in tree-ring cellulose. Earth and Planetary Science Letters 70:129–138.

Gray, J., and Thompson, P. 1976. Climatic information from $^{18}O/^{16}O$ ratios of cellulose in tree-rings. Nature 262:481–482.

Gray, J., and Thompson, P. 1977. Climatic information from $^{18}O/^{16}O$ analysis of cellulose, lignin and wholewood from tree-rings. Nature 270:708–709.

Gray, S.T., Graumlich, L.J., Betancourt, J.L., and Pederson, G.T. 2004. A tree-ring based reconstruction of the Atlantic Multidecadal Oscillation since 1567 A.D. Geophysical Research Letters 31(12): L12205, doi: 10.1029/2004GL019932.

Graybill, D.A., and Shiyatov, S.G. 1992. Dendroclimatic evidence from the northern Soviet Union. *In:* R.S. Bradley and P.D. Jones, eds., Climate since AD 1500. Routledge, London. pp. 393–414.

Greve, U., Eckstein, D., Aniol, R.W., and Scholz, F. 1986. Dendroclimatological investigations on Norway spruce under different loads of air pollution. Allaemeine Forst- und Jagdzeitung 157:174–179.

Grissino-Mayer, H.D. 1993. An updated list of species used in tree-ring research. Tree-Ring Bulletin 53:17–43.

Grissino-Mayer, H.D. 1995. Tree-ring reconstructions of climate and fire history at El Malpais National Monument, New Mexico. Dissertation, The University of Arizona, Tucson.

Grissino-Mayer, H.D. 1996. A 2129-year annual reconstruction of precipitation for northwestern New Mexico, U.S.A. *In:* J.S. Dean, D.M. Meko, and T.W. Swetnam, eds., Tree Rings, Environment, and Humanity: Proceedings of the International Conference, Tucson, Arizona, 17–21 May 1994. Radiocarbon, Tucson. pp. 191–204.

Grissino-Mayer, H.D. 2001. Evaluating crossdating accuracy: a manual and tutorial for the computer program COFECHA. Tree-Ring Research 57(2):205–221.

Grissino-Mayer, H.D. 2003. A manual and tutorial for the proper use of an increment borer. Tree-Ring Research 59(2):63–79.

Grissino-Mayer, H.D., and Fritts, H.C. 1997. The International Tree-Ring Data Bank: an enhanced global database serving the global scientific community. Holocene 7(2):235–238.

Grissino-Mayer, H.D., Swetnam, T.W., and Adams, R.K. 1997. The rare, old-aged conifers of El Malpais: their role in understanding climate change in the American Southwest. New Mexico Bureau of Mines and Mineral Resources Bulletin 156:155–161.

Grissino-Mayer, H.D., Blount, H.C., and Miller, A.C. 2001. Tree-ring dating and the ethnohistory of the naval stores industry in southern Georgia. Tree-Ring Research 57(1):3–13.

Grissino-Mayer, H.D., Cleaveland, M.K., and Sheppard, P.R. 2002. Mastering the rings. Strad 113:408–415.

Grissino-Mayer, H.D., Sheppard, P.R., and Cleaveland, M.K. 2003. Dendrochronological dating of stringed instruments: a re-evaluation. Journal of the Violin Society of America 18(2):127–174.

Grissino-Mayer, H.D., Sheppard, P.R., and Cleaveland, M.K. 2004. A dendroarchaeological re-examination of the *Messiah* violin and other instruments attributed to Antonio Stradivari. Journal of Archaeological Science 31(2):167–174.

Grissino-Mayer, H.D., Deweese, G.G., and Williams, D.A. 2005. Tree-ring dating of the Karr-Koussevitzky double bass: a case study in dendromusicology. Tree-Ring Research 61(2):77–86.

Groven, R., and Niklasson, M. 2005. Anthropogenic impact on past and present fire regimes in a boreal forest landscape of southeastern Norway. Canadian Journal of Forest Research 35:2719–2726.

Guay, R., Gagnon, R., and Morin, H. 1992. MacDendro, a new automatic and interactive tree-ring measurement system based on image processing. *In:* T.S. Bartholin, B.E. Berglund, D. Eckstein, F.H. Schweingruber, and O. Eggertsson, eds., Tree rings and Environment: Proceedings of the

International Symposium, 3–9 September 1990, Ystad, Sweden. Lundqua Report (Department of Quaternary Geology, Lund University, Sweden) 34:128–131.

Guiot, J. 1990. Methods of calibration. *In:* E.R. Cook and L.A. Kairiukstis, eds., Methods of Dendrochronology: Applications in the Environmental Sciences. Kluwer Academic Publishers, Dordrecht, the Netherlands. pp 165–178.

Guiot, J. 1991. The bootstrapped response function. Tree-Ring Bulletin 51:39–41.

Guiot, J., Nicault, A., Rathgeber, C., Edouard, J.L., Guibal, E., Pichard, G., and Till, C. 2005. Last-millennium summer-temperature variations in western Europe based on proxy data. Holocene 15(4):489–500.

Gutsell, S.L., and Johnson, E.A. 2002. Accurately ageing trees and examining their height-growth rates: implications for interpreting forest dynamics. Journal of Ecology 90:153–166.

Guyette, R., and McGinnes, E.A. 1987. Potential in using elemental concentrations in radial increment of old growth eastern red cedar to examine the chemical history of the environment. *In:* G.C. Jacoby and J.W. Hornbeck, eds., Proceedings of the International Symposium on Ecological Aspects of Tree-Ring Analysis. U.S. Department of Commerce Publication CONF-86081-44. pp. 671–680.

Guyette, R.P., and Rabeni, C.F. 1995. Climate response among growth increments of fish and trees. Oecologia 104:272–279.

Guyette, R.P., and Stambaugh, M.C. 2003. The age and density of ancient and modern oak wood in streams and sediments. International Association of Wood Anatomists Journal 24(4):345–353.

Guyette, R.P., Cutter, B.E., and Henderson, G.S. 1989. Long-term relationships between molybdenum and sulfur concentrations in red-cedar tree rings. Journal of Environmental Quality 18(3):385–389.

Guyette, R.P., Cutter, B.E., and Henderson, G.S. 1991. Long-term correlations between mining activity and levels of lead and cadmium in tree-rings of eastern red-cedar. Journal of Environmental Quality 20(1):146–150.

Guyette, R.P., Henderson, G.S., and Cutter, B.E. 1992. Reconstructing soil pH from manganese concentrations in tree-rings. Forest Science 38(4):727–737.

Guyette, R.P., Muzika, R.M., and Dey, D.C. 2002. Dynamics of an anthropogenic fire regime. Ecosystems 5:472–486.

Hadley, K.S. 1994. The role of disturbance, topography, and forest structure in the development of a mountain forest landscape. Bulletin of the Torrey Botanical Club 121(1):47–61.

Hall, G.S. 1987. Multielemental analysis of tree-rings by proton induced x-ray (PIXE) and gamma ray emission (PIGE). *In:* G.C. Jacoby and J.W. Hornbeck, eds., Proceedings of the International Symposium on Ecological Aspects of Tree-Ring Analysis. U.S. Department of Commerce Publication CONF-86081-44. pp. 681–689.

Hantemirov, R.M., Gorlanova, L.A., and Shiyatov, S.G. 2004. Extreme temperature events in summer in northwest Siberia since AD 742 inferred from tree rings. Palaeogeography, Palaeoclimatology, Palaeoecology 209(1–4):155–164.

Hart, E. 2002. Effects of woody debris on channel morphology and sediment storage in headwater streams in the Great Smoky Mountains, Tennessee–North Carolina. Physical Geography 23(6):492–510.

Hart, E. 2003. Dead wood: geomorphic effects of coarse woody debris in headwater streams, Great Smoky Mountains. Journal of the Tennessee Academy of Science 78(2):50–54.

Hartig, R. 1888. Das Fichten- und Tannenholz des bayerischen Waldes. Centralblatt f. das gesamte Forstwesen 14:357–364, 437–442.

Haury, E.W. 1962. HH-39: Recollections of a dramatic moment in Southwestern archaeology. Tree-Ring Bulletin 24(3–4):11–14.

Heinselman, J.E. 1973. Fire in the virgin forests of the Boundary Water Canoe Area, Minnesota. Quaternary Research 3:329–382.

Heizer, R.F. 1954. The first dendrochronologist. American Antiquity 22(2):186–188.

Helama, S., Schone, B.R., Black, B.A., and Dunca, E. 2006. Constructing long-term proxy series for aquatic environments with absolute dating control using a sclerochronological approach: introduction and advanced applications. Marine and Freshwater Research 57(6):591–599.

Hemming, D.L., Switsur, V.R., Waterhouse, J.S., Heaton, T.H.E., and Carter, A.H.C. 1998. Climate and the stable carbon isotope composition of tree ring cellulose: an intercomparison of three tree species. Tellus 50B: 25–32.

Hessl, A.E., and Graumlich, L.J. 2002. Interactive effects of human activities, herbivory and fire on quaking aspen (*Populus tremuloides*) age structures in western Wyoming. Journal of Biogeography 29:889–902.

Heyerdahl, E.K., and Card, V. 2000. Implications of paleorecords for ecosystem management. Trends in Ecology and Evolution 15(2):49–50.

Heyerdahl, E.K., and McKay, S.J. 2001. Condition of live fire-scarred ponderosa pine trees six years after removing partial cross sections. Tree-Ring Research 57(2):131–139.

Hildahl, V., and Reeks, W.A. 1960. Outbreaks of the forest tent caterpillar, *Malacosoma disstria* Hbn., and their effects on stands of trembling aspen in Manitoba and Saskatchewan. Canadian Entomologist 92:199–209.

Hirschboeck, K.K., Ni, F., Wood, M.L., and Woodhouse, C.A. 1996. Synoptic dendroclimatology: overview and outlook. *In:* J.S. Dean, D.M. Meko, and T.W. Swetnam, eds., Tree Rings, Environment, and Humanity: Proceedings of the International Conference, Tucson, Arizona, 17–21 May 1994. Radiocarbon, Tucson. pp. 205–223.

Hoadley, R.B. 1990. Identifying Wood: Accurate Results with Simple Tools. Taunton Press, Newtown, Connecticut. 224 pp.

Holmes, R.L. 1983. Computer-assisted quality control in tree-ring dating and measurement. Tree-Ring Bulletin 43:69–78.

Holmes, R.L., and Swetnam, T.W. 1994a. Dendroecology program library: program OUTBREAK user's manual. Unpublished document. On file with Laboratory of Tree-Ring Research, University of Arizona, Tucson. 5 pp.

Holmes, R.L., and Swetnam, T.W. 1994b. Dendroecology program library: program EVENT user's manual superposed epoch analysis in fire history studies. Unpublished document. On file with Laboratory of Tree-Ring Research, University of Arizona, Tucson. 7 pp.

Hough, F.B. 1882. The Elements of Forestry. Robert Clarke and Co., Cincinnati. 381 pp.

Huang, J.G., and Zhang, Q.B. 2007. Tree rings and climate for the last 680 years in Wulan area of northeastern Qinghai-Tibetan Plateau. Climatic Change 80:369–377.

Huber, B. 1935. Die physiologische bedeutung der ring- und zerstreut- porigkeit. Ber. Deut. Bot. Ges. 53:711–719.

Hupp, C.R. 1984. Dendrogeomorphic evidence of debris flow frequency and magnitude at Mount Shasta, California. Environmental Geology 6(2):121–128.

Hupp, C.R., Osterkamp, W.R., and Thornton, J.L. 1987. Dendrogeomorphic Evidence and Dating of Recent Debris Flows on Mount Shasta, Northern California. U.S. Geological Survey Professional Paper 1396-B. 45 pp.

Hurrell, J.W. 1995. Decadal trends in the North Atlantic Oscillation: regional temperatures and precipitation. Science 269:676–679.

Jacoby, G.C. 1997. Application of tree ring analysis to paleoseismology. Reviews of Geophysics 35(2):109–124.

Jacoby, G.C., and D'Arrigo, R.D. 1999. Tree-ring indicators of climate change at northern latitudes. World Resource Review 11(1):21–29.

Jacoby, G.C., and Ulan, L.D. 1983. Tree-ring indications of uplift at Icy Cape, Alaska, related to 1899 earthquakes. Journal of Geophysical Research 88(B11):9305–9313.

Jacoby, G.C., Sheppard, P.R., and Sieh, K.E. 1988. Irregular recurrence of large earthquakes along the San Andreas Fault: evidence from trees. Science 241:196–199.

Jacoby, G.C., Williams, P.L., and Buckley, B.M. 1992. Tree ring correlation between prehistoric landslides and abrupt tectonic events in Seattle, Washington. Science 258(5088):1621–1623.

Jacoby, G.C., Wiles, G., and D'Arrigo, R.D. 1996. Alaskan dendroclimatic variations for the past 300 years along a north-south gradient (transect). In: J.S. Dean, D.M. Meko, and T.W. Swetnam, eds., Tree Rings, Environment, and Humanity: Proceedings of the International Conference, Tucson, Arizona, 17–21 May 1994. Radiocarbon, Tucson. pp. 235–248.

Jacoby, G.C., Bunker, D.E., and Benson, B.E. 1997. Tree-ring evidence for an A.D. 1700 Cascadia earthquake in Washington and northern Oregon. Geology 25(11):999–1002.

Jacoby, G.C., Workman, K.W., and D'Arrigo, R.D. 1999. Laki eruption of 1783, tree rings, and disaster for northwest Alaska Inuit. Quaternary Science Reviews 18:1365–1371.

Jagels, R., and Telewski, F.W. 1990. Computer-aided image analysis of tree rings. In: E.R. Cook and L.A. Kairiukstis, eds., Methods of Dendrochronology: Applications in the Environmental Sciences. Kluwer Academic Publishers, Dordrecht, the Netherlands: pp. 76–93.

Jain, S., Woodhouse, C.A., and Hoerling, M.P. 2002. Multidecadal streamflow regimes in the interior western United States: implications for the vulnerability of water resources. Geophysical Research Letters 29(21):321–324.

Jansma, E. 1996. An 11,000-year tree-ring chronology of oak from the Dutch coastal region (2258–1141 B.C.). In: J.S. Dean, D.M. Meko, and T.W. Swetnam, eds., Tree Rings, Environment, and Humanity: Proceedings of the International Conference, Tucson, Arizona, 17–21 May 1994. Radiocarbon, Tucson. pp. 769–778.

Jansma, E., Hanraets, E., and Vernimmen, T. 2004. Tree-ring research on Dutch and Flemish art and furniture. In: E. Jansma, A. Bräuning, H. Gärtner, and G. Schleser, eds., Tree Rings in Archaeology, Climatology and Ecology, Vol. 2. Proceedings of the Dendrosymposium 2003. Schriften des Forschungszentrum Jülich, Reihe Umwelt 44:139–146.

Jedrysek, M.O., Krapiec, M., Skrzypek, G., Kaluzny, A., and Halas, S. 1998. An attempt to calibrate carbon and hydrogen isotope ratios in oak tree rings cellulose: the last millennium. RMZ Materials and Geoenvironment 45:82–90.

Jenkins, S.E., Guyette, R., and Rebertus, A.J. 1997. Vegetation-site relationships and fire history of a savanna-glade-woodland mosaic in the Ozarks. In: S.G. Pallardy, R.A. Cecich, H.E. Garrett, and P.S. Johnson, eds., Proceedings of the 11th Central Hardwood Forest Conference, 23–26 March 1997, Columbia, Missouri. U.S. Department of Agriculture Forest Service, GTR-NC-188. pp. 184–201.

Johnson, E.A., and Gutsell, S.L. 1994. Fire frequency models, methods and interpretations. Advances in Ecological Research 25:239–287.

Johnson, W.C. 1980. Dendrochronological sampling of Pinus oocarpa Shiede near Copan, Honduras: a preliminary note. Biotropica 12(4):315–316.

Jones, P.D., Briffa, K.R., and Schweingruber, F.H. 1995. Tree-ring evidence of the widespread effects of explosive volcanic eruptions. Geophysical Research Letters 22(11):1333–1336.

Jozsa, L. 1988. Increment Core Sampling Techniques for High-Quality Cores. Forintek Canada Corporation Special Publication No. SP-30. 26 pp.

Kaennel, M., and Schweingruber, F.H. 1995. Multilingual Glossary of Dendrochronology: Terms and Definitions in English, German, French, Spanish, Italian, Portuguese, and Russian. Paul Haupt Publishers, Berne. 467 pp.

Kairiukstis, L., and Shiyatov, S. 1990. Dendrochronology in the USSR. *In:* E.R. Cook and L.A. Kairiukstis, eds., Methods of Dendrochronology: Applications in the Environmental Sciences. Kluwer Academic Publishers, Dordrecht, the Netherlands. pp. 11–13.

Kapteyn, J.C. 1914. Tree-growth and meteorological factors. Recueil des Travaux Botaniques Neerlandais 11:70–93.

Kaye, M.W., and Swetnam, T.W. 1999. An assessment of fire, climate, and Apache history in the Sacramento Mountains, New Mexico. Physical Geography 20:305–330.

Kelly, P.E., and Larson, D.W. 1997. Dendroecological analysis of the population dynamics of an old-growth forest on cliff-faces of the Niagara Escarpment, Canada. Journal of Ecology 85:467–478.

Kelly, P.E., Cook, E.R., and Larson, D.W. 1992. Constrained growth, cambial mortality, and dendrochronology of ancient *Thuja occidentalis* on cliffs of the Niagara Escarpment: an eastern version of bristlecone pine? International Journal of Plant Science 153(1):117–127.

Kemp, M., and Walker, M. 2001. Leonardo on Painting: An Anthology of Writings by Leonardo da Vinci, with a Selection of Documents Relating to his Career as an Artist. Yale University Press, New Haven, Connecticut. 336 pp.

Kienast, F. 1982. Analytical investigations based on annual tree rings in damaged forest areas of the Valais (Rhone Valley) endangered by pollution. Geographica Helvetica 3:143–148. In German with English summary.

Kitagawa, H., and Matsumoto, E. 1995. Climatic implications of d$^{13}$C variations in a Japanese cedar (*Cryptomeria japonica*) during the last two millenia. Geophysical Research Letters 22:2155–2158.

Kitzberger, T., Veblen, T.T., and Villalba, R. 1995. Tectonic influences on tree growth in northern Patagonia, Argentina: the roles of substrate stability and climatic variation. Canadian Journal of Forest Research 25:1684–1696.

Kneeshaw, D.D., and Bergeron, Y. 1998. Canopy gap characteristics and tree replacement in the southeastern boreal forest. Ecology 79(3):783–794.

Koerber, T.W., and Wickman, B.E. 1970. Use of tree-ring measurements to evaluate impact of insect defoliation. *In:* J. Smith and J. Worrall, eds., Tree-Ring Analysis with Special References to Northwestern America. University of British Columbia Faculty Forest Bulletin 7:101–106.

Kozlowski, T.T., and Pallardy, S.G. 1997. Physiology of Woody Plants. 2nd ed. Academic Press, San Diego. 411 pp.

Krapiec, M. 1996. Subfossil oak chronology (474 BC–AD 1529) from southern Poland. *In:* J.S. Dean, D.M. Meko, and T.W. Swetnam, eds., Tree Rings, Environment, and Humanity: Proceedings of the International Conference, Tucson, Arizona, 17–21 May 1994. Radiocarbon, Tucson. pp. 813–819.

Krause, C., and Eckstein, D. 1993. Dendrochronology of roots. Dendrochronologia 11:9–23.

Krause, C., and Gagnon, R. 2006. The relationship between site and tree characteristics and the presence of wet heartwood in black spruce in the boreal forest of Quebec, Canada. Canadian Journal of Forest Research 36:1519–1526.

Krause, C., and Morin, H. 1999. Tree-ring patterns in stems and root systems of black spruce (*Picea mariana*) caused by spruce budworms. Canadian Journal of Forest Research 29(10):1583–1591.

Krause, C., and Morin, H. 2005. Adventive-root development in mature black spruce and balsam fire in the boreal forests of Quebec, Canada. Canadian Journal of Forest Research 25:2642–2654.

Krishnamurthy, R.V. 1996. Implications of a 400-year tree ring based $^{13}$C/$^{12}$C chronology. Geophysical Research Letters 23:371–374.

Krishnamurthy, R.V., and Epstein, S. 1985. Tree ring D/H ratio from Kenya, East Africa, and its palaeoclimatic significance. Nature 317:160–162.

Krueger, K.W., and Trappe, J.M. 1967. Food reserves and seasonal growth of Douglas-fir seedlings. Forest Science 13:192–202.

Kuechler, J. 1859. Das Klima von Texas. Texas Staats-Zeitung. August 6, 1859, p. 2. San Antonio. Translated and reprinted in: Campbell, T. 1949. The pioneer tree-ring work of Jacob Kuechler. Tree-Ring Bulletin 15:16–19.

Kulakowski, D., and Veblen, T.T. 2002. Influences of fire history and topography on the pattern of a severe wind blowdown in a Colorado subalpine forest. Journal of Ecology 90:806–819.

Kulakowski, D., Veblen, T.T., and Bebi, P. 2003. Effects of fire and spruce beetle outbreak legacies on the disturbance regime of a subalpine forest in Colorado. Journal of Biogeography 30:1445–1456.

Kulman, H.M. 1971. Effects of insect defoliation on growth and mortality of trees. Annual Review of Entomology 16:289–324.

Kuniholm, P.I. 2001. Dendrochronology and other applications of tree-ring studies on archaeology. *In:* D.R. Browthwell and A.M. Pollard, eds., Handbook of Archaeological Sciences. John Wiley, New York. pp. 35–46.

Kuniholm, P.I. 2003. Aegean dendrochronology project December 2003 progress report. The Malcolm and Carolyn Wiener Laboratory for Aegean and Near Eastern Dendrochronology, Cornell University, Ithaca, New York.

LaMarche, V.C., Jr. 1968. Rates of Slope Degradation as Determined from Botanical Evidence: White Mountains, California. U.S. Geological Survey Professional Paper 352-I. 45 pp.

LaMarche, V.C., Jr. 1973. Holocene climatic variations inferred from treeline fluctuations in the White Mountains, California. Quaternary Research 3:632–660.

LaMarche, V.C., Jr. 1974. Paleoclimatic inferences from long tree-ring records: intersite comparison shows climatic anomalies that may be linked to features of the general circulation. Science 183(4129):1043–1048.

LaMarche, V.C., Jr., and Fritts, H.C. 1971. Anomaly patterns of climate over the western United States, 1700–1930, derived from principal component analysis of tree-ring data. Monthly Weather Review 99:138–142.

LaMarche, V.C., Jr., and Hirschboeck, K.K. 1984. Frost rings in trees as records of major volcanic eruptions. Nature 307:121–126.

LaMarche, V.C., Jr., and Mooney, H.A. 1967. Altithermal timberline advance in western United States. Nature 213(5080):980–982.

LaMarche, V.C., Jr., and Stockton, C.W. 1974. Chronologies from temperature-sensitive bristlecone pines at upper treeline in western United States. Tree-ring Bulletin 34:21–45.

LaMarche, V.C., Jr., and Wallace, R.E. 1972. Evaluation of effects on trees of past movements on the San Andreas Fault, northern California. Geological Society of America Bulletin 83(9):2665–2676.

LaMarche, V.C., Jr., Holmes, R.L., Dunwiddie, P.W., and Drew, L.G. 1979a. Tree-ring chronologies of the Southern Hemisphere. 5. South Africa. Chronology Series V. Laboratory of Tree-Ring Research, University of Arizona, Tucson. pp. 1–27.

LaMarche, V.C., Jr., Holmes, R.L., Dunwiddie, P.W., and Drew, L.G. 1979b. Tree-ring chronologies of the Southern Hemisphere. 4. Australia. Chronology Series V. Laboratory of Tree-Ring Research, University of Arizona, Tucson. pp. 1–89.

LaMarche, V.C., Jr., Holmes, R.L., Dunwiddie, P.W., and Drew, L.G. 1979c. Tree-ring chronologies of the Southern Hemisphere. 2. Chile. Chronology Series V. Laboratory of Tree-Ring Research, University of Arizona, Tucson. pp. 1–43.

LaMarche, V.C., Jr., Holmes, R.L., Dunwiddie, P.W., and Drew, L.G. 1979d. Tree-ring chronologies of the Southern Hemisphere. 1. Argentina. Chronology Series V. Laboratory of Tree-Ring Research, University of Arizona, Tucson. pp. 1–69.

LaMarche, V.C., Jr., Holmes, R.L., Dunwiddie, P.W., and Drew, L.G. 1979e. Tree-ring chronologies of the Southern Hemisphere. 3. New Zealand. Chronology Series V. Laboratory of Tree-Ring Research, University of Arizona, Tucson. pp. 1–77.

Lambers, H., Chapin, F.S., III, and Pons, T.L. 1998. Plant Physiological Ecology. Springer, New York. 540 pp.

Lambert, G.N., Bernard, V., Doucerain, C., Girardclos, O., Lavier, C., Szepertisky, B., and Trenard, Y. 1996. French regional oak chronologies spanning more than 1000 years. *In:* J.S. Dean, D.M. Meko, and T.W. Swetnam, eds., Tree Rings, Environment, and Humanity: Proceedings of the International Conference, Tucson, Arizona, 17–21 May 1994. Radiocarbon, Tucson. pp. 821–832.

Landres, P.B., Morgan, P., and Swanson, F.J. 1999. Overview of the use of natural variability concepts in managing ecological systems. Ecological Applications 9(4):1179–1188.

Lara, A., and Villalba, R. 1993. A 3,620-year temperature record from *Fitzroya cuppressoides* tree rings in South America. Science 260:1104–1106.

Larocque, S.J., and Smith, D.J. 2005. 'Little Ice Age' proxy glacier mass balance records reconstructed from tree rings in the Mt. Waddington area, British Columbia Coast Mountains, Canada. Holocene 15(5):748–757.

Larson, D.W., and Melville, L. 1996. Stability of wood anatomy of living and Holocene *Thuja occidentalis* L. derived from exposed and submerged portions of the Niagara Escarpment. Quaternary Research 45(2):210–215.

Larson, D.W., Matthes, U., Gerrath, J.A., Gerrath, J.M., Nekola, J.C., Walker, G.L., Porembski, S., and Charlton, A. 1999. Ancient stunted trees on cliffs. Nature 398:382–383.

Larson, P.R. 1994. The Vascular Cambium: Development and Structure. Springer Verlag, New York. 725 pp.

Lavier, C., Lambert, G. 1996. Dendrochronology and works of art. *In:* J.S. Dean, D.M. Meko, and T.W. Swetnam, eds., Tree Rings, Environment, and Humanity: Proceedings of the International Conference, Tucson, Arizona, 17–21 May 1994. Radiocarbon, Tucson. pp. 343–352.

Lawrence, D.B. 1950. Estimating dates of recent glacier advances and recession rates by studying tree growth layers. Transactions of the American Geophysical Union 31:243–248.

Lawrence, J.R., and White, J.W.C. 1984. Growing season precipitation from D/H ratios of eastern white pine. Nature 311:558–560.

Laxton, R.R., and Litton, C.D. 1988. An East Midlands Master Tree-ring Chronology and Its Use for Dating Vernacular Buildings. University of Nottingham Department of Classical and Archaeological Studies (Archaeology Section) Monograph Series III. Nottingham, England.

Leavitt, S.W. 1992. Isotopes and trace elements in tree rings. Lundqua Report (Department of Quaternary Geology, Lund University, Sweden) 34:182–190.

Leavitt, S.W. 1993. Environmental information from $^{13}C/^{12}C$ ratios of wood. Geophysical Monographs 78:325–331.

Leavitt, S.W., and Danzer, S.R. 1993. Method for batch processing small wood samples to holocellulose for stable-carbon isotope analysis. Analytical Chemical 65:87–89.

Leavitt, S.W., and Lara, A. 1994. South American tree rings show declining d$^{13}$C trend. Tellus 46B:152–157.

Leavitt, S.W., and Long, A. 1984. Sampling strategy for stable carbon isotope analysis of tree rings in pine. Nature 311:145–147.

Leavitt, S.W., and Long, A. 1985. An atmospheric $^{13}C/^{12}C$ reconstruction generated through removal of climate effects from tree ring $^{13}C/^{12}C$ measurements. Tellus 35B:92–102.

LeBlanc, D.C. 1990. Relationships between breast-height and whole-stem growth indices for red spruce on Whiteface Mountain, New York. Canadian Journal of Forest Research 20:1399–1407.

LeBlanc, D.C., Raynal, D.J., and White, E.H. 1987. Acidic deposition and tree growth. 1. The use of stem analysis to study historical growth patterns. Journal of Environmental Quality 16(4):325–333.

Lehtonen, H., and Huttunen, P. 1997. History of forest fires in eastern Finland from the fifteenth century AD: the possible effects of slash-and-burn cultivation. Holocene 7:223–228.

Lertzman, K.P., Sutherland, G.D., Inselberg, A., and Saunders, S.C. 1996. Canopy gaps and the landscape mosaic in a coastal temperate rain forest. Ecology 77:1254–1270.

Lewis, E. 1873. The longevity of trees. Popular Science Monographs 3:321–334.

Lewis, M.A. 2002. Culturally modified trees as indicators of cultural activity in northern temperate rainforests. Maxwell Center for Anthropological Research Newsletter 1:4–5.

Libby, L.M., and Pandolfi, L.J. 1974. Temperature dependence of isotope ratios in tree rings. Proceedings of the National Academy of Science 71:2482–2486.

Libby, L.M., Pandolfi, L.J., Payton, P.H., Marshall, J., III, Becker, B., and Giertz-Siebenlist, V. 1976. Isotopic tree thermometers. Nature 261:284–290.

Liese, W. 1978. Bruno Huber: the pioneer of European dendrochronology. In: J. Fletcher, ed., Dendrochronology in Europe: Principles, Interpretations and Applications to Archaeology and History. Based on the symposium held at the National Maritime Museum, Greenwich, July 1977. National Maritime Museum, Greenwich, Archaeological Series No. 4; Research Laboratory for Archaeology and History of Art, Oxford University, Publication No. 2; British Arcaheological Reports International Series No. 51. pp. 1–10.

Lin, A., and Lin, S. 1998. Tree damage and surface displacement: the 1931 M 8.0 Fuyun earthquake. Journal of Geology 106(6):751–757.

Linnaeus, C. 1745. Olandska och Gothlandska Resa, etc. Stockholm. 344 pp.

Linnaeus, C. 1751. Skanska Resa, etc. Stockholm. 434 pp.

Lipp, J., and Trimborn, P. 1991. Long-term records and basic principles of tree-ring isotope data with emphasis on local environmental conditions. Palaoklimaforschung 6:105–117.

Lipp, J., Trimborn, P., Fritz, P., Moser, H., Becker, B., and Frenzel, B. 1991. Stable isotopes in tree ring cellulose and climatic change. Tellus 43B:322–330.

Little, E.L., Jr. 1971. Atlas of United States Trees. Vol. 1, Conifers and Important Hardwoods. U.S. Department of Agriculture Miscellaneous Publication 1146. 9 pp., 200 maps.

Liu, Y., Wu, X., Leavitt, S.W., and Hughes, M.K. 1996. Stable carbon isotope in tree rings from Huangling, China, and climatic variation. Science in China D 39(2):152–161. Lloyd, A.H., and Graumlich, L.J. 1997. Holocene dynamics of treeline forests in the Sierra Nevada. Ecology 78(4):1199–1210.

Loader, N.J., and Switsur, V.R. 1996. Reconstructing past environmental change using stable isotopes in tree-rings. Botanical Journal of Scotland 48:65–78.

Lomolino, M.V., Riddle, B.R., and Brown, J. 2006. Biogeography. 3rd ed. Sinauer Associates, Inc., Sunderland, Massachusetts. 845 pp.

Long, A. 1982. Stable isotopes in tree rings. In: M.K. Hughes, P.M. Kelly, J.R. Pilcher, and V.C. LaMarche Jr., eds., Climate from Tree Rings. Cambridge University Press, New York. pp. 13–18.

Lorimer, C.G., and Frelich, L.E. 1989. A method for estimating canopy disturbance frequency and intensity in dense temperate forests. Canadian Journal of Forest Research 19:651–663.

Luckman, B.H. 1988. Dating the moraines and recession of Athabasca and Dome Glaciers, Alberta, Canada. Arctic and Alpine Research 20:40–54.

Luckman, B.H. 2003. Assessment of Present, Past and Future Climate Variability in the Americas from Treeline Environments. Inter-American Institute CRN03, Annual Report 2003.

Lynch, A.M., and Swetnam, T.W. 1992. Old-growth mixed-conifer and western spruce budworm in the southern Rocky Mountains. U.S. Department of Agriculture Forest Service, GTR-RM-213.

MacDonald, G.M., and Case, R.A. 2005. Variations in the Pacific Decadal Oscillation over the past millennium. Geophysical Research Letters 32(8):L08703, doi: 10.1029/2005GL022478.

Madany, M.H., Swetnam, T.W., and West, N.E. 1982. Comparison of two approaches for determining fire dates from tree scars. Forest Science 28(4):856–861.

Malmstrom, C.M., Thompson, M.V., Juday, G., Los, S.O., Randerson, J.T., and Field, C.B. 1997. Interannual variation in global-scale net primary production: testing model estimates. Global Biogeochemical Cycles 11:367–392.

Mann, M.E., Bradley, R.S., and Hughes, M.K. 1998. Global-scale temperature patterns and climate forcing over the past six centuries. Nature 392:779–787.

Mantua, N.J., Hare, S.R., Zhang, Y., Wallace, J.M., and Francis, R.C. 1997. A Pacific interdecadal climate oscillation with impacts on salmon production. Bulletin of the American Meteorological Society 78:1069–1079.

Marchand, P.J. 1984. Dendrochronology of a fir wave. Canadian Journal of Forest Research 14(1):51–56.

Mariaux, A. 1981. Past efforts in measuring age and annual growth in tropical trees. Yale University School of Forestry and Environmental Studies Bulletin 94:20–30.

Martin, N.D., and Martin, N.M. 2001. Biotic Forest Communities of Ontario. Commonwealth Research, Belleville, Ontario. 195 pp.

Mason, R.R., and Torgerson, T.R. 1987. Dynamics of a non-outbreak population of the Douglas-fir tussock moth (Lepidoptera: Lymantriidae) in southern Oregon. Environmental Ecology 16:1217–1227.

Mason, R.R., Wickman, B.E., and Paul, H.G. 1997. Radial growth response of Douglas-fir and grand fir to larval densities of the Douglas-fir tussock moth and the western spruce budworm. Forest Science 43:194–205.

Massey, C.L. 1940. The Pandora Moth, a Periodic Pest of Western Pine Forests. U.S. Department of Agriculture Forest Service, Technical Bulletin 137. 20 pp.

Matthews, J.A. 1977. Glacier and climate fluctuations inferred from tree-growth variations over the last 250 years, central Norway. Boreas 6:1–24.

McCarroll, D., and Loader, N.J. 2004. Stable isotopes in tree rings. Quaternary Science Reviews 23:771–801.

McCarroll, D., and Pawellek, F. 1998. Stable carbon isotope ratios of latewood cellulose in *Pinus sylvestris* from northern Finland: variability and signal-strength. Holocene 8(6):675–684.

McCarroll, D., and Pawellek, F. 2001. Stable carbon isotope ratios of *Pinus sylvestris* from northern Finland and the potential for extracting a climate signal from long Fennoscandian chronologies. Holocene 11(5):517–526.

McCarthy, D.P., and Luckman, B.H. 1993. Estimating ecesis for tree-ring dating of moraines: a comparative study from the Canadian Cordillera. Arctic and Alpine Research 25:63–68.

McCarthy, D.P., Luckman, B.H., and Kelly, P.E. 1991. Sampling height-age error corrections from spruce seedlings in glacial forefields, Canadian Cordillera. Arctic and Alpine Research 23:451–455.

McCord, V.A.S. 1996. Fluvial process dendrogeomorphology: reconstruction of flood events from the southwestern United States using flood-scarred trees. In: J.S. Dean, D.M. Meko, and T.W. Swetnam, eds., Tree Rings, Environment, and Humanity: Proceedings of the International Conference, Tucson, Arizona, 17–21 May 1994. Radiocarbon, Tucson. pp. 689–699.

McCormac, F.G., Baillie, M.G.L., Pilcher, J.R., Brown, D.M., and Hoper, S.T. 1994. d$^{13}$C measurement from the Irish oak chronology. Radiocarbon 36:27–35.

McCullough, D.G., Werner, R.A., and Neumann, D. 1998. Fire and insects in northern and boreal forest ecosystems of North America. Annual Review of Entomology 43:107–127.

McLaren, B.E., and Peterson, R.O. 1994. Wolves, moose, and tree rings on Isle Royale. Science 266(5190):1555–1558.

Meisling, K.E., and Sieh, K.E. 1980. Disturbance of trees by the 1857 Fort Tejon earthquake, California. Journal of Geophysical Research 85(B6):3225–3238.

Meko, D.M., and Baisan, C.H. 2001. Pilot study of latewood-width of confers as an indicator of variability of summer rainfall in the North American Monsoon region. International Journal of Climatology 21:697–708.

Meko, D.M., Stockton, C.W., and Boggess, W.R. 1980. A tree-ring reconstruction of drought in southern California. Water Resources Bulletin 16(4):594–600.

Meko, D.M., Cook, E.R., Stahle, D.W., Stockton, C.W., and Hughes, M.K. 1993. Spatial patterns of tree-growth anomalies in the United States and southeastern Canada. Journal of Climate 6:1773–1786.

Miles, D.H., and Worthington, M.J. 1998. Sonora Pass junipers from California U.S.A.: construction of a 3,500-year chronology. *In:* V. Stravinskiene and R. Juknys, eds., Dendrochronology and Environmental Trends: Proceedings of the International Conference, 17–21 June 1998, Kaunas, Lithuania. Vytautas Magnas University Department of Environmental Sciences, Kaunas.

Mitchell, J.M., Jr., Stockton, C.W., and Meko, D.M. 1979. Evidence of a 22-year rhythm of drought in the western United States related to the Hale Solar Cycle since the 17th century. *In:* B.M. McCormac and T.A. Seliga, eds., Solar-Terrestrial Influences on Weather and Climate. D. Reidel, Dordrecht, the Netherlands. pp. 125–143.

Moberg, A., Sonechkin, D.M., Holmgren, K., Datsenko, N.M., and Karlén, W. 2005. Highly variable Northern Hemisphere temperatures reconstructed from low- and high-resolution proxy data. Nature 433:613–617.

Mobley, C.M., and Eldridge, M. 1992. Culturally modified trees in the Pacific Northwest. Arctic Anthropology 29(2):91–110.

Mora, C.I., Miller, D.L., and Grissino-Mayer, H.D. 2006. Tempest in a tree ring: paleotempestology and the record of past hurricanes. The Sedimentary Record 4(3):4–8.

Morgan, P., Aplet, G.H., Haufler, J.B., Humphries, H.C., Margaret, M.M., and Wilson, W.D. 1994. Historical range of variability: a useful tool for evaluating ecosystem change. *In:* R.L. Sampson and D.L. Adams, eds., Assessing Forest Ecosystem Health in the Inland West: Proceedings of the American Forests Scientific Workshop. Hawthorn Press, New York. pp. 87–111.

Mott, D.G., Nairn, L.D., and Cook, J.A. 1957. Radial growth in forest trees and effects of insect defoliation. Forest Science 3(3):286–304.

Motyka, R.J. 2003. Little Ice Age subsidence and post Little Ice Age uplift at Juneau, Alaska, inferred from dendrochronology and geomorphology. Quaternary Research 59(3):300–309.

Muir, J. 1911. My First Summer in the Sierra. Houghton Mifflin, Boston. 269 pp.

Munro, M.A.R., Brown, P.M., Hughes, M.K., and Garcia, E.M.R. 1996. Image analysis of tracheid dimensions for dendrochronological use. *In:* J.S. Dean, D.M. Meko, and T.W. Swetnam, eds., Tree Rings, Environment, and Humanity: Proceedings of the International Conference, Tucson, Arizona, 17–21 May 1994. Radiocarbon, Tucson. pp. 843–851.

Nash, S.E. 1997. A cutting-date estimation technique for ponderosa pine and Douglas fir wood specimens. American Antiquity 62(2):260–272.

Nash, S.E. 1999. Time, Trees, and Prehistory: Tree-Ring Dating and the Development of North American Archaeology, 1914–1950. University of Utah Press, Salt Lake City. 294 pp.

Nials, F., Gregory, D., and Graybill, D. 1989. Salt River streamflow and Hohokam irrigation systems. *In:* C. Heathington and G. Gregory, eds., The 1982–1984 Excavations at Las Colinas: Environment and Subsistence. Arizona State University Archaeological Series 162. pp. 59–78.

Nicolussi, K., Kaufmann, M., Patzelt, G., van der Plicht, J., and Thurner, A. 2005. Holocene tree-line variability in the Kauner Valley, central eastern Alps, indicated by dendrochronological analysis of living trees and subfossil logs. Vegetation History and Archaeobotany 14(3):221–234.

Niklasson, M., and Granström, A. 2000. Numbers and sizes of fires: long-term spatially explicit fire history in a Swedish boreal landscape. Ecology 81(6):1484–1499.

Nogler, P. 1981. Auskeilende und fehlende Jahrringe in absterbenden Tannen (*Abies alba* Mill.). Allgemeine Forstzeitschrift 36(28):709–711.

Okada, N., Fujiwara, T., Ohta, S., and Matsumoto, E. 1995. Stable carbon isotopes of *Chamaecyparis obtusa* grown at a high-altitude region in Japan: within and among-tree variations. *In:* S. Ohta, T. Fujii, N. Okada, M.K. Hughes, and D. Eckstein, eds., Tree-Rings: From the Past to the Future: Proceedings of the International Workshop on Asian and Pacific Dendrochronology. Forestry and Forest Products Research Institute Scientific Meeting Report 1. pp. 165–169.

O'Neill, L.C. 1963. The suppression of growth rings in jack pine in relation to defoliation by Swaine jack-pine sawfly. Canadian Journal of Botany 41:227–235.

Orvis, K.H., and Grissino-Mayer, H.D. 2002. Standardizing the reporting of abrasive papers used to surface tree-ring samples. Tree-Ring Research 58(1):47–50.

Orwig, D.A., Cogbill, C.V., Foster, D.R., and O'Keefe, J.F. 2001. Variations in old-growth structure and definitions: forest dynamics on Wachusett Mountain, Massachusetts. Ecological Applications 11(2):437–452.

Page, R. 1970. Dating episodes of faulting from tree rings: effects of the 1958 rupture of the Fairweather fault on tree growth. Geological Society of America Bulletin 81:3085–3094.

Panshin, A.J., De Zeeuw, C., and Brown, H.P. 1964. Textbook of Wood Technology. Vol. I, Structure, Identification, Uses, and Properties of the Commercial Woods of the United States. McGraw-Hill, New York. 643 pp.

Park, W.-K., and Telewski, F.W. 1993. Measuring maximum latewood density by image analysis at the cellular level. Wood and Fiber Science 25(4):326–332.

Patterson, J.E. 1929. The Pandora Moth, a Periodic Pest of the Western Pine Forests. U.S. Department of Agriculture Forest Service, Technical Bulletin 137. 20 pp.

Payette, S. 1987. Recent porcupine expansion at tree line: a dendro-ecological analysis. Canadian Journal of Zoology 65:551–557.

Payette, S., Morneau, C., Sirois, L., and Desponts, M. 1989. Recent fire history of the northern Québec biomes. Ecology 70(3):656–673.

Payette, S., Boudreau, S., Morneau, C., and Pitre, N. 2004. Long-term interactions between migratory caribou, wildfires and Nunavik hunters inferred from tree rings. Ambio 33(8):482–486.

Pearman, G.I., Francey, R.J., and Fraser, P.J.B. 1976. Climatic implications of stable carbon isotopes in tree-rings. Nature 260:771–773.

Pederson, N., Jones, R.H., and Sharitz, R.R. 1997. Age structure of old-growth loblolly pine stands in a floodplain forest. Journal of the Torrey Botanical Society 124(2):111–123.

Pederson, N., Cook, E.R., Jacoby, G.C., Peteet, D.M., and Griffin, K.L. 2004. The influence of winter temperatures on the annual radial growth of six northern range margin tree species. Dendrochronologia 22(1):7–29.

Pederson, N., D'Amato, A.W., and Orwig, D.A. 2007. Central hardwood natural history from dendrochronology: maximum ages of rarely studied species. *In:* Proceedings of the 15th Central Hardwood Conference, 27 February–1 March 2006, University of Tennessee, Knoxville. U.S. Department of Agriculture Forest Service Southern Research Station, e-General Technical Report SRS-101.

Pendall, E. 2000. Influence of precipitation seasonality on pinon pine cellulose dD values. Global Change Biology 6:287–301.

Perkins, D.L., and Swetnam, T.W. 1996. A dendroecological assessment of whitebark pine in the Sawtooth–Salmon River region, Idaho. Canadian Journal of Forest Research 26(12):2123–2133.

Phipps, R.L. 1985. Collecting, Preparing, Crossdating, and Measuring Tree Increment Cores. U.S. Geological Survey, Water Resources Investigations Report 85-4148. 48 pp.

Phipps, R.L. 2005. Some geometric constraints on ring-width trend. Tree-Ring Research 61(2):73–76.

Phipps, R.L., Ireley, D.L., and Baker, C.P. 1979. Tree Rings as Indicators of Hydrologic Change in the Great Dismal Swamp, Virginia and North Carolina. U.S. Geological Survey, Water Resources Investigations Report 78-136. pp. 1–26.

Pickett, S.T.A., and White, P.S. 1985. The Ecology of Natural Disturbance and Patch Dynamics. Academic Press, San Diego. 472 pp.

Pilcher, J.R., Baillie, M.G.L., Schmidt, B., and Becker, B. 1984. A 7,272-year tree-ring chronology for western Europe. Nature 312:150–152.

Piovesan, G., Di Filippo, A., Alessandrini, A., Biondi, F., and Schirone, E.B. 2005. Structure, dynamics and dendroecology of an old-growth *Fagus* forest in the Apennines. Journal of Vegetation Science 16:13–28.

Pollens, S. 1999. Le Messie. Journal of the Violin Society of America 16(1):77–101.

Pollens, S. 2001. Messiah redux. Journal of the Violin Society of America 17(3):159–179.

Presnall, C.C. 1933. Fire studies in the Mariposa Grove. Yosemite Nature Notes 12(3):23–24.

Pumijumnong, N., Eckstein, D., and Sass, U. 1995. Tree-ring research on *Tectona grandis* in northern Thailand. International Association of Wood Anatomists Journal 16:385–392.

Pyne, S.J. 1982. Fire in America: A Cultural History of Wildland and Rural Fire. Princeton University Press, Princeton, New Jersey. 654 pp.

Ramesh, R., Bhattacharya, S.K., and Gopalan, K. 1985. Dendroclimatological implications of isotope coherence in trees from Kashmir Valley, India. Nature 317:802–804.

Ramesh, R., Bhattacharya, S.K., and Gopalan, K. 1986. Climatic correlations in the stable isotope records of silver fir (*Abies pindrow*) tree from Kashmir, India. Earth and Planetary Science Letters 79:66–74.

Ratzeburg, J.T.C. 1866. Die Waldverderbnis, oder dauernder Schaden, welcher durch Insektenfrass, Schälen, Schlagen und Verbeissen an lebenden Waldbäumen entsteht. 2 vols. Nicolaische Verlagsbuchhandlung, Berlin.

Reid, M. 1989. The response of understorey vegetation to major canopy disturbance in the subalpine forests of Colorado. M.S. Thesis, University of Colorado, Boulder.

Robertson, I., Rolfe, J., Switsur, V.R., Carter, A.H.C., Hall, M.A., Barker, A.C., and Waterhouse, J.S. 1997a. Signal strength and climate relationships in $^{13}C/^{12}C$ ratios of tree ring cellulose from oak in southwest Finland. Geophysical Research Letters 24:1487–1490.

Robertson, I., Switsur, V.R., Carter, A.H.C., Barker, A.C., Waterhouse, J.S., Briffa, K.R., and Jones, P.D. 1997b. Signal strength and climate relationships in $^{13}C/^{12}C$ ratios of tree ring cellulose from oak in east England. Journal of Geophysical Research 102:19507–19519.

Robertson, I., Waterhouse, J.S., Barker, A.C., Carter, A.H.C., and Switsur, V.R. 2001. Oxygen isotope ratios of oak in east England: implications for reconstructing the isotopic composition of precipitation. Earth and Planetary Science Letters 191:21–31.

Roig, F.A., Villalba, R., and Ripalta, A. 1988. Climatic factors in *Discaria trinervis* growth in Argentine central Andes. Dendrochronologia 6:61–70.

Roig, F.A., Le-Quesne, C., Boninsegna, J.A., Briffa, K.R., Lara, A., Grudd, H., Jones, P.D., Villagran, C. 2001. Climate variability 50,000 years ago in mid-latitude Chile as reconstructed from tree rings. Nature 410:567–570.

Rossi, S., Deslauriers, A., Anfodillo, T., Morin, H., Saracino, A., Motta, R., and Borghetti, M. 2006. Conifers in cold environments synchronize maximum growth rate of tree-ring formation with day length. New Phytologist 170(2):301–310.

Rubino, D.L. and McCarthy, B.C. 2003. Evaluation of coarse woody debris and forest vegetation across topographic gradients in a southern Ohio forest. Forest Ecology and Management, 183(1–3):221–238.

Rubner, K. 1910. Das Hungern des Cambiums und das Aussetzen der Jahresringe. Naturw. Zeits. Forst- und Landwirtschaftliche 8:212–262.

Ruzhich, V.V., San'kov, V.A., and Dneprovskii, Y.I. 1982. The dendrochronological dating of seismo-genic ruptures in the Stanovoi Highland. Soviet Geology and Geophysics 23(8):57–63.

Ryerson, D.E., Swetnam, T.W., and Lynch, A.M. 2003. A tree-ring reconstruction of western spruce budworm outbreaks in the San Juan Mountains, Colorado, U.S.A. Canadian Journal of Forest Research 33(6):1010–1028.

Salisbury, F.B., and Ross, C.W. 1992. Plant Physiology. 4th ed. Wadsworth Publishing Co., Belmont, California. 682 pp.

Salzer, M.W. 2000. Dendroclimatology in the San Francisco Peaks region of northern Arizona, U.S.A. Dissertation, University of Arizona, Tucson. 211 pp.

Sarton, G. 1954. When was tree-ring analysis discovered? Isis 45(4):383–384.

Saurer, M., and Siegenthaler, U. 1989. $^{13}C/^{12}C$ isotope ratios in tree rings are sensitive to relative humidity. Dendrochronologia 7:9–13.

Saurer, M., Siegenthaler, U., and Schweingruber, F. 1995. The climate-carbon isotope relationship in tree rings and the significance of site conditions. Tellus 47B:320–330.

Saurer, M., Siegwolf, R., Borella, S., and Schweingruber, F. 1998a. Environmental information from stable isotopes in tree rings of *Fagus sylvatica*. *In:* M. Beniston and J.L. Innes, eds., The Impacts of Climate Variability on Forests. Springer, Berlin. pp. 241–253.

Saurer, M., Robertson, I., Siegwolf, R., and Leuenberger, M. 1998b. Oxygen isotope analysis of cellulose: an interlaboratory comparison. Analytical Chemistry 70:2074–2080.

Saurer, M., Schweingruber, F.H., Vaganov, E.A., Shiyatov, S.G., and Siegwolf, R. 2002. Spatial and temporal oxygen isotope trends at northern tree-line Eurasia. Geophysical Research Letters 29:10–14.

Savage, M., and Swetnam, T.W. 1990. Early 19th century fire decline following sheep pasturing in a Navajo ponderosa pine forest. Ecology 71(6):2374–2378.

Schiegl, W.E. 1974. Climatic significance of deuterium abundance in growth rings of *Picea*. Nature 251:582–584.

Schleser, G.H., Frielingsdorf, J., and Blair, A. 1999. Carbon isotope behaviour in wood and cellulose during artificial aging. Chemical Geology 158:121–130.

Schöngart, J., Junk, W.J., Piedade, M.T.F., Ayres, J.M., Huttermann, A., and Worbes, M. 2004. Tele-connection between tree growth in the Amazonian floodplains and the El Niño-Southern Oscillation effect. Global Change Biology 10(5):683–692.

Schöngart, J., Piedade, M.T.F., Wittmann, F., Junk, W.J., and Worbes, M. 2005. Wood growth patterns of *Macrolobium acaciifolium* (Benth.) Benth. (Fabaceae) in Amazonian black-water and white-water floodplain forests. Oecologia 145(3):454–461.

Schöngart, J., Orthmann, B., Hennenberg, K.J., Porembski, S., and Worbes, M. 2006. Climate-growth relationships of tropical tree species in West Africa and their potential for climate reconstruction. Global Change Biology 12(7):1139–1150.

Schulman, E. 1937. Some early papers on tree-rings: J.C. Kapteyn. Tree-Ring Bulletin 3:28–29.

Schulman, E. 1938. Nineteen centuries of rainfall history in the Southwest. Bulletin of the American Meteorological Society 19(5):211–216.

Schulman, E. 1954. Longevity under adversity in conifers. Science 119:396–399.

Schulman, E. 1956. Dendroclimatic Changes in Semiarid America. University of Arizona Press, Tucson. 142 pp.

Schulze, B., Wirth, C., Linke, P., Brand, W.A., Kuhlmann, I., Horna, V., and Schulze, E.D. 2004. Laser ablation-combustion-GC-IRMS: a new method for online analysis of intra-annual variation of delta C-13 in tree rings. Tree Physiology 24(11):1193–1201.

Schweingruber, F.H. 1988. Tree Rings: Basics and Applications of Dendrochronology. D. Reidel Publishing Co., Dordrecht, the Netherlands. 276 pp.

Schweingruber, F.H. 1996. Tree Rings and Environment: Dendroecology. Haupt Press, Berne. 609 pp.

Seager, R., Ting, M., Held, I., Kushnir, Y., Lu, J., Vecchi, G., Huang, H.-P., Harnik, N., Leetmaa, A., Lau, N.-C., Li, C., Velez, J., and Naik, N. 2007. Model projections of an imminent transition to a more arid climate in southwestern North America. Science 316(5828):1181–1184.

Seckendorff, A.F. 1881. Beiträge zur Kenntnis der Schwarzföhre. Mitteilung aus dem forstlichen Versuchswesen Oesterreichs. Carl Gerold Verlag, Wien. 66 pp.

Sellards, E.H., Tharp, B.C., and Hill, R.T. 1923. Investigation on the Red River Made in Connection with the Oklahoma-Texas Boundary Suit. University of Texas Bulletin No. 2327. 172 pp.

Shah, S.K., Bhattacharyya, A., and Chaudhary, V. 2007. Reconstruction of June–September precipitation based on tree-ring data of teak (Tectona grandis L.) from Hoshangabad, Madhya Pradesh, India. Dendrochronologia 25(1):57–64.

Shao, X.M., Wang, S.Z., Xu, Y., Zhu, H.F., Xu, X.G., and Xiao, Y.M. 2007. A 3500-year master tree-ring dating chronology from the northeastern part of the Qaidam Basin. Quaternary Sciences 27:477–485.

Sheppard, P.R., and Graumlich, L.J. 1996. A reflected-light video imaging system for tree-ring analysis of conifers. In: J.S. Dean, D.M. Meko, and T.W. Swetnam, eds., Tree Rings, Environment, and Humanity: Proceedings of the International Conference, Tucson, Arizona, 17–21 May 1994. Radiocarbon, Tucson. pp. 879–889.

Sheppard, P.R., and Jacoby, G.C. 1989. Application of tree-ring analysis to paleoseismology: two case studies. Geology 17:226–229.

Sheppard, P.R., and White, L.O. 1995. Tree-ring responses to the 1978 earthquake at Stephens Pass, northeastern California. Geology 23(2):109–112.

Sheppard, P.R., and Wiedenhoeft, A. 2007. An advancement in removing extraneous color from wood for low-magnification reflected-light image analysis of conifer tree rings. Wood and Fiber Science 39(1):173–183.

Sheppard, P.S., and Witten, M.L. 2005. Laser trimming tree-ring cores for dendrochemistry of metals. Tree-Ring Research 62:87–92.

Sheppard, P.R., Graumlich, L.J., and Conkey, L.E. 1996. Reflected-light image analysis of conifer tree rings for reconstructing climate. Holocene 6(1):62–68.

Sherzer, W.H. 1905. Glacial studies in the Canadian Rockies and Selkirks. Smithsonian Miscellaneous Collections 47:453–496.

Sheu, D.D., Kou, P., Chiu, C.-H., and Chen, M.-J. 1996. Variability of tree-ring $d^{13}C$ in Taiwan fir: growth effect and response to May–October temperatures. Geochimica et Cosmochimica Acta 60:171–177.

Shinn, D.A. 1978. Man and the land: an ecological history of fire and grazing on eastern Oregon rangelands. M.A. Thesis, Oregon State University, Corvallis.

Shore, T.L., Safranyik, L., Hawkes, B.C., and Taylor, S.W. 2006. Effects of the mountain pine beetle on lodgepole pine stand structure and dynamics. In: L. Safranyik and B. Wilson, eds., The Mountain Pine Beetle: A Synthesis of Biology, Management, and Impacts on Lodgepole Pine. Canadian Forest Service. pp. 95–114.

Show, S.B., and Kotok, E.I. 1924. The role of fire in the California pine forests. U.S. Department of Agriculture Bulletin 1924:1–80.

Shroder, J.F., Jr. 1978. Dendrogeomorphological analysis of mass movement on Table Cliffs Plateau, Utah. Quaternary Research 9:168–185.

Shroder, J.F., Jr. 1980. Dendrogeomorphology: review and new techniques of tree ring dating. Progress in Physical Geography 4:161–188.

Shroder, J.F., Jr., and Butler, D.R. 1987. Tree-ring analysis in the earth sciences. *In:* G.C. Jacoby and J.W. Hornbeck, eds., Proceedings of the International Symposium on Ecological Aspects of Tree-Ring Analysis, 17–21 August 1986, Marymount College, Tarrytown, New York. pp. 186–212.

Shvedov, F. 1892. The tree as a chronicle of droughts. Meteorological Herald 5:163–178. In Russian.

Sibold, J.S., Veblen, T.T., and Gonzalez, M.E. 2006. Spatial and temporal variation in historic fire regimes in subalpine forests across the Colorado Front Range in Rocky Mountain National Park, Colorado, U.S.A. Journal of Biogeography 33(4):631–647.

Sibold, J.S., Veblen, T.T., Chipko, K., Lawson, L., Mathis, E., and Scott, J. 2007. Influences of secondary disturbances on lodgepole pine stand development in Rocky Mountain National Park. Ecological Applications 17(6):1638–1655.

Siegenthaler, U. 1979. Stable hydrogen and oxygen isotopes in the water cycle. *In:* E. Jäger and J.C. Hunziker, eds., Lectures in Isotope Geology. Springer Verlag, Berlin. pp. 264–273.

Sigafoos, R.S. 1964. Botanical Evidence of Floods and Floodplain Deposits. U.S. Geological Survey Professional Paper 485-A. 35 pp.

Sigafoos, R.S., and Hendricks, E.L. 1961. Botanical Evidence of the Modern History of Nisqually Glacier, Washington. U.S. Geological Survey Professional Paper 387-A. 20 pp.

Sigafoos, R.S., and Hendricks, E.L. 1972. Recent Activity of Glaciers of Mount Rainier, Washington. U.S. Geological Survey Professional Paper 387-B. 24 pp.

Smiley, T.L. 1958. The geology and dating of Sunset Crater, Flagstaff, Arizona. *In:* R.Y. Anderson and J.W. Harshbarger, eds., Guidebook of the Black Mesa Basin, Northwestern Arizona. New Mexico Geological Society, Ninth Field Conference, Socorro, New Mexico. pp. 186–190.

Smith, D.J., and Laroque, C.P. 1996. Dendroglaciological dating of a Little Ice Age glacial advance at Moving Glacier, Vancouver Island, British Columbia. Geographie Physique et Quaternaire 50:47–55.

Smith, D.J., and Lewis, D. 2007. Dendroglaciology. *In:* S.A. Elias, ed., Encyclopedia of Quaternary Science, Vol. 2. Elsevier, Amsterdam. pp. 986–994.

Smith, K.T., and Sutherland, E.K. 1999. Fire-scar formation and compartmentalization in oak. Canadian Journal of Forest Research 29(2):166–171.

Smith, K.T., and Sutherland, E.K. 2001. Terminology and biology of fire scars in selected central hardwoods. Tree-Ring Research 57(2):141–147.

Sonninen, E., and Jungner, H. 1995. Stable carbon isotopes in tree-rings of a Scots pine (*Pinus sylvestris* L.) from northern Finland. Palaeoklimaforschung 15:121–128.

Speer, J.H. 1997. A dendrochronological record of pandora moth (*Coloradia pandora*, Blake) outbreaks in central Oregon. M.S. Thesis, University of Arizona, Tucson. 159 pp.

Speer, J.H. 2001. Oak mast history from dendrochronology: a new technique demonstrated in the southern Appalachian region. Dissertation, University of Tennessee, Knoxville. 241 pp.

Speer, J.H. 2006. Experiential Learning and Exploratory Research: The 13th Annual North American Dendroecological Fieldweek (NADEF). Indiana State University, Department of Geography, Geology, and Anthropology, Professional Paper No. 23.

Speer, J.H., and Hansen-Speer, K.H. 2007. Ecological applications of dendrochronology in archaeology. Journal of Ethnobiology 27(1):88–109.

Speer, J.H., and Holmes, R. 2004. Stem analysis on four ponderosa pine trees affected by repeated pandora moth defoliation in central Oregon. Tree-Ring Research 60(2):69–76.

Speer, J.H., Swetnam, T.W., Wickman, B.E., and Youngblood, A. 2001. Changes in pandora moth outbreak dynamics during the past 622 years. Ecology 82:679–697.

Speer, J.H., Orvis, K.H., Grissino-Mayer, H.D., Kennedy, L.M., and Horn, S.P. 2004. Assessing the dendrochronological potential of *Pinus occidentalis* Swartz in the Cordillera Central of the Dominican Republic. Holocene 14(4):563–569.

Spencer, D.A. 1964. Porcupine population fluctuations in past centuries revealed by dendrochronology. Journal of Applied Ecology 1(1):127–149.

St. George, S., and Nielsen, E. 2002. Hydroclimatic change in southern Manitoba since AD 1409 inferred from tree rings. Quaternary Research 58(2):103–111.

Stahle, D.W. 1979. Tree-ring dating of historic buildings in Arkansas. Tree-Ring Bulletin 39:1–28.

Stahle, D.W. 1996. Tree rings and ancient forest history. In: M.B. Davis, ed., Eastern Old-Growth Forests. Island Press, Washington, D.C. pp. 321–343.

Stahle, D.W. 1999. Effective strategies for the development of tropical tree-ring chronologies. International Association of Wood Anatomists Journal 20:249–253.

Stahle, D.W., and Cleaveland, M.K. 1993. Southern oscillation extremes reconstructed from tree rings of the Sierra Madre Occidental and southern Great Plains. Journal of Climate 6:129–140.

Stahle, D.W., Cleaveland, M.K., and Hehr, J.G. 1988. North Carolina climate changes reconstructed from tree rings: AD 372–1985. Science 240:1517–1519.

Stahle, D.W., Van Arsdale, R.B., and Cleaveland, M.K. 1992. Tectonic signal in baldcypress trees at Reelfoot Lake, Tennessee. Seismological Research Letters 63(3):439–447.

Stahle, D.W., Cleaveland, M.K., Blanton, D.B., Therrell, M.D., and Gay, D.A. 1998a. The lost colony and Jamestown droughts. Science 280:564–567.

Stahle, D.W., D'Arrigo, R.D., Krusic, P.J., Cleaveland, M.K., Cook, E.R., Allan, R.J., Cole, J.E., Dunbar, R.B., Therrell, M.D., Gay, D.A., Moore, M.D., Stokes, M.A., Burns, B.T., Villanueva-Diaz, J., and Thompson, L.G. 1998b. Experimental dendroclimatic reconstruction of the Southern Oscillation. Bulletin of the American Meteorological Society 79:2137–2152.

Stahle, D.W., Mushove, P.T., Cleaveland, M.K., Roig, F., and Haynes, G.A. 1999. Management implications of annual growth rings in Pterocarpus angolensis from Zimbabwe. Forest Ecology and Management 124:217–229.

Stahle, D.W., Cook, E.R., Cleaveland, M.K., Therrell, M.D., Meko, D.M., Grissino-Mayer, H.D., Watson, E., and Luckman, B.H. 2000. Tree-ring data document 16th century megadrought over North America. EOS: Transactions of the American Geophysical Union 81(12):212,125.

Stallings, W.S., Jr. 1937. Some early papers on tree-rings: J. Kuechler. Tree-Ring Bulletin 3:27–28.

Stallings, W.S., Jr. 1949. Dating Prehistoric Ruins by Tree-Rings. Rev. ed. Laboratory of Tree-Ring Research, University of Arizona, Tucson.

Stewart, O.C. 1936. Cultural Element Distributions. XIV. Northern Paiute. University of California Anthropological Records 4: 361–446.

Stockton, C.W., and Jacoby, G.C. 1976. Long-Term Surface-Water Supply and Streamflow Trends in the Upper Colorado River Basin. Lake Powell Research Project Bulletin 18. 79 pp.

Stockton, C.W., and Meko, D.M. 1975. A long-term history of drought occurrence in western United States as inferred from tree rings, Weatherwise 28(6):245–249.

Stoeckhardt, A. 1871. Untersuchungen über die schädliche Wirkung des Hütten- und Steinkohlenrauches auf das Wachstum der Pflanzen, insbesondere der Fichte und Tanne. Tharandter Forstliches Jahrbuch 21:218–254.

Stoffel, M., Lievre, I., Conus, D., Grichting, M.A., Raetzo, H., Gartner, H.W., and Monbaron, M. 2005. 400 years of debris-flow activity and triggering weather conditions: Ritigraben, Valais, Switzerland. Arctic, Antarctic, and Alpine Research 37(3):387–395.

Stokes, M.A., and Smiley, T.L. 1968. An Introduction to Tree-Ring Dating. University of Chicago Press, Chicago. 73 pp.

Stokes, M.A., and Smiley, T.L. 1996. An Introduction to Tree-Ring Dating. University of Arizona Press, Tucson. 73 pp.

Stuart, J.D., Agee, J.K., and Gara, R.I. 1989. Lodgepole pine regeneration in an old, self-perpetuating forest in south Oregon. Canadian Journal of Forest Research 19:1096–1104.

Studhalter, R.A. 1955. Tree growth: some historical chapters. The Botanical Review 21(1–3):1–72.

Studhalter, R.A. 1956. Early history of crossdating. Tree-Ring Bulletin 21(1–4):31–35.

Stuiver, M., and Braziunas, T.F. 1987. Tree cellulose $^{13}C/^{12}C$ isotope ratios and climate change. Nature 328:58–60.

Sutherland, E.K. 1997. History of fire in a southern Ohio second-growth mixed-oak forest. *In:* S.G. Pallardy, R.A. Cecich, H.E. Garrett, and P.S. Johnson, eds., Proceedings of the 11th Central Hardwood Forest Conference, 23–26 March 1997, Columbia, Missouri. U.S. Department of Agriculture Forest Service, GTR-NC-188. pp. 172–183.

Swanson, F.J., Jones, J.A., Wallin, D.O., and Cissel, J.H. 1994. Natural variability: implications for ecosystem management. *In:* M.E. Jensen and P.S. Bourgeron, tech. eds., Ecosystem Management: Principles and Applications, Vol. 2. U.S. Department of Agriculture Forest Service, Pacific Northwest Research Station, Portland, Oregon, PNW-GTR-318. pp. 89–103.

Swetnam, T.W. 1984. Peeled ponderosa pine trees: a record of inner bark utilization by Native Americans. Journal of Ethnobiology 4(2):177–190.

Swetnam, T.W. 1990. Fire history and climate in the southwestern United States. *In:* J.S. Krammes, ed., Proceedings of Symposium on Effects of Fire in Management of Southwestern U.S. Natural Resources, 15–17 November 1988, Tucson, Arizona. U.S. Department of Agriculture Forest Service, RM-GTR-191. pp. 6–17.

Swetnam, T.W., and Baisan, C.H. 1996. Historical fire regime patterns in the southwestern United States since AD 1700. *In:* C.D. Allen, ed., Fire Effects in Southwestern Forests: Proceedings of the Second La Mesa Fire Symposium. Los Alamos, New Mexico, 29–31 March 1994. U.S. Department of Agriculture Forest Service, RM-GTR-286. pp. 11–32.

Swetnam, T.W., and Betancourt, J.L. 1990. Fire–Southern Oscillation relations in the southwestern United States. Science 249:1017–1020.

Swetnam, T.W., and Lynch, A.M. 1989. A tree-ring reconstruction of western spruce budworm outbreaks in the southern Rocky Mountains. Forest Science 35(4):962–986.

Swetnam, T.W., and Lynch, A.M. 1993. Multi-century, regional-scale patterns of western spruce budworm history. Ecological Monographs 63(4):399–424.

Swetnam, T.W., Thompson, M.A., and Sutherland, E.K. 1985. Using Dendrochronology to Measure Radial Growth of Defoliated Trees. U.S. Department of Agriculture Forest Service, Agriculture Handbook 639. 39 pp.

Swetnam, T.W., Wickman, B.E., Paul, H.G., and Baisan, C.H. 1995. Historical Patterns of Western Spruce Budworm and Douglas-Fir Tussock Moth Outbreaks in the Northern Blue Mountains, Oregon, since AD 1700. U.S. Department of Agriculture Forest Service, Pacific Northwest Research Station, Portland, Oregon, PNW-RP-484. 27 pp.

Swetnam, T.W., Allen, C.D., and Betancourt, J.L. 1999. Applied historical ecology: using the past to manage for the future. Ecological Applications 9(4):1189–1206.

Switsur, V.R., Waterhouse, J.S., Field, E.M.F., Carter, A.H.C., Hall, M., Pollard, M., Robertson, I., Pilcher, J.R., and Heaton, T.H.E. 1994. Stable isotope studies of oak from the English fenland and Northern Ireland. *In:* B.M. Funnell and R.L.F. Kay, eds., Palaeoclimate of the Last Glacial/Interglacial Cycle. Natural Environment Research Council Special Publication 94/2:67–73.

Switsur, V.R., Waterhouse, J.S., Field, E.M., and Carter, A.H.C. 1996. Climatic signals from stable isotopes in oak tree-rings from East Anglia, Great Britain. *In:* J.S. Dean, D.M. Meko, and T.W. Swetnam, eds., Tree Rings, Environment, and Humanity: Proceedings of the International Conference, Tucson, Arizona, 17–21 May 1994. Radiocarbon, Tucson. pp. 637–645.

Tang, K., Feng, X., and Funkhouser, G. 1999. The d$^{13}$C of tree rings in full-bark and strip-bark bristlecone pine trees in the White Mountains of California. Global Change Biology 5:33–40.

Tang, K., Feng, X., and Ettle, G.J. 2000. The variations in dD of tree rings and the implications for climatic reconstruction. Geochimica et Cosmochimica Acta 64:1663–1673.

Tans, P., and Mook, W.G. 1980. Past atmospheric $CO_2$ levels and the $^{13}C/^{12}C$ ratios in tree rings. Tellus 32:268–283.

Tardif, J., and Bergeron, Y. 1999. Population dynamics of *Fraxinus nigra* in response to flood-level variations in northwestern Quebec. Ecological Monographs 69(1):107–125.

Tardif, J.C., Conciatori, F., Nantel, P., and Gagnon, D. 2006. Radial growth and climate responses of white oak (*Quercus alba*) and northern red oak (*Quercus rubra*) at the northern distribution limit of white oak in Quebec, Canada. Journal of Biogeography 33(9):1657–1669.

Tarr, R.S., and Martin, L. 1914. Alaskan Glacier Studies of the National Geographic Society in the Yakutat Bay, Prince William Sound and Lower Copper River Regions. National Geographic Society, Washington, D.C. 498 pp.

Taylor, S.W., Carroll, A.L., Alfaro, R.I., and Safranyik, L. 2006. Forest, climate, and mountain pine beetle outbreak dynamics in western Canada. *In:* L. Sasfranyik and B. Wilson, eds., The Mountain Pine Beetle: A Synthesis of Biology, Management, and Impacts on Lodgepole Pine. Canadian Forest Service, Pacific Forestry Center. pp. 67–94.

Telewski, F.W., Wakefield, A.H., and Mordecat, J.J. 1983. Computer-assisted image analysis of tissues of ethrel-treated *Pinus taeda* seedlings. Plant Physiology 72:177–181.

Therrell, M.D., Stahle, D.W., Ries, L.P., and Shugart, H.H. 2006. Tree-ring reconstructed rainfall variability in Zimbabwe. Climate Dynamics 26(7–8):677–685.

Thompson, D.R. 2005. Fine-scale disturbance and stand dynamics in mature spruce–subalpine fir forests of central British Columbia. M.S. Thesis, University of Northern British Columbia, Prince George.

Thompson, D.R., Daniels, L.D., and Lewis, K.J. 2007. A new dendroecological method to differentiate growth responses to fine-scale disturbance from regional-scale environmental variation. Canadian Journal of Forest Research 37:1034–1043.

Topham, J., and McCormick, D. 1997. The ring saga. The Strad 108:404–411.

Topham, J., and McCormick, D. 1998. A dendrochronological investigation of stringed instruments of the Cremonese School (1666–1757) including *The Messiah* violin attributed to Antonio Stradivari. Journal of Archaeological Science 27(3):183–192.

Topham, J., and McCormick, D. 2001. The dating game. The Strad 112:846–851.

Torrence, C., and Compo, G.P. 1998. A practical guide to wavelet analysis. Bulletin of the American Meteorological Society 79:61–78.

Touchan, R., Garfin, G.M., Meko, D.M., Funkhouser, G., Erkan, N., Hughes, M.K., and Wallis, B.S. 2003. Preliminary reconstructions of spring precipitation in southwestern Turkey from tree-ring width. International Journal of Climatology 23:157–171.

Touchan, R., Akkemik, U., Hughes, M.K., and Erkan, N. 2007. May–June precipitation reconstruction of southwestern Anatolia, Turkey, during last 900 years from tree rings. Quaternary Research 68:196–202.

Towner, R.H., Sesler, L., and Hovezak, T. 1999. Navajo culturally modified trees in the Dinétah. *In:* M.S. Duran and D.T. Kirkpatrick, eds., Diné Bíkéyah: Papers in Honor of David M. Brugge, No. 24. The Archaeological Society of New Mexico, Albuquerque. pp. 195–209.

Treydte, K., Schleser, G.H., Schweingruber, F.H., and Winiger, M. 2001. The climatic significance of $\delta^{13}C$ in subalpine spruces (Lötschental, Swiss Alps): a case study with respect to altitude, exposure and soil moisture. Tellus 53B:593–611.

Treydte, K., Schleser, G.H., Helle, G., Frank, D.V., Winiger, M., Haug, G.H., and Esper, J. 2006. The twentieth century was the wettest period in northern Pakistan over the past millennium. Nature 440:1179–1182.

Trouet, V., Haneca, K., Coppin, P., and Beeckman, H. 2001. Tree ring analysis of *Brachystegia spiciformis* and *Isoberlinia tomentosa*: evaluation of the ENSO-signal in the miombo woodland of eastern Africa. International Association of Wood Anatomists Journal 22(4):385–399.

Trouet, V., Coppin, P., and Beeckman, H. 2006. Annual growth ring patterns in *Brachystegia spiciformis* reveal influence of precipitation on tree growth. Biotropica 38(3):375–382.

Twining, A.C. 1833. On the growth of timber. American Journal of Science and Arts 24:391–393.

Vaganov, E.A., Naurazhaev, M.M., Schweingruber, F.H., Briffa, K.R., and Moell, M. 1996. An 840-year tree-ring width chronology for Taimir as an indicator of summer temperature changes. Dendrochronologia 14:193–205.

Vaganov, E.A., Hughes, M.K., Kirdyanov, A.V., Schweingruber, F.H., and Silkin, P.P. 1999. Influence of snowfall and melt timing on tree growth in subarctic Eurasia. Nature 400:149–151.

Vaganov, E.A., Hughes, M.K., Silkin, P.P., and Nesvetailo, V.D. 2004. The Tunguska event in 1908: evidence from tree-ring anatomy. Astrobiology 4(3):391–399.

Vale, T.R. 2002. Fire, Native Peoples, and the Natural Landscape. Island Press, Washington, D.C. 315 pp.

Van Arsdale, R.B., Stahle, D.W., Cleaveland, M.K., and Guccione, M.J. 1998. Earthquake signals in tree-ring data from the New Madrid seismic zone and implications for paleoseismicity. Geology 26(6):515–518.

van der Burgt, X.M. 1997. Determination of the age of *Pinus occidentalis* in La Celestina, Dominican Republic, by the use of growth rings. International Association of Wood Anatomists Journal 18:139–146.

van West, C.R., and Dean, J.S. 2000. Environmental characteristics of the A.D. 900–1300 period in the central Mesa Verde region. Kiva 66:19–44.

Vautard, R., and Ghil, M. 1989. Singular spectrum analysis in nonlinear dynamics, with applications to paleoclimatic time series. Physica D 35:395–424.

Veblen, T.T., Kitzberger, T., and Lara, A. 1992. Disturbance and forest dynamics along a transect from Andean rain forest to Patagonian shrubland. Journal of Vegetation Science 3(4):507–520.

Veblen, T.T., Hadley, K.S., Nel, E.M., Kitzberger, T., Reid, M., and Villabla, R. 1994. Disturbance regime and disturbance interactions in a Rocky Mountain subalpine forest. Journal of Ecology 82(1):125–135.

Verheyden, A. 2005. *Rhizophora mucronata* wood as a proxy for changes in environmental conditions. New Phytologist 167(2):425–435.

Verheyden, A., Kairo, J.G., Beeckman, H., and Koedam, N. 2004. Growth rings, growth ring formation and age determination in the mangrove *Rhizophora mucronata*. Annals of Botany 94:59–66.

Vetter, R.E., and Botosso, P.C. 1989. Remarks on age and growth rate determination of Amazonian trees. International Association of Wood Anatomists Bulletin 10(2):133–145.

Villalba, R., and Boninsegna, J.A. 1989. Dendrochronological studies of *Prosopis flexuosa* DC. International Association of Wood Anatomists Bulletin 10(2):155–160.

Villalba, R. Boninsegna, J.A., and Holmes, R.L. 1985. *Cedrela angustifolia* and *Juglans australis*: two new tropical species useful in dendrochronology. Tree-Ring Bulletin 45:25–35.

Villalba, R., Cook, E.R., Jacoby, G.C., D'Arrigo, R.D., Veblen, T.T., and Jones, P.D. 1998a. Tree-ring based reconstructions of northern Patagonia precipitation since AD 1600. Holocene 8(6):659–674.

Villalba, R., Grau, H.R., Boninsegna, J.A., Jacoby, G.C., and Ripalta, A. 1998b. Tree-ring evidence for long-term precipitation changes in subtropical South America. International Journal of Climatology 18:1463–1478.

Vittoz, P., Stewart, G.H., and Duncan, R.P. 2001. Earthquake impacts in old-growth *Nothofagus* forests in New Zealand. Journal of Vegetation Science 12(3):417–426.

Vroblesky, D.A., and Yanosky, T.M. 1990. Use of tree-ring chemistry to document historical ground-water contamination events. Ground Water 28(5):677–684.

Vroblesky, D.A., Yanosky, T.M., and Siegel, F.R. 2005. Increased concentrations of potassium in heartwood of trees in response to groundwater contamination. Environmental Geology 19(2):71–74.

Wagner, G. 2003. Eastern woodlands anthropogenic ecology. *In:* P.E. Minnis, ed., People and Plants in Ancient Eastern North America. Smithsonian Institution Press, Washington, D.C. pp. 126–171.

Wallace, R.E., and LaMarche, V.C., Jr. 1979. Trees as indicators of past movements on the San Andreas Fault. Earthquake Information Bulletin 2(4):127–131.

Waterhouse, J.S., Barker, A.C., Carter, A.H.C., Agafonov, L.I., and Loader, N.J. 2000. Stable carbon isotopes in Scots pine tree rings preserve a record of the flow of the River Ob. Geophysical Research Letters 27:3529–3532.

Watmough, S.A., Hutchinson, T.C., and Evans, D.R. 1998. The quantitative analysis of sugar maple tree rings by laser ablation in conjunction with ICP-MS. Journal of Environmental Quality 27(5):1087–1094.

Webb, G.E. 1983. Tree Rings and Telescopes: The Scientific Career of A.E. Douglass. University of Arizona Press, Tucson. 242 pp.

Webb, G.E. 1986. Solar physics and the origins of dendrochronology. Isis 77:291–301.

Weber, U.M., and Schweingruber, F.H. 1995. A dendroecological reconstruction of western spruce budworm outbreaks (*Choristoneura occidentalis*) in the Front Range, Colorado, from 1720 to 1986. Trees 9:204–213.

Wells, A., Duncan, R.P., and Stewart, G.H. 1998. Forest dynamics in Westland, New Zealand: the importance of large, infrequent earthquake-induced disturbance. Journal of Ecology 89(6):1006–1018.

Welsh, C. 2007. The relationship between climate and outbreak dynamics of *Dothistroma* needle blight in northwest British Columbia, Canada. M.S. Thesis, University of Northern British Columbia, Prince George. 187 pp.

Westphal, T. 2003. High-medieval urban development between the middle Elbe and the lower Oder based on dendrochronological data. *In:* G. Schleser, M. Winiger, A. Bräuning, H. Gärtner, G. Helle, E. Jansma, B. Neuwirth, and K. Treydte, eds., Tree Rings in Archaeology, Climatology, and Ecology, Vol. 1. Proceedings of the Dendrosymposium 2002. Schriften des Forschungszentrum Jülich, Reihe Umwelt 33:20–22.

Wickman, B.E. 1963. Mortality and Growth Reduction of White Fir Following Defoliation by the Douglas-Fir Tussock Moth. U.S. Department of Agriculture Forest Service, Research Paper PSW-7. 14 pp.

Wickman, B.E. 1980. Increased growth of white fire after a Douglas-fir tussock moth outbreak. Journal of Forestry 78:31–33.

Wickman, B.E., Mason, R.R., and Swetnam, T.W. 1994. Searching for long-term patterns of forest insect outbreaks. *In:* S.R. Leather, K.F.A. Walters, N.J. Mills, and A.D. Watt, eds., Individuals, Populations, and Patterns in Ecology. Intercept, Andover, U.K. pp. 251–261.

Wigley, T.M.L., Briffa, K.R., and Jones, P.D. 1984. On the average value of correlated time series, with applications in dendroclimatology and hyrometeorology. Bulletin of the American Meteorological Society 23:201–213.

Wiles, G.C., Calkin, P.E., and Jacoby, G.C. 1996. Tree-ring analysis and Quaternary geology: principles and recent applications. Geomorphology 16:259–272.

Wiles, G.C., Post, A., Muller, E.H., and Molnia, B.F. 1999. Dendrochronology and Late Holocene history of Bering Piedmont Glacier, Alaska. Quaternary Research 52:185–195.

Wiles, G.C., Barclay, D.J., Calkin, P.E., and Lowell, T.V. 2008. Century- to millennial-scale temperature variations for the last two thousand years indicated from glacial geologic records of southern Alaska. Global and Planetary Change 60:115–125.

Wilkinson, M.C. 1997. Reconstruction of historical fire regimes along an elevation and vegetation gradient in the Sacramento Mountains, New Mexico. M.S. Thesis, University of Arizona, Tucson.

Wimmer, R. 2001. Arthur Freiherr von Sechendorff-Gudent and the early history of tree-ring crossdating. Dendrochronologia 19(1):153–158.

Woodhouse, C.A. 1999. Artificial neural networks and dendroclimatic reconstructions: an example from the Front Range, Colorado, U.S.A. Holocene 9(5):521–529.

Woodhouse, C.A. 2001. A tree-ring reconstruction of streamflow for the Colorado Front Range. Journal of the American Water Resources Association 37(3):561–569.

Woodhouse, C.A., and Meko, D.M. 2009. Dendroclimatology, dendrohydrology, and water resources management. In: M.K. Hughes, T.W. Swetnam, and H.F. Diaz, eds., Dendroclimatology: Progress and Prospects. Developments in Paleoenvironmental Research, Vol. 11. Springer Verlag, Berlin.

Woodhouse, C.A., Gray, S.T., and Meko, D.M. 2006. Updated streamflow reconstructions for the Upper Colorado River basin. Water Resources Research 42:W05415, doi: 10.1029/2005WR004455.

Worbes, M. 1989. Growth rings, increment and age of trees in inundation forests, savannas and a mountain forest in the Neotropics. International Association of Wood Anatomists Bulletin 10(2):109–122.

Worbes, M. 1995. How to measure growth dynamics in tropical trees: a review. International Association of Wood Anatomists Journal 16(4):227–351.

Worbes, M. 2002. One hundred years of tree-ring research in the tropics: a brief history and an outlook to future challenges. In: P. Cherubini, ed., Tree Rings and People. Conference Proceedings, Davos, Switzerland, September 2001. Dendrochronologia 20(1–2):217–231.

Worbes, M., and Junk, W.J. 1989. Dating tropical trees by means of $^{14}$C from bomb tests. Ecology 70(2):503–507.

Worbes, M., Staschel, R., Roloff, A., and Junk, W.J. 2003. Tree ring analysis reveals age structure, dynamics and wood production of a natural forest stand in Cameroon. Forest Ecology and Management 173(1–3):105–123.

Worrall, J. 1990. Subalpine larch: Oldest trees in Canada? Forestry Chronicle 66(5):478–479.

Wurster, C.M., Patterson, W.P., and Cheatham, M.M. 1999. Advances in micromilling techniques: a new apparatus for acquiring high-resolution oxygen and carbon stable isotope values and major/minor elemental ratios from accretionary carbonate. Computers and Geosciences 25:1159–1166.

Yadav, R.R., and Kulieshius, P. 1992. Dating of earthquakes: tree ring responses to the catastrophic earthquake of 1887 in Alma-Ata Kazakhstan. The Geographical Journal 158(3):259–299.

Yamaguchi, D.K. 1983. New tree-ring dates for recent eruptions of Mount St. Helens. Quaternary Research 20:246–250.

Yamaguchi, D.K. 1991. A simple method for cross-dating increment cores from living trees. Canadian Journal of Forest Research 21:414–416.

Yamaguchi, D.K., and Hoblitt, R.P. 1995. Tree-ring dating of pre-1980 volcanic flowage deposits at Mount St. Helens, Washington. Geological Society of America Bulletin 107(9):1077–1093.

Yang, W., Spencer, R.J., and Krouse, H.R. 1996. Stable sulfur isotope hydrogeochemical studies using desert shrubs and tree rings, Death Valley, California, U.S.A. Gechemica et Cosmochimica Acta 60:3015–3022.

Yanosky, T.M., and Jarrett, R.D. 2001. Dendrochronologic evidence for the frequency and magnitude of paleofloods. In: Ancient Floods, Modern Hazards: Principles and Applications of Paleoflood Hydrology. Water Science and Application 5:77–89.

Yanosky, T.M., Hupp, C.R., and Hackney, C.T. 1995. Chloride concentrations in growth rings of Taxodium distichum in a saltwater-intruded estuary. Ecological Applications 5(3):785–792.

Yanosky, T.M., Hansen, B.P., and Schening, M.R. 2001. Use of tree rings to investigate the onset of contamination of a shallow aquifer by chlorinated hydrocarbons. Journal of Contaminant Hydrology 50:159–173.

Yapp, C.J., and Epstein, S. 1982. A re-examination of cellulose carbonbound hydrogen dD measurements and some factors affecting plant-water D/H relationships. Geochimica et Cosmochimica Acta 46:955–965.

Yarnell, S.L. 1998. The Southern Appalachians: A History of the Landscape. U.S. Department of Agriculture Forest Service, Southern Research Station GTR-SRS-18. 45 pp.

Zetterberg, P. 1990. Dendrochronological dating of a wooden causeway in Finland. Norwegian Archaeological Review 23(1–2):54–59.

Zeuner, F.E. 1958. Dating the Past: An Introduction to Geochronology. 4th ed. Methuen and Co. Ltd., London. 491 pp.

Zhang, Q.B., and Alfaro, R.I. 2002. Periodicity of two-year cycle spruce budworm outbreaks in central British Columbia: a dendro-ecological analysis. Forest Science 48(4):722–731.

Zimmermann, B., Schleser, G.H., and Brauning, A. 1997. Preliminary results of a Tibetan stable C-isotope chronology dating from 1200 to 1994. Isotopes in Environmental and Health Studies 33:157–165.

# Index

*Note:* Entries in boldface type indicate figures.

## About the Author

Jim Speer is an associate professor of geography and geology at Indiana State University. He learned dendrochronology at the Laboratory of Tree-Ring Research in Tucson, Arizona, while earning his bachelor's degree (1994) and master's degree (1997) in geology. He earned his Ph.D. in geography from the University of Tennessee in 2001. He has been teaching dendrochronology since 1997 in workshops and the classroom and has been the director of the North American Dendroecological Fieldweek since 2000. Speer is the president of the Tree-Ring Society and has received numerous awards in teaching, research, and service including the Schulman Award, the Richard L. Holmes Award for Outstanding Service to Dendrochronology, the Henry Cowles Excellence in Publication Award, and the Educational Excellence Award from the College of Arts and Sciences at Indiana State University. He has advised numerous graduate students while at Indiana State University and has published in many peer-reviewed journals, such as *Ecology, Canadian Journal of Forest Research, Tree-Ring Research, Dendrochronologia, Climate Research*, and the *Journal of Biogeography*. He currently lives in Terre Haute, Indiana, in a small rural home with his wife and two dogs.